Great Bindings
from the
Spanish Royal Collections
15th – 21st centuries

Great Bindings
from the
Spanish Royal Collections
15th – 21st centuries

DIRECTED BY
María Luisa López-Vidriero

PATRIMONIO NACIONAL

EDICIONES EL VISO

With the high patronage of His Majesty the King

Patrimonio Nacional

BOARD OF DIRECTORS

CHAIRMAN
José Rodríguez-Spiteri Palazuelo

MANAGING DIRECTOR
Alicia Pastor Mor

MEMBERS
Ana María Botella Serrano
José Luis Fernández-Quejo del Pozo
María del Carmen Iglesias Cano
Mateo Isern Estela
José María Lassalle Ruiz
María Rosario Pablos López
Jaime Pérez Renovales
Luis Reverter Gelabert
José Manuel Romero Moreno
Carlos San Basilio Pardo

SECRETARY
Juan García González-Posada

CULTURAL COMMITTEE

José Luis Álvarez Álvarez
Gonzalo Anes y Álvarez de Castrillón
Plácido Arango
Antonio Bonet Correa
María del Carmen Iglesias Cano
José María Pérez González

Great Bindings from the Spanish Royal Collections (15th–21st centuries) is the first exhibition of the outstanding bindings preserved in the Real Biblioteca of the Royal Palace and in the monastery of El Escorial and the convents of Las Huelgas, Las Descalzas and La Encarnación. It features 457 items, all belonging to the Patrimonio Nacional collections. Approximately half the works on display are books and documents; the other half are paintings, tapestries, furniture and a varied array of decorative art works.

Bindings are approached as an element of royal and courtly language which, along with other artistic disciplines, served the purpose of representation and identification. They thus helped shape an intellectual and cultural portrait of the monarchs, and books were individualised as unmistakeable property.

This collection of paramount importance, regarded as one of the most valuable in the world, attests to how and why royal books were clothed in particular bindings, what their purpose was and whose ownership they proclaimed. It also shows that the libraries of kings or infantes housed ordinary books too: it was not all singularity and brilliance, because use and the everyday have always been an inseparable part of the royal book collections.

The bindings on the books in the royal collections do not end in the exhibition rooms of the Royal Palace. Online resources, the electronic catalogue and specialised databases are a testament to the effort the Real Biblioteca has been putting into making this rich cultural heritage available to society for over two decades.

I would like to acknowledge the curator and director of the Real Biblioteca, María Luisa López-Vidriero, whose professionalism has ensured the highest level of scientific rigour, as well as the people who have contributed to this magnificent project and the various technical teams who have helped bring it to fruition.

José Rodríguez-Spiteri Palazuelo
Chairman of the Board of Directors of Patrimonio Nacional

Exhibition

SCIENTIFIC CURATOR
María Luisa López-Vidriero Abelló

ARTISTIC CURATOR
Manuel Blanco Lage

DIRECTOR, IMAGE, PROMOTION AND DEVELOPMENT
Pilar Martín-Laborda y Bergasa

DIRECTOR, CONSERVATION OF ARTISTIC
AND HISTORICAL HERITAGE
Juan Carlos de la Mata González

HEAD OF THE DEPARTMENT OF EXHIBITIONS
AND CULTURAL PROGRAMMES
Carmen Cabeza Gil-Casares

HEAD CURATOR
Paz Cabello Carro

HEAD OF THE RESTORATION DEPARTMENT
Ángel Balao González

COORDINATOR OF TEMPORARY EXHIBITIONS
Isabel Morán Suárez

REAL BIBLIOTECA DE PALACIO
María Luisa López-Vidriero Abelló

BIBLIOTECA DEL REAL MONASTERIO
DE SAN LORENZO DE EL ESCORIAL
José Luis del Valle Merino O. S. A.

PATRIMONIO NACIONAL TRANSPORTATION UNIT
Sonsoles Castillo Aguilar

PATRIMONIO NACIONAL BOOK AND DOCUMENT WORKSHOP
Amparo Gutiérrez Sánchez, Teresa Martín González,
Alba Pérez Martín

Collaborators

PROJECT AND DIRECTION OF INSTALLATION
Manuel Blanco Lage
Héctor Navarro

INSTALLATION
Exmoarte

GRAPHIC DESIGN
Roberto Turégano

GRAPHICS
Cromotex
Taller de Serigrafía

AUDIOVISUALS
Telesonic, Ostiz Audiovisuales, Digitalak

Catalogue

EDITING
Patrimonio Nacional

DIRECTION
María Luisa López-Vidriero Abelló

COORDINATION
Pablo Andrés Escapa

AUTOMATION AND ELECTRONIC RESOURCES
José Luis Rodríguez

COMPUTER RESOURCES
Jorge Soret Lois

PRODUCTION
Ediciones El Viso
Lucía Varela

DESIGN
Subiela

COVER DESIGN (PAPERBACK EDITION)
David Montoya Garrido, TTM TOTEM

TRANSLATION
Pablo Andrés Escapa, María Teresa Camps Blanco, Jenny
F. Dodman, Wade Matthews, Ian David Lewis Michael

EDITING OF ENGLISH TEXTS
Jenny F. Dodman

PHOTOGRAPHS
Antonio Ubeda, Jaume Blassi

PREPRESS
Lucam

PRINTING
Brizzolis

BINDING
Ramos

PHOTOGRAPH CREDITS
All the photographs have been supplied by
Patrimonio Nacional (Laboratorio fotográfico
de Patrimonio Nacional), except:
Fig. 1: Dijon, © Musée des Beaux-arts de Dijon
(photo: François Jay); Fig. 4: Album / Universal Images
Group; Figs. 5, 10: Cuauhtli Gutiérrez; Fig. 7: Album /
akg-images / Orsi Battaglini); Fig. 12: © Städel
Museum / ARTOTHEK

Acknowledgements

Patrimonio Nacional and the exhibition curators wish to thank the following institutions and people, as well as those who prefer to remain anonymous:

Religious communities of the convents of Las Descalzas Reales, La Encarnación, Santa Isabel and Las Huelgas and the monastery of San Lorenzo de El Escorial

José Antonio Ahijado; Mónica Alcoba; Juan José Alonso; Mercedes Alonso; Ángel de Ana; Francisco de Andrés; Juan Ramón Aparicio; Amelia Aranda; Virginia Arnaíz; Luis Baena; Pilar Baglietto; Inés Barriga; María Barrigón; Rosa Becerril; Pilar Benito; Rosario Blasco; Ignacio Calle; Paloma Callejo; Inmaculada Candil; Cristina Caro; Purificación Cereijo; José Cosials; Sagrario Criado; Belén Curiel; Carmen Díaz; Elisa Esteban; Jesús Miguel Fernández; Julián Fernández; Marta Fernández; Mª Carmen Fernández-Lascoiti; José Antonio Franco; Ana García; Faustino García; Mª Soledad García; Carmen García-Frías; Isabel Gil-Robles; José Antonio Gismera; Eloisa González; Daniel Guindulain; Amparo Gutiérrez; Eugenio Hernando; Concha Herrero; María Jesús Herrero; Santiago Herrero; David Iborra; Oriol Jané; Julián Jimenez; Javier Jordán de Urries; Dolores López; Ana Loureiro; Lourdes de Luis; Lucio Maire; Fernando Martín; Rosario Martín; Teresa Martín; Adela Martínez; Daniele Maruca; Antonio José Méndez; Concepción de Miguel; Alejandro Monreal; Francisca Morilla; Ángel Pedro Muñoz; Victoria Muñoz; Jacinto Muñoz-Reja; Cristina Mur; Héctor Navarro; José Noguera; Miguel Ángel Ortega; Teresa Ortiz; Salvador Panadero; Consuelo Parreño; Alba Pérez; Daniel Pérez; Luis Pérez de Prada; Sofía Pérez; Almudena Pérez de Tudela; Francisco del Pino; Alberto Prieto; José Javier Rivas; Esperanza Rodríguez-Arana; Juan Manuel Rojo; Antonia Ruiz; Julio Sánchez; Leticia Sánchez; Manuel Santolaya; Faustino Sanz; J. Francisco Serrano; Carmen Shallcross; Álvaro Soler; Jorge Soret; Isabel Sueiro; Carlos Torreiro; José Luis Valverde

13	Introduction María Luisa López-Vidriero
17	Bookbinding, an Artistic Language Víctor Nieto Alcalde
55	The Humble among the Distinguished Carlos Clavería Laguarda
75	Keys to the Evolution of the Armorial Bindings of Patrimonio Nacional Valentín Moreno Gallego
95	Books for Reading. Commercial Bindings in Parchment and Paper in the Era of the Handpress Nicholas Pickwoad
123	Diego Hurtado de Mendoza Anthony Hobson
149	Three Aspects of French Bindings in the Spanish National Heritage Collections Isabelle de Conihout and Pascal Ract-Madoux
191	Bodonian Bindings Pedro M. Cátedra
225	*Eadem Sed Aliter*: Uniformity and Singularity in Royal Bindings María Luisa López-Vidriero
281	From Industry to Art. Two Changes of Century in the Bindings of the Real Biblioteca Dolores Baldó
309	A Thematic Bibliography of Bookbinding in Spain (from the Nineteenth to the Twenty-First Centuries): Historiography of Contemporary Studies Concha Lois
324	References
336	Patrimonio Nacional Bindings Reproduced in This Book

Introduction

María Luisa López-Vidriero

The essays in this volume study the bindings in the royal collections in the care of Patrimonio Nacional, Spain's national heritage institution. Rather than tracing styles and artists chronologically, they provide a comprehensive view of the distinct and unique set of books, originally from various libraries, which took on a new meaning of their own when part of the king's library.

Ten different perspectives provide answers that help understand the rhetorical elements used to unify diverse books in a royal visual space. As an essential point of departure for fully grasping what can only be understood as the sum of diverse parts, the following pages interpret bookbinding as one of the various aspects of the court language employed in the symbolic construction of the royal figure.

The exhibition, opening at the Royal Palace in April 2012, embodies this cultural history-based approach to bookbinding through an analysis of the covers of books from the royal collections that is not limited to identifying tools or providing descriptions, always random, of the decoration. It shows the coherence of the court language which established a discursive correlation through the various art objects in the royal collections—an aesthetic standardisation which is expressed by each of the objects on display, with structural resources and methods of their own, and whose aim was to leave a true and lasting testimony of the king's image. The architect Manuel Blanco Lage has designed an artistic setting inseparable from the underlying idea, and far removed from a simple installation design.

Painting and tapestry, sculptures and pianos, curtains and cushions, chairs and armchairs, inkwells and bookrests come together to express a precise idea of the royal figure using similar and strictly up-to-date decorative systems. *Provenances* and *Functions* are the main underpinnings of this theoretical discourse and the objects themselves are part of a conceptual order that synchronises them, shunning the fragmentary vision of a chronological presentation. Provenance and function are two fundamental elements for understanding the king's library because it is necessary to know from what book collecting sources it draws it in order to understand what these sources become when, beyond their original uses, they take on other symbolic roles in the private palace collection.

Royal Family, Nobility, Scholarship and Learning, Spiritual Retreats, the section with which this exhibition begins, shows that the prominent role of the king as first owner is not a sustainable principle and what makes the royal library so interesting and enormously different is precisely its multiple nature. The contents of the royal library cut across many social sectors: at a particular moment, some of the books in the royal collection might originally have been acquired by a count, accompanied an infanta, been read by a widowed empress who retired to a convent, or studied for hours by a patrician or scholar. Following the development of children's literature at the end of the nineteenth century, many of the books belonging to the king's children were identical to those read by the children of their age in wealthy families throughout Europe. This fact shatters one of the recurring clichés about the royal library as the repository of a unique output and forces us to consider that exclusiveness and what makes these volumes "books from the king's private library" involves other elements that make them symbolic objects representative of royalty.

Clearly, what is exclusive about the royal library stems from these unique manuscript or printed presentation copies, exquisitely illustrated and clothed like royalty. But these items are a minority compared to the lion's share of the collection, for, in the kings' private libraries, *candour,* in the form of parchment, industrial or paperback bindings, coexists with the *luxury* of morocco leather, gold tooling, mica, velvet and moiré.

The mechanisms involved in the construction of candour, symbolised by the apparently humble and everyday parchment bindings, reveal the knowledge and wealth of resources available to the craftsmen who worked on the material makeup of those books. A specialised study of the structures of books reveals the complex economic and social processes that led bookbinders to use the skins of particular animals or to devise faster, and therefore more cost-effective, methods of stitching. Something as seemingly homogenous as a parchment binding has national and local characteristics that make it possible to distinguish, for example, the stages in the long journey of a book printed in Germany in the sixteenth century, stitched in France, bound in England and labelled in Spain, all in the short space of ten years.

The complexity of luxury is shaped in principle from tooling, binding materials and gold. The page edges and the endpapers belong to an aesthetic universe of their own which involves other industries. But ostentation can also be the absence of all such elements: bare elegance. Workshops and binders strove to create that decorative language and the study and identification of their tools allows us to attribute singular but unsigned bindings to a particular bookbinding artist. Sometimes, binders constructed these distinct covers hand in hand with printers, showing that a book could be conceived as a complex process that did not end at the press. Plantin and Bodoni—key names in the history of printing—should be studied in their other facet as printers who regarded binding as the final stage in the crafting of outstanding printed works. The French bindings executed for Prince Philip in El Escorial and the Italian ones made for the Infante Don Antonio Pascual, or for King Charles IV and his wife María Luisa exemplify this other concern of Plantin's print shop and of the palace printing house in Parma, and constitute two revelations in the royal heritage collections where, as can be seen in Lois Cabello's bibliography, the studies by bookbinding historians had focused exclusively on specific national workshops.

This select presence of foreign bindings in the Spanish royal collections attests to another of the distinctive features of the royal private library: its international character. This nature is expressed through these two manners of conceiving books as cultural objects: simplicity—always apparent—and exuberance. That is how these types of bindings were interpreted and executed at the European courts over the centuries until joining the king's private collection through the absorption of other library collections, or as the destination chosen initially by people wishing to distinguish an item intended for a royal recipient.

Notwithstanding their varied origins and diverse material characteristics, it is precisely the *functions* of these books in the king's library that triggers the process of transforming them into exclusive objects. To fulfil the different roles books were meant to play in the king's collection, royal binders or others who occasionally provided their services to the Royal Household developed aesthetic and symbolic devices to meet the expressive and representational needs of the private or chamber library. *Cultural standardisation, royal ceremonies* and the expression of the *monarchy* were unquestionably the most significant.

One of the tasks of bookbinding in the royal library was to create a harmonious court language and, in order to achieve this, bindings developed as one of many art objects, their design underpinned by the same aesthetic principles that were being expressed and shaped by the higher and decorative arts of the period. The structure of a binding, the aesthetic programme applied to its covers, displays the characteristic features of a particular architectural style. Of course, shared decorative resources unified textiles, furniture and porcelain, to the extent that the art objects in the royal collection all display the same artistic style.

The guidelines for the lives of the royal persons are set out in books, which meticulously chart the course of the ceremonies that accompany them from the moment they are born. Therefore, bindings induce and prepare the reader for the outstanding spectacle narrated in the manuscript or printed work. In the king's library, they bring solemnity to the unique celebration to which they themselves bear witness.

All in all, the main function of bindings in a royal collection is to attest to the ownership of the king or queen. We might consider this their *raison d'être*, although fortunately it is not the only one. Each monarch expressed ownership of his books in a personal manner by means of his cypher or heraldically with his coat of arms. Alfonso XIII marked his books in accordance with a singular programme of national renewal that extended far beyond cyphers or coats of arms. In 1992, the Real Biblioteca returned to this type of binding, which had been left off in 1931, with the collection derived from the Reina Sofía Prize for Ibero-American Poetry. These books by prize-winning poets form a unique set in which Spanish bookbinding artists display their creative and technical prowess, just as the royal binders did before them for centuries.

This introduction cannot end without acknowledgements and apologies, because the sheer number of names prevents me from mentioning all the people who have contributed to this undertaking to some extent with their generosity and talent. This exhibition was mounted and brought to successful completion by many colleagues—curators, archivists, restorers, photographers, administrators—from the department of conservation of artistic and historical heritage of Patrimonio Nacional, as well as Juan Carlos de la Mata, director of artistic and historical heritage, who put every effort into making it a reality.

This volume of studies stems from the reflections and expert discussions that preceded the exhibition, and from a line of research into historical bibliographical heritage that began two decades ago in the Real Biblioteca and focused on the history of royal and court culture. Close collaborators and generous contributors to this volume are the nine authors and the literary editor, Pablo Andrés, who has worked closely with an exceptional accomplice in this project: Santiago Saavedra and the publishers El Viso.

Unquestionably, research of this kind is the product of collective, patient and enthusiastic work. Among those who took part in it, José Antonio Ahijado should be remembered for meticulously combing through the archives.

Readers will be able to consult the books on which this exhibition is based in the electronic catalogue accompanying the present volume. When doing so, they should be grateful to José Luis Rodríguez, Jorge Soret and Alejandro Monreal for providing full and precise descriptions and easy access to any sort of information on types, chronology, themes or names, whether bibliographical or concerning specific copies.

I am confident that the new proposals set out in these studies, and the books that have led us to formulate them, will achieve their ultimate goal: to awaken a need and an interest in continuing to ask questions, always with a book in hand.

Bookbinding, an Artistic Language

Víctor Nieto Alcaide

Until relatively recently bookbinding, examples of which can now be seen in museums and exhibitions, has been an art that is not shown publicly but viewed privately, rather like reading, which is an intimate dialogue between book and reader. Unlike other works of art, bound books are objects which are handled and whose beauty is also appreciated through touch. Richard de Bury (1273–1345), Bishop of Durham, who was Lord Chancellor of England and an enthusiastic booklover, recommended in his *Philobiblion* that readers "treat books carefully, and ... restore them to their proper places and commend them to inviolable custody; that they may rejoice in purity while we have them in our hands, and rest securely when they are put back in their repositories".[1]

Compared to other arts, book are small objects designed to be held and touched, because we receive a tactile perception of a bound book when we grasp it in order to look at or read it. The binder Emilio Brugalla referred to this when he noted how in books the "association of the parts with the whole gives the sensation when grasping the book that the hands are holding not a polyhedral block with its straight edges and pointed corners but an exquisitely moulded form that is soft to the touch and has a perfect balance, which stimulates the emotion that is experienced in the presence of a work of art".[2]

Books, Art Objects

The various definitions of art have one feature in common, around which the purpose of Art History has progressively been shaped: the study and analysis of art objects. The history of these art objects shows how their execution does not stem from unchanging laws that allow a general principle of art to be established. For art objects span an extremely diverse range of genres and forms with many uses and functions. A fifth-century Greek sculpture, a Renaissance glass goblet, a Mudejar binding or one by Grolier, a Gothic stained-glass window, a Romanesque miniature, an Impressionist painting, a sculpture by Brancusi and a sixteenth-century Flemish tapestry are objects that apparently have nothing in common, come in different shapes and sizes, are executed in completely different materials and are used for disparate purposes. And yet they are all considered to be works of art. Because what we understand to be art encompasses a broad range of objects that are made from different forms, techniques and materials but have continued, with unequal incidence, to be part of artistic production throughout history.

Enamels, ivories, miniatures, stained glass and rich bindings were one of the most appreciated arts during the Middle Ages, although they were relegated to second place in subsequent artistic production, whereas other genres, such as sculpture and painting, together with architecture, continued to be particularly highly regarded. It was not until the nineteenth century, when the system of the arts underwent changes, that a new value was attached to the aforementioned arts.

Art is a language which is expressed plastically and visually through this diversity of objects produced to serve diverse functions ranging from the immediate practicality of a bookbinding, an outfit of clothing or a bridge, or from the representativeness of a tomb or portrait, to the apparent uselessness—albeit justified as an expression of prestige—of a necklace, a pendant or a ring. There is therefore no valid definition capable of embracing the whole range of artistic productions or "genres". However, there is another characteristic common to all the art objects included under the common denominator of art: their material and visual nature. Artistic expression is shaped by a material component which transcends the physical laws of matter and creates a different reality. In a tapestry we appreciate not only the textile matter but also the image; in a binding we perceive not only the quality and colour of the leather but its ornamentation and technical and plastic handling.

The history of the art objects we call book bindings is a combination of two aspects: technical transformations and the presence of styles in tune with those developed in other arts. Bookbinding is not an art accessible to any artist. It requires knowledge of complex techniques and this has led it to be an endogamous and introverted profession which, like other inaptly called decorative arts, was not considered a liberal art until practically the twentieth century. A few testimonies show how, during the Enlightenment, bookbinding began to be considered more than just a mechanical trade. René Martin Doudin stated in *L'Art du relieur doreur de livres*, published in 1772, that bookbinding, "although an art classified among the group of mechanical arts, may nonetheless be regarded with certain consideration owing to its privilege of being related to literature". [3]

Technical novelties are few and far between in the history of bookbinding. Another matter is the use made of these technical procedures to adapt them to different artistic languages. Gilding, for example, was used in Renaissance decoration, in fans, in neoclassical ornamentation, in the so-called "cathedral style", in Art Nouveau, in Art Déco and in contemporary decoration. What changes in the history of bookbinding is the plastic language of binding and the technical novelties inherent in the various "styles".

In ornamental aspects bookbinding has developed in parallel and in tune with the other arts. For binding is an art form that is expressed through the various artistic languages of each period. However, like clothes, bindings can be very different even if made for the same book. They can be executed in the style of the period in which the book was published, imitate this style if made long afterwards or be made in a different style consonant with the trends in vogue at the time it is bound. Bookbinding belongs to the complex world of artistic styles and in many cases is an essential reference for generally defining a style. Bindings of the so-called "curtain" [*de cortina*] type are an original design and contribution of neoclassicism. And the same is true of the so-called "Plateresque" binding or of the "cathedral style" as an expression of neo-Gothic revivals.

The different bookbinding styles trace the development of ornamental forms applied

Fig. 1
Juan de la Huerta and Antoine Le Moiturier, mourner no. 63 from the tomb of John the Fearless and Margaret of Bavaria (1443–70), alabaster. Dijon, Musée des Beaux-Arts [CA 1417, no. 63]

to books. Therefore, the compositions and decorative motifs bear a close relationship to architectural decoration, textiles, tapestries, carpets, furniture and marquetry. Binders draw from the common corpus of motifs, their use of which denotes whether they are innovative, retardataire or resistant to the introduction of new themes. Grotesques and scrolls, which became widespread in sixteenth-century binding, took over from earlier Mudejar and Gothic styles. Neoclassical bindings with their linearity and simple, neat compositions replaced the motley Baroque forms. And the same is true of Art Deco bookbinding with respect to the undulating forms of Art Nouveau and the formal autonomy of many current bindings in relation to historicist and figurative forms.

The changes the art of bookbinding has undergone are due chiefly to the taste and sensibility of the clients who have left their mark on the various languages. The bindings of the library established by Philip II at the Monastery of Escorial attest to the legacy of monastic bookbinding in a combination of royal and monastic features. The bindings of Jean Grolier, decorated with interlaced motifs and with mosaic work and gilding, reveal the exquisite taste of a collector whose books created a style that is named after its promoter. The same is true of those decorated with funereal motifs belonging to Henry III of France, who was obsessed with death,[4] and of the "curtain" style bindings of Ferdinand VII of Spain. Book bindings are therefore a language which transmits ideas and contents because

Figs. 2 and 3
Abul Qasim Mansur Firdusi, *Shah-Nama*, 1485.
Fifteenth-century Persian binding in brown sheepskin with envelope flap. RB, II/3218

> they may be regarded as the external reading of books. There is no doubt that when our gaze wanders over the shelf it is they that lead us to choose a particular volume in order to continue in its pages a tale begun

on the covers; opening the book merely amounts to carrying on reading. That is why perusing the shelves of a historical library is so telling.[5]

Any bound book on a shelf always holds a surprise if we are unaware of its contents, if it is well illustrated with prints or miniatures and if it is beautifully bound. Objects with the appearance of books but which are not books can cause greater astonishment, such as one in the library of Isabella the Catholic which bore the title *Breviario de la sed* but had no pages because it held a small barrel inside.[6]

When protected, and even when on a library shelf, books are partially hidden objects. They were concealed by protective velvet or chamois leather bags [fig. 1]. And the same is true of small pouch-type books that were worn attached to the waist, as may be seen in paintings such as the Saint Anthony executed by Martin Schongauer (*c*. 1488–91) for the church of Saint Martin in Colmar (Colmar, Musée d'Unterlinden),[7] a common type in the fifteenth century.

In some cases the protective cover added to the quality of the binding. An example from the period of Isabella the Catholic is that of *Las siete Partidas* of Alfonso X in the Biblioteca Nacional in Madrid, which creates an inverse surprise effect: the protective case of voided velvet with Moresque enamelled decoration on four brooches[8] turns out to be much richer and more sumptuous than the manuscript's Mudejar binding.

When the book comes in a protective cover, we are greeted with one surprise after another: the decoration of the boards, the headband, the headcap, the endpapers, the decoration of the edges, the beauty of the print, the text, the illuminated or printed illustrations and, sometimes, the hidden decoration of the edges which is only seen on turning the pages of the book and is invisible in its usual closed position. In this respect it is like an altarpiece protected from dust by a curtain, or a closed triptych whose interior is not visible until, on opening the doors, we are graced with the sight of the surprising beauty of the painting or sculpture in similar way to when we open a book and come into contact with its contents.

A beautifully bound book is an airtight box which holds a treasure of culture, art and knowledge. Richard de Bury stated in *Philobiblion* that books are "sacred vessels of science".[9] And Don Quixote owned "above a hundred volumes in folio, very well bound", in his prized library, the treasury of his fantasies and the origin of his adventures.[10] The world of his dreams and his fantasies, his books on chivalry, were stored in chests which were his good bindings, and stored in a library that was his most prized treasure. Bound books are beautiful objects containing condensed knowledge, hermetic in appearance. This effect is especially true of bindings featuring certain protective elements: studs at the corners and in the centre, metal corner pieces, and clasps for fastening them.

In a common type of Islamic binding the book was enclosed by an envelope flap on the left, which is an extension of the back cover of the book, as the spine of the book viewed frontally is on its right [figs. 2 and 3]. This flap encloses the textblock, forming a protective case.[11] This effect also spread inversely. Some leather-covered chests decorated with bookbinding motifs and techniques look like books, such as one that belonged to Marie de'Medici (former Whitney Hoff collection), with fanfare decoration.[12]

Books have always been symbols and visual metaphors of knowledge and wisdom. In depictions of sages of Antiquity, a period in which knowledge was preserved in scrolls, these figures are shown with books. The *School of Athens* in the Raphael Rooms of the Vatican, executed in 1509–10, draws attention to a *concordatio* between Christianity and ancient philosophy. Located in the centre of the scene holding books fastened with clasps are Plato with *Timaeus* and Aristotle with the *Ethics*, at a time in which codices did not exist [fig. 4]. The progression from scroll to codex, or to the book as we understand it today, took place long after the age of the two great philosophers, as codices became widespread between the third and fourth centuries AD.[13] The codex was a new system that facilitated the handling of texts. Codices were much faster to consult or read. With scrolls the reader had to roll and unroll them to find what he was looking for. With codices the desired text could be

Fig. 4
Raphael, *The School of Athens* (detail), 1509–10, fresco. Vatican, Stanza della Segnatura

easily located as they were made up of sheets sewn together.

Bookbinding, the first known western examples of which date from the eighth century,[14] emerged for practical reasons: to ensure their protection and preservation by sewing together quires and providing them with covers. However, as has occurred systematically and constantly in Art History, it was not long before a discovery that sprang up to meet a practical need became the support for an art object that could sometimes be outstandingly rich. In some bindings, with the incorporation of gold and silver work, ivory, enamel and precious stones, the effect of a precious box was sought, such as in the "rich bindings" of the Middle Ages [figs. 5 and 6]. These books, decorated with ivory, enamel and craftsmanship in silver and gold, belonged to the group of liturgical objects in which luxury and brilliance created visual metaphors through light and colour, embodying a set of symbolic values associated with divinity. These bindings arose in the context of a culture in which lustre made up what have been called "visual metaphors of value".[15]

Fig. 5
Silos workshop, cover of binding, c. 1165–75, gilt and chased copper, champlevé and partially cloisonné enamelwork, 23.7 x 13.7 x 1.3 cm. Madrid, Instituto Valencia de Don Juan [4251]

Fig. 6
Liber Missarum reginae Elisabeth Catholicae. Manuscript, fifteenth century. Mudejar binding covered by a taffeta bag with two enamel badges bearing the arms of Castile and Aragón dating from before the conquest of Granada (detail). RBME, Vitrinas 8

Books and Their Place

In major libraries books were not regarded solely as isolated, independent objects. The growth in the number of books affected their placement and position on library shelves. This had decisive influence on how ornament was applied to these fragments of beauty which bindings constitute.

Until the number of books multiplied rapidly with the invention of the printing press, books were placed on shelves facing front forward. Some paintings show this arrangement. A depiction by Botticelli of *Saint Augustine in his Study*, painted in 1480, shows the books arranged in the humanistic way on the shelf surrounding the saint [fig. 7]. This arrangement of the books also explains why bookshelves were sloping.

The increase in the number of books led this arrangement to fall into disuse owing to the large space required, and instead they were placed on shelves in such a way that only their spine or edges were visible. Thenceforward to the present day it has been customary to store books in this way. Some early sixteenth-century paintings show the "transition" from the humanistic way to the system described above, as in the *Vision of Saint Augustine* belonging to the series executed by Carpaccio between 1502 and 1507 for the Scuola di San Giorgio degli Schiavoni in Venice, the city where much printing took place. The saint is depicted in his study when the vision of Saint Jerome's death comes to him. The books stand in a row on a single shelf, overlapping halfway. With the new arrangement whereby only the spine or fore-edge is

Fig. 7
Sandro Botticelli. *Saint Augustine in His Study*, 1480, fresco, 152 x 112 cm. Florence, Chiesa di Ognissanti

visible, the book has become an art object that is no longer on display and is only seen when we remove it from the shelf and admire its cover.

Another problem of bookbinding in relation to book conservation in libraries was the title, which was sometimes written on a piece of paper that was glued to the spine or cover. The placement of books spine forward led the title to be displayed on this part of the book, as occurs nowadays. But this was not the only way of adding the title. In the sixteenth century it was common for the title to be written in the gilt of the edges, especially on the fore-edges, as can be seen in many of the books in

Fig. 8
Pedro Mexía, *Sylva de Varia leccion compuesta por el Magnífico cavallero Pero Mexia*. Alcalá: En casa de Juan Iñiguez de Lequerica, 1588. Renaissance calfskin binding with gold tooling executed by Juan de Sarriá for the Marquis of Moya. Edges gilded and gauffered with the title of the work and date of binding. Private collection

the library at the Monastery of El Escorial. The books in the late sixteenth-century library of the Marquis of Moya, bound by Juan de Sarriá in accordance with an agreement of 1592 and now mostly in the Biblioteca Zabálburu in Madrid,[16] are fastened with hinges, with gilt edges and the titles in medallions painted in the manner of spine labels [fig. 8]. These books are an excellent example of this type of binding adapted to a library layout underpinned by the principles of harmony and unity. This harmonious arrangement of the books was put into practice in other royal libraries. We know from Vicente Carducho that in a tower that Philip II had built on to the southeast corner of the Alcázar palace in Madrid,[17] "the books are bound curiously and uniformly on gilt shelves, in keeping with the beauty of the item".[18]

The library at the Monastery of El Escorial is an example of this type of placement [fig. 9]. Language books were initially arranged according to subject. Father Sigüenza tells of the unfortunate effect of this arrangement: "The shelf spaces were crammed with titles, which touched and covered each other, and so it was necessary for the books to be very disorganised, and the large put with the small; and as there was only one room it was very muddled and ugly."[19]

This organisation, carried out by Arias Montano, was modified by Sigüenza:

> and order to remove the ugliness that is caused by the disproportion of the books I put together all those in folio in the shelf spaces designed for them, and those in quarto in the shelf spaces for quarto size, and accordingly the rest in their own spaces, and in order for what is sought in them to be easily found, I made two catalogues: one with the names of the authors and the other with the order of these disciplines, thereby ensuring the good outward appearance and composure and the order of the sciences and faculties as regards content.[20]

Sigüenza sought a visual unity of the library in which the books could be seen to be subjected to the same order and appearance. He acknowledges this when he states of the

NEXT PAGES
Figs. 9 and 10
Interior and shelves of the library of the Royal Monastery of San Lorenzo de El Escorial

books that "it has been endeavoured they should all have the same binding, and be proportioned and in good volumes, something which I believe has not been done hitherto in any of the libraries we know of."[21] This was due to the fact that the library at the Monastery of El Escorial was part of a truly royal programme in the manner of the one set up by Francis I at Fontainebleau, for which the establishment of a "uniform formal type" was essential.[22]

The Escorial library is more than just a part of the building designed to house a book collection. It was an undertaking to which Philip II was enthusiastically dedicated and which followed a detailed programme. The location of the library in a privileged part of the Monastery steeped in symbolic connotations relative to the glorification of the sovereign, the iconographic scheme of the paintings, the scientific instruments kept there and the effect and image of the arrangement of the books in cabinets specially designed to hold them were studied with great attention. The result was a library in which all the components make up a unitary formal, ideological and functional whole.

The bindings made for the monastery library were of the "library" type in which the prevailing criteria were simplicity and functionality adapted to the very large number of volumes among which were others of different provenance with bibliophile bindings. But functionality and practicality were not the only determining factors; their placement in the shelf spaces and the design of the book shelves formed an inseparable unity in the library as a whole [fig. 10].

The books appear to be considered parts of a stage set and of an architectural arrangement designed to project an image of science as order, harmony and proportion. The bindings, subordinated to the principle of uniformity, conveyed the image of a knowledge and culture that were inseparable from power. The placement of the books represented a knowledge ordered and systematised under the authority and prestige of the king. The unity of these book bindings would have been difficult to achieve were it not for the existence of a workshop in the Monastery itself. Around 1575 Philip II established a bookbinding workshop at El Escorial, where the binder Juan de Paris, from Medina del Campo, worked for five years and Pedro Bosque for forty-eight years.[23]

It was logical to resort to the aforementioned type of binding owing to the large number of volumes and the pressing concern about giving the books in the collection an external unity. This model of binding was independent of the contents of the works and its purpose was none other than to provide the book with an appearance consonant with the rest of the library items. It should be stressed in this connection that great care was taken over the arrangement of the books on the shelves and the polychrome effect of the gilt of the outward-facing edges.[24] The gilt of the book edges harmonised with other components of the library such as "the gold leaf that predominates in the vault, especially in the cornice surrounding the hall".[25] This arrangement of the books explains the scant importance attached to spine decoration, which consists solely of the pattern of the raised cords and diagonal ornamentation in the spaces between them.

This is a medieval decorative structure and composition to which new classical decorative forms were applied. Renaissance decorative motifs were applied disparately and heterogeneously to the compositional scheme and medieval technique of blind tooling.[26] This model, which became widespread in sixteenth-century Spain, was chiefly used in the bindings of the library at El Escorial. The decoration is blind-tooled without the heat-impressed gold designs that emerged as the main novelty of Renaissance binding. It consists of various rectangles laid out concentrically with scroll decoration applied to each area with a roll. The various rectangles are joined at the corners by a single or three-line fillet. These motifs leave a central space with the supralibros of the grid of the Monastery and decorative motifs at the corners applied with a fleuron. These bindings are based on a model that combines monastic and Mudejar binding traditions with Renaissance decoration. They differ from the classicism of the Monastery's architecture in the fact the motifs decorating this book art are closer to the Plateresque style.

Style and Ornament

Before Adolf Loos conceived ornament to be an offence in 1908, decorative forms had been one of the essential components in defining styles. An artistically bound book is always an object that is decorated more or less profusely—with the exception of the mortified, plain, unornamented Jansenist bindings. Bookbinding styles thus trace the history of the different ornamental systems applied to books and of the changes they have undergone over time. However, the intense relationship the compositions of bound books enjoy with rugs, tapestries, ceiling stuccowork, *pietre dure* table tops, textiles, embroidery and glass did not always stem from a direct link with these works but from the use of themes that were part of the complex common ornamental and compositional corpus of each period, which bookbinders increased and enriched with their contributions.

It should not be forgotten that, as a rule, bookbinders were excellent craftsmen but did not possess a scholarly artistic background that enabled them to rediscover models of the past. The ordinances of the bookbinders' guild—*Ordenanzas de la comunidad de Mercaderes y encuadernadores de libros de esta Corte*—of 1762 states that "anyone who does not know how to read and write cannot be accepted as a Bookbinder or Apprentice".[27] Bookbinders' culture was that which stemmed from their contact with books as "mere objects of knowledge". And its main source of dissemination was therefore the very books that arrived in their workshops to be bound.

Bookbinding and architecture have enjoyed a close relationship through ornamentation or the representation of architectural elements, as in the case of "cathedral style" binding. Various architectural elements were also incorporated into bookbinding, such as the layout of gardens and the decorative forms conveyed

through prints. Another means of dissemination of decorative motifs and compositional forms was treatises, from which many bookbinders drew inspiration in the same way as altarpiece joiners, plasterers, embroiderers, glaziers and architects did.

Arabesques, which are abundant in sixteenth-century bookbinding [fig. 118], were disseminated through prints. One of the basic sources for ornamentation of this type was a work of 1530 by Francisque Pellegrin, *La Fleur de la Science de pourtraicture et patrons de broderie façon arabique et ytalique*, consisting of sixty plates. The very title indicates their provenance and adaptation: Islamic origin and Italian adaptation. The models of Pellegrin, an artist of Florentine origin who worked at Fontainebleau palace, where the art of ornament enjoyed great success, and was one of the main assistants of Rosso Fiorentino (1494–1540), had significant influence on various arts such as bookbinding, and not only on embroidery as the title of his work indicates.

Pellegrin's work not only borrowed motifs from Islamic art but embodied a new conception of ornament that spread to different arts.

Fig. 119
Francisco Jover, *Sanctiones ecclesiasticae tam synodicae quam pontificiae in tres classes distinctae: quarum prima, vniuersales synodos, secunda particulares, tertia pontificia decreta complectitur* .... Parisiis: apud Audoënum Paruum ..., 1555. Gold-tooled and illuminated binding (back cover). RBME, 83.IX.12

This fashion was the result of fascination for the exotic and for forms alien to western classical tradition. The library at the Monastery of El Escorial houses a binding of Aristotle's *Opera* printed at Aldo Manunzio's Venice workshop in 1495; it illustrates the use of gold-tooled arabesques with a central medallion "after the antique" representing Julius Caesar [fig. 93]. These arabesques are combined with scrolls and interlaced motifs in some of the book bindings commissioned by Jean Grolier.

Combinations of interlaced motifs characteristic of labyrinthine Mannerist decoration, whose mosaics and gilt required outstandingly expert craftsmen, played a leading role in sixteenth-century bindings [fig. 11]. Arabesques and interlaced motifs were disseminated early on through prints. Significant artists such as Albrecht Dürer, probably during his second trip to Italy (1505–7), produced six models inspired by others executed at the studio of Leonardo da Vinci[28] and applied in modified form in different decorative arts[29] [fig. 12].

Jean Grolier, a collector and bibliophile who was born in Lyon in 1479 and died in Paris in 1565, was instrumental to the flourishing and development of bindings of this kind. Grolier also possessed a magnificent coin and medal collection in keeping with the refined taste for amassing treasures that was characteristic of the great princes of the day. In this aspect Grolier has been compared to Diego Hurtado de Mendoza, a bibliophile and collector and a lover of bindings, whose library later passed to that of the Monastery of El Escorial.[30]

Fig. 12
Albrecht Dürer, *Interlace pattern*, 1505–7, woodcarving. Frankfurt, Städel Museum, Graphische Sammlung

Mudejar Bandwork

There were extensive repertoires of Islamic artistic motifs in Spain which found their way to book art. A highly original type of bookbinding called Mudejar developed during the Middle Ages and the Renaissance and was characterised by the application of ornamentation of Islamic origin to western codices.

In Mudejar bookbinding, ornamentation plays a role parallel to that of decoration in Arab and Mudejar architecture, the origin of Mudejar art.[31] All Mudejar ornamentation stems from an interpretation of Islamic models. This ornamentation was neither the reuse of an earlier model—such as the rediscovery of the classical model of Antiquity in the Renaissance period—nor a revival like those of the nineteenth century, prominent among which was neo-Mudejar. On the contrary, Mudejar decoration continued and reinterpreted a technical and artistic tradition in a synthesis of Christian and Muslim forms.

Mudejar bookbinding encompasses a heterogeneous group of works formed by a broad variety of types, generally with bandwork decoration. Despite the name by which they are called, it should not be assumed that these bindings were executed by Mudejars, Muslims who remained in Spain after the Christian reconquest. Mudejar is a stylistic term to which ethnic, social and religious connotations should not be attributed. In Mudejar bookbinding certain forms persist over time, irrespective of the limits and periods of western styles. Mudejar bookbindings are derived from the leather work executed by Muslims and Jews in Toledo, Seville and subsequently in Granada. This mastery of leather work, together with Islamic bindings no longer extant, may have been the point of departure for Mudejar bindings.[32]

Mudejar book bindings were not simply mass produced to meet a substantial demand. They were commonly found in the most important libraries belonging to the Church,

Fig. 13
Thomas Aquinas, *Regimiento de principes*. Manuscript, fifteenth century. Gothic-Mudejar binding in goatskin over boards. RB, II/3569

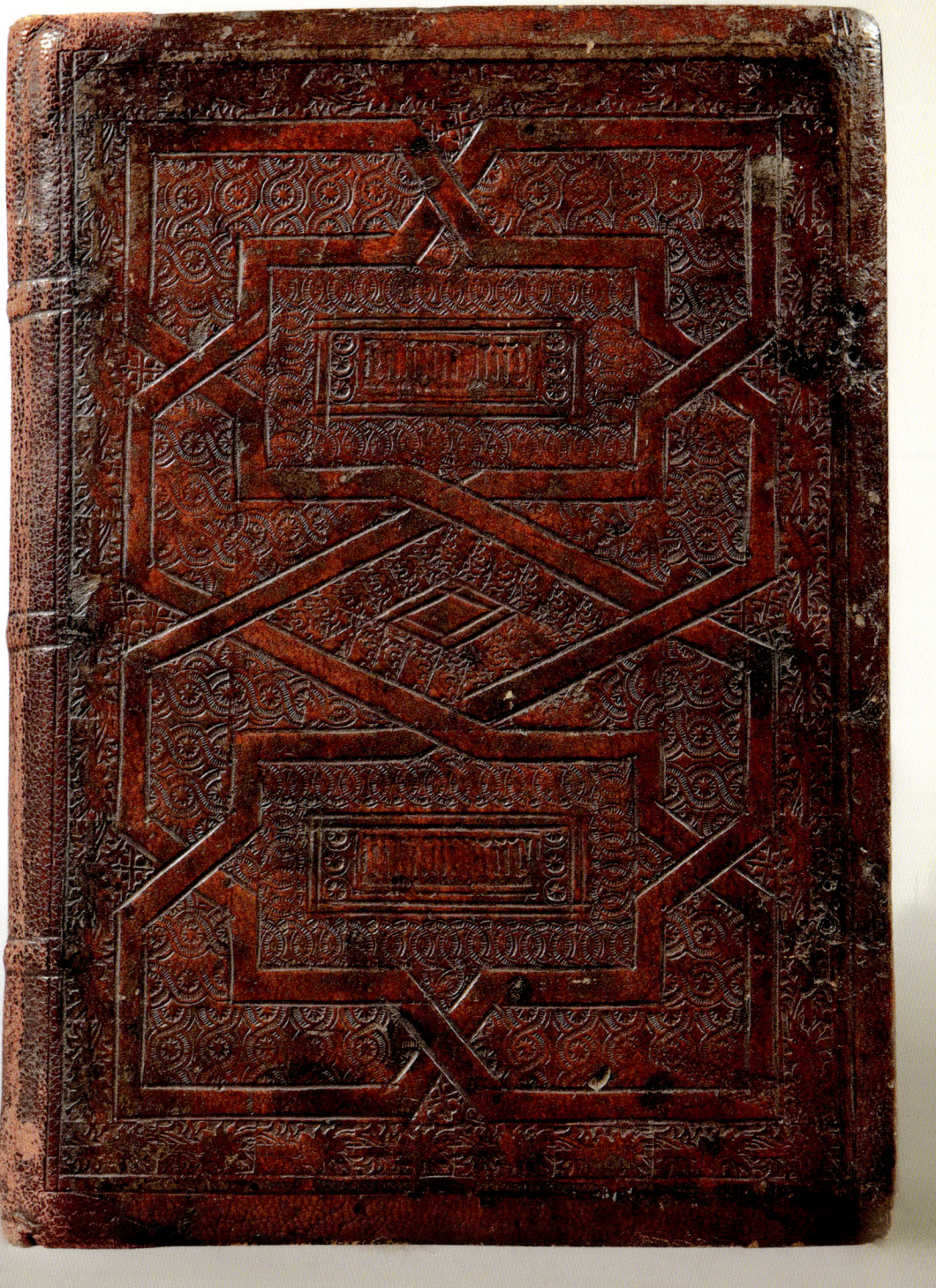

the nobility and the monarchy, such as the handsome *Breviarium Caroli V imperatoris* in the library of the Monastery of El Escorial, which is a paradigmatic example of this type of binding [figs. 14 and 15].

The connection between bookbinding ornamentation and other expressions of Mudejar art was chiefly established in woodwork such as ceilings, doors, shutters, lattices and furniture in which the main ornamental feature was compositions of interlaced bands, as in the Islamic arts. Bandwork patterns were easily adapted to book covers owing to their symmetrical, modular and serial nature. These patterns were based on repeatable geometric compositions which allowed the ornamentation to be adapted and extended to a variety of formats.[33] In order to adapt them to book format, bookbinders created their own compositions of bandwork patterns applied specifically to book covers,[34] as in the *Missale toletanum* (Madrid, Biblioteca Nacional), a perfect example of Mudejar bookbinding with a rosette in the centre and fine decoration in the spaces between the bands.

As in architecture, in Mudejar bookbinding the ornamentation is flexible and capable of being adapted to a broad diversity of formats and of incorporating decorative forms borrowed from western styles such as Gothic and Renaissance. The *Breviario de la Reina Católica* from the Chapel Royal, now in the library at El Escorial and clothed in a protective taffeta bag,[35] shows an eclectic blend of Mudejar forms and Gothic motifs executed in a period in which such combinations were common.

Figs. 14 and 15
Breviarium Caroli V imperatoris. Toledo, 1515–45. Mudejar binding with wooden boards covered in dark crimson cordovan (vol. IV) and miniature with a portrait of Charles V (fol. 1v of vol. I). RBME, Vitrinas 4–7

The consideration of Mudejar as one of the most original and typical expressions of Spanish art gradually took shape in the nineteenth century, when value began to be attached to vernacular and national styles as opposed to the universality of classicism, and fascination for new exotic models sprang up. Specifically, through the neo-Mudejar style, Orientalism played a major role in bookbinding and in the modernist movement in Catalonia.[36] The neo-Mudejar style is a systemisation characteristic of the nineteenth century—a medieval revival inspired by Spanish traditions and by a craft concept of artistic work in the context of the new value attached to the decorative arts.[37]

Earlier on, the Spanish works shown at the Exposition Universelle in Paris in 1867 featured several bindings, among them a book entitled *Arte y vocabulario árabigo* printed in Granada in 1505. In it

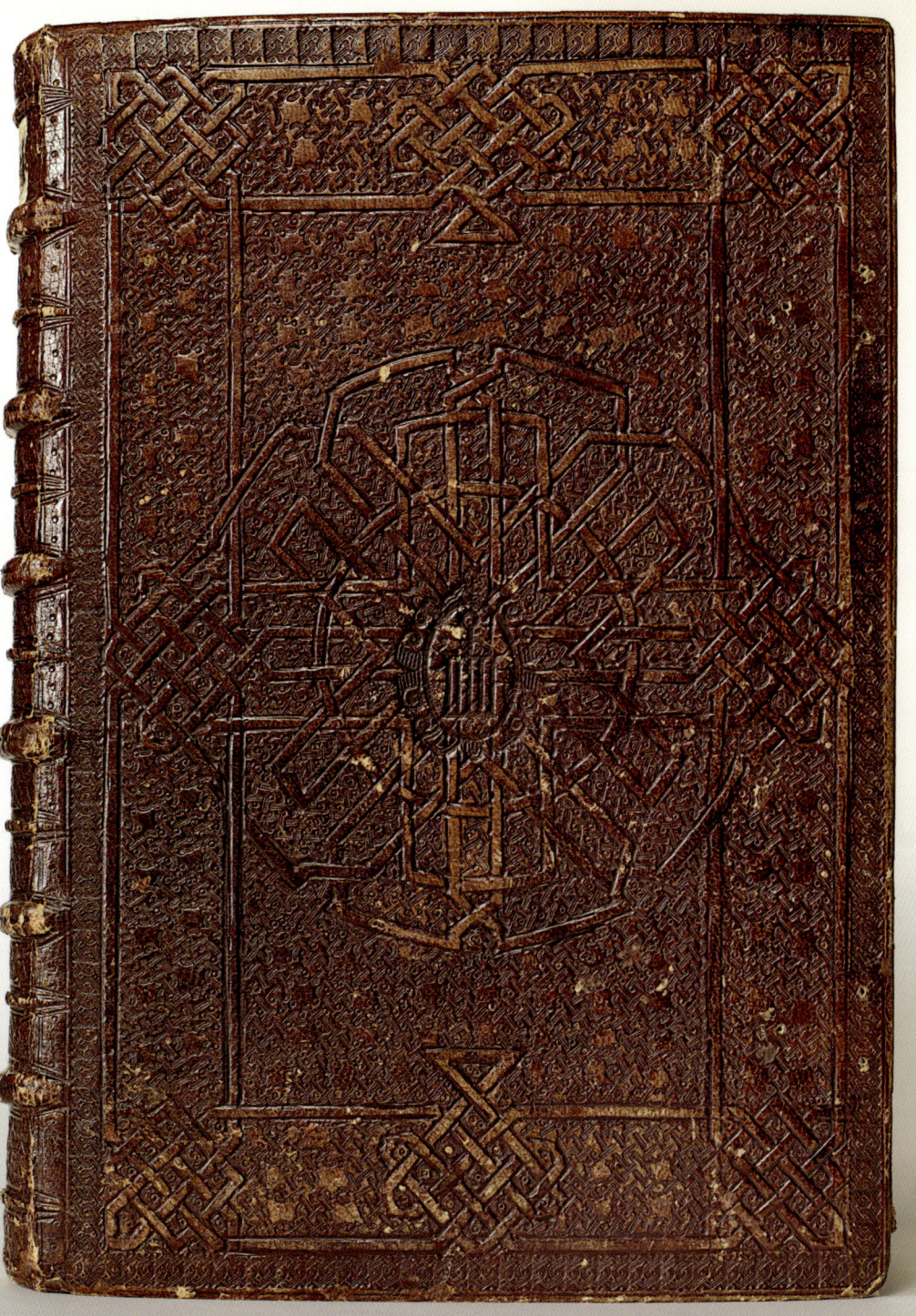

the coffering of the covers copies a detail from the Hall of the Abencerrajes in the Alhambra; the pattern on the spine and the endpapers, the tiling from the Hall of the Two Sisters; the edges, a panel from the Court of the Lions; the outer and inner squares, whose details are taken from the same building; all in all, everything represents the study of some period, in the geometrical and little known pattern of the Arabs.[38]

This is an early example of neo-Arab bookbinding whose decorative motifs reproduce those found in the Nasrid architecture of the Alhambra, in keeping with the widespread nineteenth-century trend for "Alhambrism", which had previously enjoyed considerable influence.[39]

Plateresque Grotesques and Scrollwork

Renaissance forms were introduced to Spanish bookbinding in a similar way to how they appeared in other arts through the application of classical decorative scrollwork and grotesque motifs, which became extremely widespread especially after 1480, when the *Domus Aurea* was discovered.[40]

Initially decorative motifs with a "classical" appearance were applied to some book bindings that employed medieval techniques. This phenomenon parallels the development of decoration applied to architecture: when classical ornamentation is planned for the façade—designed in the manner of an altarpiece—of a building with a Gothic structure without knowledge of the new decorative language as the ornamental features are scattered motifs disseminated through drawings, engravings and printed books. The craftsmen who applied them were master builders who, like bookbinders, had been trained in the traditional language and techniques and lacked knowledge of the classical principles and compositional systems.

A particularly illustrative example of the problems of applying Renaissance forms to bookbinding is Torello Saraina's *De origine et amplitudine civitatis Veronae*, published in Verona in 1540 and housed in the library of the Monastery of El Escorial[41] [fig. 16]. The decoration is blind tooled with scrollwork and head motifs. As it is worked with a single roll, the decoration displays adaptation problems. The motifs are repeated in each strip with the heads in vertical position in the vertical bands and positioned sideways in the horizontal bands. In order to achieve symmetry in keeping with the new classical culture, the binder would have needed a stamp or two tools, one for vertical and one for horizontal bands.

The problem has been raised of the existence of laws regulating the grotesque compositions[42] and the existence of hidden contents of what has been called "a mysterious writing".[43] This may be the case in some elaborate schemes. But in bindings these compositions

Fig. 16

Torello Saraina. *De origine et amplitudine ciuitatis Veronae* .... Veronae ...: ex officina Antonii Putelleti, 1540. Bound in wood and calfskin boards and blind decorated with tools and rolls. RBME, 39.I.37

Fig. 17
Charles Clifford, *Salamanca. University, Library Door*, 1858?, glass negative

were simply schemes after the antique. These forms were introduced to Spanish bookbinding through the same means used to spread them in other arts. Engravings, printed books and notebooks were the sources that were most widespread and had the greatest repercussions, along with models taken from works imported directly from Italy, such as tombs.

The dissemination through printmaking of these grotesque, scroll and candelabra motifs—as well as heads and warriors inspired by the study of ancient monuments and ruins—became more widespread during the sixteenth century through the engravings produced by Francesco Rosselli around 1471–90,[44] Agostino Veneziano (*c.* 1490–1540) and Giovanni Antonio de Brescia (active *c.* 1490–1525), which inspired the craftsmen who decorated the façade of Salamanca University[45] [fig. 17]. These ornamental motifs enjoyed a boom in architecture, tombs, altarpieces, the borders of stained-glass windows, miniatures, woodwork and bookbinding,[46] leading to very harsh criticism from artists who advocated a purist style. When describing the monstrance of Seville cathedral in 1587, Juan de Arfe harshly criticised the use and abuse of grotesques. Arfe, who held the Monastery of El Escorial to be the paradigm of good architecture, stated that

> everything in it displays truth and magnificence, dispensing at all times, as they are superficial, with trifling projections, *estipites*, elongated corbels, cartouches and other illusions—that, through being seen in Flemish and French papers and prints, are adopted by inconsiderate and bold artisans who, calling them inventions, adorn, or rather destroy, their works with them without concern for proportion or meaning—from which I have always fled from as a mistaken thing, following the old observation that Vitruvius and other excellent authors taught by showing the finest examples of the ancients.[47]

The use of these ornamental forms in bookbinding called for the creation of specific compositions. When the decoration is applied not with a roll but with small stamps or blocks, it reveals the difficulties of adjusting to the format of the cover, just as when stamps are used for the printed ornamentation of the pages of a book. They were a substitute for the ornamentation of many fifteenth-century bindings of Germany, Flanders and the Netherlands, executed with a single block and stamped in a press.[48] In the earliest Renaissance bindings, as there were no complete panel stamps bearing the new classical decorative motifs, these adaptations were made until the widespread use of the roll partially solved these problems of adjustment. For decoration based on a continuous strip, rolls of different widths were useful and adaptable instruments—unlike blocks, which could only stamp a motif of the same length.

As commented, in Mudejar bindings Gothic decorative motifs were inserted into the spaces between the interlaced bands. In other words, themes borrowed from different stylistic repertoires were mixed, following an eclectic ornamental criterion. As a result of this practice, Renaissance forms are likewise blended with Mudejar motifs in some bindings. The same phenomenon occurred in architecture in which diverse repertoires are mixed, giving rise to what I have called a "lack of stylistic definition".[49] Defining a Plateresque binding is thus a complex task as it usually features a mixture of Gothic, Mudejar and Renaissance motifs. This phenomenon was referred to by Diego de Sagredo, who published his *Medidas del Romano* in Toledo in 1526 in order to instruct "journeymen who wish to follow the formations of bases/columns/capitals and other pieces of ancient buildings", to whom he recommended: "And take care that you do not have the conceit to mix Roman with modern: or to seek novelties by transforming the work of one piece into another."[50]

In these bindings Renaissance motifs are the words of a language applied without syntactic structure. Motifs were used provided they were "Roman style", regardless of the disparity of their provenance. "Italian" was equivalent to "classical". The heterogeneousness and disparity of the Renaissance decorative motifs of the so-called Plateresque bookbinding style derived from the adaptation of medieval blind-tooled binding to Renaissance tastes is due to this and to the diverse sources of inspiration. Although this type of binding was very widespread in Spain, it was not exclusively "Spanish", as it was used in other countries with a medieval bookbinding tradition to which new Italian motifs were incorporated.

Books and Luxury: Marble, Curtains and Stuccowork

It has been assumed[51] that some bindings executed in Salamanca and sent by Philip II to the library at the Monastery of El Escorial were the first in which the entire covers and spine of the book display gold decoration, such as Francisco Vallés de Covarrubias' *Octo librorum Aristotelis de physica doctrina...* published in Alcalá de Henares by Andrés de Angulo in 1562. The centrepiece is octagonal, leaving four triangles which are profusely decorated in the corners of the frame.

This composition marks the start of a new decorative model which developed in the so-called fan binding that was widespread in the seventeenth century. Its origin has been sought in the French fashion for fans, but there are other arts in which similar decorative forms are found, such as lace, carpets, metalwork and, in architecture, pendentives and squinches decorated with radiating motifs to establish the transition to the circular base of cupolas. The rectangular shape of book covers facilitated the application of a central motif and four at the corners as the basis of the decoration. A type of fully decorated binding set inside a rectangle enjoyed great popularity in the eighteenth century and displays evident parallels with the art of carpet making and brocade. This effect was accentuated by the small size of the decorative motifs and their symmetrical application throughout the whole cover of the book. Examples of this type of binding are those executed by Antonio de Sancha, a bookbinder, printer and publisher who played a decisive role in Madrid between 1740 and 1790.[52] His initial works can be seen to be inspired by the traditional forms of fans, which then shift towards Italian and French Baroque forms infused with a Rococo spirit featuring a host of floral motifs that define a type of court binding characteristic of the reigns of Ferdinand VI and Charles III [fig. 18]. With Sancha the Spanish bookbinding style, which remained steeped in local traditions, became universal as it embraced the aesthetic taste of European arts of the day.

Bookbinding has never remained faithful to established repertoires; rather, it has evolved in keeping with the prevailing artistic languages of the time. Binders often created their own themes from decorative motifs of the period. Such is the case of the so-called neoclassical "curtain" bindings in Spain in which a new type of design and handling of leather were used to create an Empire-style trend.

Artistic languages, even the most radical such as neoclassicism with its strict rules, provided a source of inspiration and a stimulus rather than merely copying models. This always involved interpretation, because "imitation was not the reproduction of a model, but the elaboration of a different version of it. Antiquity is in a sense the golden branch whereby one enters the world of the arts."[53] "Curtain" bindings are an original contribution to neoclassical art, as an original emulation of monumental decoration.

These bindings incorporated new materials which accentuated their originality and established a new type of relationship with the repertoire of classical models of the day. A type of leather, the so-called *pasta valenciana,* was created during the reign of Charles IV. In *pasta valenciana* plain dye is replaced by streaking and marbled effects consonant with a fashion in the decoration of walls, altarpieces and furniture. Binding leathers come in the colour with which they left the tanning shop. Therefore, when the binder wishes to incorporate colour he must add another piece of different coloured leather, inlaying or onlaying it. Other leathers, such as *pasta valenciana,* display a mottled deco-

Fig. 18
Carissimo in Christo filio nostro Ferdinando hispaniarum Regi Catholico, Benedictus PP. XIV .... Italy (?): n. n., *c.* 1753. Rococo-style red morocco binding by Antonio Sancha. RB, I/E/84

dance with reason. *Arte de hacer el estuco jaspeado o de imitar los jaspes a poca costa y con la mayor propiedad*, a short treatise written by the prebendary of the cathedral of Ciudad Rodrigo, Ramón Pasqual Díez, and published at the royal printing house in Madrid in 1785, describes and returns to the manners of executing this decorative form.[55] On 2 March 1788 Pasqual was appointed a member of the San Fernando Royal Academy of Fine Arts together with Julián de Ayllón, a canon of Medina del Campo, and in 1792–93 he taught classes to the students of San Fernando on the application of marbling. An order issued by Floridablanca on 25 November 1777 barring altarpieces from being made of wood instead of jasper, marble or stucco[56] explains the popularity this technique enjoyed at the time—and which horrified John Ruskin, who stated in 1851: "There is not a meaner occupation for the human mind than the imitation of the stains and striae of marble and wood."[57]

ration. In Ferdinand VII's day it was applied to Empire-style bindings known as "curtain" bindings executed in Madrid, Barcelona and Valencia. In this style the predominant ornamentation was the curtain decoration in one or several corners with a pattern of gold lines and mosaic work which, together with the mottled leather, was of a hitherto unseen colourfulness[54] [fig. 19].

Mottled stuccowork imitating marble was particularly used in altarpieces. Compared to the *estofado* (gilded, painted and inscribed) decoration of altarpieces, stucco achieved an effect that was more classical and in accor-

The style of curtain binding introduced various new features such as curtain motifs, marbled leather, mosaic and classical motifs in gold. It was created by Antonio Suárez (1770–1836), who worked in Barcelona, Valencia and also Madrid, where he was made a court binder in 1803. Other binders such as Vicente Beneito in Valencia devised a style which, using common elements, brought to bookbinding a hitherto unseen originality [fig. 20]. Curtain-style decoration had been used in architectural ornamentation, as in the Pompeian ceilings of the Casita del Príncipe at El Escorial, rooms in El Pardo palace and furniture in the Hall of Ambassadors

Fig. 19
A los Reyes nuestros señores D. Fernando VII y Doña María Josefa Amalia de Saxonia, en testimonio de amor, júbilo y homenage por su venturoso enlace / la Universidad de Salamanca. [Spain]: [n. n.], [1819]. Empire-style "curtain" binding in *pasta valenciana* by Antonio Suárez. RB, I/G/354

in El Pardo palace. However, its application to bookbinding was a genuinely Spanish invention [fig. 21].

Curtains were a recurring theme in the decorative schemes of the Empire style. One of the vehicles for the dissemination of many of the themes found in the decorative arts of the nineteenth century was the catalogues of samples published at the time.[58] During the nineteenth century these catalogues were used systematically by craftsmen, master builders, decorative entrepreneurs and architects. One of the first French catalogues of standardised objects was published in 1810 and featured ornamental motifs to be executed in papier mache, mastic, terracotta, cement and other materials. Entitled *Recueil des dessins d'ornaments d'architecture de la fabrique Joseph Beunat,* it was brought out by the manufactory of Joseph Beurat, founded in Sarrebourg in 1805.[59] The catalogue was comprised of plates and the models reproduced were not labelled. It is interesting to draw attention to some in which the decoration displays close similarities to our bindings, such as those reproducing a *Bedroom* and a *Petit Boudoir*[60] and in which curtain-based decoration is a prominent feature.

BOOKBINDING, AN ARTISTIC LANGUAGE | 45

Fig. 20
Planes o Estados que manifiestan el número de pleytos, causas y expedientes ... despachados en el año 1816 .... Valencia: Benito Monfort, 1817. Empire-style "curtain" binding in *pasta valenciana* by Vicente Beneyto. RB, I/G/355

In addition to the usual definition of "cortina" [curtain], the *Diccionario de la Real Academia Española* gives another meaning according to which curtain is associated with royalty: "In the etiquette and ceremonial of the chapel royal, canopy where the king's seat of honour was."[61] In this respect, it could be related to curtain bindings, as the latter were largely executed for Ferdinand VII. Canopies and curtains played a sumptuous and decorative role. The *Recueil de decorations interieurs* (1801) by Charles Percier and Pierre-François-Léonard Fontaine shows all the lavishness of the decoration based on these features at a time when artists of the Empire style, in contrast with the simplicity of neoclassicism, "veiled the naked simplicity of geometrically shaped rooms and upholstered the walls with elaborate draperies swathed over doors and windows, sofas and beds, hung from the cornices and sometimes gathered up into the ceiling to simulate a tent".[62]

Curtain bindings eliminated the earlier decorative excesses by introducing a geometric regularity which borrowed motifs employed in other luxury arts, such as rugs and embroidery. The rug of the early seat of honour in the Chapel Royal at Aranjuez, designed by

Fig. 21
Noticia de la función fúnebre en que el Regimiento provincial de Oviedo solemnizó el once de Marzo de ... mil ochocientos diez y nueve la muerte de ... Doña María Isabel Francisca de Braganza, Reyna de España. Oviedo: Petregel y C., 1819. Empire-style "curtain" binding in red morocco. RB, XIV/2905

Pedro Cancio and embroidered by Bernardino Pandeavenas in 1799, displays these classical curtain ornaments in the corner circles and motifs of the central compartment.[63] The forms of curtain bindings are consonant with the decorative tastes of Charles IV and María Luisa of Parma, especially the ceiling and wall decorations in which silks played a prominent role and act as the genuine endpapers of the building.[64] Another example is the wall paintings featuring textile themes, executed by Vicente Gómez for the pleasure palace known as the Casa de Campo at the Royal Site of San Lorenzo.[65]

Curtain ornamentation created a new type of binding that was part of the decorative language of the period. This relationship between binding and luxurious decorative arts was not the only one. Owing to the rectangular shape of most rooms, the decoration of ceilings often consisted of stucco or plasterwork laid out around a central motif—as found in many bindings—such as, for example, the design produced by Jean Cotelle around 1640 for a Parisian ceiling rosette, which is also related to garden designs.[66] In his *Third and Fourth Book of Architecture* (1537, 1540), Sebastiano Serlio (1475–1554) had published garden designs which became models for other arts such as bookbinding [fig. 22].

Fig. 22
Sebastiano Serlio, "Gardens", in *Tercero y quarto libro de architectura.* Toledo: en casa de Iuan de Ayala, 1552. RB, XIV/21

Marbling, Paper and Abstraction

The marbling and mottling mentioned earlier create a plastic effect which is also found in the endpapers of books.[67] On opening the book the reader is surprised by the sight of the endpapers [fig. 23]. Executed in paper in intense shades, they greet us with a colourful double page before we come to the contents of the book. They are the "shirt" of the book that is worn beneath the "suit" of the binding. Some bindings have their richest and most sumptuous decoration in gold-tooled leather with mosaic ornamentation on the underside of the boards. However, it was more common to employ paper endleaves, which became widespread in Europe in the sixteenth century, although their origins can be traced back to the Far East some centuries earlier.[68] Marbled paper was being made in Europe by about 1630. The motifs of the handmade endpapers subsequently underwent a major development as they came to be printed using mechanical procedures.

Although some endpapers display figurative motifs, they usually exhibit abstract forms. An endpaper contains forms, lines and colours which give it a particular, highly original appearance. This appearance is specific to the binding and is accentuated by the fact that the binder chooses a piece of the paper more or less at random and in accordance with the size of the book. Unlike the mottled leather which imitates or emulates the forms of marble, endleaves do not imitate any motif. Their forms are autonomous, even if the endpapers used in books do not always have this meaning. Even if each one is independent

or unrepeatable, some, such as comb patterns, became forms that were representations of themselves owing to the reiterated use of the motifs.

Endleaves are not ornament as they do not contain a decorative motif applied to an object—unlike, for example, mosaic decoration or the gilt on spine and covers. They are autonomous and specific forms of binding which are not "applied" to the first sheets of the book. Endpapers are one of the first products in which form is not applied as a decoration to an object in the same way as ornamentation to architecture, the border framing a tapestry, the border of a stained-glass window or the gilt on a book's covers. Instead, endleaves are sheets of paper made independently and separately from the book and later incorporated into it. They are the "theatre curtain" which marks the start and finish of the book's performance. It is a curtain with nothing written on it and which contributes to the creation of the ritual surrounding this performance, which is reading.

The endpapers of bindings are of great importance as they are a precedent and form *avant la lettre* of what has been known since 1910 as abstraction, invented by Kandinsky initially with the aim of experimenting with dispensing with references to representation. Their use entails abstract, non-figurative forms, which have been called the "embryo of abstract art".[69]

The Crisis in the Traditional System of the Arts

Neoclassical bookbinding created a style that borrowed from classical forms and aimed to dispense with any national connotations. The 1820s saw the start of a trend which looked towards the Middle Ages and the vernacular origins of nations. Gothic forms, shunned and despised since the Renaissance, acquired a new meaning as identifying features and the recovery of a national past. In bookbinding this spirit is embodied by the so-called "cathedral style" that emerged in the early 1820s, created by Joseph Thouvenin (1791–1834).

The decoration of these bindings features Gothic architectural motifs on the book covers [fig. 24]. This did not entail the reuse of the forms of medieval Gothic binding but the invention of a new type of binding with Gothic decorative motifs that constitute one of the forms of expression of the so-called neo-Gothic style, which was disseminated on a huge scale through handmade bindings and the numerous industrial bindings.

As in other expressions of this style, in neo-Gothic bindings the Gothic models are viewed as a single unit, without distinguishing the development they had undergone between the thirteenth and fifteenth centuries. Gothic is conceived as an aesthetic category, as an anticlassical model, a seamless, non-evolving style, just as the art of the Greeks had been for the practitioners of the neoclassical style. The only aspect in which a distinction is drawn is the fact that for the first time it is distinguished from Romanesque,

Fig. 23
Carissimo in Christo filio nostro Ferdinando hispaniarum Regi Catholico, Benedictus PP. XIV .... Italy (?): n. n., *c.* 1753. Endpaper. RB, I/E/84

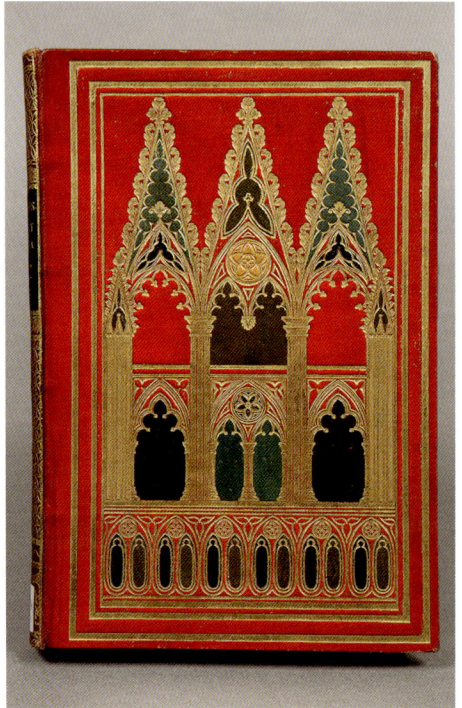

Fig. 24
Decretos del Rey Don Fernando VII: año primero de su restitucion al trono de las Españas: se refieren todas las reales resoluciones generales que se han expedido por los diferentes ministerios y consejos desde 4 de mayo de 1814 hasta fin de diciembre de igual año / por Don Fermín Martín de Balmaseda. Vol. 17. Madrid: en la Imprenta Real, 1832. Cathedral-style binding in red morocco by Antonio Suárez Jiménez. RB, I/G/241

iar with techniques, but nor can it be understood without knowledge of the technique and processes involved in its execution. The binder is not like a painter who draws and paints freely. To decorate books he uses rolls, pallets and fleurons with specific decorative motifs. The compositional changes in bookbinding are not complex but required the fashioning of tools with the new motifs. This explains why, well into the nineteenth century, neoclassical and Rococo motifs such as rocailles continued to be used. In many cases this conservatism is intentional, but in others it denotes the continuity of forms that do not deviate particularly from the tastes of the period. Rococo forms were also anticlassical and, accordingly, valid. Anticlassicism tended to appreciate these Rococo forms that were recovered by another markedly anticlassical trend, Art Nouveau, in which the influence of neo-Rococo is evident.[70]

Throughout the nineteenth century a major change took place in the hierarchical classification of the arts. The value attached to medieval styles, industrialisation and the invasion of machine-made products brought a major change in the consideration of the traditional system of the arts. The inaptly named industrial, decorative or lesser arts were differently regarded.

The system of the arts established in the Renaissance was shattered when mechanisation replaced manual labour, and books, like other arts, joined the industrialisation process. The design of many industrial bindings was excellent, albeit repeatable in editions with a large number of copies. Books came out with bindings previously designed by artists. But

which was beginning to take shape at the time. Neo-Gothic is therefore not equivalent to neo-medieval but an exclusive revival of Gothic forms.

Although bookbinding evolved in tune with other arts, many aspects of the changes it underwent can only be explained by binders' ways and systems of working. A work of art cannot be grasped simply by being famil-

Fig. 25
[Uniformes del Ejército de Rusia]. Bound in malachite and silver gilt with the royal cypher of Isabel II (1857), gift of Mariano Téllez-Girón, general and Spanish ambassador to Russia. RB, FOT/26

they were executed using mechanical procedures, and therefore now belonged in the categories of graphic and industrial design. As in all the arts in which this mechanisation process took place, artistic handmade bookbinding was reduced to an activity which was valued but isolated and reserved.

This transformation was not without contradictions and controversies.[71] It involved a change in the system of arts that was later developed extensively by the modernist movement and gave rise to a resurgence of the so-called decorative arts, among them bookbinding. In Art Nouveau the illustration of a book by Beardsley, a poster by Mucha, a lamp by Gallé or a stained-glass window by Rigalt had the same artistic value. They were objects that shaped the definition of a new style in which all the arts were involved, considered essential parts of the process of return to the idea of a single and universal style that had disappeared with neoclassicism. A new style that did not entail the imitation of early models, revivals or nostalgic glances at history.

However, in the nineteenth century revivals played an essential role in recovering, with great precision and exquisite craftsmanship, the techniques of many arts such as stained glass, enamelwork and bookbinding. From a technical viewpoint, neo-Renaissance or neo-Baroque bindings are much more perfect than works executed between the fifteenth and seventeenth centuries. They were the made by the so-called *pasticheurs* who, in parallel to the development of modern bookbinding, were intensely involved in a historicist activity owing to the survival of an academic and traditional taste which, as in the other arts, was maintained throughout the twentieth century as a clear testimony of significant resistance to the avant-garde [fig. 25].

The contribution of Art Deco bookbinding was much more than a formal renewal. It shaped a new book aesthetic from which all subsequent renewal stems, by converting into expressive elements all the components of the book from the typeface to the layout and the visual effect of the whole. Thereafter bookbinding became integrated into avant-garde concepts with an expressive and formal autonomy that caused forms to develop independently of the book's contents.

Modern bookbinding has developed as a language in tune with the contemporary arts as a whole [fig. 26]. Abstract and figurative bindings, with strict constructive rigour or heightened expressiveness, belong in an avant-garde context. There was even a break away from the traditional concept of binding when new techniques and materials were incorporated such as wood, acetate and metals, making the book a new expressive object.

An abstract binding is an expression of independence of the artistic component of the book with respect to its contents and argument. Its forms may or may not be in tune with the book itself, but they always display a formal autonomy which in no way suggests what we will find behind its covers. This is precisely because of the break with the idea of representation and, accordingly, of information about or an allusion to what it conceals. Only the titles can provide a reference to the work. But the binding is an independent object valid for its own sake. A bibliophile is a lover of books, or of books and bindings, but can

Fig. 26
Fina García Marruz, *¿De qué, silencio, eres tú silencio?* Salamanca: Universidad de Salamanca; Madrid: Patrimonio Nacional, 2011. XX Reina Sofía Prize for Ibero-American Poetry. Bound by Obradoiro Penumbra. RB, XIV/2957

also be a lover of bindings, which he collects in the same way as paintings, sculptures, drawings or prints. This phenomenon displays parallels with what has occurred in other arts such as, for example, stained glass. Stained glass has always been an architectural art which, in addition to its aesthetic character, served the function of closing a window space. In recent decades many stained-glass makers have produced independent stained glass panels, "autonomous panels" to be placed outdoors, in an architectural space, illuminated artificially from behind or in front of a window. As in bookbinding, it is the result of a process of emancipation of languages which had been fulfilling an applied function and which have secured independent spaces of their own.

---

1 BURY 2007, chap. XVII, n. p.
2 BRUGALLA 2000, 141–42.
3 DUDIN 1772, 2. NIETO ALCAIDE 2007, 27.
4 DELVAUX 1981, 10.
5 LÓPEZ-VIDRIERO 2003, 6–7.
6 As recorded in the "Inventario de los bienes muebles existentes en el Tesoro del Alcázar de Segovia, al cargo de Rodrigo de Tordesillas, hecho por el secretario Gaspar de Gricio, por mandato de Isabel la Católica" (1503): "Otro libro sin hojas, que es barril e se dize Breviario sobre la sed", in SÁNCHEZ CANTON 1950, 37; RUIZ GARCÍA. 2004, 295.
7 BARBIER 2005, 73

8 CARRIÓN 1996, 370. CRESPI DE VALLDAURA 1994, 35–47.
9 BURY 2007, chap. VIII, n. p.
10 *Don Quixote* I, VI.
11 HALDANE 1983.
12 DELVAUX 1981, 101.
13 BARBIER 2005, 38.
14 BARBIER 2005, 73.
15 GOMBRICH 1968, 25ff.
16 SÁNCHEZ MARIANA 1994, 12–18.
17 BOUZA ÁLVAREZ 2005, 39.
18 CARDUCHO 1979, 432. [Están los libros enquadernados curiosa y uniformemente en estantes dorados, en correspondencia a la hermosura de la pieza.]

19 Sigüenza 1927, II, Discurso XI, p. 411. [Los cajones llenos de títulos, que se alcanzaban y cubrían unos con otros, y así era forzoso estar los libros muy descompuestos, y grandes con chicos; y como no era más de una la pieza era una cosa muy confusa y fea.]
20 Sigüenza 1927, II, Discurso XII, 411–12. [Y por quitar la fealdad que hace la desproporción de los libros junte los de folio todos en los cajones que estaban para ellos, y los de cuarto en los de cuarto, y así los demás en sus propios senos, y para que con suma facilidad se halle lo que se busca en ellos, hice dos Catálogos: el uno de los nombres propios de los autores y el otro con el mismo orden de estas disciplinas, y se satisficiese a todo a la buena apariencia y compostura de fuera, y al orden de las Ciencias y facultades, en lo de dentro.]
21 Sigüenza 1927, II, Discurso XI, 420. [Hase procurado que tengan todos una misma encuadernación, y que hagan proporcionados y buenos tomos, lo que creo yo que hasta ahora no se ha hecho en ninguna de las librerías de que tenemos noticia.]
22 Checa Cremades 1998, 91.
23 Álvarez Turienzo 1986, 126.
24 Nieto Alcaide 1998, 46–55, and 2000, 673–78.
25 Andrés 198, 562.
26 On the problem of the Plateresque see Nieto Alcaide 1989, 11–96.
27 Hueso Rolland 1935, 165. [No podrá ser recibido para Encuadernador, ni Aprendiz ninguno que no sepa leer ni escribir.]
28 Gruber 1993a, 26–27.
29 Jordan and Constantini-Lachat 1993, 275ff.
30 Hobson 1999. A chapter of this book was published in Spanish with the title "Diego Hurtado de Mendoza" (Hobson 2000). See also the text by Hobson in this book.
31 Borras Gualix 1990, 89.
32 Álvaro Zamora 2008, 448.
33 Galay Saranana n. d., 11–12.
34 Méndez Pascual 1999, 26–55.
35 Hueso Rolland 1935, 41, pl. XIII, catalogue 66.
36 Vélez Vicente 1981, 161–99
37 Vélez Vicente 1981, 169.
38 Comisión Regia de España 1867, 128; cf. Hueso Rolland 1935, 170. [El artesonado de las tapas copia de un detalle de la Sala de los Abencerrajes de la Alhambra; el dibujo del lomo y de las guardas, los alicatados de la Sala de las dos Hermanas; el corte de una franja del Patio de los Leones; el canto y contracantos, cuyos detalles están tomados del mismo edificio; todo, en fin, representa el estudio de algún tiempo, en el geométrico y poco conocido dibujo de los árabes.]
39 Raquejo 1989.
40 Dacos 1969.
41 RBME, 39.I.37.
42 García Álvarez 2001, 103.
43 Müller Profumo 1985, 141.
44 *Italian Renaissance Prints* 2007, 42.
45 Sebastián and Cortés 1973, 43.
46 Bimbenet-Privat and Gruber 1993, 113ff.
47 Cean Bermúdez 1800, I, 61–62. See the recent study by Andrés González 2010. [Quanto en él parece, muestra verdad y magnificencia, dexando por vanas y de ningún momento las menudencias de resaltillos, estípites, mutilos, cartelas y otras burlerías, que por verse en los papeles y estampas flamencas y francesas, siguen inconsiderados y atrevidos artífices y nombrándolas invención, adornan, o por mejor decir, destruyen con ellas sus obras sin guardar proporción ni significado de lo cual como cosa mendosa he huido siempre, siguiendo la antigua observación que Vitrubio y otros excelentes autores enseñaron con demostración de los mejores ejemplos de los antiguos.]
48 López Serrano 1972, 53–54.
49 Nieto Alcaide 1989, 11–96.
50 Sagredo 1526, E, IIII. [A los oficiales que quieren seguir las formaciones de las Basas/Columnas/Capiteles/ y otras piezas de los edificios antiguos … e mira bien que no tengas presunción de mezclar romano con moderno: ni quieras buscar novedades trastocando las labores de una pieza en otra.]
51 Carrión 1994, 408.
52 López Serrano 1946, 295.
53 Fumaroli 2010, .31.
54 Lopez Serrano 1967, 22–31.
55 Pasqual Diez 1988 [facsimile edition].
56 Pasqual Diez 1988, 99.
57 Ruskin 1853, 30.
58 Negre 2004, 422.
59 Kuchly 1996. There is a reprint of Beunat's book entitled: *Empire Style Designs and Ornaments. A Reprint of Recueil des dessins d'ornements d'architecure, c. 1813* (New York, Dover Publications, 1974).
60 Pls. 70 and 71.
61 [En la etiqueta y ceremonial de la real capilla, dosel en que estaba la silla o sitial del rey.]
62 Honour 1968, 137.
63 Junquera 1979, 146; Benito García 2009b, 194–95.
64 Benito Garcia 2009a, 93–116.
65 Junquera 1979, 77ff.
66 Thornton 1986, 20, pl. 10.
67 See Earston 1983.
68 Chambers 1988, 8.
69 Stelzer 1964; Blok 1982, 13.
70 Tschudi-Madsen 1967, 66.
71 Francastel 1961, 39ff.

The Humble among the Distinguished

Carlos Clavería Laguarda

For Marco Manetti

Concerning Ignorance as One of the Fine Arts

The good and rash Naudé might well shout himself hoarse at so much flashiness, as nobody seems to take him seriously. His reflection has not gone unnoticed to those who speak of bindings with authority and knowledge, and even Hobson himself refers to it in one of his own contributions which, as usual, is far from negligible. The paragraph by the Machiavellian French librarian that provides the basis for both reflections is as follows:

> I say first and foremost that with books there is no need to go to a huge expense in binding them, it being more appropriate to save the money that might be spent on this for having them all in the largest size and in the finest edition there is to be found.[1]

Having come by those good books it is sufficient to put them in uniform, taking a conservative approach, so that they fall into line discreetly on our shelves—once again, according to the contradictory Naudé—and provided that the intention of forming a library conceals a desire, a barely aesthetic whim that yields to "the wish, for the visual enjoyment of the viewer, to cover the backs of all the books with ...". To this end it is sufficient to hire a salaried bookbinder to have everything in order "for the ornamentation of the place and the conservation of the volumes". It is fitting to add a few comments on all this, which is rather confusing, in view of how time and fashions and bookbinders and owners have given many of those good books a hard time. I will make a few observations in the margins and below: I do not like uniformed books, docile books are not convenient, I do not believe in books that are only beautiful, nor do I like books that are mutilated or at the mercy of the vanity and snobbism of the powerful. I detest the expression "visual enjoyment of viewers" when referring to libraries.[3] At this point readers may wonder what I am doing collaborating in an exhibition devoted to books in royal hands. The answer is trying to ascertain the responsibility of those royal hands (and even of other hands, if only they had known what they were dealing with) that dared leave their mark on antique books. What I do is assess the work of librarians and libraries that endeavour to ensure the "cultural enjoyment of their readers", not spectators. What I do is disagree with Naudé over the uniformity of shelves; what I do is agree in again quoting a bitter and highly intelligent reflection by a person we would not suspect of disaffection for books—namely Hipólito Escolar, when he states of bookbinding, bookbinders and their clients that "El valor de la encuadernación y de la ilustración es tanto mayor cuanto menor es la capacidad de lectura y comprensión del texto que tienen el propietario o las personas para las que se han hecho."[4]

I continue to enlist the aid of people with greater judgement to support these statements. And I return to Hobson. I believe he is being subtly ironic when he states that

> spendere molto danaro era considerato un obbligo per un gentiluomo, in un periodo in cui nuove famiglie principesche rivaleggiavano con la più vecchia aristocrazia romana per il fasto e lo splendore dei loro palazzi. È quindi logico che uno o più stemmi siano l'elemento principale di immediata attrazione sulla maggior parte delle legature e che le dorature siano spesso generose.[5]

That is, with no consideration for cultural value, scientific rigour, historical importance or even the (possible) artistic value that the skilled binder may have afforded the book. Only luxury, only ostentation, only gold assets.

Fortunately, and owing to their own competence, some of the people responsible for our current holdings know that books were made to be read rather than to be bound. What is more, I am convinced that many of them bend over backwards to promote culture or research much more than showing off.[6] It should not be too difficult to make people realise that ostentation and show, the wish to leave an invader's mark on a book, are but the simplification of a value which was initially intrinsic to books before industrialisation. I am referring to the value which others have pointed out concerning how enriching it is to find in the sixteenth century, for example, that each copy could be different according to the needs and possibilities of each buyer. A transverse richness that is reflected in the obvious fact that no two antique books are alike. So what does it matter to us that, once inside our library, all the books (whether dating from the fifteenth century or recently purchased) should be similar in form or appearance? What leads us to attach extra importance to the consideration that a good many of the books on the shelves of Mayáns y Siscar, whether from Leipzig or from Burgos, are now clothed almost identically? In the same way as whenever a compendium is made, the overall value declines, however capable and high-ranking the person who orders and directs the mutilation.[7] I am not referring to how licit it is to do so, but of the consequences of such an act.

Binding is a process—out of several that involve the manner of crafting or perfecting books before the industrial age—which escaped standardisation. A book rarely emerged from the printing house with all copies clothed in the same attire. The first paper bindings attempted by the errant printer Ratdolt are celebrated, and for a reason. Also celebrated are the memorable orange uniforms[8] of the incommensurable Bodoni. And they are celebrated for their fragility, for their originality, for their fugacity and also for their candour, for their beauty. And because when we come across them they show respect for the book, few financial resources on the part of the owner and sometimes indifference towards the value or usefulness of this book.[9]

Fortunately, however, times change and it is beginning to seem standard practice that when we come across the original fragility of a book we do not endeavour to invest it with a dignity it has perhaps not deserved, and we do not always endeavour to lay our pretentious hands on it. I do not do so (even though I may have in the past) and on the occasion of this exhibition I have come across some royal hands that encourage the infinite respect deserved by the time that can be appreciated in antique books. On eying and leafing through the catalogue of the Real Biblioteca, I was struck by the book under accession number III/7062 [fig. 28], which does not leave indifferent anyone who compares it to accession number PAS/2973 [fig. 29]. Both books contain the text of the *Spanish Constitution* of 1812; one is (very) luxuriously bound and entered the Real Biblioteca before electric light was invented (it bears a label from the period of Charles IV-Ferdinand VII). According to information provided by the Real Biblioteca, the other one was purchased in 2005. Why? It is not that they have gone mad and are afraid, for example, that one of the two copies might go missing and wish to cover themselves—or the shelves. To be able to compare what the *Constitution* looked like hot off the Cadiz press —that is, in the (almost) original state of the copy bound in paper covers—with another copy decked out in (almost) all kinds of luxuries and pomp for the use of kings and queens is extremely enriching. I can only praise this archaeology of taste, this pursuit of what things were like before we came along. I can only praise this intention to establish a dialogue which, like all dialogues, is paradoxical. The paradox is summed up by the fact that we uniform the antique book but dis-uniform the modern book. If today all the books placed on sale are the same, some will find that it makes serious sense to give them a "specific cultural or social identity"[10] or a simple personal identity by having them re-bound.

Antique books, nearly all of which were sold in signatures—also termed bound in paper—ceased to be uniform no sooner had they been purchased to be (let us hope) read, or to be later bound or protected. Each reader made his own copy a *unicum*; many collectors have made these books a uniformed set. This futile crusade of mine in defence of the original is centred not only on bindings with a coarse candour, provisional bindings "awaiting" a more definitive cover (if I may be permitted to translate the unofficial term used by the Italians); this reflection is aimed at helping readers understand why many collectors or librarians or hoarders of books decide to place their stamp on everything they own, sometimes without stopping to think about the consequences, concerned solely with values not strictly pertaining to books and at times even obsessed with a type of conduct that is not always innocent. For this purpose books have sometimes been entrusted to the hands of overly smug practitioners who are too self-engrossed and capable of defending their actions beneath the guise of art and justifying their excellence without concern for historical accountability or any other kind of responsibility. In the eighteenth century some of these binders were jealous of their own high standards and demanded measures for protecting their aristocratic skills. The Piedmontese binders who requested the king for help in establishing a Università dei Legatori di Libri in Turin acknowledged that attaining the rank of master binder was no easy task, as it required several years of apprenticeship and working one's way up the ladder, and thorough examinations and tests for mastering binding in morocco leather, sheepskin and *vitello*, with gilt, with spine bands, with fillets and with false spines. The related document, written with an endearing precision,[11] by no means makes any references to books as culture objects (allow me to simplify) and requires of aspiring bookbinders the personal attribute of being "di buoni costumi". The rest of the bureaucratic endeavour speaks of guild organisation and skilled craftsmanship, and article III of the first chapter clarifies that their work is of an importance that is beyond others' reach: we wish booksellers and printers and anyone else not belonging to our university to be barred from binding in leather and parchment (*cartapecora*), being allowed to execute "di legare alla rustica". Personally, if I had belonged to the guild, I would have asked for: respect for the historical and material life of books, respect for the marks of time, not to cut off marginal annotations, not to complete a book with facsimile leaves *animo falsificandi*, not to perfect a book in order to show off my binding—by cutting, squaring, sanding, perforating, despising the old material—to ignore the details that single out the work commissioned from my by the patron of the moment, and to have sufficient personality and dignity to advise the powerful client who pays me on what respect for antique books is based, for example.

Granted, I refer only to antique books that are to be re-bound. The task of the binder or the librarian in charge of bindings must be judged differently when dealing with books of his own time.[12] Let us speak of Bozerian, who is dead, is prestigious and was the king of technicians in the mastery of his art. The sight of a (single) book bound by Bozerian arouses admiration for his technique and his elegance: even if it is a *Polyphilus*[13] that has been clipped, washed, pressed, given gold edges and new endpapers, all traces of its nearly three hundred years of life tampered with.[14] The sight of a single book of those bound by Bozerian has a special charm. The sight of a whole shelf full of books bound by Bozerian, the complete set of his uniforms, leads me to ratify my idea that equality is impoverishing. I mean by this that the sight of one Bozerian binding may send one into ecstasy, but the sight of a whole row of small Bozerian-style octavos immediately leads one to hesitate between preferring uniformity or judging what may be an evident lack of imagination[15] as an impoverishment of everything that a (very) antique book has to offer.[16] This act of Bozerian amounts to candour, vanity, ignorance or compliance with commissions. All the clients who commissioned bindings generously held in major libraries—and in our Real Biblioteca the names Mayáns, Gondomar and the particular kings of the early nineteenth century spring to mind—should be judged both for what they preserved and for what they had destroyed. I would not go as far as saying that they should be judged for wrongdoing, but revisited for a candour that is of dubious taste or value today.[17] "Se una legatura rivela sempre qualcosa, narra sempre una storia, una legatura originale consente molto di più: ricostruire le vicende di un esemplare e talvolta anche di una edizione."[18]

How, then, should a library be begun? Or continued? Without a doubt by not despising any fragment of history, however small it might seem or however displeasing we find it. Inherited libraries, those established through power or confiscation[19] or through ostentation, are what they are and we cannot change them. All we can do is not make what we believe to be inherited mistakes, but in order to do so we need to be able to identify both mistakes and our responsibility. I do not mean by this that we should regret owning a copy of the 1812 *Constitution* in morocco leather and gilt because someone wanted it that way—and that is fine—or a *Polyphilus* "bien composé" by Derome, but rather that, as an antique book is a living organism, we should put a limit on what requires our attention in order to remain alive and continue to transmit something that cannot be manufactured: time. We cannot manufacture time. The idea is not to be slaves of something that can be avoided, such are our ambition and our short-lived tastes and desires. Even somebody as special as Angelo Maria Bandini, an eminent eighteenth-century librarian of what is now the Biblioteca Medicea Laurenziana in Florence, had material concerns worthy of being remembered. And he even wished to make clear that under his determination or responsibility books deserved to pass to posterity in good condition and in the best possible way. It is not amiss to recall in detail the concerns and fears of a librarian—whose biography shows him to be not excessively candid—reporting directly to the powerful patron:

> Avendo io con ogni diligenza nel corso della passata estate voluta da per me accudire a ristoramenti, e legature de' medesimi [codices transferred to the Laurenziana from Pitti, Santa Croce, Galleria], poiché una quantità, o erano affato privi di coperte, e erano affato guasti, e corrotti da le tarme, o legati con corde; talmenteché adesso ò il

piacere di vederli bene accomodati, distinti, e assicurati per una lunga serie di anni.[20]

Bandini, whom some call hyperbolically the first bibliophile librarian, harbours the wish that all his efforts serve for the greater glory of posterity and of his master—or, pleonastically, of his library. And to this end he does not hesitate to take in, distinguish and secure the codices which have arrived in his care through confiscation—"codici trasferiti", a seemingly kindly expression. Nobody doubts his ability to intervene for the sake of preservation or the glorious librarian's intention to give lustre to his master's power[21] or his collecting zeal. He intervenes, and greatly so, in the books but then teaches us another lesson: nothing is thrown away, everything is kept, everything is useful and everything is history.

It is known that librarians must live comfortably, at ease and with their needs well provided for. Bandini, who takes the trouble to safeguard (or not) many antique codices by candidly clothing them in eighteenth-century attire, is capable of asking his master to comply with the rules of culture, get ahead of archaeology and be capable of reading between covers. In short, Bandini has just sliced up some codices but out of historical awareness does not want to consider them dead. He therefore asks his excellency to beg his highness to provide the funds with which a librarian—still as a supplicant—may "vivere decentemente, e mantenersi galantuomo" while it is known that the work to be commissioned from him requires not doubting "l'onestà del supplicante". And to what should such a person, for whom Bandini asks so much, devote his time? To studying and conserving the pieces of binding which, as "laceri avanzi delle antique membrane" or remains of the slicing up of these old manuscripts, are small fragments of history that should be studied, handed down for posterity—conserved as if "costuma nella Vaticana di Roma" as a "cosa molto gloriosa al suo felicissimo governo". We are thus dealing with two issues: on the one hand, there is an awareness of the mutilation that aggressive intervention in an antique book entails; and on the other, there is the realisation that everything has a value and that everything must be conserved. And this is not a unique case. At the end of the nineteenth century, while those in charge of conserving some of the finest books—for example the holdings of the Biblioteca Nacional de España—were capable of rebinding a manuscript from the year 1000 with great candour (and little responsibility, unless there is an underlying explanation of which I am unaware) in marbled leather [*pasta española*], in certain parts of Germany they carefully swept away all the waste that the binders had left behind them:

> The greatest treasure of the Donaueschingen Library is one which owes its existence to its alterlife as binding waste in an early binding. ... At several times in the later nineteenth century, the Donaueschingen librarians searched old covers for ancient manuscripts waste, and turned up fragments dating to as early as the fifth century AD.[22]

But things can always take a turn for the worse, and while the Fürstenbergs amused themselves by searching for fifth-century manuscripts, Gutenberg bulls and fifteenth-century ephemerae among the waste, the most powerful markets in the book world established the fashion for washing and pressing, a taste for the paper cutter. I, who had the misfortune to exercise the profession of bookseller in a period (fortunately almost over now) in which Brugalla's Barcelona workshop was a reference point for any new book collector, have seen thousands of antique books being washed, cut, pressed, trimmed to make even and dried—that is, destroyed.[23] I have seen being put in practice the (aforementioned) expression of Goldschmidt, who in 1928 shouted himself hoarse like the poor Naudé almost three hundred years earlier, with the same effect as preaching in the wilderness:

> An equally potent agent of destruction of the ancient bindings, operating in France and elsewhere was the loving care of the wealthy abbeys for their fine libraries in the seventeenth centuries …. The same practice was observed by the great French collectors … no volume was allowed to stand on their resplendent shelves before it was smoothly created by one of the Deromes or Pasdeloups.[24]

In other words, how many conquerors of barbarity does it take for us to learn and in order not to forget that "quod non delerunt barbari delerunt Barberini"? That is, we do not lend our books to supposed researchers who present themselves cunningly in our reserve sections equipped with razors, ill intentions and tenacious hands, yet in both private and public life we have handed these books on a plate to official agents equipped with shears and gilding apparatus. And to end this section, and before ranting on too much about my complaint, I should stress that everything is relative and that I agree with Vives that there is no law so innately good that it cannot be twisted by the malice of men to serve their needs, and therefore everything said so far may be interpreted as one wishes and regarded as partial or exaggerated, but fortunately some new instruments and some new sensibilities, such as this exhibition, shed new light on the magnitude of the tragedy which, whether out of candour or out of vanity, we have all perpetuated with many of our antique books. One of these instruments deserves more than a brief mention in a footnote, so that it does not go unnoticed or unobserved. The huge effort Paul Needham has made to show how much and what valid information is to be found in the "laceri avanzi", in what we might call the suburbs of the text, the outskirts of the volume, should serve to gauge the extent of this tragedy for once and for all. I would take the liberty of advising anyone who feels candid and humble and even of slow judgement to visit the huge Index Possessorum Incunabulorum,[25] to shudder at the recent text by Petrucci Nardelli[26] and not to forget that the "binding waste" that the peculiar Bandini endeavoured to save at the aforementioned Florentine library (perhaps) still remains, but orphaned, it being unknown to whom it refers, whom to address and reason or dialogue with to clarify its origin and its importance. Because, as can be easily inferred, not everything is relevant. Petrucci Nardelli herself quotes Miglio when defining the relevant and irrelevant and even inappropriate traces that are found in the periphery of the text or in the suburbs that the binding sometimes is.[27] But leaving snippets of history to the judgement of a few seems overly risky. Who decides whether Reuchlin's portrait of Erasmus[28] on the blank sheet of an incunabulum—that blank sheet that we almost never miss!—is important? Who decides whether the variant in a margin of one of Seneca's tragedies is acceptable or not? We had best not touch books and let time be the judge of our respect, even if we are forcing ourselves to protect impertinences or reservations. Perhaps what seems redundant to us today will be a unique testimony when we are no longer here to tell of it or cut it out. And we are warned; from Naudé to De Marinis we have been warned that it is possible to be shipwrecked[29] due to the fault and art of a small watercourse. We had been warned. And nobody is free of blame:

> Così, in varie epoche, e specialmente nei due ultimi secoli, si è proceduto con disinvoltura alla sostituzione e alla conseguente distruzione delle vecchie legature. Può sembrare paradossale, ma la sostituzione e la distruzione metodica delle legature antiche è avvenuta specialmente negli istituti deputati alla conservazione del libro, nelle grandi biblioteche, nelle quali i provvedimenti amministrativi di tutela, radicali e indiscriminati, hanno causato danni molto più gravi di quelli procurati altrove dall'incuria e dall'abbandono … i libri ebbero un'altra veste, magari più ricca o più sicura della prima, ma falsa e mistificatoria, come il cattivo restauro di un'opera d'arte.[30]

It is best not to run any risks, not to tamper with books excessively: as you know, Erasmus was nearly burned for adding a comma to a Gospel.

The Pressing Urge to Be Distinguished

I very often wonder what spurs a librarian—or to a lesser extent a bookseller—to wish to form their own library parallel to the collection they are entrusted with keeping (or selling). On returning to the Real Biblioteca I again came across the fascinating figure of Mayáns y Siscar, who was distinguished insofar as he was not one of the flock and as an ex-royal.[31] It is not relevant here to point out Mayáns' intellectual standing or work as a librarian. He is mentioned here solely as an introduction to the explanation of the wishes of those who wish to organise, and above all ensure the conservation of, a library with individual[32] or private characteristics that will end up becoming public domain. Something I continue to find fascinating is that book collectors, once they have decided to publicise their obsession, should have been concerned as early as in humanistic times with the tidy arrangement and conservation of the holdings from which they dreamed of building more than just an ergastulum.[33] An example is that of Cardinal Capranica, who, on his deathbed (in 1458), insists on giving his books to the Collegium Pauperum Scolarium and demands "quod libri S.R.D. qui sunt necessarii pro dicto collegio ordinentur, deputentur et disponentur pro utilitate et commodo studentium in dicto collegio et alii uendantur."[34]

Among his more specific instructions, the cardinal orders and establishes that the librarian shall have the job of dusting the books every Saturday; and if he orders a subordinate to do so the librarian in charge must be present. Similarly, the librarian is responsible for all aspects of the conservation, restoration and binding of the volumes.[35] By halfway through the fifteenth century the penalty established for damaging or allowing a book to be damaged was immediate excommunication. These instructions for the formation and government of Cardinal Capranica's library are restrictive in nature, possibly inspired by the no less restrictive regulations dictated by Cardinal Cisneros early in the sixteenth century for the use and government of the library of the Universidad Complutense,[36] and are clear about book conservation. The librarian has the duty both to conserve the books secured with chains to the shelves and to decide on how they must be repaired.

The librarian, as a distinguished personage in his grounding and social status, thus has almost always had to decide on how the books are to be bound if they need to be bound and whether they can be entrusted to a third party who, equipped with paper cutter but not with instructions, will return to the library an object (almost certainly) different to the one originally given to him.[37] I mean by this —and I return to Mayáns—do not do with public books what you do not with your own books, or do not do with your own books (still in the Real Biblioteca, I am thinking of the Count of Gondomar) what is not done with public books, as you never know where your books can end up. I have stated elsewhere that books do not belong to us and that it is we who belong to books, those poor, long-suffering creatures which have endured the chains of medieval colleges, the tortures of humanist readers, the vanity of the Groliers of the moment, the mutilations of the Dominicans with sabbatical morals, French collectors and the ignorance of so many. That is, what do we find when a library has two copies of the same book? The Gondomar version and the Mayáns version of how that particular book should be clothed do not necessarily coincide, as may be seen in the selection of photographs I use to illustrate these reflections. And that is a good thing, as books thus inspire the aforementioned dialogue, especially when we realise that books and classics too speak to us, and not only because, as Petrarch reminds us, they are like members of the family—if it gets on well—as "nobiscum vivunt, cohabitant, colloquuntur". Let us then listen to everything they have to say to us. Let us be humble among the distinguished and refrain from invading a domain that does not belong to us and in which leaving our mark may speak ill (or well) of us. Let the librarian be distinguished among the vain and know, when performing his task of an archaeologist who has strayed from the flock, what is good taste and what is bad taste. By doing so he will educate those who go into ecstasy only over gold, and will humbly direct this ecstasy to paper covers: after all, a Sallust bound by Derome may be more handsome than one bound in paper boards, but the text is the same. And as with nearly everything, this was already pointed out by Petrarch, whom I take the insolent liberty of modifying—and resolving his varying fortunes—by adding that we would not be far wrong if, with a good book in hand, we were to treat as distinguished above all anyone who reads it; that is, we would not demand so much praise for he who believes he creates as for he who reads.

It Had Been Irrelevant, It Was Irrelevant, It Seems That It Is Starting to Be Relevant

I have written elsewhere and previously—if this is not the same thing—that it is irrelevant to ask whether or not bindings were important in early libraries.[38] From Ferdinand Columbus himself onwards, few describers of books have included details of the bindings in their catalogues or lists. Among the books collected by Isabella the Catholic there are inventories which unavoidably convey the pleasure of describing memorably beautiful items.[39] But it is irrelevant to know how many cataloguers did so: the fact that not all of them did is sufficient evidence. A twofold and outstanding case is that of the inventories of the libraries of the Marquis of Astorga, where the same books are catalogued twice: in inventory A without details; and in inventory B with a few, albeit seemingly sufficient, specifications.[40] If we had to identify the books with nothing else to go on, needless to say that inventory B would not only help establish how time has respected a particular book but it would also allow us to locate its history and place fairly easily.

It is irrelevant to know how many libraries added a sensible comment on the binding of each book when cataloguing their holdings. The tradition which combines thoroughness and passion for bookbinding is not new to what is now the Real Biblioteca. When still the Real Librería, in 1716, it invested some 16,000 *reales* in the acquisition of books, along with some 4,000 in binding expenses. The wages of the ten library officials amounted to about 64,000 *reales*. Anyone capable of doing simple sums will realise the importance of this.[41] However, reproduced beside this document is another entitled "Libros que se asientan los libros que se compran para la Biblioteca de S. Magestad 1716–1736", recording the books purchased for His Majesty's library during those years. None of the entries refers to the binding. It continued to be irrelevant, or any relevance it had was not uniform. However, the Real Biblioteca today provides extremely full information about the bindings of many (if not all) of the books and these entries can be consulted over the internet, meaning that Darwin was right and that the human species does indeed improve over the years. The Real Biblioteca is the closest proof we have that binding is an essential part of what, according the previous quote by Rodríguez-Moñino, is more than an exercise in cataloguing. Other progress to be considered is the joy derived from comparing the catalogue of incunabula of the Biblioteca Nacional in Madrid with the new catalogue of incunabula of the Biblioteca Nacional de España. There is a huge leap forward between the earlier compilation of 1945 and the one completed by Julián Martín Abad in 2010 as regards concern with individualising each entry. Indeed, the inclusion of the binding in the entry has proven to be of such importance[42] that it is reasonable to think that knowing what a particular book was like at a particular time and knowing where it is from will lead us to stop and think, at least for a second or two,[43] about how we wish to leave our mark on it and whether it needs our candour or our luxury.

Some Illustrated Comments

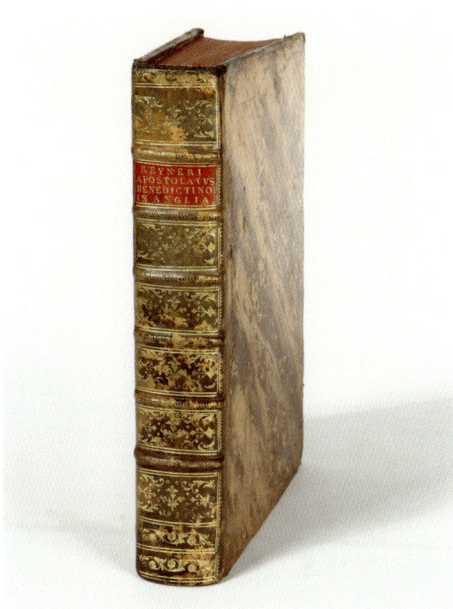

Fig. 27
Clemens Reynerus, *Apostolatus benedictorum in Anglia siue Disceptatio historica de antiquitate Ordinis Congregationisque monachorum nigrorum S. Benedicti in regno Angliae* …. Duaci: ex Officina Laurentii Kellami …, 1626. Bound in marbled leather. RB, IX/6424

This history of the feats of the Benedictines in England, of which this is the first edition, was published during the author's lifetime. It was printed in Douai, crossed the border to be read and housed by the Jesuits of Louvain, later passed into the humble hands of Mayáns y Siscar (1699–1781) and then to the distinguished possession of Charles IV and Ferdinand VI, kings of Spain. During its long journey it fell into the hands of an inexpert bookbinder who added crooked gold tooling and an erratic spine label to shoddily fashioned marbled leather [*pasta española*]. The binding is considerably later than the date of printing and was most likely executed in Spain. The book is not easy to read as it is tiresome to open. Solidity versus legibility.

Fig. 28
Constitución política de la Monarquía española: promulgada en Cádiz á 19 de marzo de 1812. Cadiz: dicho año en la Imprenta Real, [1812]. Bound in gold paper with scattered pattern in relief. RB, III/7062

Candour at the service of a political text. This binding is the epitome not of simplicity but of fragility. I cannot find an explanation for the contradiction between the precise, refined craftsmanship of the paper covering the book and how little protection it provides. Even so, it is one of the most endearing objects any reader can come by. This copy does not bear any royal stamps or marks denoting an illustrious provenance. Measuring 81 x 55 cm, it is almost a leaflet for pocket use and fast readers.

Fig. 29
Constitución política de la Monarquía española: promulgada en Cádiz á 19 de Marzo de 1812. Cadiz: dicho año en la Imprenta Real, [1812]. Bound in Empire style in red morocco. RB, PAS/2793

Luxury at the service of politics. This binding has everything: expensive leather, abundant gold tooling, silk, craftsmen with an eye for style. It is curious that a Constitution of this kind should have been given a Frenchified binding, just as the presence of the gilt ships on the spine is ironic in a text drafted not far from Trafalgar. A book is a world of its own. This example bears the royal stamps of two monarchs involved in the Peninsular War.

Figs. 30 and 31
Epistolae diuersorum philosophorum. oratorum. Rhetorum sex & viginti: quorum nominainse quenti in venies Pagina [in Greek]. Venetiis: apud Aldum, 1499. Bound in *pasta valenciana* by Miguel Ginesta Haro (I/39), bound in leather with blind tooling (I/45) and bound in *pasta valenciana* with gold tooling, possibly by Santiago Martín (I/51). RB, I/39 – I/45 – I/51

Three examples of the same incunabulum. Three ways of looking at the history of the same book. An extremely simple late nineteenth-century marbled leather binding; one from the workshop of the monastery of El Escorial whose luxury lies in the gilt edges of a period when books were displayed by the edges [fig. 31]; and a third with a semé patterned spine designed to be stylish for a modern bookshelf, when books were displayed by the spine. Each binding meets a different need, and none of the books corresponds to its age. I/51 is a centimetre shorter than I/45, and without being an aristocrat of the incunabulum, I should point out that in the former, bound at the end of the nineteenth century most likely by the court binder, the name of an early owner and reader was sliced off by the paper cutter.

Fig. 32
Marco Polo, *Historia de las grandezas y cosas marauillosas de las Prouincias Orientales ....* En Caragoça: por Angelo Tauanno, 1601. Bound in parchment. RB, VI/586

All the voyages of Marco Polo preserved in this book hardly set foot outside Aragón: the text was retouched by the eminent Bolea ("re-author" of an extremely rare *Orlando determinado*), printed in Zaragoza and most likely bound there in the seventeenth century. Several readers with Aragonese surnames wrote their names on it until it received the book stamp of Mayáns y Siscar. The volume is endearingly humble in all aspects, and spending money on it to deck it out with adornments and paraphernalia would not make it any more distinguished. As these simple parchment bindings of proletarian appearance are hardwearing by nature, none of the many owners (who were perhaps not readers) it had over the years deemed it necessary to fit it with a new binding.

Fig. 33
Etymologikon mega kata alphabeton, pany ōphelimon. En Enetíais: analōmasi … Nikoláou bla[st]ou |to|u krē[tò]s: … Annēs thyga[tr]òs t|ou| … Louka notara: … pónō dé k|aí| dexiótēti, Zacharí|ou| kalliérgou t|ou| krētós, 1499. Bound in marbled leather with gold tooling (I/2), bound in brown leather with tree marbling and gold tooling (I/3), and bound in *pasta valenciana* with gold tooling probably by Santiago Martín (I/4). RB, I/2 – I/3 – I/4

Three examples of the same book. Three different manners of viewing the world from the nineteenth century, when three different craftsmen fitted them with bindings that are modest, vulgar even, for distinguished books. What led the binders to think that they were improving on the previous bindings? I/3 has a more than illustrious provenance. Hernán Núñez de Guzmán alias Ferdinandus Pincianus alias the Comendador Griego (*c.* 1475–1553), editor of the *Biblia políglota*, purchased this book in Bologna as a student. The nineteenth-century binding does not do justice to the beauty of Kallierges' Greek type, to Pincianus' hands, to the previous binding or indeed to other signs that this distinguished volume conveys or should convey. The height of the taste that reflects a particular trend and contributes nothing (although common practice in nineteenth-century Spain, its attractiveness is dubious) is the moiré pattern the binder has added to the edges in a display of futile skill. I prefer not to discuss the yellow edges that Santiago Martín gave to I/4. Indeed, all three bindings conceal more than they show. When the books are held open, the most regrettable contrast between the beauty of their interior and the ugliness of their appearance can be seen. Could it be candour?

Fig. 34
Rodrigo Sánchez de Arévalo, bishop of Palencia, *Compendiosa historia hispánica: in qua agitur de eius situ & descriptione* .... [Romae]: Vdalricus Gallus ... eundem librim impressi, [1470]. Bound in green sheepskin with gold tooling. RB, I/119

This is one of the finest books owned by the distinguished Mayáns y Siscar (1699–1781), who not for nothing devoted to it a lengthy historical and bibliographical commentary that shows to what he extent he studied his books. The notes of the learned scholar of Valencia are later than 1733, the year Maittiare's aforementioned *Anales tipográficos* were published. The text is the work of the first Spaniard to have his writings set in print when his *Speculum* was published in Rome in 1468.

The binding recalls the Reynerus quoted *supra* [fig. 27], displaying the same lack of skill and similar leather. The book is now a solid wad of paper that is difficult to open. The binder respected the annotations and wide margins in which, thanks to the contrast between the mediocre binding—when roman type of 1470 flourished—and the excellent paper, we can appreciate that any past time was always better. At least in this case.

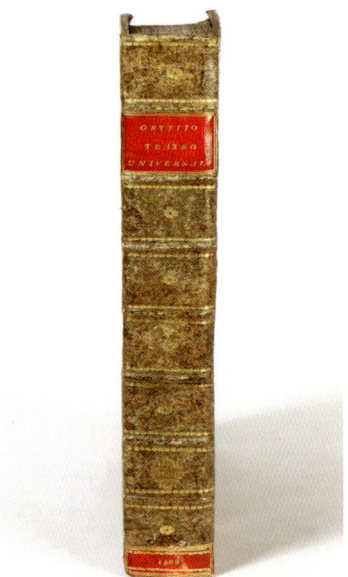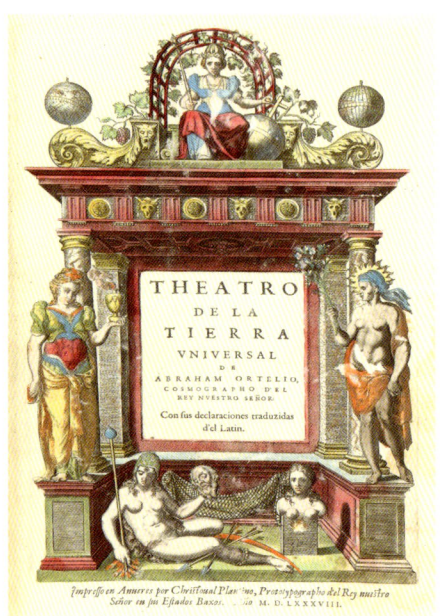

Fig. 35
Abraham Ortelius, *Theatro de la tierra universal* ....
Anveres: por Christoval Plantino, 1588. Bound in
mottled leather with gilt edges. RB, V/1553

A luxurious book dressed in humble, too humble
clothing. Humble and ugly, as it is necessary
and only fair to acknowledge that humble can
be beautiful. This aristocratic and royal copy, its
maps coloured long ago by an expert hand, has
not survived to our day without being fitted with
Spanish clothing (spine labels so often reveal the
language of the binder!) that undoubtedly dates
from after its first owner, who may have been the
great collector the Count of Gondomar. The binder
carelessly sewed the maps to the spine and did
not have the decency to mount them on guards,
thereby ruining a monumental volume. Like
many of the books from the Gondomar library,
it was bound at the beginning of the nineteenth
century at the Real Biblioteca. It has to be seen
to be believed.

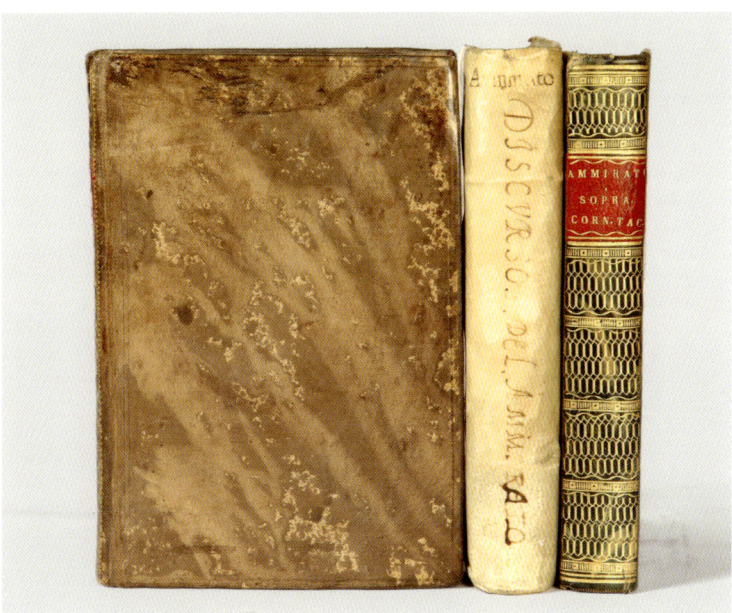

Fig. 36
Scipione Ammirato, *Discorsi del Signor Scipione Ammirato Sopra Cornelio Tacito* …. In Vinezia: per Filippo Giunti, 1599. Bound in *pasta española* with gold tooling (V/2396), bound in parchment (PAS/ARM1/24) and bound in *pasta valenciana* with gold tooling by Santiago Martín (III/340). RB, V/2396 – PAS/ARM1/24 – III/340

Three examples of the same book in the same library with different bindings. That of Mayáns, with the usual marbled leather and gilt tooled spine forming an unstable equilibrium, could be any other book in a cover without personality and, had it preserved its margins like its neighbour, we would perhaps have been able to read the notes that Mayáns himself took the trouble to write and which the binder did not take the trouble to read. The parchment-covered copy has the candour of what is most likely its first binding, imperfect and coarse, but the result of a lesser need in accordance with its objective: a uniform that is cheap but appealing. The copy bound by Santiago Martín, who made fine bindings found in the Real Biblioteca and fortunately mastered the semé technique, is an example of good craftsmanship but mass produced or without personality. It is no coincidence that he was a court binder who provided a service to any book: a supplier of quality uniforms. Compare his monotonous style with the copy of the *Epistolae diversorum philosophorum*… (RB, I/51) quoted *supra* [fig. 30]. Similar "sowing" produces similar fruit.

1 Gabriel Naudé's exclamation may be read in *Advis pour dresser une bibliothèque*. The Spanish edition is advisable. See Naudé 2008, 195. Anthony Hobson's note had been made available to those interested in 1953.
2 The figure of a royal binder at the palace would not have been new. This was the post held, for example, by Santiago Martín, two of whose works are photographed below, and whose personnel file is preserved in the Real Biblioteca. Very interesting in this connection are http://librodigital.realbiblioteca.es/index.php?bid=Martin-Santiago atque López Serrano 1943, 14–22.
3 This is perhaps why I find the so-called golden room (where the books are shown with gilt edges facing outwards) of the library at El Escorial obscene for its excessive ostentation.
4 In Escolar 1993, 325. [The value of bindings and illustrations is all the greater the smaller the capacity for reading and understanding the text of the owner or the people for whom they have been made.] It is worth recalling in this connection the satirical hyperbole in Jean Le Pautre's engraving bearing the following notice: "C'est bien le plus grand fou qui soit dans la nature que celui qui se plaist aux liures bien dorez, bien couuers, bien reliez, bien epoudrez, et ne les voit jamais que par la couuerture."
5 Hobson 1991, 13. [It was considered compulsory for a gentleman to spend a fortune in a period in which new noble families rivalled with the oldest Roman aristocracy in the pomp and splendour of their palaces. It is therefore only logical that one or several coats of arms should be the main and most immediately striking feature of most bindings and that the gilding should often be generous.]
6 Some, giving meaning to the medieval expression "explicatio non petita accusatio manifesta", even confessed not long ago that they actually read the books. Rodríguez-Moñino (1965) announced in 1963 to the astonished ears of the Hispanists at a New York meeting that, "para desgracia de ese papel de bibliógrafo, tengo la debilidad de no considerar al libro sólo como unidad catalográfica, sino como expresión material de pensamiento y sensibilidad: quiero decir que los leo".
7 The extreme case of uniformity based on a specific criterion comes to mind. The very respectable Canfora (2003, XII) points out that the citizen Barère submitted the following proposal to the *Commission* in charge of books during the French Revolution: to make a summary of all the volumes in the Bibliothèque nationale, to send these epitomes to Didot's printing house to be published in luxury editions and "bruciare tutto il resto (gli originali!)". It seems an odd manner of saving space.
8 And Bodoni's paper boards are not only orange; owing to the influence of some Spaniard we find some (perhaps even originals) that are almost violet in colour in some of the Parmesan's publications.
9 I am honoured to hold Bodoni's edition of Abbé Andrés' *Origine e progressi* ... in an uncut example, with its eight volumes in provisional boards almost violet in colour (see previous note), which had belonged to a religious institution that left it in the state in which it arrived in the nineteenth century: uncut, wrinkled from not being kept upright on the shelves, as if the product of an endearing lack of interest. Much to the delight of someone who now values books in their pristine original state. But another note should be added, albeit brief as it is not relevant to this case: should I open the book to show that I am a cultivated owner? Should I show the same disinterest as the monks who kept it for nearly two hundred years without paying the slightest attention to it? The answer is not relevant here.
10 Among the reasons Giorgio Montecchi reveals to be valid when replacing a mass-produced publisher's binding, is having a book re-bound to lengthen its life in the library "oppure per adornare, come in passato, biblioteche pubbliche o private in cerca di una specifica identità culturale e sociale", in Montecchi 2002, XI.
11 See the full text in Morazzoni 1929.
12 The advice of the IFLA on how to conserve modern books in modern libraries is sensible and respectful and bears in mind variables that are not considered when dealing with antique books. We should realise that intensively used reference books have a different use to those discussed here. The librarians responsible for general reference books often have to wage a battle against contemporary "ill-treaters of books" and their capacity for decision making and taking responsibility is much more immediate and active. On the term "ill-treaters of books" see the thought-provoking article by De Frede 2002.
13 This is an abbreviated reference to Franciscus Columna, *Hypnerotomachia Poliphili*, Venice, Aldo Manuzio, 1499.
14 Compare this devastating reflection by Mercè Dexeus (2003, 66): "la encuadernación debe ser coherente con el contenido y la cronología del libro, lo que no equivale a ser una simple copia de las encuadernaciones de la época."
15 Already pointed out by Culot 1979, 24: "Les reliures de Bozerian n'offrent pas une variété exceptionnelle de décors." The great Frenchman does not even take the trouble to compose all his bindings with detail, as "sur la reliure de Bozerian, c'est le règne de la roulette; cet outil permet de réaliser un décor plus rapidement, à moindres frais, qu'avec des petits fers." What would the meticulous and highly elaborate taste of Pietro Duedo have said about overuse of the roll? In the end the bindings commissioned by Duodo are nearly as monotonous as Bozerian's, but at least they are said to seem more elaborately executed.

16 To tell the truth, it is not much more fun to see shelves full of humble paper wraps, simple parchment covers or simple boards: the difference is that, retracing our steps, we have made a futile journey from original boredom to a new boredom with leather. And we have incurred expense and great destruction. Mercè DEXEUS 2003 puts it much better: "pocas cosas son tan poco sugerentes como una estantería con libros vestidos con idéntica encuadernación."

17 That in a moderately civilised country like Spain and in civilised libraries like our important ones an event should occur like the episode of the Rico y Sinobas collection should cause more than one person to blush and prompt retrospective acts of contrition. That is, that somebody should discover (almost) in the rubbish bin more than a thousand bookbinding scraps cannot be due to candour. I agree only partly with the bibliophile Carbonero when he states that we cannot justify such mutilation "mediante el desconocimiento, sino más bien por un sentido demasiado pragmático y poco respetuoso, cuando ni por la insensatez ...". CARBONERO 2003, 47. He is right, but I also believe that ignorance is to blame and I believe that ignorance is like sins and that its consequences are suffered by word, action and commission.

18 TUZZI 2000, 153. [If a binding always reveals anything, always tells a story, an original binding allows much more: the reconstruction of the vicissitudes of a copy and, sometimes, even of an edition.]

19 The origin of our Spanish and royal libraries is known and accepted, whereas in other countries this acceptance has yet to take place, meaning that some must reorganise their tastes and values and errors. CANFORA (2003, IX) states that "La borghesia è stata davvero la più drastica confiscatrice di ricchezze che l'Europa abbia visto all'opera", and it has thus imposed its aesthetic tastes and models on everything that has ever been part of its cultural base. We are fortunate not to have had a book bourgeoisie until only recently, and the damage can therefore be limited to the twentieth century.

20 See PINTAUDI 1990, 194. [During the course of last summer I diligently set out to have them restored and bound, for a good many were either totally lacking in covers or they were totally worn and moth eaten or held in place by cords; I thus now have the pleasure of seeing them tidily arranged, differentiated and safe for many years to come.]

21 Evidenced by another fragment of his copious correspondence when, on the subject of the catalogue he is compiling, he praises "l'Altezza Sua Reale [who] pensa providamente di tramandare alla posterità, e a tutta la colta Europa per mezzo del mio Catalogo ... tutto quello che si racchiude in questa unica, preziosa e copiosissima collezione". PINTAUDI 1990,178.

22 In *Incunabula* 1994, 13.

23 I suggest anyone with the guts to do so and a vehement if extreme attitude should take a look at the state of the famous collection of plays by Lope de Vega which, aptly and with good judgement, is now preserved in Madrid. AGUERRI 2002, 45–49. See *supra* the cross-reference in note 19.

24 GOLDSCHMIDT 1928, 14.

25 The IPI, researched and sorted by Paul Needham, is supported by the Consortium of European Research Libraries and can be consulted on the website of the CERL, where those interested can search among more than 32,000 incunabula in which various signs of identity and ownership have been traced.

26 Anyone wishing to give themselves over to anger and weariness should read the very recent PETRUCCI NARDELLI 2007. Among many other pieces of information of great and embarrassing interest, this superb monograph announced the "testimonianza di un cambianto di visual" through the words of a monk of Montecassino "che descrive l'affanno della riacquisizione di tale materiale [a collection of fragments that are binding castoffs], che i monaci, quasi per riscattare le colpe dei predecessori, sottraevano, verso la fine del xix secolo, 'dalle mani de' rilegatori di libri, e comprandole anche a peso d'oro da qualche ingordo ricettatore di cartapecore' ne riprendevano lo studio e ne curavano la conservazione nell'Archivio dell'abbazia." [It describes the endeavour to recover these materials which the monks, almost to redress their predecessors' sins, took from bookbinders at the end of the nineteenth century and, paying their weight in gold to any greedy parchment merchant, resumed the study and endeavoured to conserve what they acquired in the monastery's archives.]

27 PETRUCCI NARDELLI 2007, 146. The full quote from Miglio's article is on page 189.

28 See CARENA 2008, 241–54. On the blank sheet of an incunabulum of *Tibullus*, Reuchlin provides an account *manu propia* of the meeting with Erasmus in the Basel of 1515 when, with Frankfurt fair drawing near, the philologist gives Froben his edition of Seneca. The point I wish to make is that if this incunabulum of Latin poetry had passed through a major French library of the eighteenth century, today all these features that Carena studies in detail would not be known and the book would be a marvellous mass of morocco leather and gold, concise in its asepsis.

29 DE MARINIS 1960, I, XIX, who states that Italian bindings with a Renaissance flavour and value that circulate or remain in the world are but the [scant] remains of a devastating shipwreck.

30 In *Legature* 1977, XIV. [And so, in different periods but especially the past two centuries, antique bindings were gaily replaced, and consequently destroyed. It might seem paradoxical, but the methodical replacement and destruction of antique bindings has taken place particularly within the institutions in charge of conserving books, in major libraries where radical and indiscriminately applied administrative conservation procedures have

caused much more series damage than that derived from carelessness and neglect in other places ... books were clothed perhaps more richly or securely than they were previously, but in a false and mystifying way, like the perverse restoration of a work of art.]

31 The good Mayáns was harshly criticised for certain royal struggles. For fuller knowledge of his relationship as an intellectual with the booksellers of his period see Mestre 1993 and the later reflection by the same Mestre 2002, 219–40.

32 It should not be forgotten that what is today the royal (and public library), the Real Biblioteca, was once called the private library of HM, and that when the most varied and select holdings ended up in it, they were recorded, as we read today on the website of this library when discussing Gondomar's books, as *passing* to HM's private library as the end point of their journey.

33 Others, in contrast, are aware that some books cannot remain in the home longer than is strictly required for reading and accordingly do not take care to dress them in lasting attire. This is a lesson which is learned from the following reflection by Samuel Pepys, who is no less a collector when he buys a licentious book with a very ordinary binding in order to rid himself of it once he has read it and burn it so that it does not sully the good name of his library. From the memories of Samuel Pepys, quoted from Aries and Duby 1989, 144.

34 The will can be read, albeit requiring patience, in the Biblioteca Apostolica Vaticana, MS Vat. Lat 7971, and I quote from Aimone 2004. [May the SRD books that are necessary for the said college be ordered, classified and made available for the benefit and convenience of the students of said college, and the rest be sold.]

35 Fortunately, when it is specified that the books must be placed—speaking in the manner of Vitruvius—in a room with windows facing east, it is not clear if it must be the librarian who builds the rooms and "fenestras ferreas". We are graced with great books facing eastwards in the Real Biblioteca.

36 See Sotelo and Pacheco 2001, 127–53 for a combination of several ideas about restrictive and precautionary practices of early libraries.

37 Among the avalanche of theories on restoration and conservation, the simulated destruction recently provided by Etherington 2010 is interesting.

38 Dexeus (2003, 65) has always stressed that a book is an indivisible set of details: "el testimonio que nos aporta el libro no se limita a cuanto está relacionado con su producción, sino que incluye su trayectoria posterior hasta que llega a nuestras manos." I would venture to add that the more information we enter the more we know about the book's history.

39 That of Elisa Ruiz 2004 is.

40 See Cátedra 2002. Inventory B refers to the bindings, but does not go into much detail, at most "enquadernado en cuero colorado perfilado de oro" or, for example, "enquadernado en pergamino blanco". Illustrations of those referred to are found from pages 175 to 186. Without having seen the books as Pedro Manuel, whom I admire, has, I must confess that I do not share his affirmative opinion that the Marquis of Astorga's library "en su aspecto material era, claramente, una biblioteca exquisita".

41 I have not had the decency to investigate this information *in situ*. I have copied it from the illustration found in Santiago Páez 2004, 229.

42 I cannot help quoting as an example a collection such as the incunabula of Bayerische Staatsbibliothek, in which it is not unusual to find descriptions such as the following, each referring to different copies of the same edition: "Maroquinband auf Pappe mit Mannheimer Supralibros des Kurfürsten Karl Theodor auf Vorder- und Rückdeckel in Goldpressung, 18. Jh" and "Spätgotischer Schweinslederband auf Holz, gebunden in Rebdorf (Kyriss 28)" with a specific bibliography. Having explored our Real Biblioteca in some depth, I can confirm that we are not so far from that centre in some aspects.

43 The description of bindings in the entries of book catalogues not only signifies progress in cataloguing but is an important aspect of the commercial value of the book. I shall be brief: it is sufficient to compare the descriptions of bindings made 150 years ago for the sales of some library holdings (we might cite as an example the Hamilton collection), which, incidentally, are important, and the wealth of detail supplied nowadays in the public sales of antique books of major libraries: from Botfield to Wardington there is a choppy sea to be studied. If those who mercilessly strip down antique books do not stop to consider the historical or cultural consequences of their acts, possibly spurred by other less candid motives, perhaps they might perform acts of contrition instead of destruction.

Keys to the Evolution of the Armorial Bindings of Patrimonio Nacional

Valentín Moreno Gallego

This essay discusses twenty or so bindings from the Real Biblioteca and the Monastery of San Lorenzo el Real de El Escorial featuring armorial bearings that allow both general and specific conclusions to be drawn about constant or singular features of the heraldic emblems found on bindings in the care of Patrimonio Nacional; this applies to bindings that once belonged to members of both the royalty—to which special attention will be devoted—and the nobility.

Before printing existed, many of the codices produced during the fifteenth century, particularly in Italy, featured heraldic emblems at the foot of the text of the first folio. These emblems served a dual purpose that was both dedicatory and indicative of ownership—i.e. the artisan who had illustrated the initials generally placed there the coat of arms of the person to whom the copy was dedicated, who was obviously also the first owner of the codex and had commissioned its execution. This was the origin of the armorial supralibros, as when printing emerged it became fashionable to place this emblem on the outside to distinguish ownership of a particular copy out of many. Even elements not part of the blazon in these armorial bearings placed at the bottom of the folio were moved to the covers in the case of Italian books, such as the putti or cherubs that are found beside the coats of arms in codices and are still common in Bourbon bindings of the 1700s—centuries later—in Neapolitan-bound books, for example[1] [figs. 37 and 38].

37

This trend was also common outside Italy, as revealed by a delightful binding owned by Philip V and executed in France on a six-volume Bible in octavo, featuring the royal arms painted in a medallion and supported by putti [fig. 39]. This custom was not exclusive to members of the royalty, as it is found in other Neapolitan bindings made for the Spanish viceroys, such as for the 5th Duke of Medina de Rioseco, and later, in the seventeenth century, for the 9th Duke of Medinaceli.[2] What is more, the letterpress-printed title page evolved with respect to dedicatory practice, although it started out with a simple layout in the age of incunabula as barely a simple, brief mention of the title of the work

Fig. 37
María Jesús de Ágreda, *Sacra Rituum Congregatione... a Sanctissimo Domino Nostro Benedicto XIV deputata in causa tirasonen. beatificationis et canonizationis... Sor. Mariae á Jesu de Agreda super examine operis cui titulus Mistica Città di Dio e miracolo della Divina onnipotenza &c. ab eadem Ven. ancilla Dei conscripti*. Romae: ex Typographia Rev. Camerae Apostolicae, 1747. Neapolitan Rococo-style Italian binding in red morocco with the supralibros of Charles III (detail). RB, III/1691

Fig. 38
Ottavio Antonio Baiardi, *Prodromo delle antichita d'Ercolano alla maesta del re delle Due Sicilie Carlo infante di Spagna / di Monsignor Ottavio Antonio Bayardi* .... In Napoli: nella Regale Stampería Palatina, 1752. Neapolitan Rococo-style Italian binding in red morocco with the supralibros of Charles III (detail). RB, VIII/9704

Fig. 39
Biblia sacra vulgatae editionis. Parisiis: apud Fredericum Leonard, typographum regium, 1705. Rococo-style binding in red morocco with the painted supralibros of Philip V, in a medallion (detail). RB, IV/2966

and the author.³ A few decades after the invention of printing we find these dedicatory armorial bearings on the title pages of books, particularly in Spain, where the royal coat of arms was also used, as the new unitary monarchy controlled the publishing process by means of a royal order [*pragmática*] of 8 July 1502 barring any works from being printed without royal licence. The royal arms thus symbolised royal authorisation for publication, and sometimes filled almost the whole sheet.⁴ Among noble families of Spain the use of heraldic emblems on the covers as supralibros nearly always signified possession, and was a by no means unusual practice from the mid-sixteenth century onwards. But sometimes the presence of the emblem predates the ownership of the book because it was designed to serve as a presentation—a circumstance which again underlines the original dedicatory purpose of the heraldic emblem. In sixteenth-century Spanish society where the ideal model of lineage was "purity of blood" [*limpieza de sangre*], certified by letters patent of nobility—and in which heraldry enjoyed such a strong presence—it comes as no surprise that heraldic emblems should be have been used on the objects and assets held in highest esteem by families of noble lineage, which also asserted their status in their ancestral homes through stone carvings or in their furniture and books, according to the principle that if their coats of arms were displayed on the document that was most highly demonstrative of nobility to others, the letter patent, then why not use them in domestic life?⁵ The origin of heraldic bookplates printed on paper in turn lies in those supralibros: the latter were very costly, as the binder needed to fashion a tool bearing the coat of arms and impress

Fig. 40
Philipp Clüver, *Philippi Cluveri Sicilia antiqua ... item Sardinia et Corsica: opus post omnium curas elaboratissimum, tabulis geographicis aere expressis illustratum.* Lugduni Batavorum: ex Officina Elseviriana, 1619. Bound in mottled leather, with the supralibros of Pierre-Daniel Huet, Bishop of Avranches, in a medallion (detail).
RB, V/32

it into the leather,⁶ whereas a bookplate was much cheaper because the book's owner could affix the printed label at home, without having to deal with the master bookbinder.

It is not uncommon to find large heraldic bookplates⁷ in the early period of their existence, as their visual impact was connected with the distinctive legacy of late medieval standards and banners. Later, as a tribute to privacy, and given their domestic nature, they generally became smaller in size. And it should be borne in mind that, as occurred with manuscripts with respect to printed works, different marks of ownership coexisted on covers, in bookplates and manuscript, or simply with the owner's signature; this coexistence was very intense and it is therefore not unusual to find examples with two or even three marks of ownership [fig. 40].

The presence of Spanish royal heraldry on book covers dates from the fourteenth century, when armorial bearings appeared and became consolidated. As early as the beginning of the fourteenth century there were royal emblems of Aragón and Castile, although in general the use of heraldry on book covers did not become standardised until the fifteenth century.[8] Over the centuries the presence of constant features may be traced in the royal armorial bearings found on books, such as the recovery of certain neglected elements and the adoption of novelties that became standard practice over time, as we shall see in due course. As for the recovery of certain motifs, it was common for the new monarch to use the emblem established during the previous reign until his own heraldic model—or models— became consolidated. Some monarchs even drew not only from the previous model but from those dating from several generations earlier. This trend is found at various times, for example in the 1760s when Charles III used the shield with a circular outline newly established in Spain by Philip V, with identical quartering. Also around that time—in 1767 to be precise—Charles III used the curved-sided shield of Ferdinand VI.[9] On other occasions the borrowing from earlier models was due to particular circumstances of the place where the binding was executed or of the binder. Such is the case of a sixteenth-century binding owned by Philip II's son the Prince Don Carlos, which is based on the model used by Charles I of the quartered arms of Saint Ferdinand with the imperial eagle as an external ornament in a known binding featuring zoomorphic borders enclosed by lines of tooled artichoke and running dog motifs; the blazon is inside the central oval with the cord of Saint Francis. These covers hold a copy of the *Disputationes de indulgentiis* by Miguel de Medina[10] that was printed in Venice in 1564 and bound in Toledo, after a design identical to that used earlier by the printer Juan de Ayala in his works [fig. 41]. The presence of the imperial eagle, at least here, is due more to the fact that the work was executed in Toledo than to an intention to perpetuate the imperial model of Charles. It should be remembered that until not long earlier, 1561, the Imperial City of Toledo had been regarded as the capital of the monarchy, even though until the establishment of Madrid as the seat of court, the latter was logically located wherever the king happened to be. As we shall see further on, Philip V also used the two-headed eagle of Toledo during the early part of his reign for ideological reasons, although Gonzalo believes that its use in bindings for Don Carlos of Austria is due to the fact that it is the imperial model of Charles V—as Don Carlos was obsessed with becoming emperor like his grandfather—and we should therefore consider both possibilities.[11] Other armorial bindings featuring the imperial eagle were crafted in the Netherlands in the 1550s, and sometimes the eagle is not located in the centre of the cover but in the corners, as in one that was a gift to Charles V from his confessor in 1555.[12] The cover-title page dialectic became established in the sixteenth century with respect to royal armorial bindings. A good example is Philip II's use of the English coat of arms on book covers after marrying Mary Tudor—a few examples are preserved at San Lorenzo. The presence of

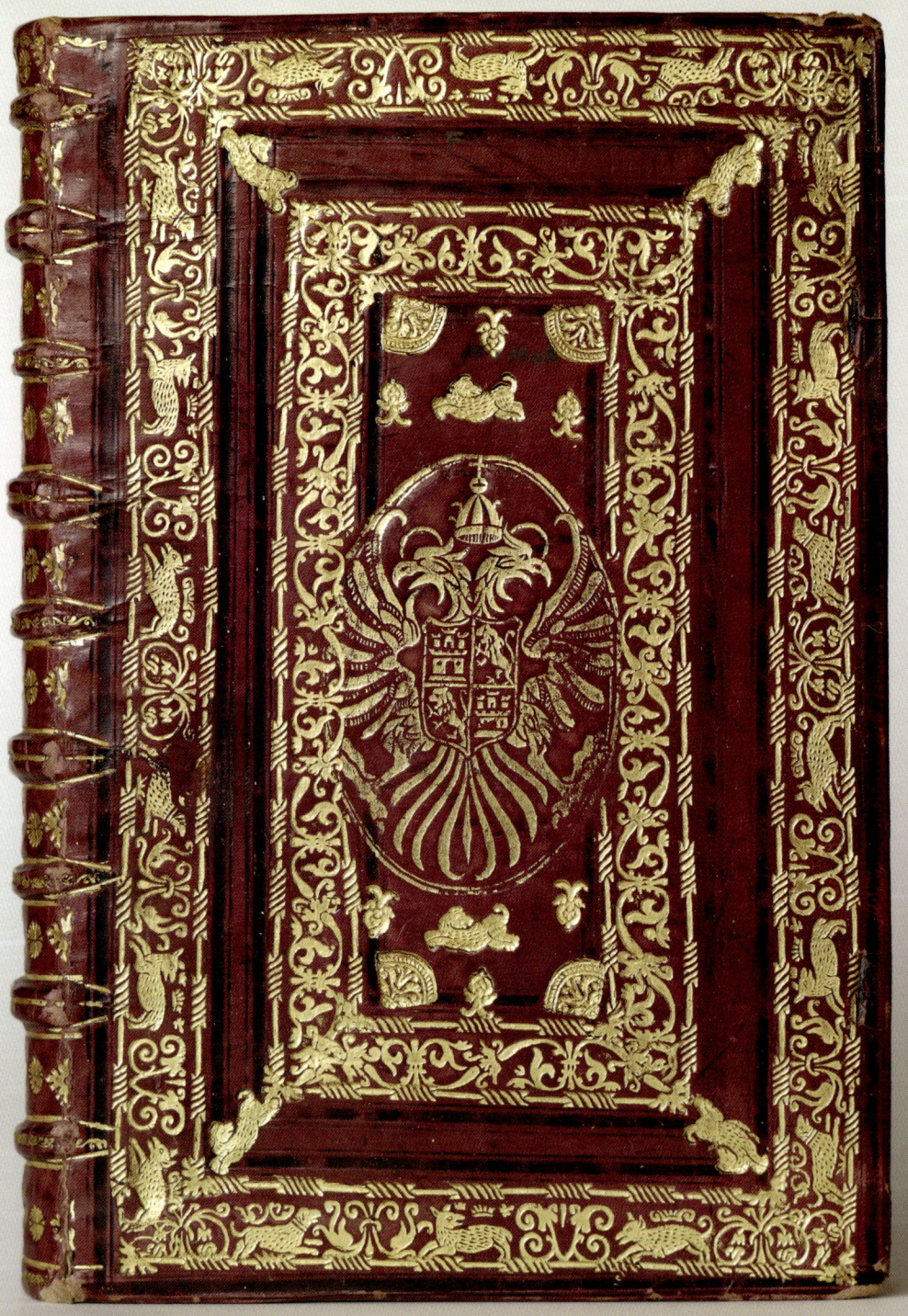

Fig. 42
Dioscorides, *Pedacio Dioscorides Anazarbeo, Acerca de la materia medicinal, y de los venenos mortiferos / traduzido de lengua griega, en la vulgar castellana, & illustrado con claras y substantiales annotationes, y con las figuras de innumeras plantas exquisitas y raras, por el doctor Andrés de Laguna ... Añadiose una tabla para hallar remedio de todo genero de enfermedades, y otras cosas curiosas, nunca antes ympressa ....* En Salamanca: por Mathias Gast, 1570. Title page with the royal coat of arms of Philip II, King of England, found on bindings made for Philip in the RBME. RB, VII/2423

Fig. 41
Miguel de Medina, *Disputationum de indulgentiis aduersus nostrae tempestatis haereticos, ad patres S. concilij Tridentini, liber unus ....* Venetiis: ex officina Stellae, Iordani Zileti, 1564. Brown in purple calfskin with gold stamped decoration and the imperial coat of arms, executed in Toledo for Carlos of Austria. RBME, 6.V.43

this coat of arms on the exterior led to its use on title pages, even decades after the monarch ceased to be the British sovereign following Mary's death in 1558, as laid down in the marriage contract. It is found on the title page of a book printed in Salamanca in 1570,[13] simply because it was one of the king's armorial bearings. This is a journey in the opposite direction to the one referred to at the beginning of the article, from codex to supralibros [fig. 42].

The quartered shield of Saint Ferdinand,[14] so called as it had been used since the period of Ferdinand III the Saint (1199–1252), particularly following the capture of Seville —although the presence of the lion dates from an earlier period, that of Alfonso XI at least (1105–1157)[15]—did not cease to be used by Spanish sovereigns and was employed particularly intensely by the Bourbons, including Alfonso XIII. The period of least frequent institutional use is the present time, as the prevailing armorial bearings are the official coat of arms of Spain and also that of His Majesty Juan Carlos I, which differs from the former in the presence of the pillars of Hercules, the saltire cross of Burgundy and the yoke and arrows at the bottom; the use of these latter elements is discussed later on. Both Isabel II and Alfonso XII very often used the quartered arms of Saint Ferdinand alone, even in very luxuriously bound works such as the book of hours of Alfonso XII, a neo-Renaissance work in the manner of Grolier, although with branch motifs characteristic of a later period, that of the first Spanish Bourbon king. This book displays the aforesaid quartered arms, also exquisitely painted on the edges, which are gauffered[16] [figs. 43 and 44].

The Bourbon quartered shield of Saint Ferdinand or "abbreviated arms" dates from

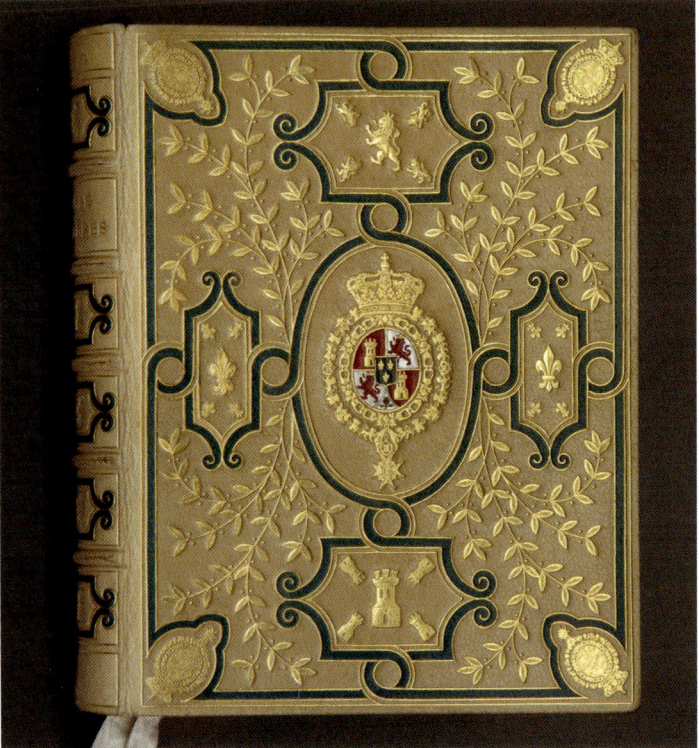 

Fig. 43
Livre d'Heures d'après les Manuscrits de la Bibliothèque Royale. Paris: Auguste Fontaine, 1878. Grolier-style neo-Renaissance binding in natural-coloured leather, signed "Chambulle-Duru" at the foot of the inner front cover, with the coat of arms—quartered shield of Saint Ferdinand— of Alfonso XII, King of Spain. RB, XIV/2922

Fig. 44
Livre d'Heures d'après les Manuscrits de la Bibliothèque Royale. Paris: Auguste Fontaine, 1878. Front edges gauffered and painted, with the quartered shield of Saint Ferdinand. RB, XIV/2922

Philip V, even in Italian bindings,[17] and features in the centre the inescutcheon emblazoned with the three fleurs-de-lis denoting lineage,[18] also known as the "French mark of difference". Following the advice of his grandfather Louis XIV, the king made only this addition to the royal arms on acceding to the Spanish throne and respected the traditional quartered shield of the Habsburgs. Philip V also used the imperial eagle of Toledo in a model identical to the present one in the aforementioned RBME,

6.V.43 [see fig. 41], even though more than a century and a half separated his reign from that of Philip II. But this feature was not recovered for aesthetic reasons, for the new Philip was particularly interested in connecting the new dynasty with the older royal legitimacy of the Visigothic kingdom of Toledo; whereas Madrid had been the Habsburg capital, Toledo had previously been the royal capital and he wished to link up with this fact. At the end of November 1700 the Council of

State even decided not to change the established order and titles of the monarch's kingdoms and dominions.[19] Indeed, Rigaud's painting in the Louvre, executed a few months later and showing the king dressed in black in the Habsburg manner with the Golden Fleece around his neck, is indicative of this interest in continuity, although logically he also sports the badge of the French Order of the Holy Spirit and the sash is not crimson but peacock blue. There are no bindings of Philip V displaying the two-headed eagle of Toledo in the Real Biblioteca because this model was used prior to 1734, the year of the fire that razed the Alcázar palace and led to the transfer to the royal public library, now the Biblioteca Nacional, of the monarch's books hitherto kept in the passage leading to the Convent of the Encarnación, which adjoined the Alcázar.[20] The design of these bindings of Philip V consists of separate polylobed compartments featuring representations of branches; visible in the centre is the two-headed eagle beneath a royal crown and with the quartered shield of Saint Ferdinand. It is curious to note that, of the sovereign's several heraldic designs, it is the only one which, with respect to the Habsburgs, does not bear the inescutcheon of lineage but only the collar of the Holy Spirit as a distinguishing feature.[21] The presence of collars belonging to chivalric orders is also a distinguishing feature: that of Saint Michel is exclusive to bindings executed in France for the Spanish Bourbons[22]—at least I have not seen it on any Spanish bindings—and the collars of the Order of Saint Januarius and of the Constaninian Order of Saint George are characteristic of Neapolitan bindings. The most obvious case of continued use of an earlier model, albeit as an imitation, is

Fig. 45
Mateo de las Nogueras y Fuente, *Oracion panegyrica, en aplauso de Maria Santissima, con el titulo de el Rosario ....* En Madrid: en la Imprenta de Lorenzo Mojados, 1743. French-style early neoclassical binding in dark crimson morocco, with the royal coat of arms of Philip V (outline of shield ending in a point) (detail). RB, PAS/2861

a binding that appears to have been executed in the period of Philip II but dates from that of Philip V. It does not even feature the fleurs-de-lis in an inescutcheon but instead incorporates the coat of arms of Portugal in the chief or upper third, while the crown is identical to many found on the title pages of printed works bearing the royal coat of arms during the reign of the previous Philip.[23]

Although the heraldry of Philip V basically perpetuated earlier models, it also made novel contributions other than the "French mark of difference". Such is the case of the emergence of the aforementioned round outline of the royal shield, which he brought from

Fig. 46
Francisco Satorre y Carbonell, *Suaristica, aristotelea, contentiosa, et experimentalis Philosophia* .... Valentiae: Chalcographiâ Josephi Thomae Lucas ..., 1755. Bound in red morocco with the English-style supralibros of Ferdinand VI (detail). RB, I/E/135

Fig. 47
Giovanni Antonio Cavazzi, *Relation historique de l'Ethiopie occidentale* .... A Paris: chez Charles-Jean-Baptiste Delespine le Fils ..., 1732. Bound in natural-coloured morocco, with a double gold fillet framing the supralibros of Paulin Prondre de Guermantes, in a medallion (detail). RB, V/2452

France,[24] and which after ceasing to be used during subsequent periods was employed sporadically by Charles III and more frequently by Charles IV.[25] A clearer case is that of Isabel II, who often displayed it on the quartered shield of Saint Ferdinand. The rectangular shield ending in a point also appeared under Philip V owing to French influence [fig. 45], as the local version was rectangular without a point. In contrast, Ferdinand VI, both as Prince of Asturias and later as king, incorporated the shield with curved sides in what is apparently a novel concept, but occasionally also used the rectangular shield ending in a point with English-type figures as external ornaments [fig. 46]. However, no less than Philip II himself used the curved-sided shield in a very similar manner when prince, at least in the 1540s in bindings by Juan Vázquez of Salamanca for Philip's so-called "rich library" [*librería rica*], which was assembled during this period by Juan Cristóbal Calvete de Estrella.[26] Nevertheless, we are inclined to think that the type used by Ferdinand is more closely connected with Italian curved-sided models and their influence than with those of his predecessor. Charles III used a different, more elongated shield of irregular lines.[27] An innovation introduced in the period of Ferdinand VI is the pennant-shaped outline, like a candle in the wind,[28] and another highly novel feature in Spain was the appearance of animals, which were common in English and French heraldry, as external elements; in addition, while Paulin-Gabriel Pronde de Guermantes (1698–1775) incorporated lions to his blazon dexter and sinister[29] [fig. 47], so did the Spanish king, adding military elements at the bottom and standards of Castile and León next to the crown—a feature which, together with the crown, was likewise innovative.[30] The lion as an external adornment might have continued to have been used, as occurred later with the pillars of Hercules, but this was not the case, even though the animal was highly representative of Spain. Indeed, a pair of lions, as in Ferdinand's arms, was chosen as the subject of the sculpture flanking the steps of the Spanish Parliament building. This arrangement is not unusual, as the same design was chosen for the Throne Room of the Royal Palace, where they are placed at the foot of the royal thrones. The lion had been the first emblem of Spanish royalty since the period of Emperor Alfonso VII (1105–1157);[31] its presence in the quarterings makes it unnecessary to repeat it in external elements. Certain other animals were also used at times as a royal emblem, such as the butterfly, which was employed by the queen dowager María Cristina of Bourbon-Two Sicilies and also by her daughter Isabel II as an infanta, who used it in bookplates during her teenage years; it is an appropriate emblem as it is a symbol of transformation. The queen used it on book covers not decoratively but emblematically, as stated earlier,[32] and this use has also been considered to denote the concept of change, transformation, as she employed the same emblem in her sentimental life with the future Duke of Riánsares, whom she secretly wedded at the end of 1833, not long after Ferdinand VII died.

The practice of combining the arms of married couples, impaling those of husband

Fig. 48

Recueil de différentes recettes. Bound in deep crimson French *veau*, with the supralibros of Anne of Austria, queen consort of Louis XIII of France, when a widow (detail). RB, II/4572

with those of the wife, became consolidated in the eighteenth century and this trend was powerfully present in the bindings of queens consort. Those of the male, the holder of the Crown, are positioned in the dexter half—in heraldry right or left is always from the point of view of the heraldic representation—and this practice become the rule thereafter until it eventually disappeared in the twentieth century. The decline is detectable by the end of the eighteenth century, as the Real Biblioteca contains supralibros of María Luisa of Parma featuring only her own blazon. Throughout the seventeenth century spouses were still represented in a partitioned shield, as is the case of Anne of Austria, wife of Louis XIII of France, and this practice sometimes continued in the eighteenth century.

Other aspects that remained were the Franciscan knotted cord with separate tassels

Fig. 49
Almanach Royal. Á Paris: De l'Imprimerie de la Veuve d'Houry, au Saint-Esprit, 1755. French Rococo-style stamped binding in brown morocco, with the impaled coat of arms of Isabella Farnese, queen consort of Philip V, when a widow (detail). RB, PAS/ARM3/50

for dowager queens, as may be seen in a copy in the Real Biblioteca, also bound for Anne of Austria—both circumstances in II/4572 [fig. 48]. An example dating from the mid-eighteenth century is a binding of Isabella Farnese as widow [fig. 49].

The Habsburg quartering continued after Philip V. Charles III repeated it, with an almost identical arrangement, even in Italian-made bindings, although the quarter of Navarra charged with the chains was occasionally incorporated. It was used subsequently by Joseph I and was reincorporated in the twentieth century, first with Alfonso XIII and systematically when Francisco Franco was head of state. The coat of arms of the constitutional monarchy continues to display the quarter of Navarra.

The dictatorship recovered the eagle of Saint John the Evangelist, which had been used earlier fairly frequently by Alfonso XIII, albeit replacing the old arms of Sicily—still used by the monarch even though they had not corresponded to territory ruled by the monarchy—with this quarter of Navarra. The use of the Sicilian arms in Alfonso's quartering is often found in royal supralibros displaying this type the eagle, although some of Alfonso's heraldic representations also display the chains of Navarra, as stated.[33] As is known, the use of the eagle of Saint John was very common during the reign of the Catholic Monarchs, as they had a special devotion to the Evangelist and adopted his distinctive animal for royal heraldry. This eagle appears not only on a host of printed works dating from Alfonso's reign but also on public buildings erected during the period, such as the main entrance of the façade of what is now Madrid city hall, in a model that combines that of Saint John and the imperial eagle of Charles V, as the bird is two-headed but its wings are not outstretched. Alfonso XIII therefore used this type of eagle in the same way as distant predecessors of his, including Philip II. The type of eagle of Saint John that was so widely used both in the reign of Alfonso XIII and during the Franco regime is almost identical to that of Philip II, including the pillars of Hercules and Charles's *Plvs Vltra* motto that can be seen on the front of a dedication to the sovereign on the reverse of the first folio of the Escorial Greek codex Σ.I.7, executed in 1564, although with the arms of Sicily and without a yoke or arrows.[34] In other respects Philip II had used the chains of Navarra occasionally when still prince,[35] as can be seen in the coat of arms on the title page of *Los veinte triunphos* by Vasco Díaz Tanco, printed in Valencia around 1535,[36] but they did not continue to be used by the Habsburgs. They were however adopted by French monarchs, as may be seen in the supralibros of the French Bourbons.[37] This was due to the fact that Henry IV incorporated French Navarra into France as Count of Foix and from this point onwards we find this blazon together with the fleurs-de-lis in French royal heraldry. To cite an example, in some bindings in the Monastery of San Lorenzo (cf. RBME, 10.V.22 [fig. 50]),[38] often all that varies is the position of the cross of the holy sepulchre and of the adjoining quarter, which descend a level, although they remain in the upper part of the blazon, and the same is true of a few Italian bindings of Charles III.[39] The cross of the holy sepulchre, of which Alfonso XIII was so fond, is also found in the woodcut of the princely shield of Philip II on the title page of *Los veinte triumphos*, showing that before being used in Italy by Charles III it was used in Spain—as also evidenced by imperial shields of Charles V found on various title pages of books—and continued throughout Philip's reign, as can be seen on many other title pages.[40]

The quartering of the aforementioned coat of arms, that of *Los veinte triumphos*, is unusual in that the first quarter, the chief, does not display the arms of Castile and León as was common practice but instead those of modern Burgundy and Austria. This variant was not so rare then; the arms of Austria and ancient Burgundy were sometimes also found in the chief of the arms used by Prince Philip but in fact the model belonged to Charles.[41]

This shield of *Los veinte triumphos* features as an external ornament a ribbon scroll bearing the motto "Plvs Vltra" adopted by the emperor—although without the pillars of Hercules—in contrast to the common model of the emperor with the imperial eagle. The pillars were recovered much later by Joseph I in his supralibros, and continued to be used by Ferdinand VII even in saddles; this borrowing enjoyed considerable success as the pillars were maintained subsequently both for the quartered shield of Saint Ferdinand and for the full coat of arms during the nineteenth and twentieth centuries. Nowadays, although present in the Spanish coat of arms, they do not feature in that of Juan Carlos I. The pillars, it should be stressed, have been maintained in the coat of arms of the Spanish state both as a monarchy and as the Second Republic, the Dictatorship and the new constitutional monarchy.

Curiously, the coat of arms found in *Los veinte triumphos* displays the saltires of Saint Andrew on each side and, hanging from them, the Golden Fleece. Their presence is logical as they are an emblem of Burgundy and the order was established in 1429 by Philip III, Duke of Burgundy and Count of Flanders. The coat of arms of Don Juan Carlos is therefore not totally original in featuring the Burgundy or saltire cross. On a few occasions Alfonso XIII had already used a royal coat of arms in the same arrangement as His Majesty today: the quartered shield of Saint Ferdinand with the Burgundian saltires.[42] Other external ornaments, such as the ribbon scroll, displaying different contents have enjoyed a more diverse presence. It is not unusual to find such scrolls on the coats of arms of Charles V and Philip II on title pages, particularly above the

Fig. 50
Regula et constitutiones Fratrum Sacri Ordinis Beatae Mariae de Mercede Redemptionis Captiuorum. [Salmanticae]: Cornelius Bonardus excudebat Salmanticae, 1588. Stamped calfskin binding executed in Salamanca for Philip III when Prince of Asturias (detail). RBME, 10.V.22

two-headed imperial eagle, and the presence of a scroll above the eagle of Saint John the Evangelist in the mid-twentieth century therefore cannot be considered a novelty either.

Ribbon scrolls have always been highly characteristic of the heraldry of bibliophiles, who place their mottos on them—we might recall, for example, Jacques August Gaspard de Thou[43]. In contrast, an external ornament which has always been used—except, as in only logical, during the Republics and the Franco period, as it is a royal attribute—is the collar of the Order of the Golden Fleece, which was immediately accepted and adopted by the new Bourbon dynasty and maintained even in Italian bindings, although there are a few exceptions among the latter.[44] The collar is also found in the heraldry of successors to the throne and is not exclusive to the king, as it is a dynastic element. It currently features in the shield of Prince Felipe.

There are therefore external ornaments which are found in royal armorial bindings, ceased to be used for a time and were subsequently recovered. Such is the case of the pillars of Hercules, which were taken up by Joseph I and widely used in the nineteenth and twentieth centuries; the ribbon scroll in the official coat of arms of Spain—during both the dictatorship and the democracy—and now surrounding the pillars bearing the "Plvs Vltra" motto, as with Charles V; and also the yoke and arrows, used by the Catholic Monarchs and during the twentieth century both in the official Spanish coat of arms in the central decades and today in the personal arms of Juan Carlos I. The personal arms of the current Spanish king feature the yoke and arrows of the Catholic Monarchs in the lower part, as in theirs, and incorporate the cross of Burgundy or St Andrew as symbols of unity, as he descends from the bloodline of Isabella and also from that of Charles and also because he wishes to accord the arms a European dimension. In some current bindings of Don Juan Carlos these elements therefore form the external ornaments of a shield with four different quarters—representing the kingdoms of Castile and León, Aragón and Navarra[45]—and not in a quartered shield of Saint Ferdinand, but in an abbreviated version which permanently adopted the chains of Navarra.

With the eighteenth-century Bourbons the quarters of the royal coat of arms continued to enjoy a territorial significance, although they no longer referred to territories that actually belonged to the Crown but to territories over which sovereignty had been lost. As King of Naples, Charles III used a shield with many quarterings—all those of the Habsburgs plus the two new ones with the fleurs-de-lis of Parma and the roundels of Tuscany, motifs which he incorporated into the Spanish royal arms giving rise to the so-called "Great Shield" [*Escudo Grande*]. But he furthermore employed that of Portugal when sometimes not even the Haps-

Fig. 51
Hermann Silberberg, *[Marche de couronnement]*, [*c.* 1902]. Bound in leather with the royal coat of arms of Alfonso XIII, King of Spain, after the *Escudo Grande* model (detail). RB, MUS/MSS/1410

burgs used the Portuguese inescutcheon following the incorporation of Portugal to the Spanish crown in 1580, as is found on RBME, 10.V.22 [fig. 50]. In this case the crown characteristic of princes of the Royal Household is used, and if it was executed for Philip III, perhaps it was considered appropriate not to include the Portuguese inescutcheon because the annexation was achieved by his father, who was still alive, meaning that he was not yet sovereign prince of Portugal. After Portugal gained its independence we find a few examples of the use of the Portuguese inescutcheon, with respect to the use of earlier models.

The fondness for using quarterings denoting territories that were no longer sovereign possessions of the Crown extended to Alfonso XIII:

Fig. 52
Antoine-Siméon-Gabriel Coffinieres, *Le Code Napoléon expliqué par les décisions suprêmes de la Cour de cassation et du Conseil d'État*. A Paris: chez Garnery, Libraire, rue de Seine, Hôtel Mirabeau; Pollet, Boulevard Bonne-Nouvelle, n. 57; Mme. Vanraest, quai Désaix, près le Palais de Justice: de l'imprimerie de J. Gratiot, 1809. Bound in red morocco with the supralibros of Joseph Bonaparte, King of Spain, showing the royal shield with a crowned ermine mantle (detail). RB, VIII/16346

a representative example is the blazon on RB, MUS/MSS/1410 [fig. 51] which features Habsburg quarters in addition to the two of Parma and Tuscany that were incorporated by Charles III, with the quartered shield of Saint Ferdinand in an inescutcheon and the three fleurs-de-lis in the centre of the latter. The last Alfonso also borrowed the emblems of the military orders for his deluxe bindings,[46] including also those executed outside Spain, such as in Paris.

As for the crowns, the use, documented as early as the sixteenth century,[47] of an open crown without half-arches for the Prince of Asturias continued to be habitual even in the eighteenth century, as we find in the case of Ferdinand VI. We have seen that both the monarch and his successor used the royal crown in the nineteenth century and only today is a distinction drawn: a crown with five half-arches for Juan Carlos I and a crown with three half-arches for Don Felipe, whose arms differ from those of his father in the use of a label in the chief, which denotes succession to the throne.

There have been charges in royal quarters which have changed their position over time. The pillars of Hercules, used by Charles V as an external ornament, as they are today, reappeared during the reign of Joseph I—a monarch who is extremely interesting from the heraldic viewpoint—in the lower half of the shield together with the two globes, as he was considered monarch of both continents, the Old and the New [fig. 52]. Charles III adopted the title of King of the Indies, but did not use the pillars in supralibros.

As for the use of the pomegranate and the pillars of Hercules, the supralibros of Joseph I's wife, Marie-Julie Clary, were very original. For example, she employed a model in which the upper part of the blazon consists of quartering identical to that used today by Don Juan Carlos—Castile, León, Aragón and Navarra—but in the lower part there are two quarters, one displaying only the pomegranate and the other only the pillars, thereby according greater importance to these heraldic charges. An inescutcheon displays the emblem of her family, not the Napoleonic eagle.[48] The pomegranate, which was incorporated following the capture of the city of Granada ["granada" means pomegranate in

Spanish] by Isabella and Ferdinand, has likewise changed position several times. The Catholic Monarchs used it enté en point, its usual position in the past centuries, but there are Habsburg coats of arms in which it features below the quartering of Saint Ferdinand, on the dexter side of the chief or between the dexter and sinister, in the manner of an inescutcheon. When the quartered arms of Saint Ferdinand feature in an inescutcheon, the pomegranate is likewise positioned at their base. And so the pomegranate was often not placed in the current enté en point of the arms—a position which, under both Hapsburgs and Bourbons, was occupied by the quarter of the lion of Flanders and that of the eagle of Tyrol, or sometimes by the eagle and the adder of Milan.

Patrimonio Nacional, in addition to royal armorial bindings, preserves examples belonging to members of the nobility. The Real Biblioteca contains many that were formerly owned by French nobles and acquired over the eighteenth century in the shipments sent from Paris. It also houses examples belonging to some of the most characteristic Spanish noble bibliophiles, such as the Marquis of Caracena and Frómista[49] and the Marquis of Moya, both of which have long been studied by scholars. The supralibros of the Marquis of Caracena, Luis de Benavides y Carrillo (1608–1668), is austere, very much in keeping with Castilian tastes, in the style of a quartered shield of Saint Ferdinand with two lions and two towers—for Benavides and Carrillo respectively—and an inescutcheon of the Bazán family,[50] but Moya's is richer and more in line with continental supralibros, enclosed in a medallion. Moya's books were bound by Juan de Sarriá of Alcalá, after being purchased from the bookseller Juan Boyer of Medina del Campo.[51]

The Marquis of Moya, Francisco Pérez de Cabrera y Bobadilla (1565–1627), sometimes used a manuscript supralibris,[52] but his arms enclosed in a medallion are more characteristic of his property[53] [fig. 53]. The use of the medallion as a supralibros has an important aesthetic connotation. We might recall that of Diego Hurtado de Mendoza, the great collector of Greek codices, who gave it a use that was not heraldic but emblematic and symbolic, placing it on an artistic plaquette in the form of a cameo. His lineage is reflected in the red and dark green of the covers, the colours of the house of the Mendozas.[54] We might also recall the famous *canevari* medallion of Giovanni Battista Grimaldi, in vogue in the

Fig. 53
Juan de Herrera, *Sumario y Breue declaracio[n] de los diseños y estampas de la fabrica de San Lorencio el Real del Escurial*. Madrid: por la viuda de Alonso Gomez, 1589. Bound in parchment by Juan de Sarriá (Alcalá de Henares, sixteenth century), with the supralibros of the Marquis of Moya, Francisco Pérez de Cabrera y Bobadilla, in a medallion (detail). RB, I/B/107

mid-sixteenth century; indeed, the Renaissance medallion is directly related to the subsequent and widespread use of the blazon as a supralibros, as the idea of the cameo on the cover is a precedent.[55] This ornamental concept gave way to the use of heraldry in supralibros, when many coats of arms were set in oval fillets that enhance them while perpetuating this ornamental character, an intention of which there is evidence both in Spain and abroad and in both the sixteenth century—for example the aforementioned supralibros of the Marquis of Moya—and the seventeenth or eighteenth, with the supralibros of De Thou or Paulin Prondre de Guermantes, framed in a broad orle of plant motifs.

At the same time many other noblemen's supralibros avoided the oval fillet or border and preferred to accord even more importance to the heraldic emblem, such as the aforementioned one of Caracena. When an armorial bearing displays many quarterings with their charges it is obvious that, in addition to the heraldic significance, the supralibros acquires a visual importance that relates it directly to Renaissance medallions. Once again, such is the case of that of Moya.

One of the first existing armorial supralibros of Spanish nobles was that of the Marquis of Astorga, Alonso Osorio. He used it from 1530 onwards in a trend spurred by the model of the supralibros of the prince, Don Felipe,[56] as there are armorial bindings of the future Philip II dating from the 1530s, in a process of assimilation similar to that of Matthias Corvinus, a pioneer in the use of the royal heraldic supralibros. The influence of the Bibliotheca Corviniana on the rest of the European courts and grandees was huge, as the king was first to adopt the systematic use of the coat of arms on the covers of his rich collection, furthermore using not just one but several heraldic models, to achieve more striking effects, and on bright backgrounds. He also introduced systematic gilding, when up until the fifteenth century blind tooling had been prevalent, with the occasional application of gold paint.[57]

Indeed, the practices of the royal households led to the formation of habits with respect to the use of heraldry in bookbinding among noble families. In the case of Spain, for example, the use of new shapes of shields for coats of arms of the nobility during the eighteenth century is closely related to the novel shapes introduced by Philip V or used by Ferdinand VI. In turn, the traditional austerity of the external ornaments in Spanish armorial bearings appearing on books was changed in the eighteenth century by the influence of continental heraldry, which was much fonder of helms, mantling and animals as ornaments as opposed to the traditional crowns or, at the most, standards at the bottom, as is likewise found in bookplates. This is a distinctive feature together with the continued use of earlier models of the previous or even earlier monarchs until the new model of the reigning monarch was shaped and consolidated. Finally, the third general feature of the development of the imagery of shields is the use and disuse of certain external ornaments and their recovery at a later date, sometimes centuries afterwards. Such is the case of the aforementioned pillars of Hercules, scrolls and the yoke and arrows, elements which have withstood empires, absolute and enlightened monarchies, dictatorships and constitutional monarchies, and today defy the future from the official coat of arms of Spain or from that of His Majesty.

1 As in RB, III/1691 [fig. 37] and VIII/9704 [fig. 38], which differ in quartering and arrangement but coincide in the putti supporting the royal crown.

2 Juan Alfonso Enríquez de Cabrera was viceroy in Naples from 1644 to 1646 and Luis Francisco de la Cerda y Aragón held the post from 1696 to 1702. Covers made for both, featuring putti, can be seen in the classic article Saltillo 1934, 2–35, nos. 15 and 17.

3 For example, in a work as significant as Fernando Mejía's *Nobiliario vero* (Seville, Pedro Brun-Juan Gentil, 1492), where woodcut shields are used for this purpose. There is one in the Real Biblioteca (I/213) and a facsimile edition in Madrid, Ministerio de Educación y Ciencia [1974]. We commented on it in connection with its significance to printed heraldic representation in Moreno Gallego 2010, 45. We also refer to this work in Moreno Gallego 2009, 18.

4 Such as, for example, *La gran conquista de Ultramar*, Salamanca: Hans Giesser, 1503 (RB, I/C/342), quoted in Moreno Gallego 2010, 48, no. 32.

5 See Moreno Gallego 2010, 55. A few allusions to letters patent of nobility, their heraldry and their subsequent influence in book practice are found in Moreno Gallego 1999, 267–88. But above all, see *Documento pintado* 2000 and Rubio de Urquía 2001.

6 The verb "timpar" is used with this meaning by Rico y Sinobas 1941.

7 To cite an example—although some were even larger—that used by Pierre-Daniel Huet, Bishop of Avranches, cf. RB, V/32, with a supralibros on the covers [fig. 40] and a large bookplate. On this library see Pélisson-Karro 1998, 107–30. This library had more than eight thousand books, see Guigard 1870–73, II, 10–11. We mention this binding, V/32, in Moreno Gallego 2009, 72, note 28.

8 See Rico y Sinobas 1941, 282 and 284 [quoted in Moreno Gallego 2009, 18].

9 For the circular model, see RB, IV/5484 (1767) and IV/1414 (1770). An example of that of Ferdinand VI is found in XIV/1703.

10 Cf. *Dispvtationvm de indvlgentiis, adversvs nostrae tempestatis haereticos, ad patres S. Concilii Tridentini ... Accessit quarti articuli symboli Apostolici interpretatio, eodem auctore*, Venetiis: Ex officina Stellae, Iordani Zileti, 1564. The copy in the Real Biblioteca at the Monastery of El Escorial (suc. RBME, 6.V.43 [fig. 41]) is reproduced in Hueso Rolland 1935, 200, ill. XXIII, no. 137. The circumstance mentioned above is commented on by Gonzalo Sánchez-Molero 2005, II, 125.

11 See Gonzalo Sánchez-Molero 2010a, 76–17; 2010b, 841–76; 2011, 47–81, especially, 62–63.

12 See Gonzalo Sánchez-Molero 2005, II, 139 (description of the book in question on p. 231). The accession number quoted is the original one "RBME, Habitación de Felipe II, nº 4", now 6.V.43.

13 Cf. RBME, 38.I.7 and 39.III.25. We refer to Mathias Gast's edition of *Dioscórides*, which bears this coat of arms on the title page (RB, VII/2423 [fig. 42]).

14 Castile, 1st and 4th, gules, three-towered crenelated castle or, masoned sable and ajouré azure; León, 2nd and 3rd, Argent, a lion rampant purpure crowned or, langued and armed gules.

15 See Menéndez Pidal 1982, 23 (quoted in Moreno Gallego 2009, 73, note 40). See also Menéndez Pidal 1988, 5–21.

16 Cf. *Livre d'Heures d'après les Manuscrits de la Bibliothèque Royale*, Paris, Auguste Fontaine, 1878 (RB, XIV/2922 [figs. 43 and 44]). On this book, see López-Vidriero 2003, 4–22. This printed work incorporates [5] sheets of vellum, manuscript and illuminated illustrations by Chambulle-Duru.

17 Cf. RB, IV/994, and a non-Italian model without an outline in RB, CS4/16, both dealt with in Moreno Gallego 2009, 126 and 91 respectively

18 For example in RB, CS4/16, reproduced in Moreno Gallego 2009, 91.

19 See Moreno Gallego 2009, 37–39 and note 105, which deals with aspects of the inescutcheon denoting lineage.

20 The model of the two-headed eagle of Philip V may be seen in Hueso Rolland 1935, ill. XLII, no. 271, and in Domínguez Bordona and Ainaud 1958, 334.

21 Juan Ainaud reproduces a cover in Domínguez Bordona and Ainaud 1958, 334, fig. 496.

22 Such is the case of RB, IX/M/6. It was made in Paris for Philip V and is reproduced in Moreno Gallego 2009, 224.

23 Cf. RB, III/501, reproduced in Moreno Gallego 2009, 119.

24 There are Paris-made examples of this model: RB, IX/M/6 (*vide supra* note 22). Shown with the collar of the French Order of Saint Michel.

25 Even as Prince of Asturias, cf. RB, PAS/ARM3/67. It is the so-called *Escudo Grande*, with the quarterings of Parma and Tuscany, reproduced in Moreno Gallego 2009, 150.

26 See Gonzalo Sánchez-Molero 1998, 110–34 which reproduces the heraldic models used by Juan Vázquez with this outline, in a model subsequently employed by other binders such as Juan de Torres. Hueso Rolland (1935, ill. XXII, no. 135) states that it dates from 1563 but it was in fact executed in 1573 as it contains the oath taken by Ferdinand as Prince of Asturias. He swore his oath at the monastery of San Jerónimo on 31 May 1573, as the title had been left vacant by the death of his half-brother Carlos of Habsburg and Avis in 1568. Also relevant is Gonzalo Sánchez-Molero 2005, 116 (on Vázquez in general, 107–21).

27 Cf. RB, I/F/1, reproduced in Moreno Gallego 2009, 139.

28 Cf. RB, IV/5124, reproduced in Moreno Gallego 2009, 131.

29 Cf. RB, V/2452 [fig. 47], see Guigard 1870–73, II, 173–74 but the information relates to the father.

30 Cf. RB, I/E/135 [fig. 46].

31 The *Chronica Adefonsi Imperatoris* refers to the use of the lion in his royal arms and flags, as pointed out by MENÉNDEZ PIDAL 1982, 23.
32 Cf. RB, I/J/68.
33 As in RB, VI/2419, with the arms of Sicily, for example in F. Giovanni da Capistrano, *Il martirio del principe degli apostoli rivendicato alla sua sede in sul gianicolo*, Seconda edizione, Roma, Tipografia Sallustiana, 1903, and the chains of Navarra in the quartered arms of Saint Ferdinand in a manuscript diploma hanging in room VI of the Real Biblioteca [inv. 10013052].
34 They are by Juan de Eucaíta and the coat of arms is reproduced in ANDRÉS 1969, ill. II.
35 *Vide supra* note 11.
36 Cf. BNE, R/16906. In a note of the entry in CCPB: "Rodríguez Moñino, *Bibliografía de Vasco Díaz Tanco*, lo cree impreso en Valencia por el propio autor antes de 1535, fecha de la muerte de Clemente VII, pues lo cita como Pontífice." He refers to the bibliography that precedes the bibliophile's edition made by Antonio of the *Palinodia de los turcos* (Orense, 1547) but Badajoz, Diputación, 1947.
37 Such as RB, IX/4714, of Louis XIII and the subsequent Louises.
38 This is *Regula et Constitutiones Fratrum sacri Ordinis Beatae Mariae de Mercede Redemptionis Captiuorum*. [Salmanticae]: Cornelius Bonardus excudebat Salmanticae, 1588, in HUESO ROLLAND 1935, 206, ill. XXVII, no. 179. It was very possibly executed in Salamanca.
39 Three Italian ones of Charles III are reproduced in MORENO GALLEGO 2009, 143–47. In the Real Biblioteca: II/1691, XIX/247, IV/252 (the latter with the chains of Navarra) and V/1990, in the quartered arms of Saint Ferdinand.
40 This is a Jerusalem cross used by the crusades in the Holy Land. Its four straight ends represent the four corners of the World, the four elements. Its use in Spanish royal heraldry is due to the fact that the title of King of Jerusalem is held by the Spanish Crown.
41 As pointed out by GONZALO SÁNCHEZ-MOLERO 2005, II, 111–12, who reports some bindings with this shield as supralibros.
42 Cf. RB, ARM 29/1078, a curious binding with applied polychrome wood.
43 Cf. RB, IX/2393, this is "Mane nobiscum domine".
44 As in RB, XIX/248, but its presence is widespread throughout all reigns.
45 Cf. RB, XIV2938, reproduced in MORENO GALLEGO 2009, 175.
46 Cf. RB, II/3863, it bears the emblem of a military order in each corner. It is by Menard.
47 Cf. RBME, 10.V.22 [fig. 50], it dates from 1588. HUESO ROLLAND 1935, ill. XXVII, no. 179. For Ferdinand VI, for example, RB, PAS/ARM3/30–31–32 and other successive entries.
48 It is an example of the type featuring the shield in a crowned ermine mantle. Cf. RB, VI/3691, reproduced in MORENO GALLEGO 2009, 183.

49 Cf. RB, VII/1786 or II/523. The latter is a singular manuscript: *Des livre d'architecture, et prospetive et fortification*, by Pierre de Poivre, executed around 1613–14, [2] shts.+70 f.+[2] shts.: paper ; 440 x 285 mm.; f. 41–42: 425 x 550 mm. It would not be surprising if it were Caracena's (1608–1668) given his military standing, see VINDEL ANGULO 1923. The owners' database of the Real Biblioteca features an entry for this object and provides a biographical sketch of Caracena.
50 The description is: or, a lion rampant or, crowned or and surrounded by a ribbon or band argent, with a bordure argent with eight cauldrons sable (Benavides); gules, a castle or ajouré azure (Carrillo); above all an escutcheon checky of fifteen pieces argent and sable (Bazán); external ornaments, marquis's crown and cross of Saint James.
51 See CASTAÑEDA 1934, 309–18, and 1958, 79–142. Later SÁNCHEZ MARIANA 1994, 12–18. Sarría's arrangement with Boyer, the bookseller from whom the marquis purchased the books, was published by PEREZ PASTOR 1895, 462–64 [no. 185] and HUESO ROLLAND 1935, 159–60. The arrangement dates from 1592.
52 As in RB, III/2352.
53 Cf. RB, I/B/107[fig. 53], for example. The description is: shield party: quartered 1 per saltire: 1) azure, a royal crown or; 2) gules, a castle or (Castile); 3) argent, a lion gules crowned or (León); 4) or, a goat sabre and crenelated bordure sabre (Cabrera); 2nd quarter: 1&4) gules, an eagle argent; 2&3) argent, a stone tower with flaming doors, windows and battlements; a bordure compony of Castile and León (Bobadilla); in an inescutcheon, argent, two cauldrons checky or and sabre, in pale (Pacheco); as an external ornament, the marquis's crown
54 There are several approaches to Diego's library, prominent among which are those of HOBSON 1993 [2001], 39–52; and HOBSON 1999. [See also the text by Hobson in this catalogue].
55 In "Heráldica y libro antiguo" [MORENO GALLEGO 2010, 59], we wrote: "El *estilo canevari*, floreciente entre 1535 y 1560 y hoy ya correctamente atribuido a Giovanni Battista Grimaldi, de planos ligeros pero con medallón en relieve al centro, también ayudó a la práctica de insertar un blasón, pues si se incorporaba en camafeo un motivo ornamental, mitológico y de gran belleza, pero decorativo al fin y al cabo, pese a su simbología, ¿por qué no iba a poner el poseedor lo que más le distinguía, que era la representación emblemática de su linaje?" For the cameo technique in bookbinding, see CLAVERIA 2006, 104–6.
56 See CÁTEDRA 2002, 20–30, (quoted by GONZALO SÁNCHEZ-MOLERO 2005, 113, no. 1685).
57 See HEVESY 1923; CSABA 1992 and DI PIETRO LOMBARDA 2002, 117–28, bibliography quoted in MORENO GALLEGO 2010, 56, note 61.

Books for Reading. Commercial Bindings in Parchment and Paper in the Era of the Handpress

Nicholas Pickwoad

Introduction

The beautifully decorated bindings which feature so powerfully in this exhibition formed part of the apanage of the royal, aristocratic, cultural and financial elites of Europe. They expressed not only the learning (actual or presumed) of their owners, but also their taste and high status. They were, however, as costly and exclusive as their owners, and can have formed only a tiny proportion of the books published and then bound for consumption across the continent of Europe and beyond. It is doubtful that even one percent of the total number of books produced were bound in such style, whilst the remaining ninety-nine percent would have been given much simpler bindings, perhaps in leather over boards with some simple decoration in the form of tooling in gold or silver foil or in blind, or, more cheaply and more numerously still, in plain parchment bindings with no decoration at all. Such bindings in parchment survive in their tens of thousands in libraries especially across southern Europe and the Americas, where bindings in parchment on books printed before the nineteenth century dominate the shelves of monastic and academic libraries, but they seldom appear in the literature of bookbinding.[1] It could be said that ninety-nine percent of the history of bookbinding concerns only one percent of the bindings made, and the other ninety-nine percent of the bindings is passed over virtually in silence. This makes it very difficult to come to firm conclusions about the history of such bindings and the parchment-covered bindings displayed in this exhibition can offer no more than an introduction to a field that is as yet largely unexplored. In addition, the collections of the Patrimonio Nacional cannot possibly offer a comprehensive selection of all the different types of such bindings that were made either in Spain or the rest of Europe, but they do allow a fascinating insight into the world of books bound for use rather than display.

It is also true that within the economics of the book trade what have come to be called "fine bindings" played only a small part in what grew rapidly into an international trade in the decades that followed the invention of printing in the 1450s, helped by the widespread use of Latin, the international language of scholarship and learning that transcended national boundaries. Along with the development of international financial instruments that allowed the major booksellers to transfer money from one part of Europe to another, the book trade also required inexpensive and lightweight ways of protecting their books as they went on their way to their customers. Books could be and often were shipped in their printed sheets, packed in barrels or bales to keep them dry, but this had risks, as the loose sheets had no protection once unpacked and were susceptible to the loss or misplacement of individual sheets that might make a book incomplete and thus unsaleable. The protection offered by the typical bindings of the period were not useful in this regard, for it was not only costly to bind and ship books that might, in the latter part of the fifteenth century, have been bound with heavy wooden boards and metal fittings, but a bookseller in one part of Europe could not necessarily predict the sort of binding that customers in another part of the continent might wish to have on their books. Faced by the demand for something different, it would appear that the binders looked to the sorts of books bound for commercial and archival work to supply this need. Throughout the medieval period, binders had developed a number of structures for what are known as stationery bindings (bindings, that is, on the blank books made for stationers rather than the printed books sold by booksellers), most of which shared the same limp parchment covers, which is to say covers that do not have rigid boards under them. The requirements of a stationery binding were simple, but well suited to their new purpose: they needed to be inexpensive yet durable and be able to be carried around without risk of damaging their contents. They did not need to be decorated—though some were [see fig. 57]—but above all, they needed to be functional.

Different binders in different countries came up with their own solutions or variations on the same solution to this demand from the book trade, and in the many differences both large and small that can be found in these bindings lies the possibility of working out their history and, to an increasing extent, as we learn more, where they were made. The differences lie in the variety of techniques used by the binders as they went about their work, which include even the personal work habits that can identify individual craftsmen. To understand these bindings, therefore, it is first essential to understand the structures and techniques used to make them.

Sewn books

A binder faced by a stack of the unbound sheets in which books were often first offered for sale had first to decide how to hold them together in the codex-form book with which we are all familiar. Traditionally, then as now, this could be done by sewing with thread through the spine-folds of the individual folded sheets of printed paper, or gatherings, to lengths of leather, parchment, white alum-tawed skin or cords, known as sewing supports, which were placed across the spine and created the raised bands so characteristic of many early books. The ends of the sewing supports, known as the sewing-support slips, would be used to attach boards or a cover to the sewn bookblock. Variations in the number and position of the supports on the spine of the books can have both economic and geographic significance. The use, for instance, of four sewing supports arranged in two pairs, placed toward the head and tail of the spine [RBME, 69.IX.25[2]], gives evidence of an international connection. It is a structure that allows a very much faster type of sewing by attaching three gatherings with each length of thread running from head to tail of the bookblock (known as three-on sewing, a type of multi-section sewing), but providing a more stable structure than that offered by supports placed at equal intervals along the spine, and it shows a Spanish binder of the late eighteenth century working under the direct influence of British bookbinders, who first used this arrangement of sewing supports, which they called "sewing wide in the middle",[3] from the 1770s.

Sewing books to sewing supports was carried out using a wide range of variant types of sewing and materials, all or any of which can offer clues as to where a binding might have been made, and therefore to where it may have been read. The material used for the sewing supports, and the way in which the supports were formed from those materials, used either single or double, and rolled, twisted, crushed, split, or with two materials combined into one, will change according to the part of Europe in which a binding was made, and its date. The type of sewing will also vary according to cost and date, with all books sewn "all-along", that is with the sewing thread emerging from each gathering at every sewing station, until the early sixteenth century, but increasingly throughout that century to be found with two shortcuts to the process: bypass sewing, in which one or more sewing supports is not sewn around in each gathering, or multi-section sewing, where two or more gatherings are secured with each length of thread between head and tail, as described in the previous paragraph. When sewing a book using a multi-section sewing technique, the binder had to be able to find in turn the centre of each gathering to be sewn, and some binders chose to do this by folding in one of the outer corners of all the sheets in either the first or second half of the gathering, at an angle, leaving a diagonal crease in the folded leaves. Occasionally the binders failed to unfold the turned-in corners, thereby accidentally preserving the deckled edges of the leaves [RBME, 65.IX.13⁴]. This technique was used by some binders in England in the eighteenth and early nineteenth centuries,[5] but its use has not previously been recorded elsewhere. Every economy such as multi-section sewing comes at a price, of course, and the faster the sewing, generally speaking, the weaker the resultant structure will be. The balance between economy and strength would have been negotiated between binder and client, and may give an indication of the status of a book within the market at the time of its binding.

It has become increasingly clear from research carried out in recent years that books were frequently offered for sale as sewn bookblocks, with endleaves and either with the edges of the bookblock uncut, or cut, to remove the uneven deckle edges of the handmade paper, which allowed endbands to be sewn to the bookblock at the head and tail of the spine. Although surviving examples of books in this state are inevitably hard to find (such unfinished bindings were never intended to survive in this unprotected state), bound books with covers often show evidence of the process, when the purchaser of a book had the binding completed, quite possibly by a different binder, by having the edges coloured, a secondary, decorative sewing in silk added to the primary sewing of the endbands and a cover or even boards and leather added to complete the binding. This could happen immediately after purchase or perhaps several or even many years later, but the appearance of an undecorated strip across the spine-end of the head and tail edges, where the pigment or gilding used for the edge decoration stopped short of the primary endbands, is usually a sign that this may have happened [figs. 54 and 55]. It can

Fig. 54
Pontificale Romanum / Clementis VIII Pont. max. iussu restitutum atque editum, nunc primùm typis Plantinianis emendatiùs recusum. Antuerpiae: ex officina Plantiniana: apud Balthasarem Moretum, & viduam Ioannis Moreti, & Io. Meursium, 1627. RBME, 61.V.13. The tailband, showing the primary sewing with colour from the later edge colouring under the silk secondary sewing.

Fig. 55
Achille Gagliardi, S. I., *Catechismo della fede cattolica, con vn compendio per fanciulli.* In Milano: nella Stamperia di Michel Tini, 1584. RB, IX/8282. A plain-cut edge gilded after the primary endband was worked, leaving a strip of exposed bookblock edge under each endband.

Fig. 56
Domingo de Soto, *Annotationes in commentarios Ioannis Feri Moguntinensis super Euangelium Ioannis*. [Salamanca]: excudebat Andreas à Portonariis, 1554. RB, I/D/163.

The spine of the longstitch binding, showing the two sets of sewing, each reinforced by a small piece of dark brown leather.

of course be the case that a book may have been sewn in one country, shipped in that state, and the binding then completed in a second country, and evidence of this will also be found where the type of cover and the sewing structure and endbands clearly belong to different traditions of bookbinding [RBME, 90.IX.17,[6] 66.IX.21[7] and 66.IX.1[8]]. Depending on the extent to which this practice was carried out, a more or less substantial number of bindings on our library shelves may be the work not only of more than one binder, but also more than one country.

Longstitch

A very popular and inexpensive alternative to sewing on sewing supports was to sew the gatherings directly though the spine of a cover made from parchment or a thick cover-paper known as cartonnage. This structure, used throughout the Middle Ages, is known in English as longstitch, and is easily recognisable, where the book has not been given a secondary cover that would hide them, by the appearance of lengths of thread running parallel to the joints on the outside of the spine [fig. 56]. This type of binding had the advantage of very low cost—it required very little more than a knife, needle and thread to make one—yet produced durable books with very flexible spines; it was for this reason that the structure was often used for music books, as the pages would lie and stay open easily. It was in common use across Europe for archival bindings, but was also used for printed books in Italy, Germany and the Low Countries [RB, PAS/ARM1/235, PAS/ARM1/238 and VIII/5334[9]], though only a handful of Spanish examples have so far been identified [fig. 56 and RB, PAS/ARM1/311[10]]. Because of its low cost, longstitch structures were often used for the more ephemeral types of publication, including almanacs, cheap devotional books, popular romances, schoolbooks (of the eight early examples located in the library of the Real Biblioteca, five are on student texts about mathematics, algebra, astronomy, rhetoric and philosophy[11]), etc. These are very often the sorts of book that did not get into the more formal libraries, and which have therefore all too often disappeared without trace, leaving only enough behind to show that they once existed.

The longstitch bindings in the exhibition raise a problem to which as yet there is only an incomplete answer, which is the extent to which Italian and Spanish bindings of the late fifteenth and sixteenth centuries so resemble each other as to make it difficult to tell them apart. It would appear to be the case that Spanish binders at first copied the work of their Italian counterparts, even down to the types of spine lining used and the complex ways in which the ties used to hold the books shut were laced through the covers. There are a few specific techniques that appear to be unique to one or other country such as the use of leather spine straps, which appears to be found only on Spanish bindings (see below), or the slotted spines found only on some Italian inboard bindings (that is bindings in which the boards are attached to the bookblock before the book is covered),[12] but other techniques are shared by both countries from at least the early sixteenth century. By the end of the century, the similarities begin to weaken and through the seventeenth century the differences become more and more evident, though this is to a large extent due to the fact that the Italian bookbinding trade evolved new and different ways to bind books in the seventeenth and eighteenth centuries, while the Spanish book trade continued to make books after a late sixteenth-century pattern well into the beginning of the nineteenth century.

The question of the similarity between the work of the two countries becomes urgent when considering books printed in a third country which have been in Spanish libraries from an early date, because the correct identification of the origin of the bindings will show the route by which the books entered the country. It can probably be safely assumed that the two books printed in Spain—Valladolid 1527 and Salamanca 1554 [RB, PAS/ARM1/311 and fig. 56]—in what appear to be rather similar-looking bindings are Spanish. The fact that both of these make use of thick tanned leather spine reinforcements for the sewing but use slightly different longstitch sewing techniques suggests that two different binders made them, but were following a general pattern (the use of the leather spine reinforcements) that may, if more can be found, turn out to be typically Spanish. The twenty-seven years that separate the dates of the two editions in these bindings suggests that the style was in use for at least three decades. There is, similarly, no reason to think that the two books printed in Venice in 1537 and 1538, now in the Real Biblioteca [RB, VIII/5334 and PAS/ARM1/235], are not in Italian bindings, as near-identical examples can be found in many Italian libraries. The 1537 edition is in a cartonnage cover with parchment reinforcements on the spine, but the 1538

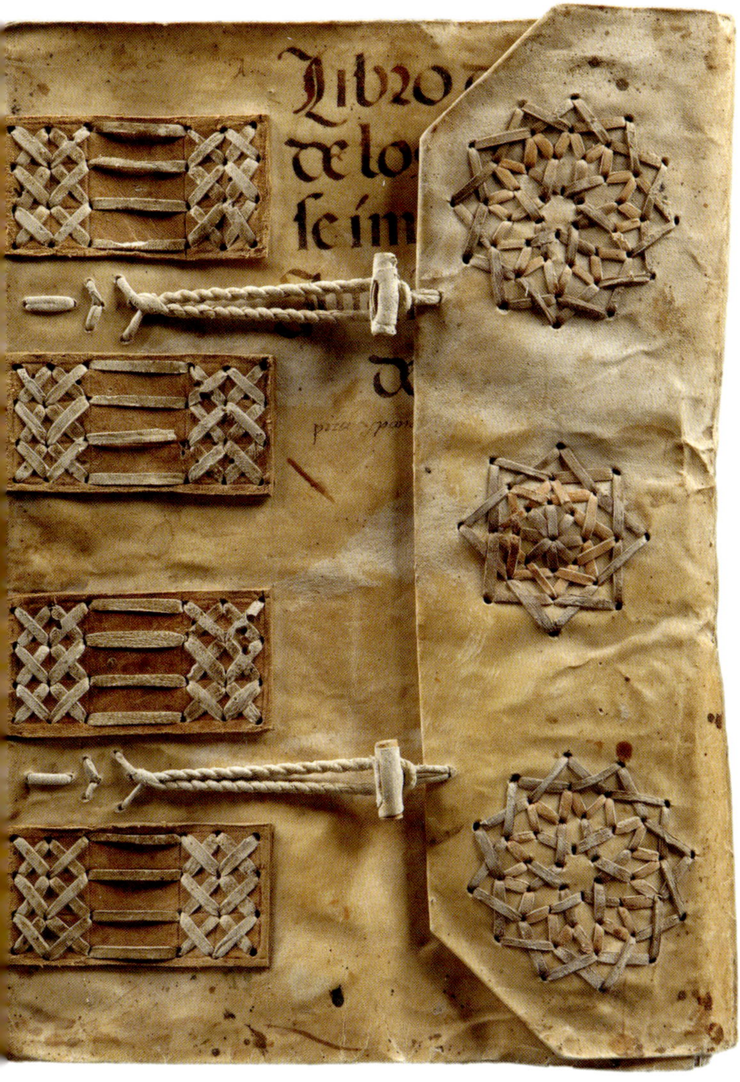

Figs. 57 and 58
Libro de memoria de los libros que se imbian a las Indias este año de 1595, [1595–1613]. RBME, 186.VI.4

The left cover and fore-edge flap, showing the leather bands across the spine secured to the cover by decorative lacing in alum-tawed skin.
The spine, showing the sewing threads of the longstitch structure worked through the leather bands placed across the spine and attached to it by the decorative lacing.

edition has a secondary cover over the cartonnage primary cover (without the reinforcements), taken from a leaf of a medieval manuscript with the text mostly washed off, in a typically Italian manner. The latter book also has ties on the fore-edge, an additional feature which, together with the secondary cover, give the book added status. It also has single-leaf text-hook endleaves at each end of the bookblock, while the 1537 edition has no endleaves at all, which very clearly indicates its low economic status. The very similar binding on a 1552 Paris edition [RB, PAS/ARM1/238] has wrapper-type endleaves folded around the textblock, a type found only on longstitch and stitched bindings, indicating an intermediate step in the cost-hierarchy of such bindings.

However, the origin of this binding and one other in the collection of the Real Biblioteca is more problematic, as the first was printed in Paris in 1552 and the other in Lyon in 1554.[13] No French longstitch bindings on printed editions have so far been recorded, and it would appear that the structure did not form part of French binding practice on printed books. For their cheapest bindings, they used instead structures which were sewn on sewing supports placed on the outside of limp parchment covers, a structure which appears only to be found on French printed books of the sixteenth and early seventeenth centuries,[14] though it has a wider, earlier currency on manuscript volumes. The Paris edition in the Real Biblioteca is in a binding which is identical in almost all details, except for the addition of endleaves, to the Venetian edition with parchment reinforcements [RB, VIII/5334]. It would therefore appear that the Paris edition arrived in Spain via Italy. However, the Lyon edition is in a very different binding, with a plain parchment cover without turn-ins that follows a pattern more typical of the Low Countries, suggesting that this book may have arrived in Spain via the Spanish Netherlands.

Longstitch structures were first used throughout Europe for archival bindings, and this use continued at least into the seventeenth century. There appears, however, to be an Iberian speciality (similar bindings are found also in Portugal, but are not recorded elsewhere) where the functional nature of the bindings is overtaken by elaborate and highly decorative lacing through the cover to secure the turn-ins. The external appearance of the bindings is however rather confusing, in that they closely resemble archival bindings made both in Spain and in the rest of Europe in which the covers were attached to bookblocks sewn on substantial sewing supports by mean of tackets. These are short lengths of cord or, more usually, animal skin, which are laced under the sewing supports and through the cover and bands of leather placed across the spine, the outer ends of which were laced to each side of the cover by means of decorative lacing, usually in white, alum-tawed skin.[15] They are therefore not longstitch bindings, as so many of the Spanish examples appear typically to have been, though the sewing thread which secures the gatherings and passes through the cover and the leather bands, might be mistaken for tackets. They are, however, structurally quite distinct.¹⁶ The example shown here dates from 1595, with a fore-edge flap decorated with three roundels of multi-coloured lacing whose original function to secure the turn-ins and the parchment reinforcement inserted under them is now disguised by the extravagant nature of the lacing [figs. 57 and 58]. Very closely similar patterns of lacing can be found in some of the volumes preserved in the archive of Toledo cathedral.¹⁷ The fore-edge flap, secured in this example with a pair of loop and toggle fastenings in alum-tawed skin, was intended to protect the bookblock of this heavily-used book and is a typical feature of account books of all sorts across Europe. It finds a pale reflection in the now mostly missing fore-edge flap on the cover of the Valladolid edition of 1527 described above [RB PAS/ARM1/311].

Stitched books

The cheapest way to hold the gatherings of a book together was to stab thread or thongs through the inner margin of the whole bookblock in a single action in a process known as stitching, as distinct from sewing through the fold. Books made this way were very quick, and therefore cheap, to make, but the result was bookblocks that did not open back to the spine folds and were therefore awkward to handle, unlike the Far-Eastern book which used a similar structure with thin flexible leaves that open without difficulty. The thicker papers used in Europe for printing, and the distortion of the paper created by the printing process, resulted in relatively inflexible leaves that required flexible structures to make them easier to handle and read. Stitching is therefore generally to be found on the cheapest books or books intended to be made ready for a rapid and immediate sale, such as the pamphlet *The Ambassador* (1603) bought by the Conde de Gondemar during, suitably enough, his time as the Spanish ambassador in London. It has a simple cover of calf parchment, no endleaves and no endbands, and represents

Fig. 59
Jean Hotman, *The Ambassador*. Printed at London: by V[alentine] S[immes] for Iames Shawe, 1603. RB, PAS/ARM4/59. Parchment binding.

Fig. 60
Christoph Gewold, *Genealogia Serenissimor. Boiariae Ducum et quorundam genuinae effigies à Wolffg. Kiliano Aug± aeri inscisae.* Augustae Vindelicorum: apud Saram Mangiam viduam, 1620. RB, IX/5080. Parchment binding showing secondary stitching (detail).

Fig. 61
Iustificacion del medio, que la señora duquesa de Medina de Rioseco propone, para el desempeño de la casa del almirante de Castilla su hijo, y paga de sus acreedores, Madrid: por Luis Sanchez ..., 1603. RBME, 67.IX.2. An alum-tawed thong stabbed through the inner margin of the bookblock (to the left), the ends of which are twisted across the spine before being laced through the cover (to the right).

one of the cheapest types of binding available in England at this time [fig. 59]. Not all stitched books are so simple, however, and large numbers were made in England in which parchment covers with turn-ins were attached to stitched bookblocks by means of an additional, secondary stitching with parchment thongs, converting a very cheap structure into something more durable and sophisticated at minimal cost. The Conde de Gondemar acquired an example of a book printed in Augsburg in 1620 with one of these bindings [RB, IX/5080[18]] and the binding tells us that he must have either bought this book in London or had it bound while he was there, though it seems, perhaps, unlikely that he would have commissioned such an inexpensive binding for himself. The parchment thongs are placed approximately where sewing supports might be expected to be found on a sewn bookblock, and this seems to be a recognisably English phenomenon, though they are easily distinguished from laced-case covers on books sewn on sewing supports as the thongs emerge from the cover at a slight distance from the spine, at the joint crease, rather than at the spine crease itself [fig. 60]. In French examples, the secondary stitching thongs are placed at the head and tail of the spine only, where endband slips might be expected to be found.

Stitching with thread is also found on Spanish books from at least the seventeenth and eighteenth centuries, but examples survive from the seventeenth century [fig. 61 and RBME, 89.VI.5[19]] in which the primary stitching was carried out with alum-tawed thongs, the ends of which were twisted together across the spine, so allowing the slips to be laced through the cover at the joint creases, making them externally identical in appearance to the more expensive books sewn on sewing supports. The bookbinding trade was not above making its cheap books look more expensive, either to please or deceive their customers, and the example preserved at the Escorial was given ties of red silk, suggesting that in Spain as in England these inexpensively constructed books may have sometimes been used for presentation purposes, made to look good for the occasion of the presentation, but at the least possible expense to the donor.

Endleaves

Before sewing or stitching the gatherings, the binder would first choose endleaves for the book, and in common with many other parts of the book, his choice would have clear cost implications. The better quality books might use several folds of new, high-quality white paper of a sort suitable for writing on, as owners of books have always wanted to write their names and notes on the flyleaves of their books, but at the other end of the scale,

as we have already seen, the cheapest books might be given no endleaves at all, thus immediately declaring their low economic status to their potential purchasers. The quality of an endleaf depends on both the quality and quantity of paper used and how it is attached to the bookblock. The endleaf which needs not only the least amount of paper to provide at least one flyleaf and the least time to attach to the book, is the single-leaf textbook endleaf. This is a single leaf of paper or parchment that is folded around a gathering at the beginning or end of the textblock, so that it will be sewn with the gathering and therefore does not need to be sewn separately. The cheapest paper would be that retrieved from another use, such as manuscript or printed waste, and examples of the latter can be found in several books in the Real Biblioteca [RB, PAS/ARM6/214[20]]. Manuscript waste from medieval manuscripts written on parchment supplied a cheap source of

Fig. 62
Johannes de Sacro Bosco, *La sphere*. A Paris: par Iehan Loys, 1546. RB, I/D/225 (1). Parchment binding (detail of endleaf).

Fig. 63
Wolfgang Musculus, [Commentariorum in Euangelistam Ioannem heptas prima [-tertia & postrema]. Basileae: apud Bartholomaeum Westhemerum, 1545. Vol. 2. RBME, 66.IX.20–21. Inside the left cover, showing the separately-sewn parchment guard. Note also the Italian/Spanish ties at the head and tail of the book, and the three-hole lacing pattern by which they are attached to the cover. The pale-coloured parchment along the fore-edge turn-in also shows an area of loose-structured skin from the belly of the goatskin from which the cover was made.

high quality parchment for binders until such manuscripts became increasingly valued for their historical or aesthetic qualities, and many sixteenth-century bindings make use of such waste for endleaves and endleaf guards, the narrow strips of parchment folded around paper endleaves to reinforce the sewing [fig. 62] as well as spine linings. One endleaf format which seems unique to French bindings uses a separately-sewn guard of parchment at the beginning or end of the bookblock, with a separately-sewn fold of paper between it and the textblock. In the example shown [fig. 63], the parchment guard has been cut from what appears to be a late medieval legal document in French, which serves to support its French provenance. It also indicates that this Basel edition of 1545 found its way to Spain via France, possibly as a sewn bookblock with its endleaves, before receiving a parchment laced-case cover in Spain.

Only one book exhibited in the exhibition has a parchment flyleaf, but that is of a very early date, and parchment is first-use, though not of the highest quality, printed in 1492 [RB, PAS/ARM1/311].

Endbands

Primary endbands, which consist of a core sewn to the gatherings across the bookblock at the head and tail of the spine, were a fundamental part of the structure of most medieval bindings, reinforcing it at its most vulnerable points, and allowing board- or cover-attachment at the head and tail of the spine by means of the endband slips. As such they were frequently used on laced-case bindings in all parts of Europe, but their absence is another clear indication of low cost, often associated with other indications of low cost, such as single-leaf text-hook endleaves [see fig. 74]. The typical late-medieval primary endband was worked without a front bead (it might or might not have a back bead), which allowed a decorative secondary sewing, usually in coloured silk threads with a front bead, to be worked around the primary sewing. The secondary sewing, as described above, could be the work of a different binder from the one responsible for working the primary endband, as it is clear that books could be sold with undecorated edges and primary endbands worked in a plain thread, both of which could then be decorated at a later date. The use of primary and secondary sewing begins to disappear in northern Europe in the second quarter of the sixteenth century, in favour of a primary sewing in coloured threads with a front bead. This does not take root in Italy until the seventeenth century, but in Spain the use of the primary sewing without a front bead, often in rather thick, naturally dark-coloured threads, survives right through to the end of the eighteenth century, a symptom of the lack of development of Spanish bookbinding from the early seventeenth century through to the second half of the eighteenth century [fig. 64].

Laced-case covers

In common with all the other parts of a binding, the parchment covers of books show a wide variety of types, quality and use across Europe. The most conspicuous difference lies in the choice of animal itself. In Italy and Spain the choice was essentially between goat and sheep, or one of the many intermediate animals that share characteristics of both, known in English as hairsheep, that is, sheep with coarse wool hairs that make the skin look much like that of the goat [fig. 65, RBME, 65.IX.10[21] and 64.IX.6,[22] and RB, PAS/ARM1/325[23]]. In northern Europe, the choice is much more likely to be calfskin [fig. 69 and RB, PAS/ARM1/304,[24] PAS/ARM1/210,[25] PAS/ARM6/146,[26] PAS/ARM4/81,[27] PAS/ARM1/109[28] and PAS/ARM1/139[29]], though sheepskin was used for the cheaper bindings [fig. 68], as sheepskin

Fig. 64
Manuel Abad Illana, *Historia del gran padre y patriarcha San Norberto, fundador del Orden candido Premonstratense* ... En Salamanca: por Eugenio Garcia de Honorato y S. Miguel ..., 1755. RBME, 64.IX.3. Detail of tailband.

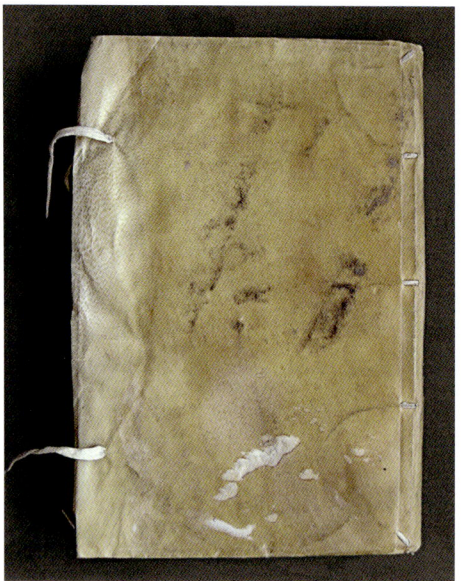

Fig. 65
Manuel Abad Illana, *Historia del gran padre y patriarcha San Norberto, fundador del Orden candido Premonstratense* .... En Salamanca: por Eugenio Garcia de Honorato y S. Miguel ..., 1755. RBME, 64.IX.3. The right cover, showing an area where the hair of the goat has been left in place during the dehairing process, and an area along the fore-edge of the pale, flanky skin from the belly of the animal.

was always the least expensive of the covering materials used for books. The quality of the skins also varies widely, and those which have faults such as flayholes [RBME, 65.IX.10] show poor quality preparation or include the weaker areas of the skin in the cover [fig. 65] reveal also their lower cost. However, the accurate identification of the animals from which these skins were taken is extremely difficult, and much remains to be learnt. It is undoubtedly the case that parchment shows evidence of the animal it comes from, such as more darkly pigmented areas which result from patches of differently-coloured hair [RBME, 64.IX.6], but while the prospect now exists of doing DNA and other analyses to decipher the type of animal and where it was reared, little or no consistent work of this sort has yet been done.

Although limp parchment covers were used on tacketed, longstitch and stitched bindings, the version known as the laced case, in which the parchment cover was attached to the bookblock by lacing the slips from the sewing supports and/or the endbands through the cover along the joints, has survived in vastly greater numbers, and is the type generally meant when the term "limp parchment binding" is used. They appear to have been a popular retail binding in the book trade throughout Europe and they have survived in large quantities in historic collections. As with the other forms of parchment binding already discussed, they were first used as archival bindings in the late Middle Ages and are found on printed books from at least the last decade of the fifteenth century, first in Italy and Spain and early in the sixteenth century in northern Europe. Because they share a superficial similarity of appearance, they are generally described in the same, simple terms (i.e. limp parchment binding), but a closer examination reveals an enormous range of differences between examples, not only from different countries, but within countries. These differences may reflect broader national styles of binding, but also the work of different workshops, or even individual craftsmen.

The archival origins of laced-case bindings are clearly visible in this exhibition in

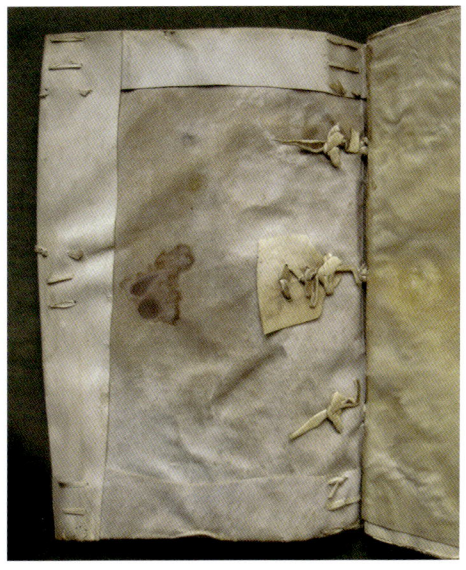

Figs. 66 and 67
Albertus de Saxonia, *Questiones subtilissime Alberti de Saxonia in libros de celo [et] mundo* .... Venetijs: Boneti d[e] locatellis Bergome[n]sis: impensa v[er]o nobilis viri Octauiani scoti, 1492. RBME, 81.IX.21. The exterior of the left cover, showing the sewing-support slips, the decorative lacing at the corners of the cover and the fastening loop, and the interior of the left cover, showing the pigmented hairside of the skin, the knotted slips and the attachment of the fastening loop.

the binding on a 1492 Venetian edition in the library of El Escorial [figs. 66 and 67] which retains the decorative lacing at the corners of each side of the cover, intended to secure the turn-ins, that was such a typical feature of account-book bindings. The binding also has a reversed cover, a common feature of some Italian and Spanish bindings of the sixteenth century, which placed the clean, creamy-white flesh-side of the skin on the outside and hid the pigmented hair-side of the skin on the inside [see also RB, PAS/ARM1/325]. It would appear that some book buyers in both Italy and Spain preferred to have their books with a clean and white external appearance, whilst others were not concerned. An early inscription records the ownership of the volume by a certain Fray Onufro of the monastery of Nuestra Señora de Guadalupe, and its Spanish origins are confirmed by a similar example recorded on a Salamanca edition of 1492 (–1495?) now in the British Library in London.[30] This latter example retains its original fore-edge flap, secured by two loop and toggle fastenings, whereas the flap on the example in the exhibition, although cut off, no doubt when the book entered the library of El Escorial and was stored fore-edge outwards, had only one. However, the Escorial volume retains uncut

Fig. 68
Johannes de Sacro Bosco, *La sphere*. A Paris: par Iehan Loys, 1546. RB, I/D/225. The exterior of the cover, showing the flat, dark brown, tanned sewing supports laced though slots cut in the coarse hairsheep parchment laced-case.

deckle edges at head, tail and fore-edge of the textblock, a rare survival on a book of this date, and one that shows that the binding on this book can be properly described as temporary, as the edges would undoubtedly have been cut if the binding was intended to be permanent. As such it is in the exact state in which it was first bought, though it is possible that the book was purchased as a sewn bookblock and that the cover was added at the request of Brother Onufro, who may not have wished for or been able to afford anything more elaborate. The knotting together of the slips of the double sewing supports inside the cover is another unusual feature.

The simplest covers found on laced-case bindings consist only of a sheet of parchment without turn-ins, a type of cover that was used across northern Europe (Germany, Flanders and England) in the first half of the sixteenth century, but survived later into the century only in Germany. Within this group of bindings, split-strap or single tanned sewing supports are more likely to be found on Flemish [fig. 68] and English bindings, whilst German bindings are more likely to use rather stiff, flat alum-tawed supports. In the second half of the century and the first half of the seventeenth century, English laced-case parchment bindings are found almost invariably with sewing supports made from a thin, soft, alum-tawed skin, sometimes reinforced across the spine with lengths of cord and with covers made from polished calf parchment with turn-ins at head, tail and fore-edge [fig. 69 and RB, PAS/ARM6/146, PAS/ARM4/81, PAS/ARM1/109 and PAS/ARM1/139]. However within this general type, several different practices can be identified, such as books with and without endbands, fore-edge cover extensions, fore-edge ties and reverse caps, as well as covers attached by the sewing-support slips only [RB, PAS/ARM1/139] or, very unusually in England, the endband slips only [RB, PAS/ARM6/146] or both types of slip [fig. 69 and RB, PAS/ARM4/81 and PAS/ARM1/109]. French practice for most of the sixteenth century does not differ greatly from English practice (it is probable that the English binders copied the French model in the second half of the sixteenth century), though perhaps with a greater use of sheep and hairsheep parchment rather than calf. By the last quarter of the century, however, French binders devised a structure which was found only in France, in which a cover lining of cartonnage was attached to the bookblock by means of the sewing-support slips before a cover of parchment was folded over the cartonnage and the endband slips were laced through both [RB, PAS/ARM1/210]. The result was a binding in which only the lacing of the endbands slips was visible from the outside, making them resemble superficially bindings in which the endband slips only were used to attach covers without cover linings, as found frequently in Italy from the mid sixteenth century onwards and in Spain in the seventeenth and eighteenth centuries if not earlier. The distinction is important, as the cover-lining appears only to have been used in France, and can therefore be used to identify French bindings.

Another source of confusion is laced-case bindings that have boards inserted into the covers on each side to reinforce them. This practice was in use across Europe from

Fig. 69
Andreas Schottus, *Itinerarii Italiae Germaniaeque libri IIII; ad haec iter Galliae et Hispaniae ....* Coloniae Agrippinae: sumptibus Bernardi Gualtheri, 1620. RB, PAS/ARM1/223. The exterior of the cover, showing the distinctive hair follicle pattern of the calf parchment used by English binders.

the late sixteenth century onwards, and was thought so typical of Dutch bindings in the seventeenth century that they were often referred to as Dutch wherever they came from (the Italians, for example, described to their own version as *al Olandese*), and there are several Spanish examples in this exhibition [fig. 84 and RBME 66.IX.15[31]]. In Flanders, however, in the late sixteenth century, a different structure was devised which is often mistaken for a laced-case binding when in fact it is an inboard structure [fig. 70]. In these bindings, the endband slips were

Fig. 70
Pierre François Sweerts, *Selectae christiani orbis deliciae ex vrbibus, templis, bibliothecis et aliunde*. Coloniae Agrippinae: sumptibus Bernardi Gualteri, 1625. RB, PAS/ARM1/304. Inside the left board, showing the parchment manuscript endleaf guard adhered to the inside of the board. The dark grey-brown colour of the board appears to be characteristic of Flemish bindings of the seventeenth century.

laced through the cover in a conventional manner (hence the mistaken identification), but the boards were attached to the sewn bookblock before the book was covered, by adhering them to parchment endleaf guards (i.e. bound in boards) rather than inserting them after the cover was attached to the bookblock (i.e. laced-case). A similar technique became a standard feature of Italian bookbinding, but only from the mid-eighteenth century, and it is not clear that the technique was used in Spain. It was certainly not used in England, and can be used to identify the origin of Catholic texts smuggled bound into England in the late sixteenth and seventeenth centuries from printing centres such as Douai and St. Omer, at a time when their importation was expressly forbidden on pain of severe penalties. The technique was also not used in France, outside the areas of modern France that once formed part of Flanders.

The strain on the lacing points along the spine of laced-case covers frequently leads to a breakdown of the parchment, especially where the weaker areas of the animal skin from the belly [RBME, 64.IX.3[32]] or behind the legs was found in these positions. Spanish binders in the sixteenth century used a technique probably, as with so many other features of these bindings, derived from archival practices, which used dark brown leather straps across the spine, secured at each end by lacing the slips through them, to act as a sort of cushion under the slip and so reduce the strain on the parchment cover [fig. 71, RBME, 91.IX.16[33] and RB, PAS/ARM1/204[34] and PAS/ARM1/135[35]]. This technique appears to be uniquely Spanish and is found from the beginning of the sixteenth century until at least as late as the 1580s. Variations in the use of the straps include whether or not there are straps at the head and tail of the spine for the endband slips to be laced through, whether the ends of the straps are cut square or canted (i.e. with the corners cut off), and whether the slips are laced out and back in within the length of the strap, or are laced back in over the ends

Fig. 71
Michele Timoteo, *In Diuinum Officium trecentum quaestiones in decem tractatus partitae* .... Venetiis: apud Franciscum Zilettum, 1581. RB, PAS/ARM1/198. The spine and exterior of the left cover, showing the dark brown tanned spine straps across the spine at both the endbands and the sewing supports.

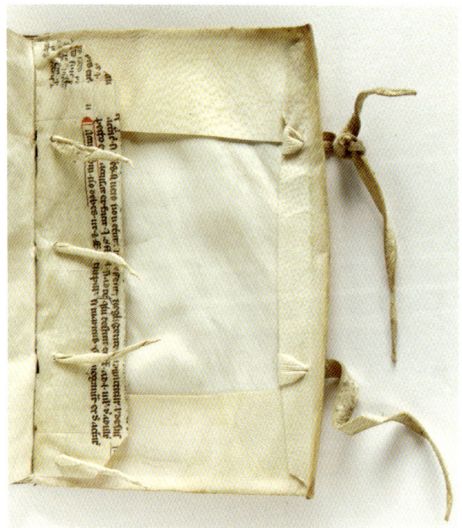

Fig. 72
Francisco Cartagena, *De Praedestinatione et reprobatione Angelorum & hominum. Tractatus in discursus duodecim diuisus* .... Romae: apud Vincentium Accoltum, 1581. RB, PAS/ARM1/135. Inside the right cover, showing the endband and sewing-support slips laced through the joint of the comb lining cut from a leaf of medieval manuscript parchment.

ends of straps with square ends and through the joints of the comb linings and the lacing paths of the fore-edge ties. The differences, the use on one of medieval manuscript parchment waste [fig. 72] and on the other of printed paper from an incunable for the comb linings, the use of single text-hook endleaves on one and two-leaf on the other may reflect economy and the availability of materials rather than a different binder, though the use of meeting fore-edge extensions on one and not on the other does suggest a slightly different approach. The manuscript hand with which they are both titled along their spines suggests that they were written by the same person, but that would most probably have been a bookseller or their first owner. It would seem likely that they are the work of the same workshop.

Another group of bindings [fig. 73 and RB, PAS/ARM6/184[36] and PAS/ARM4/43[37]] would also appear to be from the same workshop, as they too share many of the same structural features, including the use of small pieces of parchment slipped under the turns to reinforce the fore-edge tie lacing [fig. 73], the same complex lacing path through three holes in the cover to lace each of the alum-tawed fore-edge ties, the same sewing on three single alum-tawed sewing supports. All have endbands with back beads, all have knife-cut edges coloured yellow, none of them has joint creases and the titling on the spine, each in two lines of different sizes of lettering, is the same on each. However, a closer look reveals that one has a comb spine-lining of printed paper waste [fig. 73], and the other two have transverse spine-linings, one of plain paper

of the straps. All of these differences are likely to indicate the work of different binders, adding to the many other areas of variation open to the binders who made laced-case bindings. Of the books in the Real Biblioteca, two, both printed in the same year, 1581, in Italy, are very similar to each other [figs. 71 and 72], in that almost all the components are made in exactly the same way, from the shallow angle at which the endband slips are laced through the cover, the lacing of the endband and sewing-support slips over the

Fig. 73
Marcin Kromer, Bishop of Ermland, *De falsa lutheranorum siue Euangelicorum nostri temporis, et vera Christi religione libri duo primi de quatuor Polonica lingua ante octo et novem annos conscriptis atque editis, nunc recens Latina lingua donati & aucti*. Parisiis: apud Gulielmum Guillard & Almaricum Warancore, 1560. RB, PAS/ARM6/197. Inside the left cover, showing the parchment tie-lacing reinforcements under the fore-edge turn-in, the three-hole tie lacing and the joint of a comb lining made from early sixteenth-century printed waste.

[RB, PAS/ARM6/184] and the other [RB, PAS/ARM4/43] of manuscript parchment waste. It may be that these differences can be explained by the range of dates of the editions, which date from the 1550s to 1566. Within the span of perhaps a decade, the personnel in a workshop might well change, resulting in the different types of spine lining. What is quite certain, however, is that these three bindings come from a very limited geographical area, if not from the same workshop, even though the editions inside them come from Paris, Antwerp and Basel.

A fourth, ostensibly similar binding [fig. 74] on a Lyon edition of 1511 (the binding dates from the mid-century) shows several significant differences. Firstly, it has no endbands, though this is more an indication of lower economic status than necessarily of the work a different binder, and the lack of endbands is matched by the use of single-leaf text-hook endleaves. However, the fore-edge ties are laced through

Fig. 74
Xenophon, *[Select Work]*. [Lyon]: expensis honesti viri Bartholomei trot, 1511. RB, PAS/ARM1/38. Parchment binding with remains of leather fastenings.

Fig. 75
The hitherto unrecorded three-hole lacing route used for the ties.

the cover in a pattern that has not been recorded before [fig. 75], which suggests most certainly that a different hand has been at work on the binding from that (or those) which made the three bindings described above. All four bindings are made in what might be called the Italian style, and although they would not look out of place in an Italian library, they are undoubtedly Spanish.

Fastening

The attachment of the fastenings was the last task the binder had to carry out on these bindings and the majority of laced-case bindings were fitted with some kind of fastening designed to hold the covers closed around the edges of the bookblock. All of these will have fastenings on their fore-edges, but some will also have fastenings on their head and tail edges, a style which originated in Italy and is therefore found on a number of Spanish bindings [see fig. 63], as well as books from other countries where it was fashionable in the sixteenth century to look "Italian". The majority of these fastenings took the form of ties cut from alum-tawed skin, no doubt chosen because of its superior durability and softness (which made tying a bow easier and more secure). More expensive bindings, or those intended to impress their recipients as a gift, might have ties made from silk ribbons, and two bindings in the collection that are probably Italian have bi-coloured ties, in that each of the two ties is made from silk ribbons of different colours [fig. 76].

A remarkable variety of lacing patterns was used to attach the ties to the cover, with at least thirty-six different types recorded from across Europe. The greatest variety is found on Italian bindings, and given the similarities between Italian and Spanish bookbinding, it is no surprise to find that a number of the elaborate three-hole lacing patterns can be found on bindings made in both countries. It would seem likely that a binder would use one of these patterns only, possibly also using for the cheapest bindings the simplest lacing through a single hole that is found in every country of Europe. Another lacing pattern that seems to have been much used in Spain involved placing the inner end of the tie under the turn of the cover and bringing the tie around the edge of the turn-in before taking it through a hole made in the turn-in, the inner end of the tie and the outer part of the cover, thus locking it securely in place. This was also a pattern that was frequently used in France, though apparently very rarely in Italy.

Generally speaking, by the end of the sixteenth century this wide range of variant types of tie lacing had been reduced to the simplest, single-hole lacing, except in Spain, where a range of entirely different fastening types appears on limp covers which are apparently unique to Spain. The earliest of these appears to be the loop and toggle fastening, usually made from alum-tawed skin, and frequently encountered on archival bindings [see figs. 57 and 66], but which is also found on bindings on printed books [fig. 77]. A similar type of fastening, the loop and bead, is found from at least the later seventeenth century, and the beads can be made of white

Fig. 76
Ubaldino Malavolti, *I servi nobili*. In Siena: appresso Salvestro Marchetti, 1605. RB, PAS/ARM4/70. Parchment binding with silk ties of two colours.

[fig. 78] or coloured [fig. 79] glass, or coloured bone or ivory beads [fig. 80]. More often, alum-tawed thongs tied in a "turk's head" knot [fig. 81] were used in combination with loops which could be made also from alum-tawed skin, or tightly twisted cords, both of which might be coloured or even multi-coloured (strands of different colour twisted together). These loop and bead or loop and knot fastenings seem to be a particularly Spanish phenomenon, and the only examples known to me from outside Spain come from the Spanish Netherlands.

All the examples of loop fastenings in the exhibition place the loops on the fore-edge of the left cover and the beads, toggles or

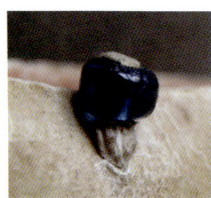

Fig. 77
Antonio Pérez, *Pentateuchum fidei, siue Volumina quinque ....* Matriti: apud Viduam Ildephonsi Martin, 1620. RBME, 70.IX.2. Detail of fastening.

Fig. 78
José de Sarabia y Lezana, *Annales de la sagrada Religion de Santo Domingo ....* En Madrid: por Juan Garcia Infanzon ...., 1709. Vol. 2. RBME, 65.IX.18–19. Detail of fastening.

Fig. 79
Bulario de la Sagrada Religion de la Hospitalidad de San Juan de Dios aprobada por San Pio Quinto .... En Madrid: en la imprenta de Geronimo de Estrada y Junco, 1702. RBME, 67.IX.4. Detail of fastening.

Fig. 80
Manuel Mariano Ribera, *Real patronato de los serenissimos señores Reyes de España en el Real y Militar Orden de Nuestra Señora dela Merced ....* Barcelona: por Pablo Campins ...., 1725. RBME, 65.IX.13. Detail of fastening.

Fig. 81
Luis de Salazar y Castro, *Historia genealógica de la casa de Silva ....* En Madrid: por Melchor Alvarez y Mateo de Llanos, 1685. Vol. 2. RBME, 64.IX.4–5. Detail of fastening.

turk's head knots on the right, following the pattern that was used in England, France, Spain and most of Italy. In the German-speaking world the direction of clasping was reversed, and although no convincing explanation for the difference has been found, it is remarkably consistent. There is at least one seventeenth-century Spanish binding where the turk's head knots are placed on the fore-edge of the left cover, but this was because the book was printed in Arabic,[38] and the binder placed the knots at the end of the text, thus reversing his normal practice to accommodate the different system of writing.

Titling

It is hard to know who was responsible for writing the titles on these bindings, as it might be done in the binder's shop, by a bookseller or by the first (and/or a subsequent) owner of the book. The choice of what to include in a title was often left to the first owner, but the consistency of the style of writing often found suggests that many were written within the book trade. The elegance and neatness of some of them suggest that they were written with the covers taken off the books, something that the laced-case binding allowed, as it could be unlaced and laced on again, so long as the outer flyleaves were not pasted to it first. Titling will also reflect the ways in which books were stored, as it was usual to write the title so that it could be easily read on the shelf, and titles can be found on any of the six outer surfaces of a book.

The majority of Spanish books in the libraries of the Patrimonio Nacional have until at least the end of the seventeenth century titles written in a large late gothic rotonda lettering along the spines, but it is difficult to know whether this indicates the horizontal or vertical storage of books, as both orientations were used from the mid-sixteenth century onwards. It may be that lettering of this sort and direction was used in order to fit the largest lettering possible on the spine and that the books were stored vertically. The collections of the Patrimonio Nacional have books dating from as late as 1759 with such lettering [RBME, 81.IX.3[39]], by which time titles written across and towards the head of the spine, which can only have been for the vertical storage of books, had become the norm. A two-volume edition of the *Directorio cathechistico* printed in Madrid in 1705 and 1708 [figs. 82 and 83] shares the title between the two volumes in a strikingly modern way that allows the title to be read continuously between the two volumes.

An elegant example on an edition of 1669 of a title written along the fore-edge from head to tail with gothic capitals and roman lower-case lettering shows also a shelf-mark number written across the head of the fore-edge, which indicates that this book was at an early date stored vertically with the fore-edge outwards [fig. 84], though whether the number was written at the same time as the title or later remains unclear. Many libraries in the sixteenth century stored their

Figs. 82 and 83
José Ortiz Cantero, *Directorio cathechistico, glossa vniversal de la doctrina Christiana ... tomo primero* and *Directorio cathechistico, el Christiano ilvstrado en la fe ... tomo segundo*. En Madrid: por Diego Martinez Abad ..., 1705–8. RBME, 73.IX.2–3. Titles written continuously from volume 1 to volume 2

 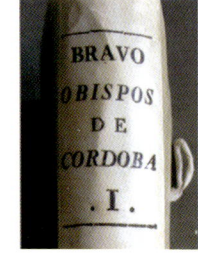

Fig. 84
Hermenegildo de San Pablo, *Origen y continuacion de el Instituto y Religion Geronimiana: fundados en los conventos de Belen en Palestina por el Maximo de los Doctores de la Iglesia ....* En Madrid: en la Imprenta Real, 1669. RBME, 66.IX.23. Title written from head to tail along the fore-edge, with a shelf mark written across the head. Note also a single surviving toggle towards the tail end of the right board.

Fig. 85
Juan Gómez Bravo, *Catalogo de los Obispos de Cordoba, y breve noticia historica de su Iglesia Catedral, y Obispado / escrito por el Doct. D. Juan Gomez Bravo ... con un Apendice de los Obispos, que lo han sido de esta Ciudad, despues de la muerte del autor de esta obra ... Tomo I.* Cordoba: en la oficina de Juan Rodriguez ..., 1778. RBME, 72.IX.10. Printed title on the spine of volume 1

books with their fore-edges outwards, and the library at El Escorial is unusual in preserving this arrangement, so that not a single book spine is visible on the shelves. This system is also used on most of the shelves in the lower, monastery library, which renders the large number of spine titles invisible, suggesting either that the storage system has changed or that the books were kept in another library before their arrival at El Escorial, or that they were perhaps purchased with the titles already written on them. It is clear that many of the bindings with fore-edge flaps or fore-edge cover extensions had them cut off on their arrival at El Escorial to expose the fore-edges of their bookblocks ready for shelving with their fore-edges outwards.

The change to writing titles across the head of the spine seems to have occurred towards the beginning of the eighteenth century, though a much wider survey of books would be needed to confirm or modify that conclusion. Unlike the earlier titles written along the spine, the change left a large area of the spine devoid of writing and on some books this provided an opportunity for decorative pen work [RBME, 96.IX.16-18,[40] 64.IX.19[41] and 66.IX.17-19[42]]. A two-volume edition printed in Cordoba in 1778 provides an unexpected combination of the old and the new, in that the binding, a traditional laced-case limp parchment binding of a sort that had remained unchanged in Spain for almost two centuries, has a title on the spine that has been printed in black ink with printers' type before the cover was attached to the book [fig. 85]. The type is one of the new-style faces introduced in the 1790s, but even at that date, printed titles on paper labels were still something of a novelty in other European countries, and to find a title printed in both roman and italic caps onto a parchment laced-case is quite remarkable. It could be said to encapsulate the revival of the book trade in Spain in the second half of the eighteenth century, when new ideas from outside Spain began to replace the old-fashioned ways of bookmaking that had survived for so long. It is a process that is paralleled at a more technical level by the sewing "wide in the middle" on a Malaga edition of 1781 [RBME, 69.IX.25], in a laced-case parchment binding with boards mentioned at the beginning of this essay.

1 The first modern re-evaluation of limp parchment bindings was written by Christopher CLARKSON 1982 [reprinted 2005].
2 Antonio Ramos, *Descripcion genealogica de la Casa de Aguayo, y lineas que se derivan de ella desde que se conquistó Andalucia por el Santo Rey D. Fernando III hasta el presente* ..., En Malaga, por el impresor de esta M.I. Ciudad, de la Dignidad Episcopal, y de la Santa Iglesia Catedral, en la Plaza, 1781.
3 The term can be found in COWIE 1828, 12.
4 Manuel Mariano Ribera, *Real patronato de los serenissimos señores Reyes de España en el Real y Militar Orden de Nuestra Señora dela Merced redencion de cautivos nueuamente ilustrado con singulares noticias*, Barcelona, por Pablo Campins ..., 1725.
5 A description of the technique can be found in COWIE 1828, 14. It should not be confused with the technique used in France and possibly elsewhere of the binder turning in the corner of a single leaf (a *témoin*) to show how much paper has been removed when the edges were cut.
6 *In Euangelium secundum Matthaeum, Marcum et Lucam commentarii ex ecclesiasticis scriptoribus collecti, nouae glossae ordinariae specimen, donec meliora Dominus* .... [Geneuae], Oliua Roberti Stephani, 1553.
7 Wolfgang Musculus, *[Commentariorum in Euangelistam Ioannem heptas prima [-tertia & postrema]*, Basileae, apud Bartholomaeum Vvesthemerum, 1545. Vol. 2. See fig. 63.
8 Johannes Brenz, *In Euangelii quod inscribitur secundum Lucam duodecim priora capita homiliae centum & decem* .... Francofurti, ex officina Petri Brubacchij, 1545.
9 See note 11.
10 Odo Magdunensis, *Libro de medicina llamado Macer, q[ue] trata de los mantenimie[n]tos, E assi mesmo d[e] todas las virtudes del Romero*, Valladolid, en casa de Miguel de eguía, 1527.
11 Pietro Pitati, *Paschales atque nouiluniorum mensurni canones* ..., Venetiis, [Lucantonio Giunta], 1537 (RB, VIII/5334); *L'algebre de Iaques Peletier du Mans,* *departie an deus Livres* ..., A Lion, par Ian de Tournes, 1554 (RB, PAS/ARM4/80); *Di Nonio Marcello ... Ragionamenti sopra la celeste sfera*, Parisiis: veneunt apud Franciscum Bartholomaeum ..., 1552 (RB, PAS/ARM1/238); *Rhetorica di Marco Tullio Cicerone*, Stampata in Vinegia, per Bartholomeo de Zanetti da Brescia: a instantia et requisitione di Messere Giouanni Giolitto da Trino, 1538 (RB, PAS/ARM1/235); *Iacobi Fabri Stapulensis Introductio in Ethicen Aristotelis*, Lovanii, ex officina Bartholomei Gravij, 1548 (RB, VIII/3680).
12 PUGLIESE 2001.
13 *L'algebre de Iaques Peletier du Mans, departie an deus Liures* ..., A Lion, par Ian de Tournes, 1554 (RB PAS/ARM4/80).
14 PICKWOAD 1995 [reprinted 2004].
15 Two Spanish examples of the use of sewing supports and tackets rather than longstitch are illustrated in *Encuadernaciones artisticas* 2009, 112–13 and 126–27, and a further example, apparently of the fifteenth century, is illustrated in PENNEY 1967, plate XLVI.
16 Two examples are illustrated in *Encuadernaciones artísticas* 2009, 122–23 and 124–25, dating from the fourteenth to the sixteenth century. Much more decorative examples can be seen in CARPALLO BAUTISTA 2010.
17 *Ibid.*
18 Christoph Gewold, *Genealogia Serenissimor. Boiariae Ducum et quorundam genuinae effigies* ..., Augustae Vindelicorum, apud Saram Mangiam viduam, 1620. See fig. 60.
19 *Traslado del testimonio autentico que el segretario de la Santa Inquisicion Suprema da del decreto que el Santo Tribunal ha hecho en favor de la Historia profetica de la Religion de Carmelitas Descalzos*, Impresso en Madrid: por Diego Diaz de la Carrera, [1640].
20 Adrien du Hecquet, *Enarrationes locupletissimae atque insigniter doctae in omnia Quadragesimae totius Euangelia* ..., Parisiis, apud Michaëlem de Roigny, 1570.
21 *Bullarium Fratrum Ordinis Minorum Sancti Francisci strictioris obervantiae discalceatarum, simulque*

Sacrarum Congregationum Decisiones spectantes ad discalceatos, ab Alexandro VI ..., Matriti, ex typographia Emmanuelis Fernandez ..., 1744–46.

22 José Vela, *Idea de la perfecta religiosa en la vida de la Ven. Madre Sor Josepha Maria Garcia, primera hija de la Real Convento de Capuchinas de la Villa de Castellon de la Plana* ..., En Valencia, en la imprenta de la Viuda de Antonio Bordazar, 1750.

23 Johann Wild, *Commentariorum Ioannis Feri in Sacrosanctum Iesu Christi Euangelium secundum Matthaeum*, Compluti, excudebat Andreas ab Angulo, 1562.

24 Pierre François Sweerts, *Selectae christiani orbis deliciae ex vrbibus, templis, bibliothecis et aliunde*, Coloniae Agrippinae: sumptibus Bernardi Gualteri, 1625. See fig. 70.

25 Pietro Aretino, *Del primo [-secondo] libro de le lettere di M. Pietro Aretino*, In Parigi, appresso Matteo il maestro ..., 1609.

26 Nicolaus Reusner, *Simbolorum Imperatorium classis prima*, Londini, apud Ioannem Billium, 1619.

27 *Thresor de sentences dorees et argentees*, A Cologny, pour Francois le Febvre, 1617.

28 Giuseppe Matteacci, *Ragionamenti politici*, In Venetia, appresso Santo Grillo & Fratelli, 1613.

29 Edmond Richer, *Emundi Richerii Obstetrix animorum hoc est Breuis et expedita ratio docendi, studendi, conuersandi, imitandi, iudicandi, componendi* ..., Francofurti, typis & impensis Ioannis Bringeri, 1617.

30 "Esta tassado este vocabulario por los muy altos muy poderosos principes el Rey la Reyna nuestros señores ..." Salamanca, 1492 (British Library, G.7655), reproduced in Thomas 1939, plate C.

31 *Regla y establecimientos de la Orden y Cavalleria del glorioso Apostol Santiago, Patron de las Spañas: con la historia del origen y principio deella*, Impresso en Madrid, en casa de Domingo Garcia Morrás, 1655.

32 Manuel Abad Illana, *Historia del gran padre y patriarcha San Norberto, fundador del Orden candido Premonstratense* ..., En Salamanca, por Eugenio Garcia de Honorato y S. Miguel ..., 1755. See figs. 64 and 65.

33 Sebastian Münster, *Silùs lsōnôt = Dictionarium trilingue* ..., Basileae, apud Henricum Petrum, 1530.

34 Etienne Aufreri, *[Obra selecta]*, Lugduni, [Vincent de Portonariis I], 1533.

35 Francisco Cartagena, *De Praedestinatione et reprobatione Angelorum & hominum. Tractatus in discursus duodecim diuisus* ..., Romae, apud Vincentium Accoltum, 1581. See fig. 72.

36 Tacite Nicolaus Zegers, *Inuentarium in Testamentum nouum, vulgo Concordantias vocant*, Antuerpiae, apud Ioannem Bellerum, sub Aquila Aurea, 1566.

37 Arethas, Archbishop of Caesarea (Cappadocia), *Aretae Caesareae Cappadociae Episcopi In D. Ioannis Apocalypsim compendiaria explanatio*, Basileae, [Michael Isingrin, *c*.1550].

38 A copy of: Abd al-Wahhab ibn Ibrahim, *Liber Tasriphi Compositio est Senis Alemami*, Rome: Ex Typographia Medicea, 1610 (Arcadian Library, London).

39 *Bullarium Ordinis Militiae de Alcantara olim S. Juliani de Pereiro* ..., Matriti, ex typographia Antonij Marin, 1759.

40 Antonio da Expectação, *A estrella Dalva, a sublimissima e sapientissima maestra da Santa Igreja, a angelica e serafica doutora mystica, Santa Theresa de Jesus, mãy e filha do Carmelo* ..., Lisboa Occidental, na officina de Joseph Antonio da Sylva ..., 1716–35.

41 Diego González Mateo, *Mystica civitas Dei vindicata ab observationibus R. D. Eusebii Amort* ..., Matriti, ex typographia Causae Venerabilis Matris Mariae à Jesu de Agreda, 1747.

42 Juan Francisco de San Antonio, *Chronicas de la apostolica Provincia de S. Gregorio de N.S.P. S. Francisco en las Islas Philipinas, China, Japon, &c* ..., Sampaloc, impressa en la imprenta de vso de la propria provincia sita en el convento de Nra. Señora de Loreto del Pueblo de Sampaloc ...: por Fr. Juan del Sotillo, 1738–44.

Diego Hurtado de Mendoza

Anthony Hobson

Diego Hurtado de Mendoza was one of an illustrious generation of Spanish Hellenists. They included Antonio Agustín, Bishop of Tarragona, famous for his work in restoring the text of Justinian's law code, Honorato Juan, bishop of Osma, Juan Páez de Castro, Gonzalo Pérez and Gerónimo Zurita. Hurtado de Mendoza stood somewhat apart from the others and his interest in Greek learning had developed independently of theirs.

He belonged to the greatest, wealthiest and most powerful family of Castile.[1] One of his forebears had been Admiral of Castile in the fourteenth century; another was High Steward to King Juan I. Mendoza support won the throne of Castile for Isabella in 1474. The head of the family became Duke of Infantado; his brother, Pedro González de Mendoza, the queen's chief minister, was rewarded with the archbishopric of Seville and a cardinal's hat. Their nephew, the Count of Tendilla, Hurtado de Mendoza's father, was one of the principal commanders in the reconquest of Granada. He held the newly captured town of Alhama, deep in Muslim territory, against Moorish counterattacks, concealing a breach in the walls with a length of painted cloth. Appointed to command the besieging forces, he was the first to plant the banner of Castile on the highest tower of the Alhambra. After the Moorish capitulation the Catholic Kings named him Captain-General of Granada for life.

Of Hurtado de Mendoza's brothers, the eldest became President of the Council of the Indies and President of the Council of Castile; Don Antonio was successively Viceroy of Mexico and of Peru; Don Bernardino was Captain-General of the galleys and Viceroy of Naples; the fourth, Don Francisco, became Bishop of Jaen and was created cardinal.

The family was pre-eminent for its literary gifts. The Count of Tendilla's grandfather, Íñigo López de Mendoza, Marquis of Santillana, although primarily a man of action, was a lyric poet of outstanding excellence. He owned the best library in Spain and had his manuscripts splendidly bound in Mudejar covers decorated with his crest.[2] Although he read French, Italian, Galician and Catalan, he knew no Greek and his Latin was uncertain, so he commissioned translations of Homer, the *Aeneid,* Ovid's *Metamorphoses* and Seneca's *Tragedies.* The Count of Tendilla had been sent on an embassy to Rome in between service on the frontiers of the Moorish kingdom. He brought back with him to Spain the Italian poet and historian Peter Martyr of Anghiera, and financed his publications. His own favourite authors were Josephus and St Augustine, and he commissioned a Castilian translation of Pius II's *History of Bohemia.* This powerful family tradition cannot have failed to influence his youngest son.

Diego Hurtado de Mendoza[3] inherited all the qualities of his highly talented family —charm, courage, boundless pride and lively intelligence—all perhaps except prudence. He was born in 1503 or 1504—the exact date is uncertain—and brought up in Granada, where the family occupied one of the Moorish palaces on the Alhambra. Granada was still a largely Muslim city. Its Moorish population had been allowed by the terms of the capitulation to keep their language, religion and dress. Tendilla had a sympathetic understanding of their wishes and tried to protect them from the Royal Council, which was pressing for forcible conversion.

Towards the end of his life Hurtado de Mendoza reminisced about his education to the royal historian, Ambrosio de Morales.[4] He declared that he had studied the "three languages" (Latin, Greek and Arabic), in Granada and Salamanca, and afterwards civil and canon law. He had travelled round much of Spain in search of antique sites and monuments. The following years were spent in Italy. Here his time was divided between military service in the summer and attendance in the winter at different universities—Rome and Padua were mentioned—where he heard lectures by Agostino Nifo and Juan Montes de Oca.

There is no reason to doubt the truth of this account, though the details are vague. It was presumably in Granada that he acquired his knowledge of Arabic. No Salamanca degree is recorded in his name. When in Italy he may well have taken part in the Spanish victory at Pavia. A Don Diego de Mendoza commanded a troop in the battle, but the name is a common one and certainty is elusive. Agostino Nifo lectured at the Sapienza in Rome; Hurtado de Mendoza could have heard him there in 1523. Nifo lectured on Averroes; Montes de Oca was a leading exponent of Averroist views. Both of them must have helped to develop Don Diego's absorbing interest in Aristotle and his commentators.

From 1532 he was in attendance at the imperial court. In the year 1535 he took part in Charles V's expedition against Tunis. Muley Hassan, the claimant supported by the Spaniards, heard of this intelligent young soldier who could speak Arabic and gave him some manuscripts.

His first diplomatic assignment followed a year later. Catherine of Aragon and Anne Boleyn both being dead, Charles V was able to recognise Henry VIII's marriage to Jane Seymour. Don Diego was sent with an experienced diplomat to England to propose a marriage between Princess Mary and Charles's brother-in-law, the Infante of Portugal. Following Jane Seymour's death he was instructed to offer Henry VIII the hand of Charles's niece, the widowed Duchess of Milan. Henry rejected both offers. After about seven months in England, Hurtado de Mendoza returned via Flanders to the imperial court in Toledo. In April 1539 he received the news that he was to proceed as ambassador to Venice.

The seven years of his Venetian embassy was the period of his library's fastest growth. Venice was then the principal centre of the international trade in Greek manuscripts. New texts reached the West through the Republic's territories in the Greek islands and its enclaves on the mainland. In Venice itself there were three great Greek collections: Bessarion's manuscripts in St Mark's, Cardinal Grimani's in S. Antonio di Castello and a third collection in the Dominican convent of SS. Giovanni e Paolo. Capable scribes from the Greek colony centred on S. Giorgio dei Greci were available to copy them.

Don Diego lost little time in making use of these opportunities. The earliest manuscript transcribed for him which bears a date was completed in 1541,[5] but already in September of the previous year Bartolomeo Cavalcanti had reported to the Florentine scholar Piero Vettori that "all these rare books [in Venetian libraries] are being copied, or will be copied, for the ambassadors of the Emperor and of the King [of France]".[6] What had launched Hurtado de Mendoza into an all-out campaign of acquisition was almost certainly the example of the French ambassador. Guillaume Pellicier, Bishop of Montpellier, the representative of Charles V's greatest enemy, had been employing as many as ten or twelve Greek scribes at a time. Though part of their output was intended for his own collection, it was well known that most of the manuscripts were to join the library Francis I was assembling at Fontainebleau.[7] Don Diego set out, single-handed, to form for Spain a collection to rival the one being brought together by the French king's diplomatic agents.

Three qualities are needed to carry to completion any great enterprise, Arnoldus Arlenius observed when dedicating to Hurtado de Mendoza his edition of Josephus: will, ability and diligent application. Of those who combined all three qualities, he informed the dedicatee, "you are easily the foremost".[8]

Arnout van Eynthouts, always known by a hybrid version of his name as Arnoldus Arlenius Peraxylus, had entered Don Diego's service towards the end of 1542.[9] A Netherlander from s'Hertogenbosh, he had studied in Paris, Ferrara and Bologna and become a first-rate Greek scholar. For the previous five years, while attending the University of Bologna, he had earned a living by bookselling and by acting as a scout for the printers of Basle.

Antonio Agustín was under the impression that Arlenius had been engaged as a copyist.[10] This was a misapprehension. His duties were those of a librarian, to search out new texts and to organise the work of transcription. In 1543 he travelled to the Frankfurt New Year Fair. In subsequent years he made two journeys to Florence. On the second occasion he was accompanied by a team of Greek scribes and stayed for three months while copies were made of manuscripts in the Bibliotheca Laurenziana. He also compiled a catalogue of Mendoza's Greek collection. The original is lost, but a copy in the hand of Jean Matal, Agustín's close collaborator and later secretary, is in Cambridge University Library.[11] It shows that Mendoza succeeded in acquiring, almost entirely during the course of his Venetian embassy, two hundred and fifty-eight Greek manuscripts and one in Hebrew. The latter could not be read and was left untitled in the list.

Where had the manuscripts come from? Initially, from commissioning Greeks to copy exemplars in Venetian libraries: Don Diego employed about eight scribes.[12] With one of them his relations were particularly close. Agustín reported that two bookmen were lodged by Mendoza in the imperial embassy: Arlenius and a Greek scribe.[13] The name of the latter was not recorded, but he was certainly Andronicus Nucius. One other scribe, Nicolas Murmuris, probably copied as many manuscripts as Nucius, but Nucius was the only one to state in his colophons that he had carried out the work of transcription of the emperor's ambassador, Diego Hurtado de Mendoza.[14]

Andronicus Nucius was a native of Corfu who had taken refuge in Venice after the Turkish siege of 1537. There he translated Aesop's *Fables* into demotic Greek and edited a ritual listing the days of feasting and of fast in the Greek Church.[15] From 1541 he was employed by Don Diego.[16] In 1545 he attached himself to the embassy of Gerard Van Veltwick, who was travelling to Istanbul as the emperor's envoy. He returned across Europe to Flanders, continuing from there on a new mission to England. On arrival he found that an expedition was being fitted out against the Scots. Impulsively he joined it and took part in the campaign. When it was over he crossed to France with a company of Greek mercenaries, proceeding thence to Italy where he intended to visit Rome before returning to Venice. His account of his travels, contained in one Bodleian and two other manuscripts, all three incomplete, breaks off at this point.[17] It is in some ways a disappointing document, as it opens after he left Venice and so contains no account of Hurtado de Mendoza or his library.

The exemplars to be copied were principally found among Bessarion's manuscripts in the library of St Mark's. Mendoza had free access to the library and permission to borrow from it. Andronicus Nucius copied Appian's Roman history from an exemplar in SS. Giovanni e Paolo,[18] and advantage was taken of the services of Valriano Albini, librarian of S. Antonio di Castello, who supplemented his income by copying the manuscripts in his care.[19]

Information is less easy to come by about the second source of supply. Arlenius declared that Mendoza had "the most exquisite and rarest codices brought to light like buried treasure both in Italy and in Greece".[20] It is probable that some of the more common texts—Sophocles, Aristophanes, Manuel Moschopoulos's grammar—were present in Italian copies. A partial list of thirty-eight manuscripts dating probably from 1544 and consisting overwhelmingly of modern transcripts end with six "very ancient books bought recently".[21] They were all of biblical or patristic works, characteristic of the manuscripts which continued to reach Venice from its Greek colonies, except one, a highly prized fourteenth- or fifteenth-century collection of Byzantine law.[22]

Antonius Eparchus, the principal Venetian dealer in Greek manuscripts, was known to Mendoza and was doubtless one of his suppliers. The ambassador's collection included a manuscript in the dealer's hand of a rare medical vade mecum, *The Travellers' Handbook*, translated into Greek from an Arabic original and from Greek into Latin by Eparchus.[23] Fourteen of Don Diego's manuscripts are in blind-tooled bindings by a man whom Eparchus employed to bind a group of manuscripts he sold to Augsburg. With one exception the bindings, of pinky-red goatskin over wooden boards with western (not Greek) sewing, form a homogeneous group,[24] though as the entries are scattered through Arlenius's catalogue they may not have been acquired in a single transaction.

The really desirable early manuscripts of unpublished texts could only be obtained from Greece and the Levant. Don Diego determined on two bold moves to secure them. During the wars on the frontier of the Moorish kingdom his father had sent back a female captive, a relation of the Sultan, without demanding a ransom. The Emir of Granada had responded to this chivalrous gesture by releasing twenty priests and thirty knights.[25] The ambassador repeated the same tactic. He ransomed a Turkish prisoner of war and dispatched him to Süleyman the Magnificent, letting it be known, in answer to the Grand Turk's enquiry, that he would welcome in exchange a consignment of food for the Venetians and Greek manuscripts for himself. A ship loaded with corn and carrying six boxes of manuscripts duly arrived. The story, related to Ambrosio de Morales,[26] is confirmed by an inscription in a large twelfth-century manuscript of the Old Testament.[27] It records that an entry in Hurtado de Mendoza's hand in his catalogue stated that the volume had been found in the bookcases of Cantacuzenus and sent by the emperor of the Turks. Süleyman had evidently raided the famous Greek collection of the Phanariot millionaire, Michael Cantacuzenus,[28] to reward the Spanish ambassador.

On 6 February 1543, Jean Matal wrote from Venice to Antonio Agustín giving the news that Don Diego had sent Nicolas Sophianus to Mount Athos in search of unpublished Greek manuscripts to be brought back or copied.[29] Sophianus, of a noble family of Corfu, was the most intelligent and enterprising man of letters in the Greek colony in

Venice. Employed as librarian by Cardinal Ridolfi in Rome and later as a scribe by Georges de Selve, Pellicier's predecessor as French ambassador to Venice, he had collaborated with a young Italian author on a comedy performed before the pope and the emperor, contributing a dialogue in demotic, and had designed a fount of type to be used in Rome in Cardinal Marcello Cervini's ambitious programme of printing unpublished Greek texts.[30] He had returned from Rome only shortly before leaving for Greece. His journey was expected to last for seven months, and he was indeed back in Venice by 19 September, when he executed a power of attorney.[31]

Sophianus left no account of where he went or what he succeeded in buying. Perhaps the answer given to two Anglican clergymen who visited Athos in search of manuscripts in 1801, that "a substantial number of their manuscripts had already been sold to the Venetians", preserves a lingering memory of his visit.[32] Some conjecture can however be made as to what he brought back. Arlenius's catalogue is not arranged alphabetically or by subject. It appears to have been added to as new acquisitions arrived. In the first hundred entries *recentes*, recent transcripts, predominate. A block of thirty entries follows, largely of older manuscripts with only three *recentes*. A similar block of mostly older manuscripts, with only five *recentes*, occurs between numbers 200 and 250. The latter group, of forty volumes or so, including the twelfth-century Bible already mentioned, may represent the sultan's gift, the former one, of less than thirty, Sophianus's rather meagre takings.[33] Times had become harder for book hunters since Janus Lascaris had brought back two hundred manuscripts for Lorenzo the Magnificent half a century earlier.[34]

Don Diego had devised idiosyncratic bindings for the Greek manuscripts transcribed for him and for more than sixty printed books. They were in parti-coloured goatskin, the upper cover red, the lower one black [see fig. 90]. The majority were decorated with a double-line frame in gilt and blind, with fleurons at the inner and outer corners and a gilt plaquette in the centre [fig. 86]. Thirteen plaquettes were used, some of them after the antique, one after Giovanni Bernardi da Castelbolognese but the majority after Valerio Belli. Fifteen books, mostly octavos and all but one from the Aldine Press, were decorated with a vertical grid of gilt lines [figs. 87 and 88].

The man responsible, known as the "Mendoza Binder" (his real name was probably Andrea di Lorenzo), was the leading bookbinder in Venice from c. 1520 to 1555. He seems to have been closely connected with the Greek colony in Venice and to have spoken at least some demotic. Before working for Hurtado de Mendoza, he had bound Greek manuscripts for the young Francesco Barozzi, of a Venetian family resident in Crete, and for Francis I's library in Fontainebleau, and been employed by the principal bookshop selling Aldine Press books. From 1530 his was the chief workshop providing bindings for *Commissioni*, sets of standard instructions issued in the doge's name to members of patrician families appointed to posts in Venice's dependent provinces.

fig. 86
Theophilactus Simocattus, *Historia de rebus gestis Mauricii imperatoris*. Manuscript, 1453. Binding with gold tooling and plaquettes by the "Mendoza Binder".
BME, Φ.I.12

Figs. 87 and 88
Dante Alighieri, *Comedia del diuino poeta Danthe Alig[hieri] con la dotta e leggiadra spositione di Christophoro Lan[dino] aggiuntaui di nuouo vna copiosissima tauola ....*

Vinegia: ad instantia di M. Gioanni Giolitto da Trino,
[15]36. Bound in goatskin with vertical lines and plaquettes
(back and front covers) by the "Mendoza Binder".
BME, 24.XIII.13

Not all Don Diego's bindings were by this man. He owned three by the "Fugger Binder" [figs. 89 and 90], a craftsman so called from his chief client, the Augsburg banker Johann Jakob Fugger, and a copy of Alessandro Caravia, *Il sogno di Caravia* (Venice, 1541), probably a present from the author, bound by the "Emblematic Binder" [fig. 91].[35]

The collection, assembled from all these sources, was already of major importance by 1543, when the Swiss bibliographer Conrad Gesner visited Venice. He was shown Arlenius´s catalogue and subsequently listed one hundred and twenty-five works as unpublished in his *Bibliotheca Universalis*.[36] As the collection had reached no more than about two-thirds of its final extent at the time of his visit,[37] this total was a considerable underestimate.

Don Diego profited from Venice's status as the major entrepot for the Eastern trade by acquiring also one hundred and fifty-three Arabic manuscripts.[38]

Contemporaries were greatly impressed by the energy and application which Don Diego devoted to studying his manuscripts. When he arrived in Venice his knowledge of Greek was faulty. This was rapidly corrected. As soon as he finished transacting his diplomatic business, a Venetian gentleman attached to the embassy reported,

> [he] studies continuously, and in this short time has improved so much that he understands Aristotle and other Greek authors by himself, and soon will be a great man in Greek. As for Latin, there is no one in these parts who understands it as well as he does .... [He also] studies mathematics and often himself demonstrates the demonstrations to his own teacher.[39]

The teacher in question appears to have been Niccolò Tartaglia, a brilliant self-taught mathematician, translator of Euclid into the vernacular and pioneer of the science of artillery. His *Quesiti, et inventioni diverse,* printed in Venice in 1546, ranges over many subjects, ballistics, surveying, tactics and fortification, as well as arithmetic, algebra and geometry. The seventh and eighth books, on the pseudo-Aristotelian *Mechanica* and on weights, take the form of dialogues with Don Diego.[40]

Juan Páez de Castro, a young Spanish Hellenist setting out on a grand tour of Italian libraries, gives a charming account of the ambassador's enthusiasm. Don Diego had enlisted him in Trent to help with his Castilian translation of the *Mechanica*. "We are now discovering the meaning of Aristotle's *Mechanica*", Páez de Castro wrote to the Aragonese historian, Gerónimo Zurita, "making much of it clear, as he has a romance translation and has glossed it. I think that I will be some help to him. He never sees me without saying, 'To our studies, señor Joan Páez' .... He is a great Aristotelian and mathematician. He knows Latin and Greek as no one else does ...."[41]

Don Diego was generous with his manuscripts. He wanted them to be published and made available to scholars. "You want to share them with all diligent and upright men," Arlenius observed, "... You allowed me to explore and investigate them on condition that I should arrange to have presented to the public anything I thought worth printing."[42]

Figs. 89 and 90
Albert Krantz, *Wandalia*. Coloniae Agrippinae: Iohannes Soter alias Heil ex Bentzheim & socij impresserunt, 1519. Bound in red and black goatskin with gold tooling and plaquettes (front cover and spine) by the "Fugger Binder". RBME, 42.VI.24

Full use was made of Arlenius's links with publishing houses in Basle. He edited Josephus and Polybius from Hurtado de Mendoza's manuscripts. The *editio princeps* of the former was printed by Froben and Episcopius in 1544, the latter by Herwagen in 1549, an edition containing for the first time the epitome of books VII to XVII. A transcript of a twelfth-century manuscript in St Mark's, containing the *Contra gentes* of Theophilus, Bishop of Antioch, was lent to Gesner's friend, Johann Fries, to be printed in Basle. Don Diego never recovered it. It was bought in Venice in the 1590s by Sir Ralph Winwood and given to the Bodleian Library.[43]

Hurtado de Mendoza was able to help two foreign visitors to Italy. His young compatriot, Antonio Agustín, the future Archbishop of Tarragona, shortly to become celebrated for his contribution to the study of Roman law, was at the time of Don Diego's embassy attending Andrea Alciato's lectures in Bologna. He spent the autumn vacation of 1539 in Venice as the ambassador's guest. Four years later he returned. In the interval he had obtained his doctorate and decided to undertake private research. He was aware of the corrupt and unreliable state of the texts of the *Corpus Juris* and was anxious to consult the sixth-century Codex Pisanus of the Digest. This was kept as a precious relic in Florence, closely guarded behind bars in the Palazzo Vecchio. Through the generosity of Lelio Torelli, who was preparing a complete edition, and perhaps backed by a recommendation from Hurtado de Mendoza, he gained access to the manuscript and aided by Jean Matal completed the collation in three months.[44]

In the summer of 1543 he was back in Venice to see through the press the *Emendationes et opiniones* embodying the results of his research.[45] His attention now turned to the *Novellae*, the constitutions promulgated by Justinian and his successors after the publication of the Codex. He was delighted to discover in St Mark's Library Bessarion's manuscript, the most complete one known, of the Greek collection of one hundred and sixty-eight *Novellae*.[46] Don Diego arranged for its loan and with the help of Arlenius and "another Greek bookman" (presumably Andronicus Nucius) Agustín collated it in the ambassador's palace against Haloander's edition (Nuremberg, 1531) and provided for the constitutions lacking in the printed text to be transcribed.[47]

Antoine Perrenot de Granvelle, the future cardinal, was a Franc-Comtois, like Matal, from Besançon, and a contemporary of Agustín. The son of the emperor's minister, Nicolas Perrenot, he had been carefully schooled by his father for the imperial service. In early 1543, when he first met Hurtado de Mendoza, he was still only 25, but had been Bishop of Arras for four years. The two men were colleagues with the emperor's ambassador to Rome, Juan Fernández, Marquis of Aguilar, on a mission to Trent to conduct preliminary discussions about the projected Council.[48]

The bishop and the ambassador formed a lasting friendship. Don Diego seems to have used the opportunity to introduce the younger man to the pleasures of bibliophily and the opportunities afforded by the Venetian book-trade. He gave Granvelle a copy of the Aldine Terence of 1541 in a binding with his own arms,[49] and six works by the Dominican Crisostomo Javelli, a respected commentator on Aristotle, in his idiosyncratic bicoloured plaquette bindings.[50] Some years later Granvelle ordered a large consignment of books in gilt bindings from Venice, as well as a few Greek manuscripts bound by the "Mendoza" or the "Fugger Binder".[51]

Hurtado de Mendoza gave help and encouragement to other scholars working on subjects that interested him. He lent Vincenzo Maggi a manuscript for the latter's work on Aristotle's *Poetica*,[52] he offered to finance the publication of a commentary on the *Physics* by the theologian Francisco Herrera,[53] and provided information for Giacomo Gastaldi's great wall-map of Spain;[54] Alessandro

fig. 91
Alessandro Caravia, *Il sogno dil Caravia*. In Vinegia: nelle case di Giouann'Antonio di Nicolini da Sabbio, 1541. Gold-tooled binding by the "Emblematic Binder". RBME, Mesa 11-II-7

Piccolomini, who was making an Italian paraphrase of the *Mechanica*, was lodged in the imperial embassy in Rome;[55] Benedetto Varchi, at the time a student in Padua, and a Florentine exile, Jacopo Nardi, were encouraged to translate Aristotle and Livy. But authors' dedications are marked by a tone of formality. There is no mention of affability or munificence. Instead they speak of Hurtado de Mendoza's high birth, great office and profound learning. Don Diego was very conscious of his rank as a member of one of the premier families of Spain. He welcomed into his palace social equals like Cardinal Benedetto Accolti or Spanish scholars of *hidalgo* families like Antonio Agustín and Páez de Castro; Paolo Manuzio might be admitted for a philosophical discussion,[56] but others were kept at a distance.

Greek scribes, a librarian, plaquette bindings, the cost of older manuscripts, a buying agent sent specially to the Levant, all this involved expense. Don Diego was not a rich man. His inherited portion as a younger son had been commuted with his brother for a capital sum of only three thousand ducats, less than his annual salary as an ambassador. His need for money became increasingly urgent. He complained that his salary arrived late from Milan and begged to be made Bishop of Calahorra, or failing that of Cuenca, or failing that of Jaen. His concentrated campaign of acquisition was fuelled by enthusiasm and dedication, but not by large supplies of ready cash. Charles V eventually rescued him with a present of nine thousand *scudi* to pay his debts.[57] Nevertheless, when he was transferred to Rome he could not afford to take Arlenius with him.

In February 1545 Don Diego was appointed the emperor's representative to the Council of Trent. He arrived in Trent the following month bringing with him his Greek manuscripts and many printed books. They were made freely available and created a considerable stir, as no one else had thought of equipping the Council with the Greek works the Fathers might need to consult. Several were lent to Cardinal Marcello Cervini, one of the three papal legates to the Council.[58] Gentien Hervet, a French ecclesiastic attached to his household, edited the dialogue *Ammonius* by Zacharias of Mytilene from Hurtado de Mendoza's manuscript now in the Bodleian.[59]

Juan Páez de Castro arrived in Trent in July, was introduced to the ambassador and given the run of his library. A close friendship followed. By August he was seeing Don Diego every day and his house was full of borrowed books and manuscripts, as many as he wanted, as well as the ambassador's notebooks. A few days later he left for Venice to bring back a copy of the Aldine Aristotle, with all the Greek commentators and some of the Latin ones, particularly Averroes and Aquinas. That winter, "dum sub nivibus stupet alma tellus", he told Zurita, there was to be a great academy of learned men to study Aristotle.[60]

But that winter Don Diego was absent, suffering from malaria. Páez de Castro devoted himself to the text of Aristotle, followed by Plato, unpublished commentaries of Proclus, and Galen, which he read in conjunction with Vesalius's *De humani corporis fabrica*. Aristotle however engaged the major part of his attention. He declared that he had made wonderful discoveries; he had the benefit of the best appara-

Fig. 92
Aristotle, *Opera*. Basileae: Johannes Oporinus, 1538. With notes by Hurtado de Mendoza and Páez de Castro. Pinerolo, Oblati di Maria Vergine, MD.A.5.1-2.

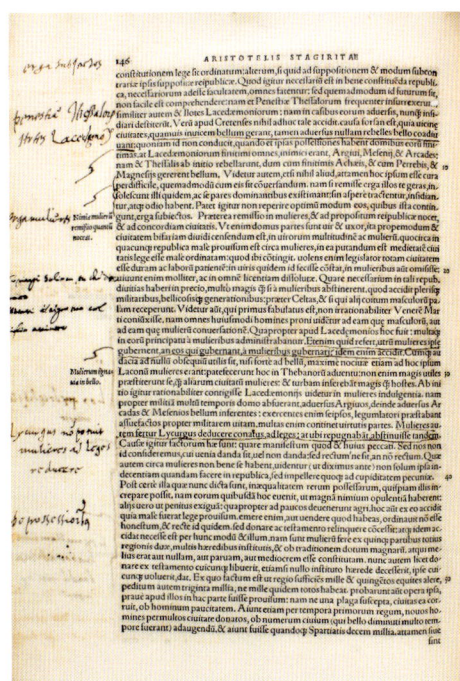

tus any Christian had ever enjoyed and had the texts in a more correct form than anyone had possessed outside the Greek Empire for eight hundred years.[61] Don Diego owned the *editio princeps* of Aristotle, with a second copy of the first volume, and four copies of the 1531 and later Basle editions. The margins of the 1531 edition were used to record variant readings.[62]

A record of this collaboration has been discovered by Prof. Francesco Malaguzzi in a small ecclesiastical library in Piedmont.[63] It is a copy of Aristotle's *Opera*, in Latin translation, edited by Philip Melancthon, 2 vols. (Basle, Johann Oporinus, 1538). The *De naturali ascultatione, Meteorologica, De anima, Ethica ad Nicomachum, Magna Moralia, Politica* and *Oeconomica* are profusely annotated in Latin by Hurtado de Mendoza [fig. 92]. He has also written two marginal notes in Greek, one in Hebrew and twenty-eight in Arabic. The annotations by Páez de Castro are considerably fewer. For unknown reasons the volume was left behind when its owner returned to Spain. It next belonged to Girolamo Marcello de Gubernatis (1633–1713).[64] Although born in Sospel on the present Franco-Italian frontier and holding office in the duchy of Savoy, he spent fifteen years in Rome and may have acquired the book there.

In May 1546 the ambassador returned to Trent, and immediately Páez de Castro declared that "truly in the whole of Italy there is no better conversation than here".[65] Don Diego made a great impression in Trent. "Everyone believes", Páez de Castro reported, "that after the Council His Majesty will make him a bishop and His Holiness a cardinal."[66] Don Diego, who had a Jewish mistress in Venice, was perhaps, as Graux remarks, rather too worldly to have made a model bishop or cardinal.[67] Instead the Emperor appointed him ambassador in Rome.

A grave charge has blackened Don Diego's reputation. He has been accused of stealing manuscripts from the Library of St Mark's.[68] Venetian suspicions were aroused early. George

Tanner, a future professor of Greek in Vienna, spent the best part of two years in Venice in 1554–55. During this time he was only allowed to visit the Marciana once. He blamed the restrictions on the "iniquities" of the ambassador. "Access to the Marciana is granted to very few", he reported, "as two years ago Don Diego Mendoza filched books from libraries all over Italy and rarely returned important books he had been lent."[69]

It is true that Don Diego could be high-handed. He asked Páez de Castro to bring a manuscript of Dionysius of Halicarnassus's treatise *On the Ancient Orators* to Trent even if it had a chain attached.[70] He had liberal borrowing rights from the Marciana and took out twenty-four Greek manuscripts in 1545 and 15646, including some of major importance.[71] Nevertheless the accusation appears to be unfounded. All his loans were properly registered and duly returned. The evidence against him is weak: two manuscripts in the Escorial with notes or longer passages in Bessarion's hand,[72] of which one is not in Arlenius's catalogue and must have been acquired after he left Venice, while the other never belonged to the Marciana,[73] and three volumes of Gregory of Nyssa's works, destroyed in the Escorial fire but said to have belonged to Bessarion.[74] They were perhaps copies, as Bessarion's manuscripts of the Greek Father are still present in Venice.[75] The slander may have originated because manuscripts were mislaid and it was easy to blame a foreigner who had enjoyed exceptional licence to borrow.[76]

Don Diego reached Rome and was received by the pope in April 157. A nucleus of learned Spaniards was already resident in the city. They included Antonio Agustín, by this time one of the Auditors of the Rota, his scholarly friends Juan de Arce and Francisco Torres, both of Palencia, and the erudite doctor Andrés de Laguna, whose translations of Galen and Aristotle and corrections to Janus Cornarius's edition of the writers on agriculture Don Diego owned.[77] In August, as well as ambassador to the Holy See, he was appointed Governor of Siena.

He continued to collect, though at a reduced rate. An eleventh-century manuscript of the Greek writers on military tactics, which had belonged to the Perugian professor Francesco Maturanzio, was obtained from the monastery of S. Pietro in Perugia.[78] In December 1547 Valeriano Albini, who by this time had moved to Rome, borrowed a manuscript of the Alexandrian geometer Pappus and other mathematicians from the Vatican and returned it the following April, after completing a transcript for the ambassador.[79]

An incident involving Hurtado de Mendoza is related in Cardinal Cervini's correspondence with his secretary, Guglielmo Sirleto. As the Council proceeded in Trent Cervini needed to know the opinions of the Greek Fathers on a variety of subjects: the sacraments, the doctrines of grace and justification, the merits of virginity. He sent pressing requests to Sirleto to have copies of Vatican or other exemplars made and sent to him. The problem was to find reliable Greek scribes in Rome. Sirleto engaged a certain Georgius to copy the Acts of the Council of Ephesus from a manuscript lent from the Library of St Mark's. Georgius had finished only half when he was carried off to Siena by Don Diego. He was thought to have taken one gathering with him, a matter of some embarrassment to Sirleto as the Venetian ambassador was already pressing for the manuscript's return. Fortunately Georgius was innocent of this offence; he had left the missing gathering "in the hands of Don Diego's scribe".[80] The scribe in question was probably the Corfiote, Joannes Mauromates, who copied two manuscripts for the ambassador in 1548. Don Diego, however, had no exclusive right to his services. From the following year he was chiefly employed by the Cardinal of Burgos, Francisco de Mendoza y Bobadilla.[81]

It has been said that "the true collectors of the 16th and 17th centuries ... formed many valuable and justly famous collections. These were not, however, collections or rare books, but general collections. The rare books were included ... 'as an added grace'".[82] This is not wholly true of Hurtado de Medoza, who showed

Fig. 93
Aristotle, *Opera, graece*. Venetiis: Aldus Manutius, 1495, vol. I. The dedication copy to Alberto Pio, Prince of Carpi. Venetian plaquette binding. RBME, 54.IV.3

an interest in dedication, association or specially bound copies, and it is certainly not true of Fulvio Orsini. Don Diego acquired three interesting volumes, probably in Rome. They were the dedication copy to Alberto Pio, Prince of Carpi, of volume I of the Aldine Aristotle, in a Venetian plaquette binding, perhaps obtained from the dedicatee's son, Cardinal Rodolfo Pio [fig. 93];[83] the dedication copy to the French Cardinal Robert Britto of the 1508 Rome edition of Ptolemy, in a gilt binding of red goatskin [fig. 94];[84] and the first edition of Sannazaro's *De partu Virginis* (1526), one of two known copies in a presentation binding with a medallion of the author by Girolamo Santacroce on the upper cover and the obverse of the same medal, representing the Nativity, on the lower one. The binding has suffered and of the two medallions only part of lower one survives [fig. 95].[85] The Aristotle was a natural acquisition for the ambassador, but though keenly interested in vernacular verse, he never showed any special interest in neo-Latin poetry. He may have bought the Sannazaro, and perhaps the Ptolemy, as much for their associations and bindings as for their contents.

It is curious that in spite of Don Diego's reputation as a diplomat he failed in his principal task in each of his appointments. In Venice he was unable to persuade the Venetians not to make peace with the Turks; nor, when in Rome, was he able to prevent the General Council of the Church being moved from Trent to Bologna. His high-handed actions as Governor of Siena provoked the Sienese to rebel and drive out the Spanish garrison. Don Diego returned to Spain, and although granted a pension, created knight of Alcántara, and twice appointed Commissary General of a Spanish fleet, he was debarred from further high office. He had left Rome in a hurry, "escaping his creditors [and] trusting his books and [antiquities] ... to the mercy of his friends".[86] One of the Greek manuscripts is later found in the collection of Cardinal Sirleto,[87] and of the two hundred and fifty-eight in Arlenius's catalogue about two dozen never reached the Escorial, and may have been lost in the upheaval. Of the printed books, he may have most regretted the loss of the 1538 Basle Aristotle which he had studied and annotated with Páez de Castro.

The latter part of his life contained many disappointments. For sixteen years he was largely unemployed, a condition that must have been galling to a man of his energy and intellectual vigour. In 1568 there was a scandalous scene in the royal palace, a fight between Don Diego and another courtier. Swords were drawn; there was an uproar. Philip II was outraged. Both protagonists were arrested and imprisoned, Don Diego in the castle La Mota at Medina del Campo. After six months' imprisonment he was exiled to Granada, arriving there when the Morisco revolt had just broken out. He solaced his exile by collecting Arabic manuscripts and by writing an account of the revolt in a style much influenced by

Fig. 94
Claudius Ptolemy, *Geographia*. Roma: Bernardino dei Vitali for Evangelista Tosini, 1508. The dedication copy to Cardinal Robert Britto. Bound in red goatskin with gold tooling. RBME, 69.V.5

Fig. 95
Iacopo Sannazzaro, *De partu Virginis*.
Neapoli: per Antonium Fretiam Corinaldinum ...,
1526. Bound in red goatskin with plaquettes.
RBME, 64.VI.13

his study of ancient authors, especially Thucydides. It is the work by which he is now chiefly remembered.[88]

Some years earlier he had been summoned to give evidence before the Inquisition in the trial of Fray Bartolomé de Carranza, the ill-starred Archbishop of Toledo. He was again interrogated in 1573 by the Secretary of the Holy Office about a heretical print of the Crucifixion.[89] It was perhaps after one or other of these occasions that his library was submitted to censorship.[90] Passages were inked out, and pages excised or pasted together; books may have been confiscated or destroyed. Certainly the Lutheran works, which the ambassador had provided for the instruction of the Church Fathers in Trent, had disappeared before the library reached the Escorial, and the owner thought it prudent to anticipate the visitation by tearing Luther's prologue out of the first printing of the Koran.[91]

Nevertheless the collection escaped surprisingly lightly. There is no reason to suspect that Hurtado de Mendoza's beliefs were not entirely orthodox, but his library had been formed during the more tolerant era of Charles V's reign and contained many books that fell under the ban of the former Inquisitor General, Michele Ghislieri, Pope Pius V. Don Diego owned works on subjects—astrology and prognostication—condemned by the Roman Index of 1559;[92] books by prohibited authors—Georgius Agricola, Aretino, Brucioli, Grynaeus, Ulrich von Hutten, Machiavelli, Lukas Loss, Jakob Schegk and Jakob Ziegler; and works specifically forbidden—the *Decameron*, Marcantonio Flaminio's paraphrase of the Psalms, the Koran, the *Dialogues* of Lucian and the edition of the Bible printed in Lyons for Antoine Vincent in 1545. Antonio Roselli's *Monarchia* appears to have been jettisoned and Sixt Birck's edition of Cicero, *De officiis*, was excised, but Conrad Gesner's *Thesaurus de remediis secretis* slipped through under the cloak of pseudonymity. He was allowed to keep a Lyonese edition of the Mainz Franciscan Johann Wild's commentary on St John's Gospel, although the book's sale in Spain was forbidden by the Inquisition, and must have felt on safer ground in adding the same author's commentary on Matthew in an expurgated edition prepared by order of the Inquisitor General, Archbishop Fernando de Valdes. Even this work however incurred a later Inquisitor's censure.[93]

Books from the Protestant presses of Basle were comprehensively banned by the Roman Index. Don Diego owned more than a hundred, ten per cent of his known collection. Among them were works edited or translated by proscribed Northern scholars, Erasmus's editions of Ambrose, Augustine, and Jerome, Wolfgang Musculus's of Basil and Cyril, Beatus Rhenanus's of Tacitus and the church historians, translations by Janus Cornarius. Erasmus was a special case. Every one of his writings was forbidden. Yet Hurtado de Mendoza was allowed to keep the Basle edition of the collected works, though in a severely expurgated form.[94]

These years of banishment were not happy ones. Don Diego, who had spent his life in the service of the Crown, was distressed to be the object of the king's displeasure. In 1573 Philip II let it be known that he would be interested in acquiring the library for the Escorial. Don Diego took this message as implying that a pardon would be granted. He had no doubt intended to leave the books as a family possession. The vernacular literature had already been deposited with the Duke of Infantado, the head of the senior branch. The other books, which had been scattered in different locations, were now brought together at Alcalá de Henares. Don Diego was allowed to go to Madrid in 1574 to answer questions about financial irregularities in Venice and Siena. From there he could visit Alcalá and was delighted to see the books again in one place. He had been dusting them, he told Zurita, and looking to see if the mice had got at them and was happy to find them in good condition. There were uncommon authors among them, of whom he'd found no record; he was amazed by the number he'd read, even though, he added modestly, he'd learnt nothing from them.[95]

By the summer of the following year Don Diego was dying. His will, dated 9 August 1575, left all his possessions to the king. A few days later Philip II grudgingly pardoned him. He died on 14 August.

The library was conveyed to the Escorial in the following summer. Two hundred and fifty-six Greek manuscripts entered the royal collection, thirty-two Hebrew and two hundred and fifty-five Arabic.[96] The two hundred and seventy Latin manuscripts varied greatly in quality and interest. There was a humanistic Lactantius, a Cicero, *De officiis*, and a Statius,[97] the last two probably from the Veneto, but others were imperfect and undistinguished. Don Diego evidently regarded them as mere adjuncts to the Greek collection. Only the Cicero and a Virgil show[98] signs of having been studied.

The printed books are more difficult to estimate. The only complete inventory perished in the Escorial fire of 1671. What survives is a partial copy, of the theology, philosophy and some of the mathematics, supplemented by two other, even more incomplete, lists. Our knowledge of Don Diego's holdings of medicine, law, history, rhetoric, poetry and grammar is fragmentary and accidental. Nevertheless it has been possible to recover almost one thousand two hundred titles, out of an original total perhaps of about two thousand, and some of the main features of his collecting interests can be discerned.

Philosophy was his chief love and Aristotle his principal interest. His collection of manuscripts of Aristotle and Plato and of the commentators on both amazed scholars.[99] He owned eighty-six printed editions of works by (or attributed to) Aristotle and one hundred and four volumes of ancient, medieval and more recent commentary, paraphrase, or epitome, with three indexes. A Latin paraphrase of the whole of Aristotle was planned, but abandoned after one work. He did however complete a translation of the *Mechanica* into Castilian.[100] In this, as in other sections, favourite books were signalised by special bindings.

Plato was represented by three editions of the works, one extensively annotated and specially bound, and by manuscripts of major commentators.[101] The collector did not limit himself to the greatest names. He also owned manuscripts of Maximus Tyrius, Plotinus and Sextus Empiricus, all recent transcripts no doubt specially commissioned.[102] Among later philosophers his teacher, Agostino Nifo, was prominent.

Biblical commentaries, books on faith and morals, sermons and anti-Lutheran tracts form a large theological category. The Aldine Greek Bible and Agostino Steuco's elucidation of passages in the Vulgate Pentateuch were distinguished by plaquette bindings.

Mathematics, headed by six editions of Euclid's *Elements*, was held in strength. Some sheets of calculations are still present, loosely inserted into Girolamo Cardano's book on arithmetic. Marginal notes, many in Greek, are evidence that the section on the *Mechanica* in the *Opuscula* of Niccolò Leonico Tomeo was attentively studied. Astronomy and cosmography were another strongly held section with a wide selection of Jewish, Muslim and Christian authors. The first edition of Copernicus's *De revolutionibus orbium coelestium* could compete for acceptance with the *De Meteoris* of the anti-Copernican Michael Stanhuf, a believer in signs and portents. The distinction of a special binding was awarded, not to Copernicus, but to Firmicus Maternus, Regiomontanus, Petrus Apianus, Simon Grynaeus, Johann Stoeffer, and Jakob Ziegler. Don Diego took a professional interest in astrology—after arriving in Rome he reported that the astrologers predicted the pope's death in 1548[103]—and demonstrated a special regard for the *Summa astrologiae judicialis* of the English exponent, John Eastwood.

History was important to him, with nineteen works (twenty if one includes Guillaume Budé's *De asse*) in plaquette bindings. Agustín had no doubt stimulated his interest in Roman law. Nine editions, in ten volumes, of the *Codex, Digest,* and *Novellae* were specially bound. Dioscorides, Galen, the simples prescribed by Serapion, Averroes and Rhazes, and a vellum copy of Vesalius figured in the medical section.

Their Mudejar bindings identify two books from his childhood. He must have learnt

Greek from an edition of Chrysoloras's *Erotemata* together with other elementary works on grammar printed in Alcalá; Ovid's *Art of Love* points to an early taste for poetry, not unexpected in a man who was himself to become a poet.[104] Classical authors in Aldine editions, Dante and Bembo were given stately bindings. Xenophon was a favourite author. Don Diego's manuscript of the *Cyropaedia* was one of the two earliest known and he was vexed when refused permission by Pietro Bembo to borrow his manuscripts for Xenophon and Aristotle. He repaid the cardinal by speaking slightingly of his learning, antiquities and garden.[105]

The library had been predominantly formed during the ambassador's six years in Venice. Only seventeen per cent of the identified books were printed after his departure. He must have been a regular customer at the shops in the Merceria of various members of the Scoto family for the philosophical works they published. More popular Italian works could have been picked up at bookstalls all over the city. Spanish literature on the contrary is surprisingly lacking, or has not come to light; only the *Carcel de Amor* of Diego Hernández de San Pedro in Italian translation, Ausías March's poems in Valencian, the *Coplas* of the Infante Dom Pedro of Portugal and the *Cancionero* of Pedro Manuel de Ximénez de Urrea. Indeed, Spanish books comprised hardly more than two per cent of the collection. Even during the last twenty-two years of his life, spent almost entirely in Spain, he preferred to buy books printed in Lyons, Paris or Antwerp.[106]

Hurtado de Mendoza was a fine linguist, an omnivorous reader and a collector with a wide range of interests. He had impressive holdings of philosophy, science and mathematics, medicine and vernacular literature. That he succeeded in forming a collection of international importance though himself relatively poor makes his achievement all the more remarkable. Nor was he devoid of bibliophilic instincts, even though he might write in one of his poems,

> I'll fling my books on the ground
> I'll open or close whichever one I please.[107]

It does not sound very bibliophilic behaviour. But he certainly minded about the script and the margins in the Greek manuscripts copied for him, and the bindings he commissioned are notable for the simplicity of their gilt ornament and the classical beauty of their plaquettes.

1 NADER 1979.
2 SCHIFF 1905, repr. 1970; *Exposición Mendoza del Infantado* 1958; REICHENBERGER 1969, 5–34.
3 For his life see GONZÁLEZ PALENCIA AND MELE 1941–43 and SPIVAKOVSKY 1970.
4 MORALES 1575, dedication.
5 RBME, *cod. graec.* 134, T.I.14.
6 CAVALCANTI 1967, 95.
7 DELISLE 1868, I, 151–54; IRIGOIN 1977, II, 399–415.
8 JOSEPHUS 1544, dedication, *2r.
9 JENNY 1964, 5–45.
10 ANDRÉS 1804, 134.
11 Cambridge University Library, Add. Ms. 565. Cf. HOBSON 1975a, 33–61.
12 Andronicus Nucius, Nicolas Murmuris, Georgius Bevaines, Joannes Mauromates, Petrus Karnavaka, Nicolas Marulus Gaïtanus, and at least two anonymous ones.
13 ANDRÉS 1804, 13, quoted by GRAUX 1880, 189, n. 2.
14 LEGRAND 1885, I, 242; ANDRÉS 1965, II, 19; III, 132. On Nucius's life, GRAUX 1880, 190–92.
15 LEGRAND 1885, I, nos. 103, 114; II, no. 238.
16 See above, n. 5.
17 FOUCAULT 1962. The English part of the journey was published with an English translation by the Revd J. A. Cramer for the Camden Society (London, 1841). Cf. FOUCAULT 1972, 102–3.
18 RBME, *cod. graec.* 143, T.II.4.
19 RBME, *cod. graec.* 247, 346 and 131.
20 JOSEPHUS 1544, dedication, *2r. See above, n. 8.
21 Vat. lat. 3958, fols. 232–34; ANDRÉS 1961, 382–89. Of the thirty-eight manuscripts twenty-four either survive in the Escorial and are transcripts of the 1540s or are described in ANDRÉS (1968) as "recentes"; four are undated, and only four are "antiqui" apart from the six "qui[!] nuper emit". One is dated 1544: Nicomachus Gerasenus, *Arithmetica* (RBME, *cod. graec.* 351). The list cannot therefore represent "the primitive nucleus of the collection, c. 1530–40", as Gregorio de ANDRÉS (1961, 382) suggested.
22 RBME, *cod. graec.* 30, R.II.11.
23 RBME, &.II.9. The author, kindly identified for me by Mr Paul Quarrie, was Abu Ja'far Ahmad ibn Ibrahim.
24 The exception is an Aristophanes, Y.III.16, bound in dark brown goatskin *alla greca*. Dr Nicholas PICKWOAD (1991, 60) has pointed out that the leather traditionally described as goatskin may often be the hide of the hairy sheep, also known as Persian morocco.
25 GONZÁLEZ PALENCIA AND MELE 1941–43, I, 9.
26 MORALES 1575, dedication. A list in Milan, Biblioteca Ambrosiana, E 60 sup., fols. 52–63, includes thirty-one titles headed "Librorum quos dono acceipt à Turca index". They agree with those on the list printed by GRAUX (1880, 383–85) and are equally fictitious (GRAUX 1880, 177–81).
27 RBME, *cod. graec.* 514, w.I.13.
28 RUNCIMAN 1968, 197.

29 ANDRÉS 1804, 167. Eighteen years later Giovanni Battista Amalteo stated that Sophianus had told him he had made two visits to Greece for Don Diego (GRAUX 1880, 174).
30 TINTO 1965, 171–75; 1970, 285–93. PETTAS 1974, 206–13. PASCHINI 1958, 203, 223.
31 HOBSON 1979, 280–81. Sophianus had returned by the time of Gesner's visit to Venice: GRAUX 1880, 171, n. 3.
32 ST CLAIR 1983, 77.
33 The total of older manuscripts in Arlenius's catalogue is 106, but several of these were certainly of Italian origin (e.g. RBME, *cod. graec.* 502, copied at Carpi in 1523). The dates of forty-seven manuscripts are not recorded.
34 MÜLLER 1884, 333f; SPEAKE 1993, 325–30.
35 THOMAS 1954, 474–80; HOBSON 1999, chap. 5. The Caravia binding was reported to me by Mme Isabelle de Conihout.
36 GRAUX 1880, 387–400. Of the titles queried by GRAUX (245–46), the Chrysostom *Homiliae* is RBME, *cod. graec.* 529 and the Eutecnius RBME, *cod. graec.* 77. For Arlenius's own collection cf. HOBSON 1975a, 36–37.
37 He mentions nothing after no. 173 in Arlenius's catalogue.
38 HOBSON 1975a, 36.
39 GONZÁLEZ PALENCIA and MELE 1941–43, I, 283–84.
40 ROSE AND DRAKE 1971, 85–87. A translation of book VII of Tartaglia's *Quesiti*, containing the dialogue with Hurtado de Mendoza, is printed in DRAKE AND DRABKIN 1969, 104–43.
41 Páez de Castro, letter of August 1545: DORMER 1680, 463–64, quoted in part by GONZÁLEZ PALENCIA AND MELE 1941–43, I, 285.
42 JOSEPHUS 1544, dedication, *2v.
43 GRAUX 1880, 225. Oxford, Bodleian Library, Auct. E. I. 11.
44 ZULUETA 1939; HOBSON 1975a; CRAWFORD 1993. Cf. AGUSTÍN 1980, 81, 82, 83, etc. FERRARY 1992.
45 AGUSTÍN 1543.
46 Venice, Biblioteca Nazionale Marciana, *cod. graec.* 179.
47 Agustín's annotated copy of Haloander is RBME, 82.VI.4. Hurtado de Mendoza's copy, partly corrected from the Marciana MS, is RBME, M.10.I.21.
48 VAN DURME 1953. There is a Spanish translation (1957).
49 Manchester, John Rylands Manchester University Library, 8614. The book is inscribed: "Dittacus Mendocius D. D. Perrenoto Ep[iscop]o Atrib[atensi]".
50 Besançon, Bibliothèque de la Ville, 228182–5.
51 HOBSON 1999, 117–20.
52 MADIUS AND LOMBARDUS 1550; cf. PORRO 1983, 317.
53 VAZQUEZ AND ROSE 1935, 124; GONZÁLEZ PALENCIA AND MELE 1941–43, II, 109.
54 *Alli Spettatori Salute Questa e la vera descrittione di tutta la Spagna....* Venice, 1544; TOOLEY 1939, 43, no. 527; MARCEL 1899, 186–87. The late Lord Wardington kindly drew my attention to this map.

55 PICCOLOMINI 1547. The dedication of the second work to Mendoza (*Commentarium de certitudine mathematicarum disciplinarum*) is dated: "*Romae ex aedibus ipsis tuis*".
56 CICERO, *De Philosophia*, ed. Paolo Manuzio, Venice, apud Aldi filios, 1541, dedication, repr. GONZÁLEZ PALENCIA AND MELE 1941–43, III, 271–75. Accolti was staying with Mendoza at the time. Arlenius's edition of Lycophron, *Alexandra* (Basle: Oporinus, 1546), is dedicated to Accolti. For the dedication copy in a Bolognese binding (BL, C.47.I.14) see NIXON 1956, 52; FOOT 1978–2010, I, 303.
57 DORMER 1680, 474–75.
58 *Concilium Tridentinum: Diariorum, Actorum, Epistularum, Tractatuum Nova Collectio*, ed. Goerresgesellschaft (Freiburg i.B., 1901), I, 166, 187, 229.
59 GRAUX 1880, 248, 407. The manuscript is Ms. Auct. E. I.11; cf. HOBSON 1975b, 33–36. The work was printed in Venice by Nicolò Bascarini for Melchiorre Sessa in 1546.
60 Páez de Castro, letters to Zurita of 10 August "9" [*vere* 19?] August 1545. DORMER 1680, 461–65.
61 Páez de Castro, letters of 14 December 1545, 25 March 1546, and 17 February 1547. DORMER 1680, 465–68, 470–71, 476–77.
62 RBME, 25.III.11.
63 Pinerolo, Oblati di Maria Vergine. MALAGUZZI 2008, 84–85.
64 BERTARELLI AND PRIOR 1902, 218.
65 Páez de Castro, letter of 8 June 1546. DORMER 1680, 471–73.
66 Páez de Castro, letter of 10 August 1545. DORMER 1680, 463.
67 GRAUX 1880, 167.
68 The latest account is given by ZORZI 1987, 112–14.
69 BIBL 1898, 385–430.
70 Páez de Castro did what he was told. GRAUX 1880, 192, 405.
71 OMONT 1887, 651–86; GRAUX 1880, 408–413; HARLFINGER 1971, 82.
72 RBME, *cod. graec.* 72, S.I.12 y 100, S.III.1; LABOWSKY 1979, 484–85. Madrid, BN, Ms N 15 did not belong to Mendoza.
73 It is not LABOWSKY (1979), B.555 (= C.53).
74 ANDRÉS 1968, nos. 551, 552, 554.
75 Venice, Biblioteca Marciana, *cod. graec.* 66, 67, 68, 69 and 496 (= LABOWSKY 1979, B.170, 266, 684, 267 and 201).
76 Books had already in the fifteenth century been lent out and not returned (COGGIOLA 1908, 52). CASTELLANI (1896–97, 311–377) lists manuscripts of Bessarion in other libraries. FOSCARINI 1752, 63–65; ANDRÉS 1790–93, III, 54–57; VALENTINELLI 1868–73, I, 46–47, and GRAUX 1880, 182–85, all defended Hurtado de Mendoza against the slander.
77 HOBSON 1975a; MAICAS 1986; BATAILLON 1991, I, 722 (on Laguna). Andrés de Laguna's, *Castigationes in tralationem octo ultimorum librorum De re rustica* was printed in Cologne in 1543 by Johann von Aich (RBME 9.VI.27).
78 HOFFMANN 1983, 91, 100–3, 118–19. The manuscript was in 2 vols. One was secured by Hurtado de Mendoza (RBME, *cod. graec.* 281 [y.III.11]); the other passed through the hands of Prospero Podiani and Fulvio Orsini into the Farnese collection (Naples III.C.26). FABRI DE PEIRESC (1992, 225) searched in vain for the Escorial manuscript.
79 The Vatican exemplar (Vat. gr. 218) and Escorial copy (*cod. graec.* 300, y.I.7) contain books V–VIII of Pappus. Hurtado de Mendoza already owned books II–IV (book I is lost) copied by Valeriano Albini in 1545 (RBME, *cod. graec.* 131, T.I.11). TREWEEK 1957, 195–233.
80 Sirleto, letters to Cervini of 29 February and 21 March 1548: Vat. lat. 6177, fols. 127–28, 131–32. "Georgius" was probably Georgius Bevaines.
81 The manuscripts are RBME, *cod. graec.* 194, and astronomical and arithmetical collection (F.I.16) and *cod. graec.* 305, Asclepius Trallianus, *In Aristotelis metaphysica* (y.I.12). For Mauromates, VOGEL AND GARDTHAUSEN 1909 (re-ed. Hildesheim, 1966), 177–78.
82 BATTS 1975, 282 The words in quotation marks are from A. W. POLLARD's article, "Book-Collecting", in the *Encyclopedia Britannica*, 11th edition.
83 RBME, 54.IV.3. Cf. THOMAS 1954, fig. 363; DE MARINIS 1960, III, no. 2694, tav. CCCCLXXIV; HOBSON 1989, 105, 221, fig. 84.
84 RBME, 69.V.5. Cf. HOBSON 1989, 123.
85 RBME, 64.VI.13. Cf. HOBSON 1989, 112, 226, fig. 91.
86 SPIVAKOVSKY 1970, 305.
87 Vat. gr. 1444.
88 Diego Hurtado de Mendoza, *Guerra de Granada* (1st ed. Lisbon, 1627). An English translation by Martin Shuttleworth was published by the Folio Society in 1982.
89 LLORENTE 1817–18, III, 245–57; MENÉNDEZ Y PELAYO 1945, V, 53–54; GONZÁLEZ PALENCIA AND MELE 1941–43, II, 382; SPIVAKOVSKY 1970, 345.
90 That the books were censored before reaching the Escorial is proved by the copy of Musler's *Oratio de liberalibus artibus* (Venice, 1538). Faced by a book whose title page had been removed, Gracián made a guess and entered it in the inventory as a work on the institutions of the Empire (ANDRÉS 1964, 318, no. 1584: "in explicationem institutionum imperialium"). The library was frequently censored in later years when in the Escorial.
91 *Koran*, trans. Robert of Ketton, Basle, Johann Oporinus, 1543. RBME, 57.IX.15.
92 REUSCH 1886, 176–208; BUJANDA, DAVIGNON AND STANEK 1990.
93 The commentary on St John is no longer present. That on St Matthew is RBME, 81.IV.10. Cf. MORISSE 1995, 159–74.
94 RBME, 45.IV.5–11.
95 Diego Hurtado de Mendoza, letter of 18 November 1574. DORMER 1680, 503.

96 Andrés 1916–65, VII (1964), 237–323.
97 RBME, b.I.16, T.III.19 and f.III.11.
98 RBME, S.II.15.
99 Páez de Castro, letter to Honorato Juan. Graux 1880, 404–5.
100 RBME, f.III.15 and f.III.27. Zarco Cuevas 1924, I, 142–43. The translation was published by Foulché-Delbosc 1898, 365–405. It was dedicated to the Duke of Alba.
101 Graux 1880, 405. Dr James Hankins kindly drew my attention to commentaries on the *Gorgias* and *Euthydemus* (which he identified as excerpts from Ficino's *argumenta* preceding the dialogues in the editions of his Latin translations of Plato) in RBME, K.III.8. Antolín (1910, II, 530) suggested that they were by Hurtado de Mendoza. The manuscript, in a scribal hand of the second half of the sixteenth century, did not belong to him, and the attribution appears unfounded.
102 Andrés 1916–65, VII (1964), 265–66, nos. 373, 386, 388, 390.
103 González Palencia and Mele 1941–43, II, 83.
104 Madrid, BN, R.1305; RBME, 85.VII.19.
105 Graux 1880, 169–70 [Quoted from a letter from Páez de Castro to Zurita (Trent, 8 June 1546). Dormer 1680, 472.]. The manuscript is of the tenth century and had belonged to the Great Lavra on Mount Athos. It is now RBME, *cod. graec.* 174, T.III.14.
106 The import of vernacular books printed abroad was restricted in 1558: *Novísima Recopilación de las leyes de España*, Madrid, 1805, IV, 123.
107 Quoted by Spivakovsky 1970, 335.

Three Aspects of French Bindings in the Spanish National Heritage Collections

Isabelle de Conihout and Pascal Ract-Madoux

For María Luisa

I
Diplomacy and Bookbinding: Sixteenth-Century French Bindings at El Escorial

A Gift from Francis I to Charles V?

During the visit to the royal Monastery of San Lorenzo de El Escorial, which constituted one of the great moments of the International Seminar on databases of historical bindings organised by María Luisa López-Vidriero in 2008, our attention was caught by a volume in a Parisian cover from the early 1540s: an edition of Budé, bound in blue morocco, which was peculiar in having its title gilded on the spine [figs. 96 and 97]. The volume came from the "Chamber of Charles V". Now it was known from T. Kimball Brooker's study that the only French bindings that have a title gilded on the spine before 1547 are those belonging to the private library of Francis I. Could the Escorial volume have been a gift from Francis I to Charles V? It is necessary at this point to provide a brief reminder of the relations between these two monarchs, as well as an overview of Parisian bookbinding from 1540 to 1547.

Diplomatic Relations, First Period: Charles V-Francis I, 1515–47

At first sight the contentious relations entertained by the two greatest of Christian princes, who were very nearly contemporaries, during more than a quarter of a century make the hypothesis rather improbable. The struggle for supremacy that pitted the one against the other of the two grand European monarchies during the greater part of the sixteenth century was inflamed by personal rivalry, "the impossible duel" in which Francis and Charles confronted one another.[1]

Charles, the heir to chivalric Burgundian culture, used to read the *Chevalier délibéré* by Olivier de la Marche (the last great chronicler of the Burgundian court), half romance of chivalry, half mirror of princes, of which he possessed a fine copy during his reclusion at Yuste. It was to him that Erasmus dedicated his *Institution of a Christian Prince*, while the political project of the Habsburgs was much influenced by the pacifism and the political evangelism of the Rotterdam humanist. Francis I, on the contrary, was a Renaissance prince, for whom reason of State was all-important.

Charles, Duke of Burgundy from the proclamation of his coming of age in 1515 —the same year as that of Francis I, who had just succeeded Louis XII as king of France— won the battle of Marignano, and soon after became King of Castile and Aragon in 1516. A polite neutrality was established between the two young princes, both preoccupied by securing their inheritances, which was regulated by the treaties of Noyon in 1516 and Cambrai in 1517.

After the imperial election in 1519, however, the two men became permanently opposed to one another: "Though they were not at war, even so it could not be said that they were at peace."[2] The war begun in Italy came to an end with the disaster at Pavia in 1525 and the capture of Francis I. Some difficult negotiations resulted in the treaty of Madrid in January 1526, but to gain his freedom Francis I was forced to accept that his two sons should become hostages of Charles V. No sooner liberated, he went back on the undertakings he had given under constraint, which provoked the fury of Charles V and meant for the young princes a worsening of conditions in their captivity, despite the interventions of Charles V's wife and his sister Eleanor, who was affianced to Francis according to the terms of the treaty of Madrid.

Only the intervention of Louise of Savoy and Margaret of Austria achieved the Ladies' Peace in 1529 and the freeing of the young French princes through a very large ransom and the restitution of the Burgundian jewel, as well as the reliquary of the Fleur-de-Lys —later destroyed in the fire at the Alcazar in Madrid. On 7 July 1530 Francis I, widower of Claude of France since 1524, married Charles's sister Eleanor, herself the widow of the King of Portugal.

Nonetheless their relations underwent a further deterioration in 1536 with the French invasion of Savoy and Charles V's offensive speech in front of Pope Paul III, followed by Charles's dramatic devastation of Provence. The attempts at mediation by the papacy resulted in the truce of Nice in June 1538, concluded theoretically for ten years, but which only lasted for four.

This duel without quarter, however, had some periods of respite, sketchy attempts at agreement, brief moments propitious for diplomatic presents. If one omits the very temporary reconciliation in September 1525, when Charles V paid a visit to Francis I, gravely ill in his Madrid prison, the main improvement in relations occurred between the summer of 1538 and 1541.

Their interview at Aigues-Mortes,[3] the port from which St Louis had sailed on his crusades—the place had been chosen for its highly symbolic significance—owed nothing to pontifical mediation, but more to an impulsive act by Francis I who, scorning the rules of security, arrived at the encounter with Charles V accompanied by a limited escort on board a very small ship. The two princes "embraced each other standing on the poop deck", and Charles V could do no other than repay Francis's visit by going ashore. The emperor knelt and embraced the dauphin —an apology for the imprisonment he suffered from 1526 to 1530. The sumptuous banquet was followed by a surprise visit, organised by Queen Eleanor, for Francis I to proceed to the chamber of Charles V where exchanges of gifts and of the orders of the Golden Fleece and St Michael were made. It was to Queen Eleanor and her ally the constable of Montmorency that this sudden change of fortune was due.

The good relations established in 1538 persisted. At the end of 1539, Charles V was obliged to travel across the kingdom of France in order to check the uprising in his birthplace, Ghent.[4] It was not without hesitation that the land route had been chosen in preference to a sea voyage, considered to be more dangerous. Strict guarantees had been demanded of the King of France and his eventual successor the dauphin in order to avoid an attack on the emperor or pressures to force him to settle delicate matters like that of the Milanese duchy in a direction more favourable to France. Welcomed by Francis I's sons and the constable of Montmorency, Charles V, in mourning for his spouse who had died a few months earlier, made his way northwards with a reduced escort, splendidly received by the various towns through which he passed, Bayonne, Bordeaux, Poitiers and Loches, where on 12 December 1539 he met Francis I. The itinerary had been arranged so as to show the emperor the great artistic achievements of the realm: Chambord, Fontainebleau where Christmas was celebrated, the Louvre where Charles V was lodged in the pavilion of the Stoves—decorated for the occasion by Rosso and Le Primatice—and Chantilly. Thence he made his way through the northern towns towards Ghent, where he arrived on 14 February. The journey had taken three months. It was a great flourish of triumphal entries and festivities, of poems and songs that recalled that Charles V's mother tongue was French. Clément Marot provided several pieces including *L'Adieu de France à l'Empereur*. For the entry into Paris, Hugues Salel composed the famous *Chasse royale* that described the united efforts of the monarchs to overcome the wild boar of Discord. Claude Chappuis, who was also Francis I's librarian, offered his *Complainte de Mars*.

It appeared that the Spaniards had judged too severely the licence and disorder in the French court, and had been relieved to revisit the imperial lands. Francis I's undertaking not to bring up any political questions during the journey had been respected, and it was only after Charles V's crossing of the frontier that the negotiations were renewed, once more unsuccessfully, with a view to reaching an accommodation over the duchy of Milan.

In 1541 the assassination, on the orders of the imperial governor of the Milanese duchy, of two French ambassadors aroused the protestations of Francis I, who did not dare, however, to attack his rival during the expedition against Algiers. It was only on 12 July 1542 that war was solemnly declared. The dauphin and Annebault descended on Roussillon and Perpignan, while the Duke of Orleans and the Duke of Guise marched on Luxemburg. Francis I took the conflict to the heart of Germany in support of William of Juliers, Duke of Cleves, who had married Jeanne of Albret.

The brilliant French victory at Cérisoles on the Italian front on 14 April 1544 made scarcely any impact. It only served to limit the consequences of the second invasion of France by Charles V in Champagne and the threat of a revenge attack by the English.

The peace of Crépy on 18 September 1544, which set a provisional limit to the confrontation, was severely criticised by both camps. But its secret articles reveal a real reconciliation between the monarchs in the domain of religion and politics: Charles V agreed at last to bestow the title of Duke of Milan on Charles, the youngest son of Francis I, and the emperor received him in Brussels as a son. But the death of the young prince on 9 September 1545 put everything into question once more. The time had come for Henry VIII of England and Francis I to adopt a mutual anti-Habsburg strategy, based on the alliance with the protestant German princes (which Charles V would crush at Mühlberg in 1547). The death of Francis I in 1547 put a temporary end to the conflict which had lasted for more than twenty years.

Bookbinding in Paris 1540–47

It was in 1540 that there suddenly appeared on the Paris scene bindings of unheard-of luxury and refinement.[5] Up to then the Paris bindings with gold tooling were usually pale imitations of Italian bindings. In that year Robert Estienne presented to Francis I the dedication copy on vellum of his bible in large folio. Everything is stupefying in these two volumes: the morocco leather, then very novel in Paris; the adornments (one is covered with large gold motifs), totally original and different for each volume; and the dazzling richness of the whole effect.

At the same time three Parisian workshops, Picard, Roffet and the "Salel binder" started a production of great elegance, totally new and very carefully executed.

It was Jean Grolier (1489–1565), considered to be the first great bibliophile in France, who was the prime mover of this changeover. At first treasurer at Milan, he assembled there a collection of magnificently bound books. Sentenced later in Paris, he was imprisoned, and his first library was sold in 1536. Having recovered his freedom and his status, in 1540 Grolier ordered from his bookseller Jean Picard

Fig. 96
Volumes bound in Paris in the early 1540s with gilt titles on the spine, preserved in the Real Biblioteca del Monasterio de San Lorenzo de El Escorial

the first bindings of a long series (two hundred and fifty Picard bindings for Grolier are known today). Picard, or rather his gilder, reinvented himself ceaselessly, alternating sobriety and sophistication in structures both simple and complex. He showed a surprising capacity for innovation that often went hand in hand with perfect execution.

A little later, Francis I had begun a programme of binding, entrusted to Roffet, with less care for luxury and elegance (the bindings are in calf and never in morocco), while adopting gilded titles on the spines and not on the front like Grolier's. Roffet and his contemporary the Salel binder produced a certain number of deluxe or presentation volumes, principally for the king and his entourage. In their workshops, too, elegance and innovation are the rule.

A fourth workshop, inferior to the three principal ones, but very active, has been named "the Pecking Crow binder" after a frequently used tool. This binder also worked for several important personages.

The Eighteen Escorial Bindings

Returning to the Escorial and the copy of Budé in blue morocco from the "Chamber of Charles V" [fig. 97], we learned that this appellation did not refer to an attested provenance but was a recent bibliographical reconstruction. Yet the hypothesis of the Francis I–Charles V connection remained no less well founded. Our research at the Escorial[6] indeed allowed us to discover seventeen other volumes, very elegantly bound in Paris at the beginning of the 1540s, which lacked a mark of provenance. This group of eighteen volumes is extremely interesting for a number of reasons:

First, by dint of their luxury and elegance, they are close to the style Grolier was commissioning at the same time for his second library, with new tools, the frequent use of morocco, and adornments that vary from volume to volume.

Second, the author's name (accompanied by the title of the work if necessary) is gilded on the spines of the eighteen volumes [fig. 96]. At the start of the 1540s, as we have already stated, one single customer had made that choice: Francis I, for a set of books bound by Roffet between 1539 most probably and the beginning of 1541. According to T. Kimball Brooker, who has brilliantly studied that set,[7] there could be only one other example in French binding before 1547, the dedication copy for Francis I of Robert Estienne's 1538–40 bible, already cited. He adds that for Francis I himself this practice was abandoned in 1541. Third, the colours (white, shades of blue, citron, brown, bronze green and black) remained unchanged, or almost so.

Lastly these bindings, although they form a homogenous set, emerged from three different binderies: Picard, Roffet and Pecking Crow. We have divided the volumes into four groups. The first three correspond to the three workshops we have mentioned. For the fourth group, which we have called the "cocktail group", curiously the gilder has used tools belonging to all three workshops. Was there urgency to deliver all or part of these bindings?

Here is the list of the eighteen volumes, grouped by workshop:

97
illaume Budé, *Libri V de Asse*. Venetiis: in
ibus Aldi, et Andreae Asulani soceri, 1522.
nd in dark blue morocco. RBME, 177.IV.14

GROUP 1: PICARD

Budé, *De Asse*, Venice, 1522, 4º, darkish blue morocco [fig. 97].

Lucretius, *De Rerum naturæ*, Lyons, 1534, 8º, mid-blue morocco [fig. 98].

Cicero, *Orationum volumen primum*, Paris, 1538, 8º, darkish blue morocco [fig. 99].

Cicero, *Orationum volumen tertium*, Paris, 1532, 8º, darkish blue morocco [fig. 100].

Cicero, *Ad Atticum*, Paris, 1532, 8º, blue morocco [fig. 101].

Mantuanus, *Secunda pars Operum*, Paris (1507?), 8º, calf originally painted black (upper cover missing)

GROUP 2: ROFFET

Politian, *Opera*; *Alter tomus*, Lyons, 1536–37, 8º, 2 vols, deluxe white sheepskin [figs. 102 and 103].

Erasmus, *In Evangelium Matthæi Paraphrasis* ...; *Marci* ...; *Lucae* ..., Basle, 1540, 8º, 2 vols., deluxe white sheepskin.

Cyprianus, *Opera*, Lyons, 1537, 8º, calf originally painted black.

GROUP 3: PECKING CROW

Thomas Aquinas, *Principis ac sacre scripture*, Lyons, 1520, 8º, calf originally painted black [fig. 104].

GROUP 4 (COCKTAIL)

Quintilian, *Institutionum oratoriarum*, Lyons, 1536, 8º calf originally painted black [fig. 105].

Aulus Gellius, *Noctes atticæ*, Lyons, 1534, 8º, bronze green morocco [fig. 106].

Macrobius, *In Somnium Scipionis*, Lyons, 1532, 8º, bronze green morocco [fig. 107].

Cicero, *Rhetoricorum ... ad Herennium*, Paris, 1539, 8º, bronze green morocco [fig. 108].

Budé, *Annotatationes ... in ... Pandectarum*, Basle, 1534, 8º, very pale citron morocco [fig. 109].

Juvenal, *Satyræ*; Sannazar, *Opera omnia*, Lyons, 1538/1536, 8º, brown morocco [fig. 110].

Fig. 98
Titus Lucretius Carus, *De rerum natura libri VI*. Lugduni: apud Seb. Gryphium, 1534. Bound in mid-blue morocco. RBME, 16.V.31

Fig. 99
Marcus Tullius Cicero, *M. T. Ciceronis orationum: volumen primum*. Parisiis: apud Simonem Colinaeum, 1538. Bound in dark blue morocco. RBME, 63.IV.2

Fig. 100
Marcus Tullius Cicero, *M. T. Ciceronis orationum: volumen tertium*. Parisiis: apud Simone[m] Colinaeum, 1532. Bound in dark blue morocco. RBME, 63.IV.3

Fig. 101
Marcus Tullius Cicero, *M. Tullii Ciceronis ad Titum Pomponium Atticum, ad M. Brutum & ad Quintum fratrem, epistolaru[m] libri XX: diligentissime recogniti, cum latina eorum interpretatione, quae in iis ipsis epistolis graece scripta sunt ....* Parisiis: apud Simonem Colinaeum, 1532. Bound in blue morocco. RBME, 75.IV.3

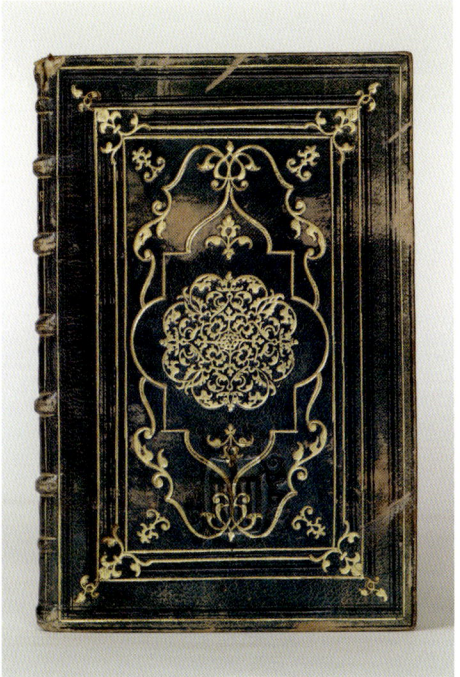

98

99

100

101

Figs. 102 and 103
Angelo Poliziano, *Opera* .... Lugduni: apud Seb. Gryphium, 1536–37, 3 tomes in 2 vols. Bound in white sheepskin with different gold ornamentation on each volume.
RBME, 37.VI.31–32

Fig. 104
Thomas Aquinas, *Principis ac sacre scripture sinceri interp[re]tis Commentarij in Soliloq[ui]a, sive hymnos davidicos* .... Lugdu[ni]: In edibus Jacobi myt: impensis Jacobi q. Fra[n]scici de giu[n]ta et sociorum florentinoru[m], 1520. Bound in calfskin originally painted black.
RBME, 177.V.11

A Gift, from Whom and for Whom?

If the peculiarity common to these bindings—the title gilded on the spine—necessarily points to the court of Francis I as the source of this order to the binders, the precise details of it remain unknown. It is extremely difficult to extrapolate from the printing dates of the volumes, since it is probable that these eighteen bindings represent only a part of a group that must have been considerably larger. The publication date of 1540 of several of the volumes rules out the idea that they were sent to Charles V after his journey through France. The gift is more likely to have been made in the following months, in 1540, 1541 or at the beginning of 1542 (as stated above, war would be officially declared on 12 July 1542).

The volumes have no armorial bearings, nor do they figure in any of the published inventories of the Spanish royal libraries.[8] Were they sent to Charles V personally? The choice of authors (Erasmus, Cicero, Latin poets

Fig. 105
Marcus Fabius Quintilianus, *Institutionum oratoriarum libri XII*. Lugduni: apud Seb. Gryphium, 1536. Bound in bronze green morocco. RBME, 80.IV.1

Fig. 106
Aulus Gellius, *Noctes Atticae*. Lugduni: apud Seb. Gryphium, 1534. Bound in bronze green morocco. RBME, 56.IV.22

Fig. 107
Ambrosius Aurelius Theodosius Macrobius, *In Somnium Scipionis libri II; Saturnaliorum libri VII*. Excud. Lugd.: Seb. Gryphius Germ., 1532. Bound in bronze green morocco. RBME, 56.IV.23

Fig. 108
Marcus Tullius Cicero, *M. Tullij Ciceronis Rhetoricorum libri quatuor ad Herennium*. Parisiis: ex officina Simonis Colinaei, 1539. Bound in bronze green morocco. RBME, 80.IV.5

Fig. 109
Guillaume Budé, *Annotationes Gulielmi Budaei ... in quatuor & viginti Pandectarum libros...: per autore[m] diligentissime recognitae & auctae*. Basileae: apud Thomam Volffium, 1534. Bound in citron morocco. RBME, 74.IV.10

Fig. 110
Decius Junius Juvenal, *Satyrae iam recens recognitae, simul ac adnotatiunculis, quae breuis commentarij uice esse possint, illustratae*. Lugduni: apud Seb. Gryphium, 1538; Iacopo Sannazaro, *Opera omnia ...*. Lugduni: apud Seb. Gryphium, 1536. Bound in brown morocco. RBME, 17.V.1

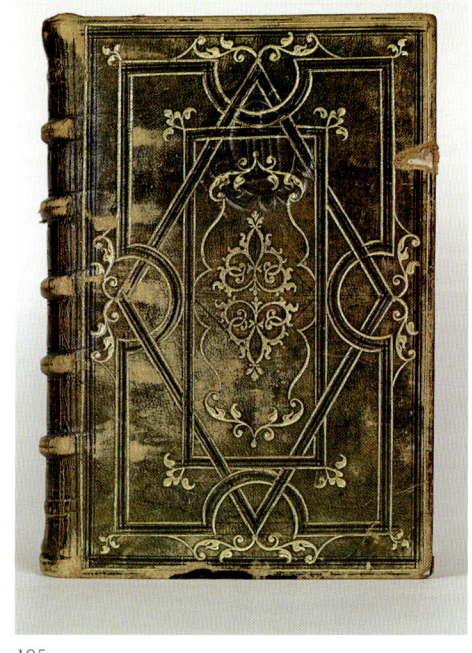

105

108

106

107

109

110

and neo-Latin Christian poets like Sannazar) leads us to associate these volumes with the intellectual programme established at the same time for the future Philip II. Charles V had received an upbringing more medieval than humanistic. He took care to give his son, entrusted after the death of his mother in 1539 to various tutors, of whom the principal one was Calvete de Estrella, an education more in line with the spirit of the Renaissance.[9]

According to this hypothesis, it is very likely that the designer of this small library, bound in Paris for the young Prince Philip, was not the king but rather his wife Eleanor, "my favourite sister" as Charles V called her.[10] The eldest of the six children of Philip the Fair and Joan of Castile, she had been brought up at Malines by their aunt Margaret of Austria. A cultivated princess, Latinist, musician and singer, she was also a huntress and a dancer with equal distinction and was, in spite of the friendship her brother bore for her, used unsparingly by him as a pawn in his matrimonial politicking. Despite having been widowed as the result of her brief marriage to King Manuel of Portugal, she never obtained the right to marry her admirer, the Count Palatine Frederick II. Engaged to Francis I in January 1526, she had to wait until July 1530 to marry the King of France. A fastidious princess, conscious of her rank, her solemn entrance into Paris and her coronation were described in a famous book printed by Geoffroy Tory.[11]

If her husband scarcely loved her, they seemed to have shared the same interests in art and book collections. Her relations with Portugal allowed her to procure exotica and objects of mother-of-pearl for Francis I's cabinet of curiosities. Her letters to her sister, Mary of Hungary, who visited her in 1538, are a mine of information about the artistic and architectural enterprises of the French court. She had little influence in politics, except just at the moment of the rapprochement between years 1538 and 1540. That would be once more the case after the treaty of Crépy; Eleanor paid an official visit to the court at Brussels where she made a triumphal entry on 22 October 1544.

There is a last possibility: could the bindings that concern us have been carried out for Eleanor? After the death of Francis I she withdrew to the Brussels court of her sister Mary of Hungary, where, possessing a very large fortune, she devoted herself to the patronage of those arts she particularly appreciated: portraiture (cf. Anthonis Mor's portrait of her preserved in the convent of the Descalzas Reales in Madrid, inv. PN 00612060), goldsmithery, tapestry and books (illuminated manuscripts and editions of books of devotion in Spanish by Nutius of Antwerp in the 1550s). The two sisters, Mary and Eleanor, retired to Spain with Charles V in 1556, where Eleanor died on 18 February 1558. Her only daughter, who stayed in Portugal, inherited her collections, but it seems very unlikely that the eighteen Escorial bindings had belonged to her.

Our hypothesis, therefore, is that they were presented by Francis I or by Queen Eleanor to Charles V for the education of Prince Philip after the journey he made from 1539 to 1540, and before the resumption of hostilities in July 1542. Nevertheless the gift could yet be dated to the brief rapprochement that followed the peace of Crépy.

A Binding by the Great Gilder

At the start of our research in the Escorial we were expecting to find bindings dating to the years following the peace of Cateau-Cambrésis (1559) and the marriage of Elizabeth, daughter of Henry II and Catherine of Medici, to Philip II. Without imagining it in the least, we came across some presents from the time of Francis I, and two extraordinary French bindings from the third quarter of the sixteenth century, pointed out by Spanish researchers but still unknown in France: the Paulus Jovius and the Baïf of Philip II.

The first, a magnificent binding splendidly adorned with the arms of King Philip I and Queen Mary I of England, is comparable to the finest bindings executed for Henry II, Francis I's son and successor. It covers a copy of the original edition, published at Lyons by Guillaume Rouille in two tomes that appeared successively in 1552 and 1555, of the French translation of Paulus Jovius's *Histories* by Denys Sauvage, the royal historiographer [fig. 111].[12] The work recounts the historic and diplomatic events that occurred from 1494 to 1547, and deals mainly with the Italian wars and the relations between France and Italy. The bicolour binding—citron morocco and black paint—offers a particularly spectacular decoration, spread over the entire cover, with ribbons and ringlets around a central cartouche left blank. The arms of Philip are painted on the upper field, those of Mary Tudor on the lower. Both tomes are bound in one very thick volume, the spine is wide enough to carry a decoration matching that of the two fields, particularly well executed. The ensemble constitutes one of the finest specimens of Parisian binding in the reign of Henry II.

Bookbinding in Paris 1547–59

Francis I died in March 1547, three years after having launched the creation of the royal library at Fontainebleau and a great bookbinding venture. Henry II was less interested in books than his father, but, somewhat despite himself, he was to dominate that second period, while Grolier, who seemed to be less anxious to augment his library, was rivalled by his protégé Thomas Mahieu. The creation of the Fontainebleau library was almost finished in 1552[13] and it was essentially the books accessed from that year which gained for Henry II the reputation of being the greatest owner of deluxe bindings who had ever existed in France. Indeed, it was a small number of magnificently adorned bindings, commissioned by the royal library between 1552 and 1559, to which should be added the bindings of some copies dedicated to Henry II. For these bindings the inventive power of the decorator, who seemed to have a magical touch, was as dazzling as the work of the gilder.

Gommar Estienne, appointed binder to the king in 1547 and presumed creator of all Henry II's bindings, is considered the great craftsman of the reign. But the true artist was the prodigious gilder who worked for him, traditionally known as the Great Gilder of Henry II. Rather strangely, only twenty-six bindings are identified today as having been executed by Gommar Estienne for Grolier, although Thomas Mahieu had given him much more work to do: the majority of the covers commissioned by Mahieu and dating from around 1550 to 1560 are by him. On them can be made out Mahieu's first device, or the famous complex monogram brilliantly deciphered by Nixon, which contains his name and the same motto.

Another very active workshop (*c.* 1548–56), that of the Cupid's Bow binder—thus named after an emblematic tool—also worked for Grolier (at least fifty bindings) and for many other collectors. But, with very few exceptions, its output is inferior to that of Gommar Estienne. We shall refer to it in the following chapter concerning Plantin.

Let us return to the Paulus Jovius volume, about which the same question can be posed as for the Roffet-Picard bindings of the 1540s: how could such a gift have been made at a time when the two countries were at war?

Diplomatic Relations, Second Period: Charles V, Later Philip II, against Henry II, 1547–59

The veiled hostility of 1547–51 was followed by open conflict. The political edifice built by Charles V rapidly broke down between 1552 and 1555, when all his adversaries (France, the sultan, the Barbary pirates, the German protestant princes) were united at the instigation of Henry II, who did not forgive the emperor for his four years of imprisonment in Castile. The King of France conducted an aggressive policy, the principal purpose of which was to install a French prince on the ducal throne of Milan.

In April 1552, as part of the German expedition, the French king occupied the three bishoprics of Toul, Metz and Verdun. Charles V, cut off at Innsbruck, only saved his skin by means of a humiliating flight. He gathered an immense army and in October began the siege of Metz, where Francis of Guise was trapped—an irredeemable mistake reminiscent of the siege of Nancy that had proved fatal to Charles the Bold. The siege was lifted in December, and a discredited Charles took refuge in Brussels wrapped in melancholy.

The military campaigns of the two following years, 1553 and 1554, conducted in different theatres (Italy, Corsica, the frontiers of France and of the Empire) did not prove decisive. But Charles V's real master-stroke was diplomatic, with the marriage of his son Philip to Mary Tudor, Queen of England, in July 1554.

Nevertheless the beginning of a dialogue existed alongside the hostilities, notably through the mediation of England. The French ambassador in London, Antoine de Noailles, and his brother Francis offered themselves to Mary Tudor and her king consort as mediators. Queen Mary, with Charles V's agreement, accepted their role in January 1555. The first round of negotiations at the La Marck conference ended in failure.[14]

Fig. 111
Paulus Jovius, *Histoires de Paolo Iovio ... sur les choses faictes et auenues de son temps en toutes les parties du monde*. À Lion: chez Guillaume Rouille ..., 1552–55. Bound in citron morocco with black paint, with the arms of Philip II and Mary Tudor. RBME, 40.I.13

The military impotence shown in the campaign that followed and the exhaustion of the opposing armies led to a second attempt to make peace: Francis of Noailles crossed the Channel once more in June 1555 and remained in London until mid-August, pressed by Mary I and Philip I of England—impatient to disengage from his father's policy—to obtain instructions that would permit the start of fresh negotiations.

The meetings that were held from December 1555 to February 1556 resulted in the treaty of Vaucelles, which was more favourable to Henry II. While the details were being worked out, Philip left London for Brussels where the complex transfer of powers was taking place: Charles V ceded the Low Countries to Philip on 25 October (but the very Spanish prince was unable to utter the few words in French that his Flemish subjects expected). On 16 January 1556 it was the turn of the Spanish kingdoms to be transferred to him, making him Philip II of Spain.

One of the most delicate points to be settled after the negotiations at Vaucelles was the fate of the great lords who were prisoners of war (the constable of Montmorency's son, d'Andelot, Villars, Silly and La Marck on the French side, and the Duke of Arschot and Mansfield on the imperial side). This matter of the exchange of prisoners also led to a glorious episode in the history of Parisian bookbinding.

The Duke of Arschot, Philip III of Croy (1526–1595), was captured by the French in 1553 after a skirmish and imprisoned at Vincennes, whence he managed to escape in May 1556. There are extant three French bindings produced for him during his captivity, all dated 1555, which bear his monogram and mottos (including "Jy parviendray, Croy"), the first preserved in the Pierpoint Morgan Library, the two others in private hands.[15] We can add to these three a fourth uncatalogued binding, found by us in the Vatican library, which also bears the date 1555 and the Croy devices.[16]

The second distinguished prisoner from the imperial side, Count Ernest de Mansfield (1517–1604), who formed part of Charles V's escort from the time of the journey to Ghent in 1540, was captured in 1552, imprisoned at Vincennes and only released in 1557. He was quite harshly treated on the orders of the constable of Montmorency, who wanted his own son to be handed over. His journal reveals that he spent his time in captivity reading, and no fewer than twenty-two bindings are known to have been executed for him in Paris,[17] which bear his motto "Force m'est trop" and a marguerite and constitute a splendid ensemble of Parisian bindings.

Howard Nixon, the great historian of bookbinding, has turned this episode into the theme of his introduction to the catalogue of sixteenth-century bindings in the Pierpoint Morgan library. He imagines himself transported back to Vincennes in 1554, present at a meeting between the commissioners of bindings in that period: the two prisoners, their gaoler the constable of Montmorency, and their visitors, the cardinal of Lorraine and the two Farnese princes, at that time the presumed commissioners of the Grimaldi bindings. Only missing from that meeting was Granvelle, fierce enemy of France except in the domain of bookbinding, and surely Grolier too!

Let us return to our survey of diplomatic relations, in search of possible lulls propitious for the exchange of gifts. The truce of Vaucelles was contested too quickly by the warmongers in both camps. On assuming full power, Philip II changed his attitude and desired to resume hostilities. The conflict began once more, and a new balance was imposed in 1557–58 by force of arms, a last tragic episode that would be brought to a conclusion in 1559, paradoxically by the most durable accord of the sixteenth century. The battle of St Quentin (10 August 1557) saw the triumph of the Spanish monarchy, leaving France open to attack and Paris ill-protected. Henry II's prestige —and credit—collapsed. He succeeded however in recovering himself, and a risky campaign by the Duke of Guise allowed him to capture Calais in January 1558. He negotiated the marriage of Mary Stuart to the dauphin and thus saved face. In 1558 the military successes (Thionville, the battle of the Dunes) restored the balance. The two great armies confronted one another all that summer without undertaking more than skirmishes: the time had come to make peace.

At the end of a diplomatic marathon— temporarily interrupted by the death of Mary Tudor on 17 November 1558—which lasted for four months in two successive venues (Cercamp from October to November 1558, then Le Cateau-Cambrésis from February to April 1559), the final agreement was reached at the cost of important concessions by France and opened the way to reconciliation. The peace of Cateau-Cambrésis confirmed the treaty of Cambrai and the renunciation of the duchy of Burgundy by the heir to its ancient dukes, at the same time putting an end to the Italian ambitions of the kings of France.

The tragic grandeur of the withdrawal of Charles V (his departure for Yuste took place in September 1556) was celebrated in France as a victory. He died there on 21 September 1558.

Just at that moment, could the Paulus Jovius have been presented as a gift, between June 1555 (date of the dedication) and November 1558 (date of Mary Tudor's death)? Stylistically the binding seems to be closer to Vaucelles than to Cercamp, to the 1555–56 negotiations than to those of the autumn of 1558. The respites were too short for the binding to have been carried to England by François de Noailles in June 1555. The most probable moment was during the negotiations leading to the truce of Vaucelles, for which the support of Mary I and her husband Philip I of England were actively sought. The Bibliotèque nationale of France, inheritor of the Bibliotèque Royale at Fontainebleau, does not possess a royal copy of the Paulus Jovius edition, although it was dedicated to Catherine of Medici and Margaret of Berry, sister of Henry II. Could the copy sent to Philip and Mary have been the gift copy intended for Henry II, delivered without having yet had the gilded arms of the French sovereign applied to its cover, then reconverted or "recycled", given the urgent need for a diplomatic gift?

The Baïf Copy Bound in Red Morocco with the Fanfare Decoration, Presented to Philip II in 1573

The natural son of a great ambassador, Lazare de Baïf, by a Venetian lady, Jean Antoine de Baïf (1532–1589) received a very carefully designed humanistic education, ending his studies in the humanities under Jean Dorat together with Ronsard and du Bellay. He was one of the prominent members of the Pléiade in the poetic domain (his *Amours* in 1552 and his *Amours de Francine* in 1555) and in the theatre (*Le Brave*, an adaptation of Plautus's *Miles gloriosus*, 1567, a version composed in alexandrines of Sophocles's *Antigone*, and an adaptation of Terence's *Eunuch*). He attempted to unite poetry and music in an honourable restoration of classical prosody. This project entranced Charles IX, who allowed Baïf and his friend the musician Thibault de Courville to found the Academy of Poetry and Music in 1570. It was above all at the court of Charles IX that Baïf enjoyed increasing favour. He also assumed the task of reassembling his earlier work in a collected edition, the *Œuvres en rime*, published in Paris between 1572 and 1573. Dedicated to Charles IX, the compilation contains nine books of *Poèmes*, nine books of *Amours*, five books of *Jeux* (comedies, tragedies) and five books of *Passe-temps* (short pieces, epigrams, occasional verses). It was therefore at the moment of his highest favour at the French court that Baïf decided to offer to the potentates of that world copies of his publication, in very luxurious bindings accompanied by presentational epistles calligraphed on vellum.

José Luis Sánchez-Molero,[18] who discovered this copy [fig. 112], has studied the dedicatory sonnet and has also established the circumstances of the gift, passed on in June 1573 by Philip II to Gabriel de Zayas, thence to Antonio Gracián the king's secretary, who recorded the gift in his journal on 23 June. The calligraphic *envoi*, which heads the beginning of the printed dedication to the king, recalls that Baïf was registered in his father the ambassador's lineage: "Filippo Hispaniarum Regi Catolico Ianus Antonius Baifus Lazari Filius DD."

Fig. 112
Jean-Antoine de Baïf, *Euvres en rime*. A Paris: pour Lucas Breyer ..., 1572–73. 4 vols. Bound in red morocco. RBME, Mesa 5.II.11–14

These four magnificent volumes had arrived in Spain by diplomatic courier and it was the French ambassador in Madrid, Jean de Vivonne, who had them sent on to Zayas. Yet their reception was lukewarm. The policy of closure and the atrocities of the St Bartholomew's Day massacre—August 1572—gave way at the French court to a more tolerant attitude towards the Huguenots, a tendency which Spain deplored.

Baïf also sent a copy of his *Euvres en rime* to Catherine de Medici, and the following year he sent his *Étrenes de poezie fransoeze* to the emperor Maximilian II. For these three presentation copies Baïf ordered superb fanfare bindings at one of the best workshops of that time, which G.D. Hobson has called the Plumed Heart, after a frequently used tool.[19] The fanfare decoration that began about 1568—and named thus after a pastiche executed for Charles Nodier by his binder Thouvenin in 1829—remained the dominant decoration up to the middle of the seventeenth century.

II
The Plantin Bindings Preserved at El Escorial: from Antwerp or Paris?

Plantin as Binder[20]

The most famous printer in the Low Countries, Christopher Plantin (1520–1589) was of French origin and settled in Antwerp, the real economic capital of Charles V's empire, in 1548 or 1549. According to his own account, he first worked as a binder, but abandoned that craft in 1555, as the result of an accident, in favour of printing:

> J'ay le metier eleu
> Qui m'a nourri en liant des volumes
> L'estoc receu après m'a emeu
> De les escrire a la presse sans plumes.[21]

The same version appears in an earlier text, *l'Ode à Philippe II* (the copy is dedicated to Philip II, in a binding on which we shall comment later) discovered in 1965 at the Escorial), in which he boasts of having been encouraged to compose "some little verses" to the glory of Philip II, then "in a few days, in the same hand, write them, print them and bind them".

This testimony was confirmed by his descendants in 1604 (see below). It is also attested by various contemporary accounts, among them one by the humanist Juan Martín Cordero. He relates, thirty years after the events, that he commissioned a binding from Plantin to present to Mary Tudor on a copy of his translation of Vida's *Christiade* (Antwerp, Martin Nucio, 1554) "because he was from Paris and a very clever binder". Various records and documents from the archives dating from 1552 to 1554, in which Plantin is named as "lyeur des livres et merchant, bourgeois manant de la ville d'Anvers" [bookbinder and merchant, a citizen from the town of Antwerp], all lead to the same conclusion.

The contrast between the abundance of accounts that attest to his business and his training as a binder (Plantin had been apprenticed to a bookseller in Caen, to Robert Macé II, who was probably above all a binder) and the absence of typical bindings on the books that emerged from his presses, intrigued researchers for a long time, up to the studies by Rudbeck in 1914. It was he who proposed the attribution to Plantin of two bindings with gilt and painted decoration (a volume of Seneca's *Flores* of 1555 and a copy of the book by Calvete de Estrella, Philip II's tutor, recounting the journeys of his royal pupil in Italy and Germany between 1548 and 1551, *El felicissimo viaje*, 1552). Later, in 1937, Vanheyden "provided the demonstration that was wanting", by adding to that attribution the bindings of two presentation copies, one to Charles V, the other to Philip II, of a book dedicated to the glory of Charles V, translated into Latin by a Flemish author and printed at Antwerp in 1550.

Several successive studies, following the intuitions of Rudbeck and Vanheyden, have permitted the establishment of a list, based on the identification of the gilding work, which today amounts to fifty-one bindings. The most important publications after those of Ilse Schunke, who identified fifteen new bindings, being those of Georges Colin, who then alone with the great English specialist Howard Nixon appears in the seminal article published in the *Studia Bibliographica in honorem Herman de la Fontaine Verwey* in 1966. In that study Colin and Nixon proposed to add to the twenty-four bindings already attributed to Plantin eighteen new ones, of which nine were discovered at the Escorial. These covers, in order not to break the numeration established in the earlier studies, were numbered in the order of their discovery from 1 to 42. A regrouping by types of decoration, and above all by the date and place of the edition, permitted the authors to pronounce their conclusion: all these bindings had been executed by Plantin the binder before he had renounced that craft to take up printing.

The few studies that have appeared since 1966 have not materially affected the picture. Colin, in the volume of studies presented to Nixon in 1975, brought to light nine new entries, numbered 43 to 51.[22] In another article that appeared in 1990 he underlined the great importance of the settings of the Spanish court in the dedications and the recipients of the presentations copies bound by Plantin (Charles V and Philip II, Granvelle, but also le Croy Duke of Arschot, whom we mentioned in the preceding section, and the secretary of State Gonzalo Pérez), and he concentrated especially on the later period (after 1564) for which detailed account-books have survived.[23] Finally, the exhibition at the Plantin Museum in 2005 mounted for the first time a combined display of many of these bindings.[24]

An Enigmatic Binder

Thus according to Colin and Nixon (henceforth cited as CN) a group of fifty-one bindings are likely to have been executed by Plantin himself at Antwerp between 1549 and 1556, but this hypothesis may be placed in doubt. We propose a different scenario, in three phases which correspond to three groups (A, B and C).

GROUP A (1549–55): A PARISIAN BINDERY

CN 28 Ariosto, Urrea, *Orlando furioso*, Antwerp, 1549; copy dedicated to Prince Philip, with an added sheet [fig. 117].

CN 29 Tarafa, *De origine, ac rebus gestis Regum Hispaniæ liber*, Antwerp, 1553; presentation copy with the arms of Spain painted on the front cover [figs. 113 and 114].

CN 30 *Rerum à Carolo V*, Antwerp, 1554: assumed to be Prince Philip's copy [fig. 115].

CN 31 Jover, *Sanctiones ecclesiasticæ*, Paris, 1555; dedication copy with added sheet painted with the arms of Philip and Mary Tudor [fig. 11].

CN 32, Juan de Mena, *Las Trezientas*, Antwerp; gift copy to Gonzalo Pérez.

CN 33 Bruto, *De rebus a Carolo V*, Antwerp, 1555; copy dedicated to Prince Philip with gilded inscription [fig. 116].

We link to this group A from the Escorial the following bindings from the Colin-Nixon list; we have included only those we have personally examined or those of which we have been able to examine a reproduction of sufficient quality: 2, 3, 4, 6, 7, 8, 12, 14, 15, 18, 19, 20, 21, 37 and 43.

Fig. 115
Rerum à Carolo V Caesare Augusto in Africa bello gestarum commentarij: elegantissimis iconibus ad historiam accommodis illustrati ... Antuerpiae: apud Ioan. Bellerum ..., 1554. RBME, 40.VI.18

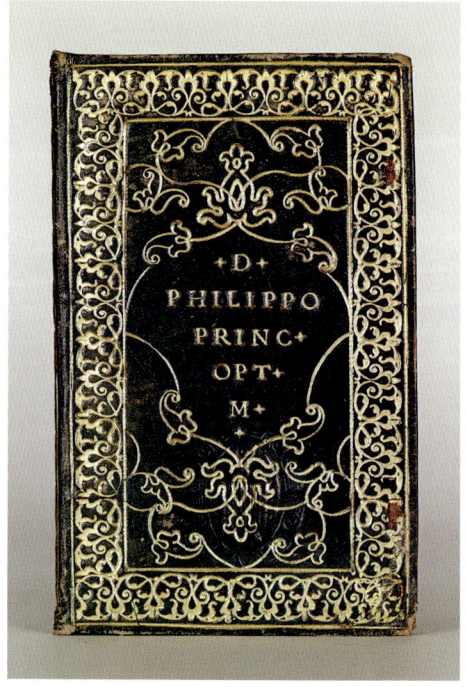

Fig. 116
Gian Michele Bruto, *De rebus a Carolo V Caesare Romanorum Imperatore gestis, Ioannis Michaëlis Bruti oratio.* Antuerpiae: apud Ioannem Bellerum ..., 1555. Bound in blue morocco. RBME, 39.VI.12

PREVIOUS PAGES

Figs. 113 and 114
Francisco Tarafa, *De origine ac rebus gestis Regum Hispaniae liber, multarum rerum cognitione refertus.* Antuerpiae: in aedibus Ioannis Steelsij, 1553. Illuminated binding with the royal coat of arms (back and front covers). RBME, 40.VI.13

Fig. 117
Ludovico Ariosto, *Orlando furioso: dirigido al Principe Don Philipe nuestro Señor / traduzido en romance castellano por Don Ieronymo de Vrrea.* Imprimiose en ... Anuers: en casa de Martin Nucio, 1549. RBME, 30.V.24

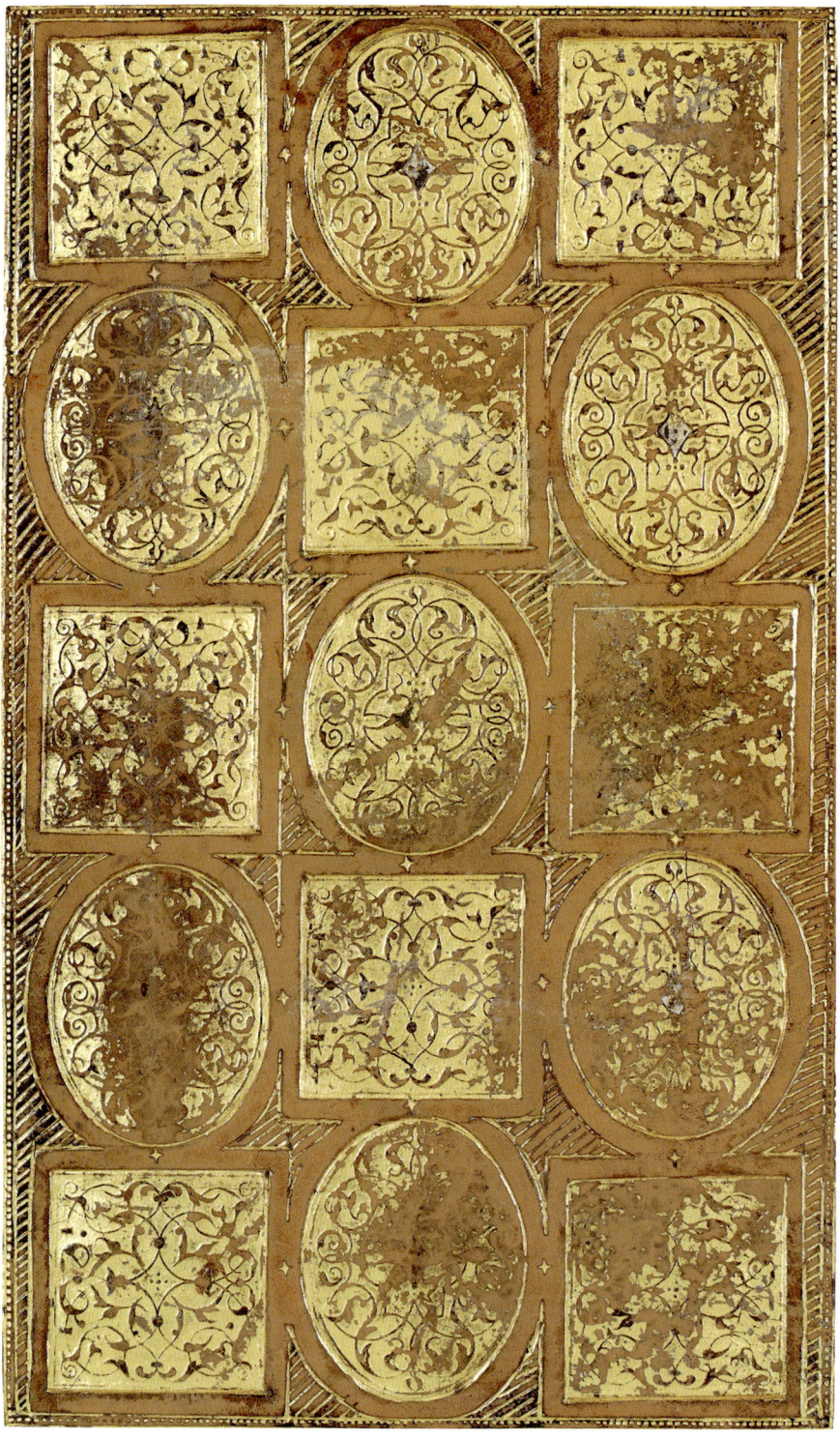

GROUP B (END OF 1555–56): THE ANTWERP
WORKSHOP I. THE APPEARANCE OF STAMPS

CN 25 Plantin, *Ode à Philippe II*, Antwerp, 1556; dedication copy [fig. 119].

CN 27 Calvete de Estrella, *Felicíssimo viaje*, Antwerp 1552; binding commissioned in 1556 by the author, who may have presented this copy to Gonzalo Pérez, most of whose books were accessed at the Escorial library in 1571 [fig. 118].

We attach to group B from the Escorial three bindings that are in the Colin-Nixon list, as well as another uncatalogued volume.

CN 26 Dioscorides, *Acerca de la materia medicinal*, Antwerp, 1555; a copy dedicated to prince Philip, printed on vellum and illuminated.

CN 51 Dioscorides, *Acerca de la material medicinal*, Antwerp, 1555; presentation copy to Gonzalo Pérez, very probably bound after February 1556, the month when Pérez was appointed Secretary of State by Philip II.

CN 22 Biesius, *De Republica libri IV*, Antwerp, 1556; presentation copy for cardinal Granvelle.

Calvete de Estrella, *Felicíssimo viaje*, Antwerp, 1552: presentation copy to Federico Badoer, Venetian ambassador to the court of Charles V and then of Philip II, with a gilt inscription dated 1556 (private collection).

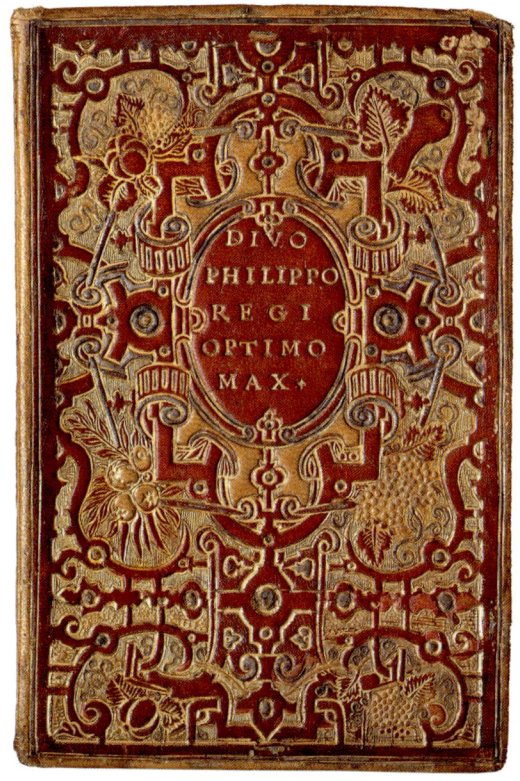

Fig. 119
Cristopher Plantin, *Ode au trespuissant et serenissime Prince Philippe II ... Colit ardua virtus*. [Antuerpiae: Christophe Plantin, 1556]. Bound by Christopher Plantin.
RBME, Mesa 9.II.6

Fig. 118
Juan Cristóbal Calvete de Estrella, *El felicissimo viaie del muy alto y muy Poderoso Principe Don Phelippe, Hijo d'el Emperador Don Carlos Quinto Maximo, desde España à sus tierras dela baxa Alemaña, con la descripcion de todos los Estados de Brabante y Flandes / escrito en quatro libros por Iuan Christoual Caluete de Estrella ....* En Anuers: en casa de Martin Nucio, 1552. RBME, 34.I.

GROUP C (1557–58): THE ANTWERP BINDERY 2. THE TOOLS OF THE CUPID'S BOW WORKSHOP

This group brings together six bindings from the Escorial that do not figure in the Colin-Nixon list.

Pannormia seu Decretum ..., Louvain, 1557; copy dedicated to Philip II [fig. 122].

Cordero, *Los siete libros de Flauio Josefo*, Antwerp, 1557; copy dedicated to Philip II with painted coat of arms: his on the front cover, Mary Tudor's on the back [fig. 123].

Goltz, *Vivae omnium*, Antwerp, 1557; copy dedicated to Philip II with his coat of arms painted on the front cover [fig. 120].

Orozco, *Ad responsa prudentum commentarij*, Salamanca 1558; copy dedicated to Philip II with his coat of arms painted on the front cover and an inscription gilded on the back [fig. 121].

Fazello, *De rebus Siculis decades duae*, Palermo, May 1558; copy dedicated to Philip II with his coat of arms and those of Mary Tudor painted on the front cover [fig. 124].

Agylaeus, *Quae in novellis* ..., Cologne, 1558; copy dedicated to Philip II.

Group C also contains two other bindings from the Escorial on later Plantin printings (1590 and 1595), for the decoration of which the Cupid's Bow tools were employed, still in use at that date in an Antwerp bindery.

Hopper, *Seduardus, sive de vera jurisprudentia*, Antwerp, 1590; copy dedicated to Philip II.

Bochius, *Descriptio publicae gratulationis*, Antwerp, 1595; presentation copy to Philip II.

Fig. 120
Hubertus Goltzius, *Viuae omnium fere imperatorum imagines a C. Iulio Caes. vsque ad Carolum V et Ferdinandum eius fratrem ex antiquis veterum numismatis solertissime, non vt olim ab aliis, sed vere ac fideliter adumbratae, necnon eorundem vitae, acta, mores, virtutes, vitia, suis coloribus historico penicillo delineatae* .... Excus. Antuerpiae: cura & aere Huberti Goltz ...: in officina Aegidij Copenij ..., 1557. Binding with the painted royal coat of arms. RBME, 40.IV.5

Fig. 121
Juan de Orozco, *Ad responsa prudentum commentarij*. Salmanticae: in aedibus Andreae Portonariis ..., 1558. Binding with the illuminated royal coat of arms. RBME, 32.IV.1

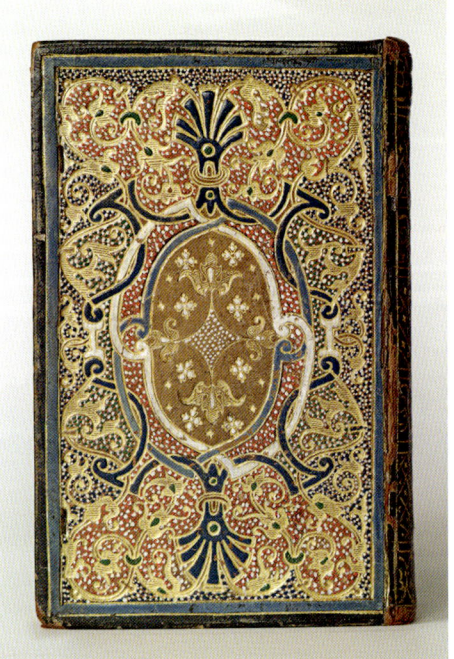

Fig. 122
Ivo, bishop of Chartres, *Pannormia, seu Decretum, D. Iuonis Carnothensis episcopi restitutu[m], correctum, & emendatum / opera & diligentia Melchioris à Vosmediano* .... Louanii: ex officina Antonij Maria Bergagne ..., 1557. RBME, 25.VI.20

Fig. 123
Flavius Josephus, *Los siete libros de Flauio Iosefo los quales contienen las guerras de los Iudios, y la destrucion de Hierusalem y d'el templo / traduzidos agora nueuamente segun la verdad de la historia por Iuan Martin Cordero* .... En Anuers: en casa de Martin Nucio ..., 1557. Binding with the painted royal coat of arms. RBME, 33.V.17

Here we set out our objections to the conclusions of Colin and Nixon. Some forty volumes in their list certainly constitute a very homogenous group (Antwerp printings, Spanish authors, Spanish dedicatees or owners, similar decorative style), but the presence of others is harder to explain, or cannot be explained at all. The binding most evidently foreign to this homogenous group is the one that bears the device and emblems of Henry II, preserved in Oxford (CN 41).[25]

It covers a book of hours printed in 1549 by Regnauld and Claude Chaudière. It is unprecedented and furthermore totally improbable that a book printed in Paris and meant for Henry II should have been sent abroad to be bound. And even more unlikely in view of the absolute evidence that the copy was presented to the king by Chaudière. The elegant and skilfully designed decoration includes two wide bows and an emblem; it also bears eight impressions of the small Cupid's

Fig. 124
Tommaso Fazello, *De rebus Siculis decades duae* ....
Panormi: ex officina Ioannis Matthaei Maydae,
1558. Bound in green and red morocco.
RBME, 60.IX.13

Bow tool after which the workshop that possessed it has been named.

This Cupid's Bow tool, present on the binding of the Hours belonging to Henry II, was used in Paris up to 1556, and could not in any event have been found in Antwerp in 1549. This binding therefore belongs to the Parisian Cupid's Bow workshop or to another very near to it, and has nothing to do with Plantin. The other thirteen tools used on the Henry II binding are likewise Parisian. This last point is crucial because many of them were used frequently or very frequently on the bindings listed in our group A.

From what is known of Plantin's beginnings (attestations and indications that tally with one another), he was a binder but not a gilder. These are two completely different skills. It is possible that Plantin himself bound all or part of the fifty-one volumes, at least up to the time of his accident (which probably occurred at the end of 1554 or the beginning of 1555). It seems impossible on the other hand that he would have been capable of carrying out with his own hands the very elaborate gilt decorations in the period from 1549 to 1555 (our group A). The know-how essential for a good gilder takes a long time to acquire. And Plantin's stay in Paris was very short indeed. Nonetheless he may have learned to gild some "boxes and coffrets" covered in calf or morocco, such as those alluded to by Balthasar Moretus in a letter of 1604: "When the late Christopher Plantin arrived in Antwerp in 1549, he was engaged at first in binding books and in making boxes and coffrets which he covered in leather and gilded, and which he incrusted with leather patches of many colours with remarkable skill."

Since no one in Antwerp was capable of gilding bindings in the Parisian manner, Plantin had only two options: to have recourse to a Paris bindery, or to send to a Parisian gilder books previously bound in Antwerp. It is therefore reasonable to suggest that all the bindings in group A were decorated in Paris by the Cupid's Bow binder, the work of the binding proper having possibly been carried out in Antwerp by Plantin himself (prior to the accident in 1554 or 1555), or under his supervision.

The only binding certainly executed by Plantin is the cover (group B) of his *Ode à Philippe II* of 28 January 1556 (some verses of his own invention in which he states that he was able "in a few days, with his own hand, to write, print and bind them") [fig. 119]. The decoration consisted of a very strange panel-stamped design that is asymmetric and clumsy, the antithesis of Parisian taste, and appears to be the result of an accumulation of elements resembling nothing at all. There is such a complete divide between the decoration of the bindings in group A and that of the cover of the *Ode* that it is very difficult to believe that the same workshop could have produced them. It must have been an improvisation of Plantin himself who, probably in a hurry to send his masterpiece to Philip II, had no other solution to hand. Some very similar stamped designs appeared at the same time on four bindings of the same group B. These were probably intended for some other use: the décor of gilded "boxes and coffrets" which was Plantin's speciality.

Plantin was better inspired (but perhaps he was following the instructions of the customer) when he executed, on a copy of the *Viaje* probably intended for Pérez [fig. 118], a highly ingenious semé pattern on two small, very elegant stamps, one of which also adorns the *Ode*.

In 1557 and 1558, in a dramatic turn of events, the Antwerp workshop produced six remarkable bindings (our group C) whose decoration featured two Parisian tools employed on the "Plantin" bindings in group A, as well as some new tools that formed part of the Cupid's Bow bindery. These bindings, decorated by a competent gilder, were not taken into account by Colin and Nixon.[26] On the other hand, they did study two bindings (on Plantin printings) executed nearly forty years later, on which the decoration includes some tools from the same sources. Nixon very correctly concluded that the Parisian Cupid's Bow workshop had ceased to exist, probably in 1556, and that part of its tools had turned up in Antwerp.

For our part we are convinced that the six uncatalogued bindings in the Escorial were executed in an Antwerp workshop belonging to Plantin or patronised by him.

We end this section with an extraordinary binding, without a cover on the spine, which is certainly Parisian and which covers the dedication copy to Philip II of a work printed in Barcelona in 1561 by Claude Bornat (Alfonsus, *Dialogi de immortalitate animae*, Barcelona, 1561) [fig. 125].

Only four sixteenth-century French bindings with uncovered spines had appeared until now, all made for a corpus such as the one in the Escorial. At first we thought that

Fig. 125
Pedro Alfonso de Burgos, *Dialogi de immortalitate animae* .... Barcinone: apud Claudium Bornat, 1561. French "spineless" binding. RBME, 6.V.54

Plantin could have served as intermediary for the commissioning of this binding in Paris, but it was more probably Claude Bornat who himself took charge of it, since in 1564 the dedication copy to Philip II of another work published by him, in a Spanish binding on this occasion, is half-decorated with the same very elegant stamp-impressed design.

Conclusion

These two sections dedicated to French sixteenth-century bindings or bindings executed according to the French taste, which are preserved at the Escorial, now have an unexpected epilogue attached to them. A month after we delivered our text, Isabelle de Conihout, while taking part in the colloquium on *Documenting the early modern Book World: Inventories and Catalogues in manuscript and print* organised from 7 to 9 July 2011 by the University of St Andrews in Scotland, heard the very interesting paper given by Kevin Stevens (University of Nevada) titled "The lost library of Catherine of Austria (1507–1578) and the Milan connection". In it the author set out his discovery in the Milanese archives of a contract from 1540 (1541 N.S.) between the Milanese bookseller Andrea Calvo and the Portuguese businessman Gonzalo Gomes. The bookseller undertook to deliver in the short space of six weeks more than two hundred volumes in Greek, Latin and Italian ("volgare") in good bindings. The contract specified that the octavo volumes should be bound with gilt decoration ("legati in oro") and in different colours (red, blue, green and black). The scholar who made this splendid discovery supposes that the order was destined for the library of Catherine of Austria, the youngest sister of Charles V, who succeeded Eleanor as Queen of Portugal.

But the connections that Gomes must equally have had with Eleanor cause us to venture an alternative explanation: could it not have been yet another book order for the young Prince Philip? That this Italian commission came from Eleanor or from Catherine, the coincidence of the dates, the very short space of time for its completion set by the customer (which recalls the speed that caused the mixture of tools from several binderies used on some of the Paris bindings of about 1540 preserved at the Escorial), the gilt decoration required for the octavo books, and the choice of colours similar to that we have stated earlier, make this hypothesis quite likely. But only the publication of this contract by Kevin Stevens and the study of the titles ordered will allow us to find out more about the matter.

III
A Dazzling Collection of Eighteenth-Century French Mosaic Bindings Preserved in the Real Biblioteca in Madrid

The Duke of Anjou, grandson of Louis XIV, acceded to the Spanish throne as Philip V in 1700, and his son Ferdinand (1712–1759) succeeded him in 1746.

In that same year, Pierre-Paul Dubuisson, son of a great Parisian binder, became a master binder and invented a new type of binding, in white calf impressed with panel stamps and then hand-painted in green with red latticework.[27] A second stage was reached two years later: a royal almanac of 1749, bound in white calf for Ferdinand VI, preserved in the Real Biblioteca [fig. 127], bears the same latticework painted red which fills the spaces left vacant between the tooling of the corners and the central panel with mosaics, the latter in the form of a radiant star surrounding the coat of arms painted on mica.

A single copy of the 1749 almanac in mosaic binding by Pierre-Paul Dubuisson had been recognised up to now, with the arms of Amelot de Chaillou, preserved in the national archives in Paris. These two covers are the first known mosaic bindings by Pierre-Paul Dubuisson on royal almanacs, the series of which continued until his death in 1762, and they constitute a moment of perfection in the history of French binding.

Given that the almanacs made for Louis XV seem to have disappeared—only one is known up to the present day, for the year 1752[28]—the Real Biblioteca in Madrid is unique in possessing a series of ten of these extraordinary bindings (1749–58), all executed by Pierre-Paul Dubuisson for Ferdinand VI [fig. 126]. This series can only be compared to the less dazzling group of eight almanacs in mosaic covers bound by another great Parisian binder, Padeloup, with the armorial bearings of Bournonville, preserved in France in the municipal library at Dijon.[29]

Pierre-Paul Dubuisson, born around 1725, was the spoilt son of one of the main Parisian gilders, who doubled as a sharp businessman. Endowed by his father with the sum of fifteen thousand *livres*, he married a haberdasher's daughter in 1749,[30] and this probably led to his entrée into that circle which directed him towards his speciality, deluxe bindings, employing unusual and refined materials—white calf, mica, mother-of-pearl and spangles—always leaving a large field for the coats of arms of their owners, elegantly executed and prominently set. On Padeloup's death in 1758, he was appointed binder to the king, only twelve years after joining that guild. He was then only about thirty-three years old.

But the speciality in which he would have wished to make his mark was heraldry. At his death in 1762, his widow petitioned the Marquise de Pompadour in order to obtain her husband's pension, proposing moreover

Fig. 126
Almanach Royal. À Paris: De l'Imprimerie
de la Veuve d'Houry, au Saint-Esprit, 1749–58.
Bindings by Pierre-Paul Dubuisson.
RB, PAS/ARM3/44–53

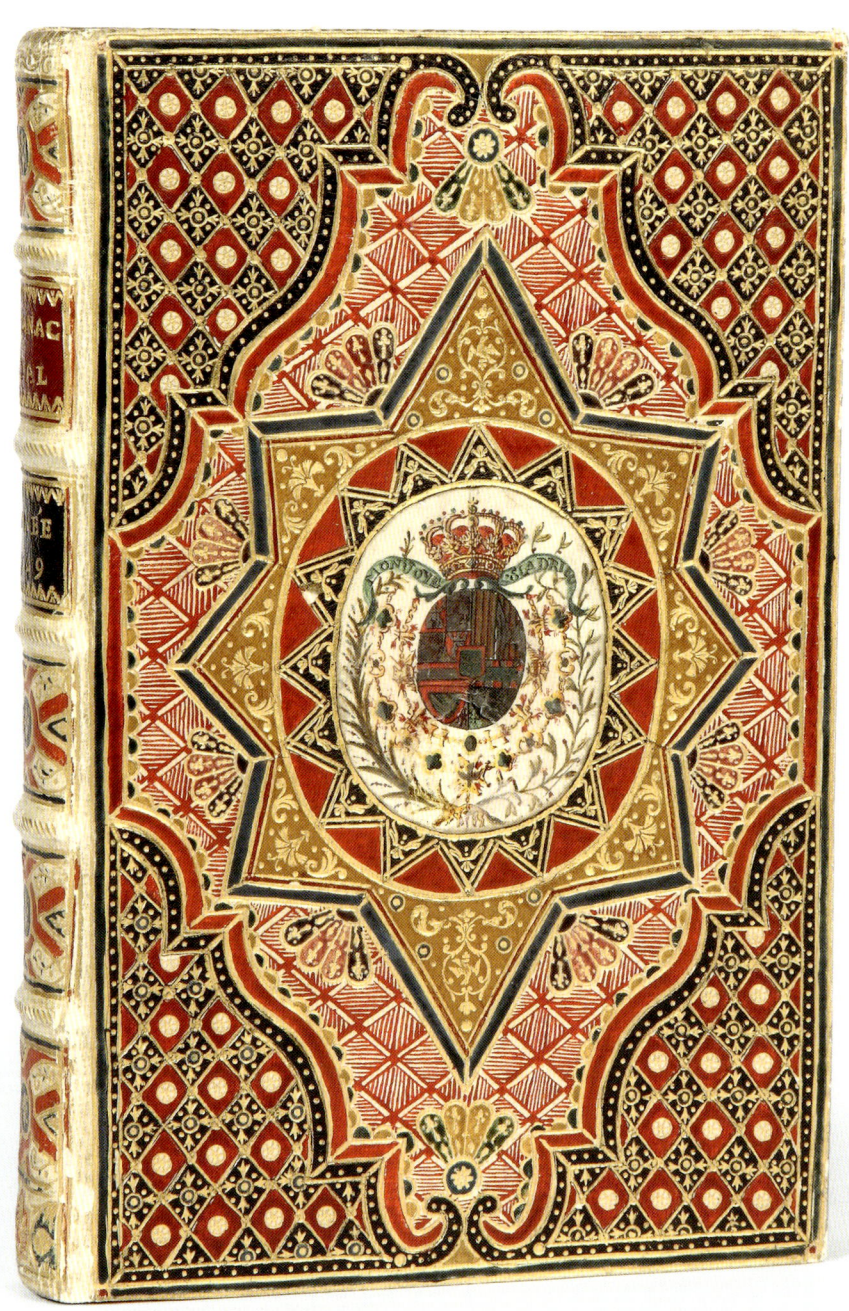

Fig. 127
Almanach Royal: année 1749. Á Paris: De l'Imprimerie de la Veuve d'Houry, au Saint-Esprit, 1749. Mosaic binding in ivory, blue, ochre, black and red leather with a few painted details by Pierre-Paul Dubuisson.
RB, PAS/ARM3/44

Fig. 128
Label of Pierre-Paul Dubuisson on *Almanach Royal: année 1749*. Á Paris: De l'Imprimerie de la Veuve d'Houry, au Saint-Esprit, 1749. RB, PAS/ARM3/44

Fig. 129
Label of Pierre-Paul Dubuisson on *Almanach Royal: année 1753*. Á Paris: De l'Imprimerie de la Veuve d'Houry, au Saint-Esprit, 1753. RB, PAS/ARM3/48

that she acquire the considerable heraldic collection of the deceased, which Pierre-Paul Dubuisson had gathered at great personal expense, to the point, she said, of having "affected his fortune".

It was in the eighteenth century, at first in the great workshops, that the practice developed of signing the bindings—by gilding and stamping the name of the binder or by attaching engraved labels glued to the inside cover of the volume. As far as Pierre-Paul Dubuisson was concerned, he used three ornamented labels, in different formats. The first of these is present in the 1749 almanac, the second in that of 1753 [figs. 128 and 129].

1 BÉLY 2001, 75–84; BENNASSAR 1995, 229–36; SALLMANN 2004; JACQUART 1981.
2 Guillaume du Bellay, quoted by C. PAILLARD, 1879.
3 LE PERSON, 2005, 1–27.
4 SAULNIER 1960, 207–33.
5 Since Michon's little book of 1951—excellent, but necessarily out of date—no other serious work has appeared that provides an overall account of French production in the skill of bookbinding. For the sixteenth century, see NIXON 1971 and HOBSON 1989 and 1999.
6 We are grateful to Padre Losé Luis del Valle, director of the Real Biblioteca del Monasterio de San Lorenzo de El Escorial, for his hospitality and for assisting us with our research.
7 BROOKER 1997, 33–91.
8 CHECA 2010.
9 GONZALO SÁNCHEZ-MOLERO 1998.
10 JORDAN GSCHWEND AND WILSON-CHEVALIER 2007, 341–80; JORDAN GSCHWEND 2010, 2569–92.
11 DEPROUW 2011,
12 RBME, 40.I.13. CHECA 1997, 92–93.
13 LAFFITTE AND LE BARS 1999.
14 HAAN, 2010.
15 NIXON, 1971; for Croy, no. 33; for Mansfeld, no. 32; and for the imaginary meeting at Vincennes, p. XI.
16 To be published by Isabelle de Conihout in the proceedings of the CERL colloquium, *La stampa romana nella Roma dei Papi e in Europa*, Vatican City, Biblioteca Apostolica Romana, November 2011 (in press).
17 VEKENE 1978; MOUSSET AND DE JONGE 2007.
18 GONZALO SÁNCHEZ-MOLERO 2006, 553–61.
19 HOBSON 1970, nos. 82a and 94a for the other examples given by Baïf.
20 See essentially the article by NIXON AND COLIN 1968, 56–89. For the list of earlier studies, see VOET 1969–72, 15, n. 3.
21 [I chose the craft / which nourished me in binding volumes / The blow I suffered later moved me / to write them on the press without pens.]
22 COLIN 1975, 58–64.
23 COLIN 1990, 346–59.
24 COCKX-INDESTEGE AND STORM VAN LEEUWEN 2005.
25 NIXON ((1971), who had probably felt that the attribution to Plantin of the Oxford Book of Hours was rather puzzling ("at first sight this binding appears suspect") did not have occasion, in his masterly catalogue of the bindings in the Pierpoint Morgan library, published in 1971, to return to this question.
26 They are probably the bindings alluded to in COLIN AND NIXON 1968, 87.
27 This is the copy Res 8°, Lc 25-18 (1747 Double).
28 MICHON 1956, no. 242. After the sale of the Danon Collection, 21 March 1973, no. 15.
29 *Ibid.*, 96.
30 The marriage contract was discovered by LE BRIS (2002, 828).

Bodonian Bindings

Pedro M. Cátedra

"Puo esser certo che qui Lei e stimatissimo sopra tutti li typographi del mondo dal 1450 in qua, e che tutti sono una mandra di cogl… riguardo al gran Bodoni."[1] Such exaggerated and colloquial terms are used by Benito Agüera to express to Giambattista Bodoni [fig. 130] the opinion held of him in 1787 by the Madrid court, where there were even expectations that at some point the Parma-based Piedmontese printer would finish putting his printing house in order, appraise it and offer it to the Crown, and that he would hopefully move to the Spanish capital.

The plan failed to materialise, but the printer sought after, secured and proudly displayed the title of Printer to His Catholic Majesty from January 1782 onwards. It is therefore not surprising that the collection of Bodonian editions in the Real Biblioteca is now among the greatest in Spain—if not in number at least in quality and representativeness, as most of the copies are special and chosen for their intended recipients. Indeed, many were selected in Parma to be sent to members of Spanish royalty via the protocol of the duchy or by Bodoni himself, either alone or in conjunction with the authors or promoters of the books. They are therefore usually examples of the most limited editions printed on the finest paper and sometimes personalised with a brief dedicatory note to the intended recipient, and—most relevant to this article—often clothed in fine quality bindings. But the holdings of the Real Biblioteca also include special copies

Fig. 130
Francesco Rosaspina after Andrea Appiani, "Retrato de Giambattista Bodoni", copperplate engraving, in *Manuale tipografico del cavaliere Giambattista Bodoni*. Parma: presso la Vedova, 1818. RB, IV/5477

arising from other circumstances such as the bibliophilism of the people who assembled these collections, among them the Infante Don Antonio Pascual of Bourbon, some of whose Bodonian books are part of the Real Biblioteca.[2] Apart from the acquisitions made by Don Antonio, there are records of purchases or plans for large purchases of Bodoni editions, such as the attempt made in 1787 on the initiative of Father Fernando Scío, then tutor of the future Charles IV's children and also *direttore* of Charles's library when Prince of Asturias, on whose orders he assembled a collection of more than fifteen thousand volumes that was to feature all the finest examples of classical, Spanish, French, English, German and Italian literature.[3] Agüera acts as an intermediary between Bodoni and the tutor, to whom he had spoken of the printer and his books and whom he had invited to examine some in the Count of Floridablanca's library, especially the rarest and most coveted such as the first Anacreon of 1784 and the very delicate Longo translated by Aníbal Caro and published in 1786. Scío must have had a high opinion of them and Agüera procured on his behalf all the books Bodoni brought out, with the sole condition—which is particularly relevant to the context dealt with here—that they be sent "senza legare a motivo del suo genio [of the prince] di legarli qua".[4] It is true that there was a ban on importing bound books in order to foster and protect Spanish craft production, but in this case the acquisition of books in gatherings or bound in paper covers can be explained by the future Charles IV's preference for the Madrid workshops such as that of Sancha, among others, which offered bindings like some of those on the Bodoni editions shown in the exhibition. Nor do we know what came of other plans for large-scale acquisitions which I deal with in the extended version of this essay.

Agüera was among the group of Spaniards who had served Charles III in diplomatic posts in Italy, including the legation in Parma, where several of them proved very sensitive to the duchy's new cultural scene that had taken shape during the mandate of ministers such as Guillaume du Tillot and José Agustín del Llano, the former a Frenchman with close ties to the court of Spain, where he lived, and the latter a Spaniard. The most outstanding Spanish diplomats who served a stint in Parma did not take long to strike up a relationship with Bodoni, and some developed genuine friendships. It is therefore hardly surprising that one of the first recorded examples of the presentation to Spaniards of books printed by him should be the sending of four copies of the *Epithalamia exoticis linguis reddita* at the end of 1775 to prominent politicians and diplomats connected in some way or another with Italy or, more specifically, with the Roman legation. The list of the recipients of these four books sent to Spain is headed by the Infante Don Gabriel of Bourbon, a bibliophile but somewhat less than in his youth. It also includes the aforementioned Marquis of Llano; the Marquis of Grimaldi, then first Secretary of State of the Spanish Crown; Manuel de Roda, ambassador to the city from 1758 to 1765; and his pupil José Nicolás de Azara, who soon became Bodoni's patron and closest Spanish friend. Bodoni's initial circle of Spanish friends and mentors gradually extended to other high-ranking officials based in Madrid, such as the two Moñino brothers and Eugenio de Llaguno, whose relationship I discuss at length in another essay. Some of them, especially Azara, wished to involve Bodoni in the cultural projects of the reign of Charles III, and strove to bring him or his typefaces to the printing house of the Real Biblioteca, which was founded when Santander was librarian.

Even though these plans came to nothing, Bodoni's fame progressively grew in Spain as a result of their announcement, and his books arrived more or less regularly at the palace. Most of these presentation volumes were bound in Parma on the printer's instructions. They provide an insight into one of the least known aspects of the history of books in Parma in Bodoni's day—bookbinding, and specifically the craftsmen who worked for him, especially the one who was perhaps his closest collaborator and who is mentioned here for the first time thanks to the only signed binding by him we have located to date.

In the monograph mentioned in note 1, from which this essay draws, I established the specifications and type of binding executed in Parma for the books printed by Bodini on the basis of the examples in the Real Biblioteca, and also attempted to determine the relationship or direct involvement of the printer in what, after all, may have been the extension of his material and artistic plans for books. I also established in this connection some types of series bindings, which are not the usual pale orange or brick-red printer's boards but are executed in leather and denote a homogeneous aesthetic project in some cases and even the existence of a workshop or group of binders who may perhaps be the successors of Laferté or other French or Parmesan binders. However, I only have enough room here to refer to the books on display, which represent some of the usual types produced by the binderies that worked for Bodoni, which I will discuss in chronological order rather than by type.

Bindings from the Times of Laferté and Other Workshops (1765–90)

The art of bookbinding flourished in Parma along with other government-promoted cultural projects, namely the establishment of the Biblioteca Palatina, the University and the

Stamperia Reale. Although, of course, bookbinding in Parma and in connection with its library is documented before the aforementioned cultural reforms, it could be said that it is also a lesser but necessary sister art to these major Enlightenment developments. In 1765 the great librarian Paciudi arranged the hiring of a French binder with a with a well-known surname, Antoine Louis Laferté,[5] who was given official commissions very early on; his initiative and the bindery he established probably breathed new life into bookbinding in Parma, although the existing records are gradually revealing the existence of accomplished craftsmen who cannot be proven to have served apprenticeships under Laferté.

The first of the Bodonian books selected for this exhibition is one of the rarest he printed and furthermore documents the first appearance of his newly acquired title linking him to the Spanish Crown. The title page of the *Essai de caracteres russes gravés et fondus par Jean Baptiste Bodoni Typographe de S. M. le Roi d'Espagne Directeur de l'Imprimerie Royale & Membre de l'Academie des Beaux Arts à Parme*, in folio size and printed in 1782 (RB IV/169), consciously publishes novelty and is striking for its bold composition all in roman and capital forms of chancery characters [fig. 131]. Bodoni seems to want to raise his status above that of craftsman and official by showing off his posts and honours, beginning with the one linking him to the Spanish Crown: "Typographe de S. M. le Roi d'Espagne | Directeur de l'Imprimerie Royale | & Membre de l'Academie des Beaux Arts | à Parme."

This fourth "typography manual" was published on the occasion of the visit paid to Parma by the Grand Duke Paul, eldest son of Empress Catherine of Russia and future Paul I, and his wife Maria of Württemberg. It contains eight variants of roman Cyrillic typefaces, followed by ten capital alphabets, all presented in descending order of size, plus a *Gratulatio* in Russian and Latin written by Father Paciaudi. Bodoni must have presented his work to the illustrious spouses in the presence of the entire court of Parma during the visit they presumably paid to the Stamperia on 13 April 1782.[6]

But Bodoni not only aimed to please the prince and princess just as he did with King Gustav III of Denmark in 1784 when he presented him with the small $\Psi\pi o\mu\acute{\epsilon}\nu\alpha$ *Parmense in adventu Gustavi III Sueciae Regis*, also in the Real Biblioteca (RB, IX/9687) and bound in the same manner as the *Essai*. He furthermore wished to sound out the possibility of selling typefaces in Russia, which was then undergoing a cultural expansion thanks to the westernising projects promoted by the Tsarina Catherine. We know this from the references to this enterprise in letters exchanged by Azara and the printer, which are one of the main sources of information on Bodoni. Indeed, after describing the work as "sorprendente e che gli fa infinito onore",[7] Azara expresses his doubts about the success of the project and the interest of the aforesaid persons, and therefore later on recommends Bodoni be prudent, refrain from sending matrixes or typefaces to Russia unless directly commissioned by the tsarina, and wait for groundwork to be laid by the recently appointed Spanish ambassador Felipe Fonsdeviela y Ondeano, Marquis of La Torre, also from Aragón and shortly to travel to Russia.[8] Bodoni must have planned to act as he had done

Fig. 131
Giambattista Bodoni, *Essai de caracteres russes gravés et fondus par Jean Baptiste Bodoni ....* [Parma: n. n.], 1782. Title page. RB, IV/160

Bodoni in the Real Biblioteca that features a type of binding to which, with variants, Bodoni remained faithful throughout his lifetime.

The binding is of the kind known in France as *demi-reliure*, or as *all'impostura* in the Italian terminology of Bodoni's day.[9] Leather, in this case red morocco, is used only for the spine, and the boards are covered with leather-look paper in a similar colour, seeking a homogeneous effect which is accentuated, on the one hand, by reducing the area of the part in leather, which barely covers the back and does not extend to the boards—unlike in half-binding—and also by concealing the join with a roll or line, in this case a triple fillet which, on both covers, forms the inner side of a rectangle whose corners are stamped with the usual rosette.

The copy in the Real Biblioteca belonged to the Infante Don Antonio, whose stamp is displayed on the title page, although it also bears the bookplates of Charles IV and Ferdinand VII. However, it is possible that Bodoni may have presented it to Charles III in gratitude for his recent appointment, as he did with other prominent people such as Floridablanca, sending copies with perhaps a similar but less magnificent binding.[10] The tooling used in the ornamentation of the spine panels, of which the central one continued to feature in later bindings, and the similarities with other copies of the same work such as the one with accession no. Coll. Bod. 165 in the Biblioteca Palatina, denote an economical, more or less mass-produced type of binding used by the printer for works which, as in this case, may be regarded as stemming from his own initiative and intended for a very limited number of people. Indeed, in the three aforementioned bindings,

or would do with other sovereign dynasties of Europe, namely those of Savoy, Portugal and Spain, to which he sent his matrixes, placing his trust in the discretion of their rulers. In the case of Spain—at least as regards the last flow of shipments to the minister Urquijo in 1800—despite the Crown treasury shortfalls, these efforts paid off thanks to the part played, among others, by one of his most effective contacts, José Esteban de Mendizábal, who had served in the secretary's office under Azara in Rome.

But this volume is mentioned here not only for all these reasons and because it is one of Bodoni's rarest typography manuals but also because it is the earliest book by the two on the *Essai* and the one on *Ψπομένα*, we find Bodoni's name on the spine label in what was a manner of making his presence known and the first step towards what became his institutionalised signature on a second label in the series bindings produced by the private printing house from the end of the eighties, which I have discussed elsewhere.

This type of *all'impostura* binding was long-lasting and we find examples dating from the ninth decade of the eighteenth century, such as those in the Real Biblioteca, to after Bodoni's death; it was therefore used both for single volumes or series with the same title, which allows us to classify it as one of Bodoni's characteristic types of binding.

Domenico Guarnaschelli, Bodoni's Binder

Apart from Guarnaschelli, a name which is emerging today in connection with eighteenth-century bookbinding in Parma, scholars have referred to several of Laferté's *giovani* [apprentices] who must have begun training under him no sooner than they arrived in Parma. One of the first to be documented is Antonio Sidoli, who unfortunately did not prosper in his vocation.[11] Giuseppe Signifredi did considerably better for himself. His connections with the Parma library are documented by specific payments, and it would now be feasible to identify other works as his in the same library on the basis of works that can be attributed to him with certainty.[12] There are other binders, however, whom Bodoni held in esteem and who, on the basis of early references to them, may perhaps have made up a different group to that of Laferté, as a result of which we should perhaps play down the importance of the central role so far attributed to the Frenchman in the bookbinding scene of Parma. I discuss this question more extensively elsewhere.

The pupil of Laferté who most interests us here is the maker of the binding for the Horace published in 1791, the next book on show. It is of paramount importance because it marks the start of Bodoni's endeavour, under the aegis of the Spaniard Azara, to renew the aesthetic of neoclassical books. The binder is identified by the signature that occupies the whole fore-edge square of the back cover, separating each word with a small tooled flower: "DOMENICO GUARNASCHELLI LEGATORE DI LIBRI" [fig. 132]. Guarnaschelli was hitherto a completely unknown figure in the history of Italian bookbinding —a fact which is particularly surprising in view of some of the examples of his output such as the one discussed here, which evidences his skill, and also because his output, which we could now begin to catalogue, must have been abundant. It is true that this anonymity, widespread in the world of early bookbinding, may also be due in this case to his almost exclusive dedication to a small circle of Parmesan clients, beginning with the highest authority, Duke Ferdinand, in whose library at Colorno Guarnaschelli invested his time. This circle also included Giambattista Bodoni, who, as we shall see, considered him a subordinate of his own, and many of whose books—among them several of those on show here—were bound by Guarnaschelli in Parma before being presented as gifts or sold, and another client, the bookseller Blanchon.

Fig. 132
Quintus Horatius Flaccus, *Q. Horatii Flacci Opera*. Parma: in aedibus Palatinis, typis Bodonianis, 1791. Signature of Domenico Guarnaschelli on fore-edge square of back cover. RB, IX/7185

Although thorough research, which I intend to conduct, into the administrative records of the duchy and Bodoni's own archives or a systematic search through the notarial documents of the period will undoubtedly provide a clearer picture of the so far vague figure of Guarnaschelli and his relationship with his colleagues, especially Signifredi, an initial sketch should begin with the 1791 copy of the Horace. I therefore refer readers to the monograph mentioned in note 1 for some biographical aspects of the man we can consider Bodoni's bookbinder in the 1790s.

The origins of the edition of Horace[13] are Azara's fondness for the poet. In July 1786 he confided to Bodoni that all devotees have their "saint", and that he entrusts himself to Saint Horace, "che è il mio protettore favorito". He goes on to criticise bitterly John Pine's edition (London, 1733), which is as particular in its text as it is in its makeup, for it is not printed with type: rather, the text and illustrations are combined on printed copper plates. He considers it so "scelerata" [despicable] for its excessive ornamentation that he wishes to make amends for his hero with a new edition "così magnifica, che non si fosse mai veduta la simile".[14] Part of its greatness would lie in the fact that it would feature engravings of archaeological remains at the head of each page composition together with an embellishment—it should be remembered that discoveries were constantly being made at the time, some promoted by Azara himself—to both clarify and adorn the text.[15] Although the edition Azara has in mind is not entirely original—Pine endeavoured to give his own profuse ornamentation the same origin and use—this first proposal is interesting because it clearly combines the literary and antiquarian facets of the Spanish diplomat and also in part because it does not yet properly define the idea, which subsequently materialised, of a purely neoclassical book without concessions to late Baroque, based on the elimination of illustrations and concerned solely with the sobriety of the clean text harmonised with a page layout displaying a perfect balance between black and the corresponding blanks [fig. 134]. Azara matured this project and these aesthetic principles over the following years and, having forgotten his initial idea, rejected Bodoni's proposal of incorporating ornamentation or engravings: "Per l'amor di Dio, non pensi Lei ad imbrattare il nostro Orazio con rami ne ornati d'incisione, giachè tutta la bellezza à de consistere nella tipografia e purità di testo."[16] Some of the works carefully produced by Bodoni at the Stamperia Reale still smacked of Rococo owing above all to the headpieces and embellishments; the aforementioned book by Pine even had a certain amount of influence on Bodoni's work. The products supervised by Azara from the early eighties onwards are practically the only examples of the more excluding neoclassical and Empire text-only forms that became established following the Horace of 1791. It should be stressed that Bodoni was just as much a great printer as he was a keen businessman who had no qualms about going along with or pandering to the various prevailing tastes of the age—or, indeed, about following the orders of those who commissioned an edition from him. Although we are discussing the Bodonian aesthetic, we should not forget that underlying this programme are, of course, the models established by great English printers such as Baskerville and Foulis and even Didot, although he replicated them to improve on them; and also the advice of Azara when it came to materialising "his" books of Greco-Latin classics—Anacreon, Horace, Virgil, Greek elegiac poets—or Italians such as Tasso, Dante and Petrarch, the publication of which also incidentally started out as an enterprise proposed by the Spanish ambassador, who intended to dedicate it to King Charles IV.

Magnificence came to be combined with exclusivity: in a letter to Bodoni of December 1788, Azara informs him that he wishes to finance the printing of the Horace and, aside from the copies intended for the Duke of Parma and his library, wants to ensure that "non uscisse veruna copia assolutamente"[17] without his supervision. By March 1789 work has already begun with Azara's choice of the characters from among two samples sent by Bodoni; he simply makes the observation that "per un in folio il carattere dev'essere un po grosso; altrimenti, comparisce meschino e gracile e fatica la vista"[18] and leaves Bodoni to choose the paper and the *mise en page*. By May 1789 Bodoni has cast new typefaces for the Horace and Azara is pleased about this, but urges the printer: "Fissiamoci una volta."[19] At the end of July Azara finalises aspects of the print run and text with Bodoni: he definitely decides to finance the edition and dedicate it to his friend Moñino, the Count of Floridablanca; he establishes that the special edition on parchment will consist of four copies including one for the printer, whom he allows to decide on the number to be printed on paper—months later he states that he considers three hundred sufficient—in order to place on sale those which Azara does not need as gifts for his friends; and finally, he gives instructions on what text Bodoni can base himself in order to compose it,[20] from which we may deduce the method to be used, which involves working on the proofs Bodoni will send and making the corrections he and his collaborators deem appropriate on the basis of other opinions and *ope ingenii*. Owing to the doubts raised to Azara and his collaborators concerning the text by the abbés Visconti, Fea and Arteaga, on receiving the first proofs at the end of August 1789 the diplomat adds to the printer's Horatian sources by sending him the only volume he has of Janus' edition printed in Leipzig, stating that he will endeavour to procure the rest in Germany through Bodoni and two agents; meanwhile, the printer replies that there is nobody in Parma he can use to adapt the text, and that the best solution would be for him to be sent a good printed original of Horace with the related corrections to the text and punctuation.[21] By the beginning of 1790 these books have still not arrived and Azara wonders when he will be able to set to work—"mettere mano"—on the production.[22] For his part, Bodoni chooses the middle path and decides to take as a model the Baskerville edition he has in the library, in order not to continue delaying a project in which he too has made investments, as the Horace was to be the first product of, and therefore a showcase for, his private printing house, in which he had already made a sizeable investment by purchasing the materials used for the large-scale enterprise of printing the Livorno *Encyclopédie*. However, when Janus' edition arrives, Azara gives his final instructions for it to be followed and, after the text had been composed and the first corrections made, for him to be sent the proofs so that "his abbés" can go over them, although he changes his mind in the same letter owing to an observation by Visconti and tells Bodoni to go ahead with the Baskerville edition corrected by Talbott.[23] Following this decision, the work progressed considerably.

The circumstances of the publication deserve not merely an article but an entire book to be devoted to them. But let us focus on what is most relevant, which is the binding. When the printing is nearing completion in May 1791, Azara states that he wishes to have ten copies "ben legati" [well bound] and is keeping the rest for himself bound "in buoni cartoni" [in good paper boards], although he does not specify the characteristics.[24] By July the book is entirely finished and printed. Azara instructs him to prepare a copy "ben legato" for the king—on another occasion he describes it as "più magnifico"—and a dozen ordinary ones for friends, to be sent to Spain via Barcelona. Bodoni announces to him shortly afterwards the shipment of forty-eight copies on handmade paper bound in paper boards; meanwhile he informs him that the copies on vellum paper, "carta d'Annonay", are being bound "all'inglese, e in marrochino verde, giachè de' rossi non se ne trovano". He adds that "io non so come riusciranno perchè il migliore Bibliopega che noi avevam qui è partito improvvisamente e sento che egli trovasi nella stamperia del Seminario di Padova". He then asks for instructions concerning the other copies to be sent to Spain, "mentre io mi affretterò di farle preparare quella che è destinata pel Re, e mi lusingo che sarà in pronto allorchè avrò riscontro di questa mia".[25] Early in September Azara tells him that he is waiting for the forty-eight copies, plus the one for the king, which he will personally arrange to be sent from Rome.[26] The books arrive at the end of September, and apart from his displeasure at finding that some mistakes have not been corrected, Azara complains about his embarrassment on showing a copy to some friends and seeing that the binder, in an act of intolerable "trascuratezza" [negligence], has ruined several copies by forgetting to stitch or disarranging some bifolio; it is feared that if this has also happened to the copies already distributed both from Parma and in Rome, it will be a disgrace for Bodoni and for himself.[27]

I deduce that the copies in which Azara found uncorrected mistakes and omissions are those bound in cardboard. Certainly, no such mistakes and omissions are found today in the one in the Real Biblioteca which we could identify in principle[28] as the one sent to Charles IV. Those intended for Spain, presumably including this one, arrived at Barcelona harbour in February 1792, as Azara comments to Bodoni, whom he informs in another letter that the "Horaces" arrived the day before Floridablanca was overthrown, and that he has asked the Count of Aranda to present to the king on his behalf the copy intended for him.[29] He had written to Floridablanca earlier, stating that he hoped that his Horace had arrived and asking for privileges for the printer:

> Acabo de saber que el navío que llevaba mis Horacios había llegado a Barcelona, de cuyo cajón no tenía noticias hace dos meses…. El Horacio ha despertado un entusiasmo grande en toda Italia y aun más en Inglaterra, de donde recibo cartas sin número. Bodoni ha fijado con esta obra su reputación y hace época en los anales tipográficos. Ud., que le hizo dar el título de tipógrafo del Rey, perfeccione la obra proponiendo a Su Majestad que le dé una pensioncilla para que no viva con solo la miseria de Parma, que es vergonzosa; y con verdad puedo decir a Ud. que, sin las ayudas de este pobre diablo, este gran artista se hallaría todavía en la oscuridad. Por más apuros que tengamos, un pequeño auxilio no nos hará más pobres ni más ricos; y en pocas cosas lo podrá emplear el Rey que le hagan tanto honor.[30]

However, the allowance was granted a couple of years later, on 22 July 1793, after the printer cultivated relations with new minister Godoy and his circle; it was the Prince of Peace himself, as Godoy was known, who informed him of the royal decision, "en atención al distinguido mérito de Vm., tan conocido en toda Europa por los que aman y saben estimar las artes y para dar a Vm. una prueba de lo mucho que ha apreciado el Rey las magníficas obras que ha enviado Vm. en diferentes ocasiones".[31]

The list of these publications should include the Horace, the execution of which will be dealt with in the following lines. The present copy is one of those printed on the excellent vellum paper of Annonay, in a somewhat larger format than those printed on the well-calendered laid paper used for the ordinary edition. As is known, Azara also ordered three or four copies printed on fine parchment, but he never thought to send any of these or any of the others that he had had printed on this support, because "non ne ànno idea e le stimano meno che in buona carta; questo gusto non à penetrato ancora nella mia Arabia"[32]—perhaps an unfair judgement.[33]

Guarnaschelli's work is also governed by the principle of sobriety—I do not know whether this is because of financial constraints or because his artistic creativity failed to attain the heights then being achieved in other countries such as England and France, where the new neoclassical styles of the Empire period were taking off [fig. 133]. Perhaps the plainness of the covers is an indication of this change, even though the two gold-tooled motifs at the corners and pointing to the centre are only too reminiscent of the style of Baroque dentelle border bindings that were common to the school of Laferté. Certainly, no modifications are made to the *longue durée* French Baroque design on the spine, which is characteristic of Laferté's bindery. Nevertheless, I believe there are evident signs of artistic intentions and rigour, such as, for example, the overall quality of the gilding, which denotes a bold choice of tools with fine lines and a considerable number of volutes that are nevertheless executed without unsightly build-ups of materials and fairly expertly, the end result not being marred by double impressions.

But perhaps the most evident act of artistic intention is the signing of the book. Although other Parmesan binders did so, beginning with Laferté and continuing with Signifredi, another of his *boys*, Guarnaschelli did so in one of the least frequent manners,[34] without the—whether or not feigned—concealment usually found in the act of signing a binding: as we have seen, he adds his full name in gold lettering whose spacing and size ensure that it occupies the full extension of the fore-edge square of the back cover of the book, the most striking place when viewed from the outside, as when one goes to open it to begin examining it the binder's identity becomes apparent at first sight. The resulting effect is a wish to be associated with what was universally considered the work of art of Bodoni's printing house. Guarnaschelli thus proclaims his own craftsmanship loud and clear and links himself to the name of the printer, which is displayed on the spine, and partly also to that of the donor of the copy, José Nicolás de Azara. Of course both men must have agreed and thought fit that Guarnaschelli, following the disappearance of Laferté's bindery where he had worked anonymously, should be made known to the Spanish court —who knows, perhaps dreaming of some reward and recognition, or offering his services in this peculiar umbilical relationship and web of common political and economic aims that is still apparent between the subjects of the Duke of Parma and the Spanish monarchs, and which also partly explains Bodoni's importance in our country.

Although, as Bodoni tells Azara, red morocco is hard to come by, this luxurious leather is used to cover the book, which is generally well constructed. Guarnaschelli would have begun by decorating the spine, which was usually the first part of a book to be gilded, with the pattern of the seven bands establishing the six panels and the head and tail spaces. The bands are blind stamped and decorated with spiral volutes applied with a pallet or roll. Not counting the two panels that bear the labels, the remaining six rectangular spaces are delimited by single-line and cat's tooth rolls; their four corners are stamped with an acanthus branch tooled design, which is not one of the most characteristic owing to its function and geometrical form. I have rarely seen such tools used in the bindings produced by the workshop of Laferté and subsequently of his followers, whose output features few specialised tools but plenty of multiple-use volutes or vegetal motifs. The centre of the panels is occupied by what can be considered a typical centrepiece, with a plant and fleur-de-lis motif;[35] two aligned dots mark the top and bottom of the central motif and serve as a guide

Fig. 133
Quintus Horatius Flaccus, *Q. Horatii Flacci Opera*.
Parma: in aedibus Palatinis, typis Bodonianis, 1791.
Bound in red morocco with gold tooling by Domenico
Guarnaschelli. RB, IX/7185

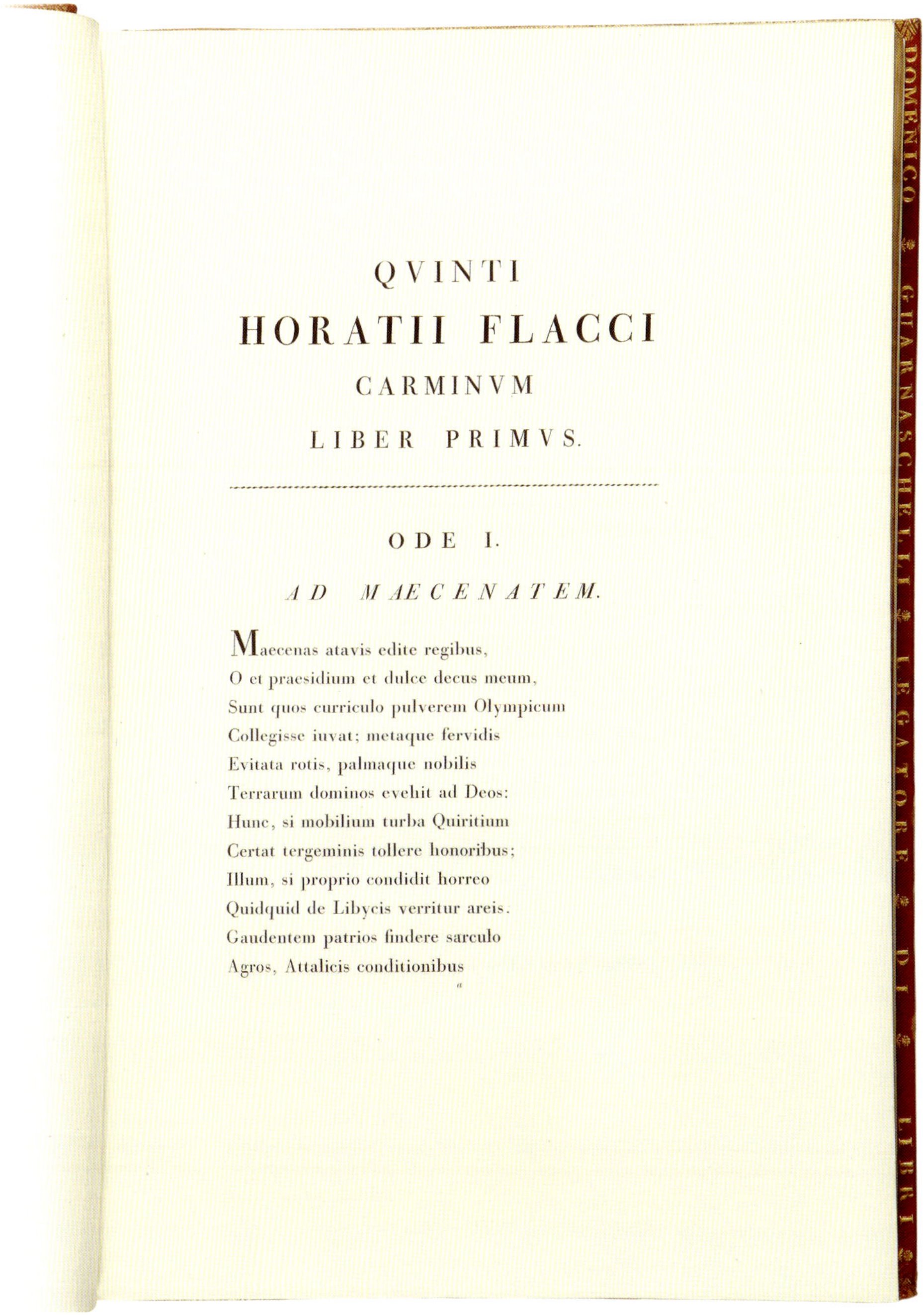

QVINTI
HORATII FLACCI
CARMINVM

LIBER PRIMVS.

ODE I.

AD MAECENATEM.

Maecenas atavis edite regibus,
O et praesidium et dulce decus meum,
Sunt quos curriculo pulverem Olympicum
Collegisse iuvat; metaque fervidis
Evitata rotis, palmaque nobilis
Terrarum dominos evehit ad Deos:
Hunc, si mobilium turba Quiritium
Certat tergeminis tollere honoribus;
Illum, si proprio condidit horreo
Quidquid de Libycis verritur areis.
Gaudentem patrios findere sarculo
Agros, Attalicis conditionibus

a

Fig. 134
Quintus Horatius Flaccus, *Q. Horatii Flacci Opera*.
Parma: in aedibus Palatinis, typis Bodonianis,
1791. RB, IX/7185

for its correct positioning. The right and left sides are occupied by small spiked fleur-de-lis tooled designs flanked by a composition of two small tools, a star and a radiating circle. At the head of the spine is a pallet or roll with the "dog passant" and, at the tail end, two of the same kind separated by single-line and cat's tooth rolls.

Two upper panels, the second and third, are occupied by a double label in green morocco decorated in gold, as was customary, with individual tools. It can be seen from the blurred D in the second line of the lower label that the binder has "gone over" the letter again. This title form became customary in what I consider to be series bindings, and the fact that Bodoni's name features explicitly and always in the same manner on several copies of the same book indicates that this is the work of the printer, wishing to accentuate his prominence.

The covers are decorated with a simple design, framed with a border of three fillets with the usual rosette in the corners to conceal the uneven intersection of the fillets, as matching roll-decorated corner pieces are not used. In the inner corners of the border, pointing towards the centre of the cover, is a gold-tooled design consisting of two motifs, a fleur-de-lis with branches and a pomegranate. In the centre of the cover is the royal coat of arms used by Charles III during the reign of Charles IV, based on the so-called *escudo grande* [great shield], i.e. featuring the two new quarters incorporated by Charles III when he arrived in Spain from Naples in 1760, the bezants of Tuscany and the fleurs-de-lis of Parma.[36] Beneath this coat of arms is the supralibros of the Infante Don Antonio ("s.d.s.i.d.a.", monogram of "soy del serenísimo infante don antonio"). Both the stamp and the coat of arms have the appearance of additions as they are impressed differently to the rest of the ornamentation. At least I am sure this is true of the supralibros and more than likely of the coat of arms, although the difference in the gold tones of the coat of arms and the overall design could be explained by the impression technique. The endleaves are made of moiré paper with spiral motifs; the squares display gold roll decoration consisting of a zigzag motif alternating with vine leaves, except for the one with the binder's signature. The edges of the boards are worked with a roll of alternating lozenges and bezants. The headbands are tooled with thick transverse lines.

The Real Biblioteca preserves many similar Bodonian books bound by Guarnaschelli and dating from those years. Their homogeneousness may have been due to the fact that they were mass produced or based on the same design; what is more, they bear the bookplate of the Infante Don Antonio.[37] Around 1793 the Crown granted the printer a new favour: on 2 July he was awarded a yearly allowance that strengthened his ties with Charles IV, the king's family and the Spanish rulers. We have seen that Azara proposed this to Floridablanca on sending him a copy of the Horace, and that he was going to send his own copy to Charles IV. In the end it was Godoy who informed the printer of the award of the allowance on 2 July 1793.

I shall now go on to examine what I consider to be if not Bodoni's most original production—similar products are documented both in Italy and in other parts of Europe, both earlier and later than those examined here—perhaps his favourite output. This is the kind which, among others, is found in several of the copies of the other essential books printed by Bodoni and shown here, the two of Kempis' *De imitatione Christi* (1793) and the *Pitture di Antonio Allegri detto il Correggio* (1800), the binding of which is identified by Bodoni when referring to this particular example as being bound "all'inglese".

The oldest surviving Parmesan bindings of this kind are the two copies of Kempis' work which were intended, and personalised with a printed inscription, for King Charles IV and Queen María Luisa of Parma [figs 135 and 136]. Although the book came out with the date 1793 on the title page, Bodoni would have been working on the magnificent folio size *De imitatione Christi libri quatuor* at the ducal printing house, "typis bodonianis", for some time. In a Latin dedication to the heir of Parma, Don Ferdinand's son Don Luis of Bourbon, in handsome cursive characters, "I. B. Bodonius Hispaniarum Regis Typographus"—no doubt composed by an intermediary—he tells this prince, born in 1773, that from the time he started his printing endeavours he had always planned to honour the monumental works of sacred literature with his typefaces and now had the opportunity to do so with one of the most prestigious; this work was furthermore a favourite of Don Luis himself thanks to the education he had received from Adeodato Turchi, then Bishop of Parma, whom he praised in a generous note.

However, it does not appear that Bodoni's main reason for choosing this book was its undisputable spiritual significance or the fact that the Kempis may perhaps have been more to the liking of Don Luis's father, the duke. The choice of this particular title and his intention to produce a splendid book "non sine aliquo peculiari nitore atque elegantia",[38] as he writes in the dedication, should be regarded more as a chapter in his own particular "typographic" history in which his established rivalry with Pierre Didot plays a fundamental role. In the second volume of his work, the printer's friend and biographer, Giuseppe De Lama, published a letter from the printer to the Minister of State, Count Cesare Ventura, requesting permission to dedicate his book to Don Luis. In it he refers to the "gara" [competition] Bodoni had been involved in with the French for some time; he specifically mentions Didot's edition of "quel celebratissimo *De imitatione Christi*" and states that Bodoni has been working on an edition of the same work belonging to his series of Latin classics, in respect of which "forse l'Italia sarà imparziale nel portar giudizio fra lo stampatore parigino ed il parmense".[39]

Didot's edition of the Kempis came out in 1788, preceded by a "typographi monitum" citing his own printing and publishing history in order to justify the publication of this work, which is aimed at presenting the first characters cast by his son Henri, in *petit-parangon* size. In a note at the end of the *monitum* he boasts about the support, which Bodoni very soon began to use too: "Opum exaratum chartis quas vocant *vélin*, eductis ex officina *Montgolfier* patris et filii, ex oppido dicto Annonay, cum primis litterarum typis romanis, cudente Henrico Didot, secundo ex natis P. Fr. Didot."[40]

Bodoni must have considered this prologue pretentious to say the least, and I do not know whether he also interpreted it as a new challenge posed by the Frenchman, who around that time had issued the subscription leaflet for his edition of Demosthenes (1790) providing examples of his new Greek characters and boasting about its quality and beauty—no doubt sensitive to the recent showing off of his Parmesan rival, who had just published several of his Greek classics with different characters and, more importantly, a specific manual or repertoire of Greek typefaces.

Bodoni's response to Didot's presumptuousness about the new Greek typeface was highly explicit and clear in the prologue to the Callimachus of 1791,[41] and his reaction to the Kempis is no less evident, albeit implicit. There are a number of contrasting parallels in the prologues of Didot and Bodoni, which would not have gone unnoticed to readers. In the *monitum* Didot traces his own history and accomplishments in the art of printing, in an exercise of self-praise. For example, he builds on the presumptuous and clichéd quote from Terence—"Quadraginta fere abhinc annos rei librariæ deditus, nihil quod ad illam pertineret alienum a me putans, omnes omnino illius partes complexus sum"[42]—and goes on to boast of the acquisition of an encyclopaedic knowledge of antique and modern books on a broad variety of disciplines. Bodoni—naturally without the slightest mention of Didot's publications or his *gara* with them—counterattacks the Frenchman's conceitedness by professing his humility and, in the opening lines, establishes the aim of his equally lengthy track record in printing: to make available to his peers the "Sacrarum Litterarum monumenta … meis formis magnifice splendideque descripta",[43] as if providing a divine service. Didot goes on to speak of his experience in casting typefaces from 1783, of how his own son, unbeknown to him, had taken up the same profession, cutting and casting some *petit-parangon* characters which, being the young apprentice's first accomplishments, the father wished to protect and almost honour by publishing the Kempis in them. Bodoni's ironic response to this description of father-son apprenticeship, which is more boastful and ridiculous than endearing and undermines such a prestigious book, is summed up by the following inversion: after devoting himself to perfecting it "omni studio ac labore" and, thanks to God, finding himself mature and very capable in his art, he considered himself in a position to bring out an illustrious and exquisite edition "divinorum librorum", as a public testimony to his gratitude to God, for which he was choosing *De imitatione Christi*, praising it and stressing its importance in half a page.

His technical response, although implicit, is no less evident. He casts and composes the text with a new *parangon* character which, rivalling that of Didot junior, is much fuller and more angular and even. Particularly striking, for example, is the perfect balance between Bodoni's small capitals and roman type and the contrast between Didot's typefaces. He also teaches the Frenchmen a significant lesson in *mise en page* and composition, for which, as I have found in other cases, he proceeds to replicate Didot's, thereby drawing attention to the flaws or choices of composition and printing which can end up disfiguring the Frenchman's page layout, especially compared to that of Bodoni. Among other things, in Didot's work there is a noticeable lack of proportion between the font size and the size of the printed area and the paper; Bodoni chooses full folio size—460 mm high—compared to Didot's imperial 4to resulting from the folds of Annonay paper (350 mm, uncut, in the copy on view). Also evident is the evenness and perfect alignment of Bodoni's typefaces, none of which, incidentally, I have found to be damaged; the regularity of the word spacing and alternating blanks is obvious, as is the proportion of the interlinear spacing. All this further heightens the crammed, unbalanced impression one has of Didot's composition and the contrast intentionally sought by Bodoni, not to mention other, even graphic details, such as the use of V in place of U in titles in capitals, which infuses with classical elegance the rendering of a Latin text that Bodoni—perhaps in an ironic jab at the Frenchman's choice—claims in his prologue to be part of his series of classic authors.

The binding of the two examples housed in the Real Biblioteca and now on show [figs. 135 and 136] may be attributed in principle to Domenico Guarnaschelli. The leather used in both is dyed calfskin. The spine, with seven raised bands outlined in blind tooling and decorated in gold using the same pallet or roll with a spiral volute motif found on the Horace, has six rectangular panels delimited by two-line pallets or rolls forming a rectangular composition; at the four corners, tool number 6; in the centre of the panels a small gold-tooled flower or rosette within a garland. The only difference found between the two copies of the Kempis as regards spine decoration is that the one intended for the queen [fig. 135] features a dot inside each of the four sides at the centre, whereas this space is left blank in the one for the king [fig. 136]. The dog passant pallet or roll is used at the head of the spine of copy IV/7196, as in the Horace, and at the tail is the same double pallet or roll separated by a two-line pallet or roll. The same pallet is used at the head and tail of copy IX/8413, double at the tail and separated by a two-line pallet or roll. The spine label is double with gold lettering executed with individual tools for each of the letters and with similar double impression flaws mentioned previously in the title of the Horace. In both copies the upper label in red morocco leather contains the title of the work and the lower label, in blue morocco, the name of the printer and the year. Needless to say this is a Bourbon colour combination.

Above all it is the decoration of the covers that identifies and gives character to the style of the binding. It is distinguished by the differently dyed leather and the gold tooling, which draws attention to these differences. As we can see, both books were bound with a certain amount of coordination, which is clear in the dying of the leather: the king's copy [fig. 136] was first hand dyed and subsequently stained with hyssop to give a granite-like finish; the spine and a rectangular band extending over front and back cover were marbled with a paintbrush in shades of green and ochre. The colours are inverted on the queen's copy [fig. 135]. The gold of the covers basically highlights the coloured bands, which in the king's copy are delimited by three-line rolls joined at the inner

Fig. 135
Attributed to Thomas a Kempis, *De imitatione Christi libri quatuor*. Parmae: in aedibus Palatinis, typis Bodonianis, 1793. Bound in leather with green and ochre mottling and gold tooling. RB, IX/8413

Fig. 136
Attributed to Thomas a Kempis, *De imitatione Christi libri quatuor*. Parmae: in aedibus Palatinis, typis Bodonianis, 1793. Bound in granite-like leather with green and ochre mottling and gold tooling. RB, IX/7196

and outer corners by the same rosette used for the Horace, as we have seen previously and in several other bindings, whereas the queen's copy displays roll decoration consisting of a central line flanked by two lines of cat's tooth. In the first copy, for example, the four inner corners of each cover are decorated with a tool commonly used by Guarnaschelli and also featured on that of the queen, although here it is extended with another. The edges of the paper are gilded and the interior is covered with moiré endpapers with a natural marbled design in several colours; a roll bearing a design also characteristic of the bindery is used on the squares. The board edges are marked with a two-line roll; and the headbands with tools with thick diagonal lines.

Certainly, an examination of the bindings on the two copies in the Real Biblioteca, which display ornamental elements previously found on the Horace, might allow us to attribute them to Bodoni's binder, Guarnaschelli, who was perhaps also responsible for the copy whose binding is praised by Azaro. The personalised printed dedication found at the beginning of each one shows that they are the copies sent to the king and queen, which were furthermore accompanied from Parma by letters from the Duke Don Ferdinand to the Spanish monarchs. Nevertheless, it was Bodoni himself who ensured that the books arrived in Madrid, enlisting the aid of Llaguno, whom he asked to arrange for Godoy to present them to the king and queen on his behalf. The letters exchanged also enable us to identify this type of binding as what Bodoni defines as *all'inglese*, which is described in greater detail in the essay on which the present article is based and in which I also analyse other examples in the Real Biblioteca.[44]

Of them we have also chosen for the exhibition the Real Biblioteca's example of Bodoni's new tour de force and one of the most important of his output: the folio-size book of the *Pitture di Antonio Allegri detto il Correggio esistenti nel Monistero di San Paolo*, which came out in 1800 after a long process [fig. 137]. It is one of Bodoni's few books in which the illustrations are the essential part, as its purpose was to make known the outstanding frescoes painted by the young Correggio in the apartments decorated on the instructions of the abbess, Giovanna di Piacenza, for her use in the aforementioned convent in Parma. The book we can admire today, in two issues in folio and quarto sizes, is the end result of a long process that documents the genesis of the printer's idea—which, as nearly always, depended on other initiatives—and the various changes the project underwent over the course of more than five years. The copy housed in the Real Biblioteca and on show here is the folio issue and is extraordinary in every way—for its support (it is one of the few to be printed on vellum paper with engravings on thick paper) and for its intended recipient, King Charles IV. It features a neoclassical typographic title page typical of Bodoni, the dedication—actually written by Tomasso Valperga di Calusso—the description of the Camera di San Paolo printed in different characters for each of the three languages in which it is published, Italian, French and

Spanish (making it one of the rare Spanish texts printed by Bodoni) and the thirty-four plates reproducing details of Correggio's frescoes, preceded by an allegorical frontispiece. The drawings from which the engravings were made were executed by the Portuguese Francisco Vieira and were engraved by Rosaspina using a technique that has sometimes confused the inexperienced. The present copy contains the engravings in sanguine, which have more nuances—the *sfumature* to which Bodoni refers when discussing them—and are more attractive compared to another issue in black.

Once again, the mentions found in the correspondence of Azara and Bodoni are among the earliest references to a publication disseminating the rediscovered frescoes of Correggio. The Spanish diplomat, to whom, as Corrado Mingardi suggests, Mengs might have mentioned the work and suggested the authorship, according to Ireneo Affò, after viewing the paintings on passing through Parma,[45] was the first person who seems to have taken the initiative to reproduce or encourage the reproduction of the whole iconographic scheme. Indeed, by 1790 he had arranged for the issuing of permits—the convent was still owned by the Benedictine nuns—from the Parmesan authorities, the Infante Don Ferdinand and the Prime Minister Count Cesare Ventura, all of whom must have approved the project "di fare incidere in rame i quadri di Correggio, che sono in codesto convento di monache. Li faranno copiare e poi mi manderano le copie, e sarano incisse da Volpato e Morghen a conto loro".[46] It is evident from these words from Azara to Bodoni that the former intends simply to publish a series of prints by famous engravers and that the printer was therefore not part of the initial project. But things did not go as Azara had hoped, as in February 1791 he asks Bodoni if the reproduction work is under way: "Malgrado le promesse fattemi di farli incidere, temo che non se ne facia niente, giachè vedo che in Parma non cè altro che Bodoni, che facia."[47] Apart from this considerable apathy, no less of an impediment to the project was the reluctance of Bishop Turchi, who "imbroglia l'affare" on several pretexts.[48] Indeed, Azara, with his reputation for a religious sceptic and priest-hater, did not get on well with the bishop and conveys this enmity in the many ironic comments to this effect in his letters, some of which we have examined earlier. In the same letter he regrets that, having gone to this trouble "per puro amore dell'Arte", it should not be possible to take the project forward.[49]

When the Spaniard writes that Bodoni is the only one in Parma who is doing anything he is in fact prophesising; for as on other occasions, the printer's keen eye for certain business opportunities or for self-promotion eventually led him to consider bringing out the edition of engraved reproductions himself accompanied by explanatory texts on what was by then the painter's legendary early work. Bodoni's own project for the publication began to fall into place in 1794; a few scholars of Parma had visited the Camera in July, in addition to Vieira and Rosaspina, who eventually executed the drawings and engravings published by Bodoni. But the current characteristics of what had initially been intended (and failed) as a book to be presented during the wedding of Maria

Antonietta of Bourbon Parma—third child of the Duke Don Ferdinand and, incidentally, a lover of painting—and later became a book to commemorate the birth in Madrid of Don Ferdinand's grandson and heir of the Duchy, progressively took shape in Bodoni's mind from the second half of 1795 onwards, not without doubts and changes, as we know from a letter from Vieira to Rosaspina of 11 September that year. Vieira discloses that the printer is thinking of publishing engravings of the entire surviving oeuvre of Correggio in Parma, including the frescoes of the Camera di San Paolo, the drawings of which the Portuguese had been keeping since visiting it, with a few comments in verse by Giovanni Gerardo De Rossi, director of the Portuguese school in Rome and author of the poems of the *Scherzi*. He had in mind a book of pictures and poems similar in format and design to this work,[50] a copy of which is included in the exhibition. Vieira began working on the main paintings of Parma but Bodoni also ruled out this idea at an early stage, although he used these drawings by Vieira in another important work of his, *Le più insigni pitture parmensi* (1809, although not distributed until after his death in 1813), and together with his collaborators, the Portuguese and Rosaspina, concentrated on preparing the *Pitture* of the Camera di San Pablo.

The work of the two artists, directed by Bodoni, became hectic. As the frescoes of the Camera had aroused much expectation in the art world and interest had not waned in bringing out more or less full sets of prints illustrating the main motifs, Bodoni repeatedly urged his collaborators to act with utmost discretion. Meanwhile plans changed for the destination of the book—an aspect of crucial relevance to its dissemination, above all because Bodoni was orchestrating his role of ducal printer to the benefit of his own fame by devising publications of special importance for special occasions related to the ducal family, as we have seen earlier in other cases. And so, while on 18 September 1795 Bodoni discloses to Vieira that he is thinking of dedicating the work to the duke's daughter to mark her wedding, a few days later, on receiving news of the heir Don Luis's wedding to María Luisa of Bourbon on 28 August at the royal site of San Ildefonso, he discards the initial plan and decides "pubblicare questa camera del Correggio con una descrizione italiana, spagnola, francese, ed inglese",[51] and to present the book to the spouses when they returned to the states of Parma.[52] Their return was delayed and Bodoni accordingly slowed down the publication, although the engravings were ready by August 1796. All that remained was to complete the iconographical series with Vieira's allegorical frontispiece, which Rosaspina later engraved in 1798,[53] and to start composing and printing the descriptive introduction to the Camera, which had been entrusted to De Rossi and which Bodoni was waiting for in Parma in September 1796.[54] As we have seen, the Italian original was also to be published in French, Spanish and English, although the latter version must have finally been ruled out; nevertheless, when commissioning the Spanish version in December 1797, Bodoni tells Azara he is waiting for the English version to arrive from London.[55]

Apart from the requisite of the arrival in Parma of the infante and his wife, nor did

Fig. 137
Giovanni Gherardo De Rossi, *Pitture di Antonio Allegri detto il Correggio esistenti in Parma nel Monistero di San Paolo.* Parma: nel Regal Palazzo co' tipi Bodoniani, 1800. Bound in mottled leather with gold tooling. RB, VIII/219

the new political circumstances of 1796, what with the French invasion and the resulting disruption to movement and trade in Italy, overly encourage Bodoni to bring out a book to which subscribers did not appear to be reacting very enthusiastically, despite the interest it had aroused; by the beginning of 1796 barely thirty had committed themselves to purchasing the book following the first subscription campaign. Despite the progress made and the fact that the description —the last requisite for publishing the book— was already in press, the printer hesitated whether to go ahead with it.

However, an event that took place in the ducal family at last encouraged him to give definitive impetus to the publication: the birth of Carlos Luis Fernando of Bourbon, son of the heir to the duchy, Don Luis, and María Luisa of Bourbon, daughter of Charles IV and María Luisa of Parma, at the Royal Palace of Madrid on 22 December 1799. As Bodoni writes to Rosaspina, although he was waiting for the parents to return, as there was no scheduled date he therefore decided to take the opportunity "per render pubblica un'opera che da varii anni si aspetta con impazienza"[56] and dedicate the book to the new mother. In the end both parents were the intended recipients—no doubt he was forced to change his mind owing to the conditions of the authorisation he had previously requested from the duke regarding the dedication—and he thus used the same the formula of *service* employed earlier to commemorate the baptism of the newborn's father, the publication of one of his first typography manuals, the *Iscrizioni esotiche* (1774); and which he would later repeat for the birth of Napoleon's son the King of Rome, the very rare *Cimelio tipografico-pittorico* of 1811, in which the texts and plates of Rossi's *Scherzi* were used to make up a new typography manual, the last one to be published in the printer's lifetime.

Bodoni needed to speed up the final stages of production. He obtained from Rosaspina the engravings required to complete a portion of copies and finished printing the descriptions in all three languages—in press by November 1799—by the end of 1799 or beginning of 1800. A few days after learning of the good news, he commissioned the dedication, to which he nevertheless put his own name, from the famous Tommaso Valperga di Calusso, his advisor over the course of many years on editorial enterprises involving Greek and Latin classics, among others. Indeed, this dedicatory letter features at the beginning of each of the three versions of the description. The French version of the description and dedication is by Giuseppe De Lama, as Bodoni comments to Calusso in a letter of 25 March and the translator himself states in his Bodonian catalogue.[57] In the same letter to the Piedmontese he also states that he hopes to have printed by Easter the Spanish version, "che è riuscita assai gradevole all'Infante Nostro, che ne volle far lettura di tutte tre".[58] De Lama himself provides us with the name of the Spanish translator, Esteban de Arteaga. Indeed, in December 1797 the printer had enlisted the help of Azara, for whom Arteaga worked, to request the translation, entrusting him with not disclosing it to anyone; the translation was ready at the end of the following January.[59] It is De Lama who tells us that the Spanish version of the dedication is by Francesco Baroni; although a younger man, he was a friend of the printer and the members of his closest circle, such as De Lama himself, and also a collector of Bodoni editions placed on sale in 1817 after his death.[60]

In order to complete the copies of the book, Bodoni had to commission sets of engravings and the frontispiece illustration progressively from Rosaspina, who was working in Bologna. By August 1800 he had put together the presentation copies and sent to Madrid seven books "elegantemente legate all'inglese" [elegantly bound in English style] for the Crown prince and his wife, to whom they were dedicated; for King Charles IV; for Queen María Luisa of Parma; for the Infante Don Antonio; for the Prime Minister Mariano Luis de Urquijo; and for Esteban Mendizábal, then third secretary of the office of the Secretary of State, who after working with Azara in Rome had developed a closer relationship with Bodoni.[61] Many documentary records survive of the vicissitudes suffered by these copies in such troubled times as the year 1800.[62] After the first shipment went missing, he sent further copies of the book to the court, this time using a more secure means—in the luggage of Manuel Salabert, who wrote from Bologna offering to take the books and entrust them to his father, the Marquis of Torrecillas, to present them to the king and queen and other authorities. Bodoni accepted his offer and specifies the contents of the two boxes of books on 22 September: "Nella 1ª si contengono due copie legate all'inglese della *Descrizione* della famosa camera dipinta dal celebre Correggio in Parma. Ed avanti al frontispizio d'ognuna si trova una intitolazione stampata. La prima è per sua maestà il Re, la seconda è destinata per sua maestà la Regina."[63] This time the books did reach their intended recipients, who had them by the end of November. It goes without saying that Bodoni, as was his custom, had also taken advantage of the need to resend them to position himself and adapt once again to the authorities and latest developments in those unsettled times—the political downfalls and rises that occurred during the transition from 1800 to 1801, from Godoy to Urquijo, and from the latter to Cevallos, and with Godoy again outshining them all.

Of the two copies intended for the king and queen, the Real Biblioteca preserves the one now on display [fig. 137], which is one of the few copies whose text is printed on the new vellum-like paper from the manufactories of Pietro Miliani in Fabriano, and the engravings on paper of the same type that is much stronger and whiter than that of the ordinary edition in folio size. It is a truly royal copy, which furthermore preserves the dedication to Queen María Luisa of Parma and, of course, the "English-style" binding mentioned by Bodoni.

The binding has the same air of the characteristic, accomplished style of the Parma bindery. For example, compared to the two copies of the Kempis, the spine is more sober with only six raised bands instead of seven; the seven panels, each delimited only by a three-line pallet in the upper and lower part, are decorated with the same tool and without further gold ornamentation except for that of the single label in red morocco with the title in gold lettering impressed with individual tools. In view of a number of details referred to in the monograph from which this article is taken, this English-style binding could have been produced jointly at the workshop possibly run by Laferté's two pupils, Guarnaschelli and Signifredi.[64] The base leather of the spine and boards is also stained with hyssop; the marbling, however, is more elaborate than in the copies of the Kempis, because it displays two concentric borders, a narrow, finely speckled outer border delimited on the outside by a single-line roll and on the inside by roll-impressed cat's tooth and a single line, and an inner border in green—creating the impression of mosaic—delimited on the outer side by a roll tool of two wavy lines and on the inner side by one of three straight lines. At the corners of the green-dyed border and pointing to the centre is the same composition found on the queen's copy of the Kempis and on one of the bindings attributed to Signifredi. The edges are gilded; on the inner covers, endpapers very proficiently marbled in a herringbone pattern with predominant shades of blue, unlike any examined so far; on the squares, a roll pattern documented earlier in Parma; and on the edges of the boards, two-line rolls.

Other Bodonian Bindings and for the "Bodonis" in the Real Biblioteca

Azara died in 1804; the already scant international influence of the Spanish Crown had also been rapidly waning, and it was forced to give up Parma and hand over other territories to France. Bodoni, sharply adapting to the circumstances, ceased to look to Spain; as was only natural, he had decided to accept the protection of Napoleon's rulers, who gave fresh impetus to his ambitions. He soon replaced the official protection of the King of Spain with that of the Viceroy of Italy, the aforementioned Beauharnais, Napoleon's adoptive son. He justifies these changes in a letter dating from earlier than 1808—perhaps 1806—referring to the mismanagement of the Spanish diplomats, especially that Blasco de Orozco, ambassador to Turin, and leaves no doubts as to where his loyalties now lie:

> Altrettanto increscevole mi è riuscita l'inesattezza delle espresioni colle quali il prelodato Ministro ispano accenna di averlo addimandato a Madrid. Poiché in quel dì benavventurato che l'augusto principe Eugenio, mio nuovo padrone e signore, ebbe la degnazione di accogliermi sotto l'alto suo padrocinio e noverarmi fra suoi certissimi servidori, io le dissi candidamente che già da gran tempo era decorato del titolo di tipografo di camera del monarca ibero, e che percepiva già da varii anni non tenue pensione. Degnossi allora l'ottimo umanissimo Viceré di accertarmi coll'innata sua clemenza ch'egli stesso avrebbe fatto ricercare l'opportuno permesso onde poter passare al suo servizio colla continuazione della medesima tanto lena e vigoria donde tramandare alla più tarda posterità l'augusto suo imperial nome con qualche opera degna di cedro, e che il tempo edace non disgruggera sì presto.[65]

We do not know whether Napoleon's adoptive son, Eugene, took this action or whether it was aimed at Charles IV or Joseph I. Indeed, the former royal printer to His Catholic Majesty, with the temporary change of dynasty in Spain and despite the earlier promises of exclusive loyalty, offered his services to Joseph Bonaparte—whom he would have met in Parma in 1797 during the latter's ambassadorship—soon afterwards, in 1811, in an attempt to recover his position and wages, presenting his case as a continuation of the earlier Bourbon privileges; it was the same year that Bodoni spares no praise for the French elites in Italy in the aforementioned magnificent and extremely rare *Cimelio tipografico-pittorico* commemorating the birth of the emperor's son and in the first volume belonging to the series of his French classics, La Rochefoucauld's *Maximes*, dedicated to Fernando Marescalchi, Minister of Foreign Affairs of the Kingdom of Italy, and in the French version of the *Songe de Poliphile*, dedicated to the Queen of Naples, General Murat's wife.

As a result of the foregoing, books ceased to arrive at the palace from Parma during the final years of Charles IV's reign; and those that arrived during the reign of Joseph I—to whom it is only logical that Bodoni or his mentors would have sent the most significant—were removed from the country or lost along with his possessions when he abandoned Spain.

Bodoni died on 30 November 1813. The fall of Napoleon and the ensuing political changes, which brought the restoration of the Duchy of Parma under Marie Louise of Austria, who made her entry in 1816, and the return to the Spanish throne of the Bourbons at the end of 1813, also changed the strategies of the printer's successors. Apart from De Lama's monograph and bibliography published in 1816 and the collection of the works of Mazza, few important books other than those begun by Bodoni were published during the time the printing house was run by his widow, Paola Margherita dell'Aglio. After working on it for years, Bodoni left unpublished one of his valuable works, the *Manuale tipografico del cavaliere Giambattista Bodoni*, which was published by his widow—"presso la Vedova"—as we read on the title page, in two excellent volumes in quarto format. To comment on what Bodoni wrote in his prologue or go into detail about its contents and characteristics would offend the knowledge of the reader, who is well aware of the importance of this publication in the history of books. A month after the work was presented to the duchess, who had deigned to accept the widow's dedication, the copy sent to King Ferdinand VII arrived in Madrid. Personalised with a printed dedicatory note and a letter from its sender, it had left Parma on the 13th of the month. The person entrusted with "inoltrarlo" [dispatching it] was Eusebio Bardaxí y Azara, nephew of Nicolás and then ambassador in Turin, from where he had the copy sent on to Madrid. This copy is now housed in the Real Biblioteca and on display in the exhibition [fig. 138]. If we examine the list of copies sold and given away by Bodoni's widow until 1820, we find that Bardaxí, a diplomat and nephew of Azara, was the recipient of another copy. A few days later, perhaps in accordance with the political significance of the act of presentation, the book was sent to Charles IV in exile in Rome, where he died the following year.[66] It is clear that Bodoni's firm is grateful and, above all, is endeavouring to re-establish the earlier relations that are again predominant in Europe.

Through his secretary, Ferdinand VII sends his thanks from Sacedón on 18 July in a rather curt letter[67] which does not precisely shine amid the corpus of enthusiastic acknowledgements, some of them generous—the duchess gives him a timepiece, the tsar a ring, the King of Sardinia another ring, the Grand Duke of Tuscany a chain, the pope two gold medals and others wish to give in cash the one hundred *livres* that is the selling price of the book—which Ciavarella received for his prologue of the first facsimile edition of the *Manuale* brought out by Franco Maria Ricci. I believe I am not imagining it when I read between the lines his Catholic Majesty's lack of interest in these objects that were so admired by his grandfather, his uncles, their advisers and somewhat more than him his father. We should therefore perhaps not be surprised that only three names linked to the Catholic Monarchy—Ferdinand VII, Ambassador Bardaxí and Charles IV—should feature on the list of recipients of gift copies and that there is not a single Spaniard among those who spent the handsome sum the two volumes fetched by the time they came out, compared to the presence of Italian and French bibliophiles and booksellers such as Renouard, who purchased eleven copies, as well as their English counterparts.

The *Manuale* in the Real Biblioteca is preserved in the same state in which it was sent from Parma, still displaying the printed *ad personam*, and bound in boards covered in paper with the appearance of morocco leather; the spine is divided into five sections by double rows of horizontal lines worked with a roll, with no further ornament than the small circle indicating the volume number; in the second panel the title and author's name are impressed in gold with individual tools in capitals, and the one at the base displays the printer's name and the year. The boards are framed with two-line rolls; the endpapers are made of strong, deep blue paper [fig. 138]. It is thus the only original paper-covered Bodoni binding housed in the Real Biblioteca. Most of the copies issued in Parma were like this one; compared to the present copy, the only difference I find is that not all display the gold frame on the covers.

Appreciation for paper-covered Bodoni editions is not only a modern-day phenomenon; indeed, in the printer's own day many collectors preserved the books in *cartoncino arancione*, with moiré paper or, like the present copy, red morocco-like paper. As the copies bound in printer's boards were generally uncut, the volume had the same appearance as when it was released from the printing house, without any loss of margins. This pristine condition gradually became a requirement of collectors, which the printer himself encouraged and managed to establish, perhaps because the simplicity of the binding better showed off the quality or importance of his work, which could also be extended to the *all'impostura* bindings of the grander copies that Bodoni himself prepared for important libraries or occasions.

The Real Biblioteca's Bodoni editions examined so far and on display in the exhibition include neither all the main examples of his feverish output nor all those Bodoni sent to Madrid. For example, Tasso's *La Gerusalemme liberate*, dated 1794 on the title page—even though in October that year he was still waiting to be able to add the dedication to King

Charles IV, whose authorisation had been sought by Count Ventura—is one of the essential works from the most productive years of his private printing house. Five editions, as Bodoni calls them, were published simultaneously, all of them dedicated to the King of Spain as one of the tributes with which he wished to express his gratitude for the allowance granted to him in 1793. He states this in the subscription "manifesto" for the series of classics he planned bring out, of which Dante's *Commedia* and the songs of Petrarch were actually published, in addition to *La Gerusalemme*. The rarest—and, certainly, most magnificent—of these editions, consisting of less than one hundred copies on vellum-like paper in three volumes in folio size, with two verses of the poem per page in italics, is not preserved in the Real Biblioteca. However, there is a copy of the first and most representative edition, in two volumes in large folio size printed on laid paper with three verses in roman per page; the print run totalled one hundred and fifty copies, one hundred of which were allotted to subscribers. *Ad calcem*, Bodoni thought of sending two copies, the first of this edition, to Madrid, one for the king and the other for Godoy, together with the compilation of the works of the Latin elegiac poets that Azara had arranged to be bound in Parma for the king and instructed Bodoni to send through the Spanish consul in Livorno.[68] He had to abandon this idea owing to the insecurity of all transport in Italy and the Mediterranean at the time. Taking up the offers of a certain chaplain, Luigi del Fiume, who was returning to Spain after a stay in Parma as part of the retinue of the minister, Count Ventura, he had eight copies bound "magnificamente all'inglese" for the king and queen and other prominent members of the court and entrusted them to the "prete" [priest] in June 1795. Fiume tricked him and, as Bodoni himself tells his friend Mendizábal years later, "non lo presentò in mio nome, anzì furono smarrite le lettere che accompagnavano la mia non indifferente offerta. Il prete ottenè non so qual pensione ecclesiastica, ed io non ho mai avuto il menomo riscontro su i libri predetti."[69] Sometime afterwards Azara did not waste the opportunity to remind him implicitly of the consequences of taking the initiative of sending books to Madrid at his own risk and expense,[70] something which, in the hasty and self-seeking race to offer his *services* with a view to securing

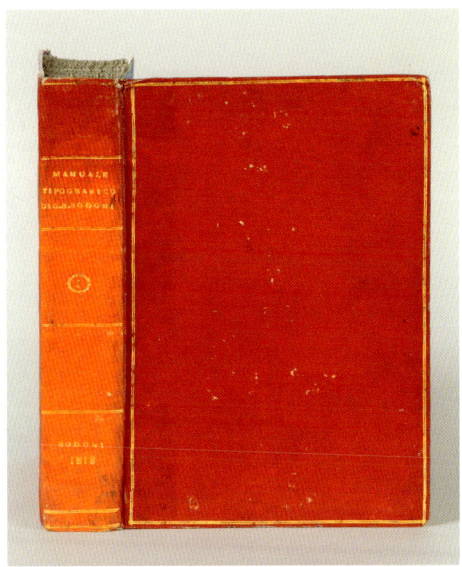

Fig. 138
Giambattista Bodoni, *Manuale tipografico del cavaliere Giambattista Bodoni*. Parma: presso la Vedova, 1818. Bound in red printer's boards with gold tooling. Vol. I. RB, IV/5477

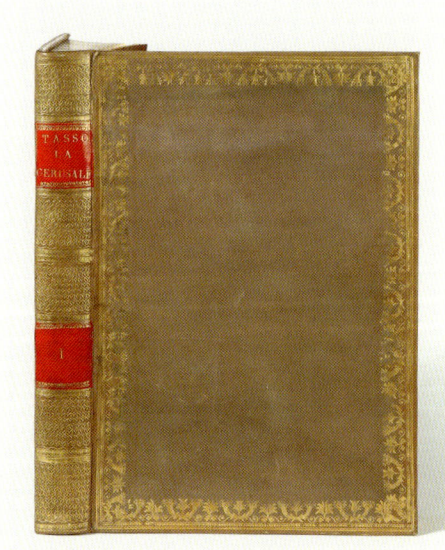

Fig. 139
Torquato Tasso, *La Gerusalemme liberata*. Parma: nel Regal Palazzo co'tipi Bodoniani, 1794. Bound in morocco with gold tooling. Vol. I. RB, VIII/6120

honours and privileges, could prove as hazardous as it might be beneficial.

Indeed, the copy in the Real Biblioteca of *La Gerusalemme liberata di Torquato Tasso* [fig. 139], on show in this exhibition, is not one of those bound in what Bodoni refers to as the English style; rather, it displays the same characteristics as the books in the library of the Infante Don Antonio which, initially acquired in paper covers, were then bound in Madrid, like two other works also on show, the *Scherzi poetici e pittorici* of 1795, with a text by Giovanni Gherardo De Rossi and illustrations by Teixeira engraved by Rosaspina [fig. 140], and the Τρυφιοδορου Αιγυπτιου του γραμματικου Ιλιου αλωσις published the following year in two editions in quarto and small folio size [figs. 141 and 142]. We have seen earlier how Bodoni is asked to send even some of the books he presents as gifts unbound; in one case the explanation given is that they will take up less space during transportation, but in others the recipients are stated to prefer Madrid bindings. Following the completion of the 1793 edition of the Virgil, the second of the Latin classics sponsored by Azara, the latter describes the impression it caused on arriving in Madrid bound in paper boards, as requested, and Godoy's haste in presenting it to the king, once "Sancia famosso legatore lo ricoprisse".[71] This is the copy housed in the Real Biblioteca and currently on show, which evidences the craftsmanship and the ornamentation used by Gabriel Sancha (XI/3445 and 3446).

It seems evident that in Madrid clients preferred local bookbinding which, judging from these copies, was gradually shifting away from the more Baroque features still found in the Parma-bound copies and towards the purely neoclassical styles that were then becoming fashionable in other parts of Europe. Roll-worked designs on the covers and ornamentation on spines without raised bands were inspired by the same classical elements —amphorae, lamps, Greek and Roman borders— that were the basis of the ornamentation which would soon find its way to other greater and lesser arts. We may therefore speak of a certain readjustment of the bindings for Bodonian books in Europe. In the case of Spain, one swallow does not make a summer, and the example of Don Antonio, himself a lover of binding, cannot be extended to other Spaniards who completed their collections of Bodoni editions in Spanish binderies.

Fig. 140
Giovanni Gherardo De Rossi, *Scherzi poetici e pittorici*. Parma: co'tipi Bodoniani, 1795. Bound in *pasta valenciana* with gold tooling by Santiago Martín. RB, VIII/2322

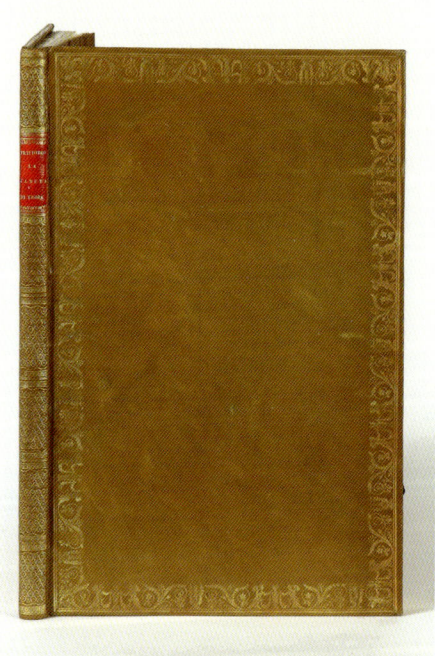

However, certain trends may be noted in the cases of France and England. It is common to find in libraries and even on the antique market a fairly sober type of neoclassical binding for Bodoni books, especially for his issues of classical authors, executed by Kalthoeber or Pyne to mention two of the great English binders. They display striking similarities to the much more abundant examples by Jean-Claude Bozérian, whose bindings for Bodoni books were also mass produced—"par masses", as Beraldi put it. It is likely that Bodoni, who was familiar with the Bozérians' work, liked this very sober, very neoclassical type of binding that was so appropriate to his books, although we know that he turned down Renouard's offer to have a series of his books in octavo bound in Paris, claiming that he did not wish to offend the binders of Parma. This renunciation of innovation out of loyalty to people like Domenico Guarnaschelli and the other craftsmen of Parma, whose style might prove somewhat archaic over time, honoured him, although it could also be judged as a hindrance to the prestige of Bodoni's editions in Europe and, of course, to the development of the art of binding in Parma.

Fig. 141
Tryphiodorus, *Tryphiodorou Aigyptiou tou grammatikou Iliou alosis.* Parmae: in Aedibus Palatinis, Typis Bodonianis, 1796. Leather binding with gold tooling by Santiago Martín. RB, XIX/8290

Fig. 142
Tryphiodorus, *Tryphiodorou Aigyptiou tou grammatikou Iliou alosis.* Parmae: in Aedibus Palatinis, Typis Bodonianis, 1797. Leather binding with gold tooling by Francisco Cifuentes. RB, VIII/6130

1 [It is quite true that here you are the most highly appreciated of all printers of the world from 1450 to today, and that they are all a bunch of ... compared to the great Bodoni.] This article is a much abbreviated version of the essay originally written for this volume, which is too extensive and is due to be published elsewhere (see, in the bibliography, CATEDRA in press [a]). The letters and documents used as sources, when no specific bibliographic details are provided, will be progressively published in the several volumes of my *G. B. Bodoni y los españoles,* the first of which has already come out (CATEDRA 2010). The research was conducted as part of the project *Público, libro, innovación tipográfica y bibliofilia internacional en el Siglo de las Luces: Bodoni y España,* carried out at the University of Salamanca with the support of the Ministerio de Ciencia e Innovación (FFI2011–23223). Part of the necessary time spent in national and foreign libraries was financed by grant PR2010-0558 from the "Subprograma de estancias de movilidad de profesores e investigadores españoles en centros extranjeros de enseñanza superior e investigación", Ministerio de Educación.
2 The Bodonian library of the Infante Don Antonio and the involvement of Bodoni and the Spanish booksellers in its formation are dealt with in greater detail in a monograph (CATEDRA in press [b]).
3 The plan would have been to overhaul the existing library of which the surviving catalogue of 1782 has been published and studied by LÓPEZ-VIDRIERO 2002.
4 [Unbound in order to please [the Prince's] fondness for having them bound here.]
5 See BERTINI 1983, 42–46; and also GORRERI 1994, 49–51—this monograph is the most complete on Laferté in Parma—and, more recently, CAROSELLI 2010, 55–56. I am grateful to Dr Giuseppe Bertini and Dr Silvana Gorreri for their attention and advice, and also to Federicho Macchi for providing the essential information that I include in the extended version of this essay.
6 On this, the visit and the production of the book see MINGARDI 1990.
7 [Surprising, and which honours him infinitely.]
8 CIAVARELLA 1979, I, 55–57. Despite the value of Ciavarella's meritorious edition, we are working on a new edition of this essential correspondence.
9 For further details, see CATEDRA in press [a].
10 See CATEDRA in press [b].
11 GORRERI 1994, 55–59.
12 The most extensive and recent contribution on this binder is CAROSELLI 2010, 55 and ff. For other bindings, see CATEDRA in press [a].
13 Apart from the aforementioned, see the references provided by GOTOR 1992
14 [So superb that nothing further be known of the aforesaid.]
15 CIAVARELLA 1979, I, 115.

16 *Ibid.,* II, 35. [For love of God, let it not occur to you to sully our Horace with frills or engraved adornments, as all its beauty must lie in the print and cleanness of the text.]
17 *Ibid.,* I, 140. [Not a single copy should be released.]
18 *Ibid.,* II, 10. [For folio size the character should be fairly thick, otherwise it is weak and without force and tiresome to read.]
19 *Ibid.,* II, 14. [Let us decide for once and for all.]
20 *Ibid.,* II, 21.
21 *Ibid.,* II, 23
22 *Ibid.,* II, 30.
23 *Ibid.,* II, 33.
24 *Ibid.,* II, 48.
25 *Ibid,.* II, 51. [In English style, in green morocco because there is no red .... I do not know how it will come out because the best binder we had left without notice and I gather that he is at the printing house of Padua Seminary ... meanwhile I shall make haste to have the king's copy ready, and I am pleased to say that it will be ready as soon as I have checked mine.]
26 *Ibid.,* II, 56.
27 *Ibid.,* II, 58.
28 See, however, CATEDRA in press [a].
29 CIAVARELLA 1979, II, 64.
30 JIMENO PUYOL 2010, 1792. [I have just found out that the ship carrying my Horaces, the shipment of which I have not had news of for two months, had arrived in Barcelona .... The Horace has aroused great enthusiasm all over Italy and even more in England, from which I receive countless letters. Bodoni has established his reputation with this work and is marking a new era in the annals of printing. You, who had him awarded the title of printer to the king, pray perfect the deed by proposing that His Majesty grant him a small allowance so that he does not live solely with the pittance from Parma, which is a disgrace; and truly, I can say that, without the help of this poor soul, this great artist would still remain in obscurity. Whatever hardship we are experiencing, a little help will not make us any poorer or any richer; and there are few things in which the king could use it so honourably.]
31 [In view of the distinguished merit of your honour, who is so well known throughout Europe by those who love the arts and hold them in high esteem, and as a token of how much the king has appreciated the magnificent works you have sent him on different occasions.]
32 CATEDRA 2010, 42–43. [They have no idea and appreciate them less than on good paper; this taste has not yet caught on in my Arabia.]
33 See CATEDRA in press [a] and [b].
34 There are few similar cases. I am grateful to Dr Federico Macchi for making known to me the signature of the binder Antonio Cantoni, active in Bergamo from 1666 to *c.*1700, who placed his name on the inner edge of the front cover and the city where

35. he exercised his profession in the place where Guarnaschelli's name is.
35. I discuss these tools individually in Catedra in press [a].
36. I am grateful to Valentin Moreno of the Real Biblioteca for his expert definition of this coat of arms. See Moreno 2008, 42–45, 139, ill. 48.
37. See, however, Catedra in press [a].
38. [Not without a certain peculiar splendour and elegance.]
39. De Lama 1816, II, 80. [Perhaps Italy may be impartial when judging the Parisian printer and the one of Parma.]
40. [Work written on paper called vellum, from the workshop of Montgolfier (father and son), in the town which bears the name of Annonay, with the first roman characters cast by Henri Didot, the second son of Pierre-François Didot.]
41. For this matter and Bodoni's reaction, see Catedra in press [c].
42. [Forty years practically dedicated to books, judging that nothing concerning them is alien to me, encompassing each and every one of their aspects.]
43. [The monuments of the sacred writings superbly and magnificently composed with my characters.]
44. Catedra in press [a].
45. Mingardi 1994, 208. We refer to this work for various aspects of the production of the original drawings and of the vicissitudes of Bodoni's edition, and also to the more recent Raggi 2005. On the subject of the apartments, an essential reference work continues to be the compilation by Barocelli 1988, which reproduces various documents including some of those published by Bodoni and his circle, to which I refer here.
46. Ciavarella 1979, II, 42. [To have engraved the paintings of Correggio which are in this convent of nuns. They will copy them and then send me the copies and Volpato and Moghen will make the engravings themselves.]
47. Ibid., II, 44. [Despite promising me they would be engraved, I fear that nothing has been done; as far as I can see, the only one who is doing anything in Parma is Bodoni.]
48. Ibid., II, 45. [Is complicating matters.]
49. Raggi 2005, 48.
50. Ibid., 54, who transcribes in a note the letter from Vieira housed in the Biblioteca Comunale de Forlì, Fondo Piancastelli, Carte Romagne 397.519.
51. [To publish this Camera of Correggio with a description in Italian, Spanish, French and English.]
52. As he writes to Rosaspina (Servolini 1958, 115).
53. The production process is reconstructed in detail by Raggi 2005, 52–62 from the letters exchanged by the three parties.
54. Servolini 1958, 183.
55. Ciavarella 1979, II, 133.
56. Servolini 1958, 250. [In order to make known a work which has been impatiently awaited for several years.]
57. De Lama 1816, II, 139.
58. Ciravegna 1942, 237). [Which has so greatly pleased our Infante who wishes to read all three … bound in English style with great elegance.]
59. Ciavarella 1979, II, 134.
60. For further information on his role in this publication and his relationship with the Spanish diplomats, see Catedra in press [a].
61. Ciavarella 1979, II, 158.
62. Catedra in press [a].
63. [The first includes two copies bound in English style of the *Descrizione* of the famous Camera painted by the celebrated Correggio in Parma. At the front of each one is a printed dedication. The first is for his majesty the king, the second is addressed to her majesty the queen.]
64. Catedra in press [a].
65. [Equally unbearable do I find the vagueness of the expressions with which the celebrated Spanish minister indicates that he has sent it to Madrid. After that blessed day in which the august Prince Eugene, my new patron and lord, deigned to accord me his high protection and count me among his most certain servants, I ingenuously mentioned to him that long ago I had been distinguished with the title of royal printer to the King of Spain, and that I had enjoyed a by no means insignificant allowance for some years. The great and very human viceroy deigned to assure me with his innate clemency that he himself would have given orders for the appropriate permit to be sought in order that I may pass into his service preserving the same enthusiasm and vigour needed to have his august imperial name transcend to posterity with some work worthy of being remembered and which cruel time should not destroy within a short period.]
66. Ciavarella 1965, 38.
67. See Catedra in press [a].
68. Ciavarella 1979, II, 99.
69. [He did not present it on my behalf to say the least, and the letters which accompanied the by no means lukewarm offering were mislaid. The priest earned for himself some ecclesiastical allowance and I have received absolutely nothing for the said books.]
70. Ciavarella 1979, II, 120.
71. Ibid., II, 90. [Sancha, a famous binder, has re-bound it.]

Eadem Sed Aliter: Uniformity and Singularity in Royal Bindings

María Luisa López-Vidriero

Difference within the Multiple. Luxury in Similarity

The private royal library, in accordance with the symbolic role it is required to play in shaping the emblematic image of the royal figure, articulates a precise material language capable of meeting these allegorical needs for which it was created. A book's binding plays a primary role in this undertaking: it is the first and last part of a book to be seen and receives the initial and final contact of the reader's hands. This inaugural character makes the binding a privileged surface and an ideal terrain for establishing codes that immediately distinguish and identify the royal person's books.

Associating royal bookbinding with precious metals and stones, exquisite leathers and gold tooling is both typical and inevitable. A glance at the inventories of the Hapsburgs sweeps away any doubt about the value their bindings had for the appraisers. The amount of gold and silver was so significant that it was priced by weight, just like the pearls, rubies or diamonds that adorned these bindings. The covers of missals, books of hours, psalm books and entertainment books were luxury and saleable goods owing to the extraordinary richness of their composition, in the same way as tapestries, candlesticks, necklaces or trinkets.

And yet neither the inventories nor the catalogues, nor indeed the monarchs' own book collections, allow them to be considered as such.

While studies and research have concentrated mainly—almost exclusively—on outstanding examples of royal bookbinding, and their visual appeal has made these bindings favourite subjects of coffee-table books and magazine articles, as well as irresistible items for any exhibition, most of the bindings in the royal libraries are of a different sort. Neither showcases of materials nor displays of luxury, they fulfil the function of royal bindings: to distinguish all the king's books unmistakeably through a single language.

In these book covers, the principles of distinction and luxury are approached in a different way: royal bindings are serial, but they are repetitive only to the eyes of those who, disappointed by their apparent normalcy, do not take the time to discover their exceptional artistry, in which stylistic devices—materials, tools and supralibros—have been used with precise craftsmanship to create a corpus.

The challenge faced by these bindings is the opposite to that of rich bindings: they are part of a precise programme conceived to distinguish a whole as if it were a unit. Their luxury lies in their extension and sustainability. They do not seek to distinguish a particular book among a thousand, but rather to make clear that the lasting solemnity of the king's library is their responsibility, and that these bindings embody the meaning of a unique and distinctive book collection.

Since its formation, the personal, private or chamber library offers abundant examples of serial bindings that form large, differentiated sets which are in keeping with the aesthetic of the time, sensitive to the addition of new materials, and extremely interesting in that they are programmatic proposals established for a specific representation of a royal figure.

From this standpoint, an analysis of royal bindings by reigns reveals aspects of the workshops of the craftsmen appointed as royal binders that cast their profession in a new and fairer light, closer to the reality of their trade, and help provide a more legitimate understanding of the Real Biblioteca's collection of artistic and historical bindings.

Court bookbinders held their posts and maintained their workshops thanks to these special but mass-produced bindings—in that respect we should consider them pre-industrial—that provided them with a steady income and a permanent relationship that was a constant source of earnings and promotion. The king's library was considered a preferential client because it offered stable work—and the opportunity to work with its outstanding holdings—to bookbinding artists capable of rising to the challenge of displaying their art by clothing unique pieces.

The studies on palace bindings listed in Concha Lois's exhaustive bibliography unmistakeably show that, in the past, court bindings have been approached in a positivist manner, focusing on marks of ownership—bookplates and supralibros—and the most exceptional pieces crafted by outstanding binders. Those studies concentrate on the main features of the collection, in accordance with an approach based on an elementary concept of bibliographical treasures and, although valuable in other ways, they cannot provide an understanding of the exceptional cultural phenomenon that is entailed by the existence of a collection of royal bindings in the private royal library.

A reconstruction of this part of the history of palace bookbinding, in which archival documentation is combined with locating the books themselves and making exhaustive descriptions and comparative and sequential studies of binders' tools, draws on many fields of knowledge, as well as advances in computer processing and digitisation. It is yet another example of how a cultural analysis of bibliographical heritage is significant when the research is approached as a team effort. This has allowed me to avoid exhaustive, tiresome-to-read descriptions of each binding in the footnotes, in order to focus this article on specific information relevant to this research. All the details of the ornamentation and the classification of the tools may be found in the automated database of the Real Biblioteca.[1]

Systematic Identification: Pascual Carsi Vidal, Santiago Martín and Pedro Pastor

The phenomenon of identifying cultural and sumptuary goods is associated with the royal person and forms a part of our understanding of royal collecting. As vast as the existence of the private libraries, it requires certain limits to be set. The present study is therefore confined to the Contemporary Era.

The study of these books has allowed us to pinpoint the common traits shared by royal bindings during that period. The durability of these material and bibliographical elements leads them to be considered the basis for two hundred years of precise practice and, accordingly, a reliable guideline for analysing the work of royal bookbinders with respect to this other facet.

Binders' tools play a leading role among the lasting features of court bindings and, as we shall see, they pose one of the main problems when attempting to attribute work to particular binders. The fact that specific tools—rolls, fleurons, pallets and gouges—continued to be used over the years suggests that they were institutional property available to the court binders. Others were the personal property of each binder and can be identified as such. There were also tools that became fashionable and were therefore copied, making them difficult to tell apart. Finally, we must consider tools that were inherited or passed down from one binder to another. And these different types could coincide in a single binding.

Identifying the tools is essential to determining authorship because, owing to the nature of these bindings, binders tended not to sign or label them except on rare occasions.

The dyed sheepskins—*pastas*—used for binding are another common feature that binders attempted to maintain in accordance with particular models, even though there are clear differences from one workshop to another. Granite-marbled sheepskins and the mottled sheepskins known as *pastas valencianas* (in brown or green tones) and *pastas españolas* took precedence over the introduction of new materials and half-binding.

Bookbinders' bills—an essential research tool—also offer an invaluable insight into the technical vocabulary employed by these professionals when referring to types of work and materials. It was their way of referring to specific kinds of bindings, without necessarily mentioning tooled decoration; the mention of one book bound in a particular manner allowed the rest to be listed simply with an *idem*. This vocabulary bears little resemblance to the terms used nowadays to designate types of binding in accordance with their materials and craftsmanship.

Lastly, within these common features, we must consider the existence of specific book genres that received serial court bindings. Along with the general collection—in which manuscripts and printed works received the same consideration for this type of binding—there is also a distinctive and preferential core consisting of official publications produced by the Imprenta Real [royal printing house] and intended for official use in the court, celebratory editions for royal events, for example, and periodical works such as guides or almanacs. Once again, binders' invoices allow us to trace the production, quantification and fees charged for those serial bindings that distinguish sets of copies of an edition according to the sector of the court for which it is intended.

This approach to royal bindings does not aim to compile an exhaustive list of the binders themselves. The names and works of the craftsmen who are not dealt with here are mentioned in footnotes, waiting to occupy the pages of a forthcoming book.[2]

A key date in the process of systematically identifying the books in the king's private library is 1819. That year Santiago Martín embarked on the large-scale endeavour of pasting to them the bookplate designed in 1808 for the collection of Charles IV. Political events had kept these bookplates from being affixed when Felix Amat y Pont was chief librarian of the Real Biblioteca Privada.[3] When Ferdinand VII returned to the throne, the interrupted work at the private library was resumed, ushering in one of the most brilliant periods for the collection. The incorporation of the holdings of major libraries during the final years of Charles IV's reign—those of the Count of Gondomar, the *colegios mayores* or university residences of Salamanca, Francisco de Bruna, Joaquín Ibáñez García and the Secretaría de Gracia y Justicia de Indias—made it necessary to devise a means of visual standardisation to ensure that books received from private owners were associated with the king by their outward appearance. Pascual Carsi Vidal and Santiago Martín personify that link: their professional careers in the private royal library started out at precisely that time and were marked by the fortunes of war.

Pascual Carsi Vidal

Pascual Carsi received the honours and entitlement to wear the uniform of the *Real Furriera* [the office of the Royal Household in charge of keys, furniture and effects] under the same conditions as the chief officers of the Imprenta Real. By then, he was already bookbinder to HM and to the royal printing house. At the same time, on 7 July 1799, it was confirmed that his rank was equivalent to that of an assistant of the *Furriera* and he received the title of chamber bookbinder, placing him on a par with the chief officers of the Imprenta Real, as chamber printer and stamper.

He was sworn in on 16 July 1799. An acquittance dated 15 July indicated that the treasurer had already paid him the corresponding six thousand five hundred and sixteen *maravedíes* to which he was entitled.

He was unable to bill the work he did between 1806 and 1808 until after the war, in July 1814. It came to ten thousand nine hundred and three *reales* for one hundred and twenty-seven titles, many of which comprised several volumes. One of the jobs listed, for which he charged two-thousand *reales*, is described as follows: "For classifying the works belonging to HM and boxing them in forty-three crates, on which one journeyman, two hands and Carsi himself spent thirty-five days."[4] These were the books from the royal collection that were packed in 1808 to be sent to the infantes Don Fernando (Ferdinand VII), Don Carlos and Don Antonio Pascual at Talleyrand Castle in Valençay, where they remained during their exile. Carsi's widow, María Clark, received this payment years later, in 1819.

Carsi's bills document the binding of one hundred and thirty-one titles. With the exception of manuscripts bound in red morocco—in the second part of *Historia general*, "deluxe" is specified—the bindings are serial and made of calfskin, fine calfskin, dyed sheepskin, fine dyed sheepskin and finely marbled leather.

The *Guías de forasteros* or foreigners' guides were already distinguished as special items. Carsi began buying and binding them for Ferdinand VII while the latter was still Prince of Asturias and he delivered them on 31 December 1807. They constitute a finished example of the unique among the serial in courtly language: two deluxe copies with their cases (112 *reales* each), twelve fine copies (34 *reales* apiece), five medium-fine copies (30 *reales* each) and twenty-seven ordinary ones (20 *reales* each).[5]

In 1816, Carsi also billed the queen for his services. Along with his binding work, there are other tasks generally performed by royal bookbinders as part of their duties: desk tops in bottle-green morocco leather with gold tooling, as well as book spines simulating large folio-sized books to adorn her bookshelves. In 1818, he billed for making portfolios for music that also stood out for their luxury: in folio size, in red morocco with gilt edges; in deluxe and "less deluxe" dyed sheepskin. Several of his bills would remain unpaid and his son, Pascual Carsi Clark, eventually received the three thousand and fifty-two *reales* in 1819. A year later, Carsi's son began billing his own work.[6]

The price of Pascual Carsi's luxury work skyrocketed over the following thirty years. In 1850, the Valencian edition of Scio's Bible that had belonged to Cardinal Luis de Borbón y Vallabriga, bound by Carsi in morocco with gilt edges, was acquired through Poupart for one thousand three hundred and twenty *reales*.[7]

Santiago Martín

In 1804, Santiago Martín based his application for the post of royal bookbinder on the recognition due for his having bound the manuscripts of the king's private library in the Juego de Pelota workshop.

In 1803, Fernando Scio San Miguel, chief librarian of the Real Biblioteca Particular, had chosen him to execute the "delicate binding" of numerous manuscripts from the *colegios mayores* of Salamanca. In his application, Martín recalls with pride his very successful completion of this assignment, resulting in bindings comparable "to the most delicate English ones".[8] The consolidation of the differentiated serial image of the books of the Real Biblioteca was the responsibility of his workshop, a process of identification ratified by a supralibros with the king's cypher "CIIII" on the spine and the new heraldic bookplate systematically placed inside the covers of manuscript and printed works.

The professional pride he displays in his request is accompanied by a list of needs that beg for compassion: a widowed mother and a lack of tools to exercise his profession with the expertise of which he has proven himself capable. This appeal to pity, a long-standing tactic at court, provides a basic insight into how bookbinding functioned—both for representative purposes and for everyday use—in the private royal library. It sheds light on the use of "institutional" tools to standardise production—a practice that has often led certain bindings to be attributed to specific binders because these tools were held to be the property of a particular binder.

Martín's application, dating from early November 1804, was dealt with immediately, and he was appointed chamber bookbinder on 11 November. The Duke of Aliaga was commissioned on 19 December to swear him in. He was initially supposed to take oath of office at Aliaga's residence on the 23rd of the month at ten in the morning, but the session was postponed because Martín had not yet paid the tax associated with his appointment. Martín paid the corresponding fee, known as the *media anata*, in February 1805 and on the 12th the Duke of Aliaga arranged for him to be sworn in two days later in the presence of the *Grefier general* [assistant comptroller].[9]

In 1816, Santiago Martín sent a new report to the king. The basis of his new petition was the same as thirteen years earlier: proven professionalism and evident poverty.[10]

The twenty *reales* per day that he had been paid for systematically binding the collection of Charles IV's manuscripts had ensured his upkeep until the French invasion forced him to flee, leaving behind his family, his home and his workshop in the Juego de Pelota. He lost most of his tools in the process. Once again, as before the Peninsular War, Martín found himself without resources. In his petition, he asked to return to work, caring for and binding the king's books in exchange for whatever wages they saw fit.

The office of the *Sumiller* [chief officer of the royal chamber] supported his petition, stressing that a person of high repute was needed to maintain the collection and, at the same time, bind books within the palace, even in the library itself.[11] The invoices he submitted as chamber bookbinder in December 1816 refer to the work he performed repairing, cleaning and polishing all the books in rooms 11, 12 and 13 of the king's library. For the library of the king's second wife, Queen María Isabel Francisca of Braganza, he made twenty-four volumes of mock books in large folio size, bound in morocco leather, to cover the doors. This involved eleven weeks' work, amounting to a total of sixty days with the help of between three and four journeymen.[12]

The bookbinder's work involved more than just books and writing implements and extended to the furniture itself. Not only were his skills required to make trompe-l'oeil bookshelves: morocco leather, tooling and gold decoration also served to cover the monarchs' desks. Martín worked with cabinetmakers to outfit the king's furniture in a fashion similar to his books, as did his successor Antonio Suárez, who made a desk for Ferdinand VII that is still in the collection.[13]

During those same years, Martín concentrated on serial bindings for older printed works, including the collection of the Count of Gondomar. In 1819, he presented a bill for three thousand five hundred and ninety-five *reales* for the days his craftsmen spent cutting out thirty-seven thousand coats of arms and affixing them to the books in HM's chamber library.[14] That same year, he bound official periodicals, a preferred type of printed matter for serial royal bindings because it allowed the key variants of this kind of binding to be combined: standardisation and distinction. The uniform size and sequential nature of these annual publications made it possible to treat them as a whole in which the binder could nevertheless play with differences. In that sense, the royal binders' designs for them can be considered models for future artistic bindings of larger-format books.

Santiago Martín bound the *Guías de litigantes* and *Estados militares* in morocco leather with protective cases, charging seventy and ninety *reales* for them respectively.[15] His specialisation in the serial and distinctive binding of guidebooks continued throughout his career, and in the years that ensued his bills would include this exclusive work that began at the Imprenta Real, where he acquired specially printed and engraved materials which, combined with his binding work, resulted in a unique product. In 1820, his bill lists three full sets of "Guías compradas en papel" [guides purchased in paper]. It also specifies the separate purchase of portraits of their majesties and illuminated title pages for the *Guías de forasteros*, *Estados Militares*, *Guías de la Real Hacienda* and ecclesiastic guides. Martín produced special bindings featuring portraits of the monarchs and illuminated title pages, for which he charged thirty *reales*.

In fact, the Imprenta Real had some special components—engraved portraits of the monarch and illuminated frontispieces costing six *reales* per engraving or five per colour frontispiece—which bookbinders could insert, fold, mount and gild in order to provide the luxury binding with an eye-catching print that, although multiple within its singularity,

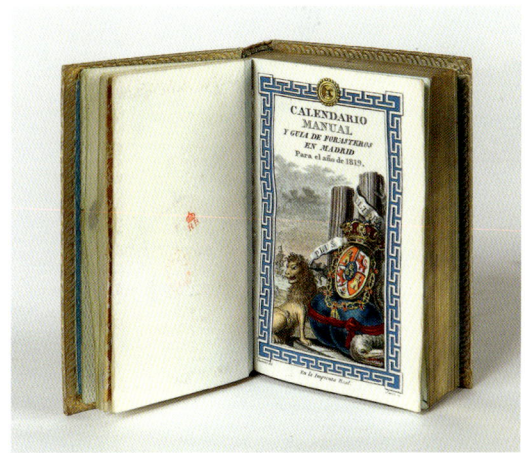

Figs. 143 and 144
[*Guía de forasteros de Madrid*]. Madrid: [n. n.], 1819. Portraits of Ferdinand VII and María Isabel of Braganza and illustrated title page. RB, CS/4/1

would give the owner and collector the sensation of possessing a unique object. The *Calendario manual* of 1819, featuring a "curtain" binding in white morocco, portraits of Ferdinand VII and María Isabel Francisca in gold decorative borders [fig. 143], a coloured title page [fig. 144] and a coloured map printed

Fig. 145
[Guía de forasteros de Madrid].
Madrid: [n. n.],
1815. RB, CS/4/1

on blue paper, is a superb example of the "false truly unique" in a collection filled with such works. The incorporation of materials of unequal value in these luxury bindings is part of that same strategy: morocco, *pasta valenciana* and granite-marbled sheepskin are combined with the same degree of ostentation[16] [figs. 145 and 146].

This is not the only way in which bookbinders played with serial and exclusive binding. Often, there is no difference between the tools used on luxury and serial bindings and, in that respect, the king's rich bindings are treated as serial ones. Such is the case of a report that minister Colomarde presented to the king years later, in 1826. Santiago Martín bound it in red morocco decorated with the same tools that were used in ordinary bindings—and continued to be used after his death by Pedro Pastor—along with specific, highly elaborate curtain and Pompeian tools he only employed in luxury bindings.[17]

Ferdinand VII also required Martín's services as a maker of serial bindings to bind books in representative editions—"Don Quixote" and "Sallust in Spanish"—to be sent abroad as gifts of state. These were special, though multiple, pieces and quite costly. Each volume of *Don Quixote* cost one hundred and seventy *reales* and the *Sallust* two hundred. The only detail mentioned in their bill is the material, which was morocco leather. The packaging and their four shipping crates were also made by Martín, who charged eighty *reales* for them in a separate bill.[18]

Between July 1834 and December 1825, Santiago Martín submitted invoices totalling twenty-one thousand four hundred and fifty-one *reales*. He continued to combine his work as a book agent and custodian of the library

Fig. 146
[Guía de forasteros de Madrid].
Madrid: [n. n.], 1819. RB, CS/4/1

with his duties as royal binder. He acquired printed matter for Ferdinand VII—our attention is drawn by twenty-two romance novels—and cleaned the books in the Real Biblioteca around the summer and winter solstices. His bookbinding bills reveal the sociological changes then taking place in reading habits in the king's private library: collections of loose papers—the ones grouped under "Spain", "Spain in 1820 to 1823", are one example—and numerous newspaper titles began to play a leading role in the list of what was distinguished and standardised in the king's private library through royal binding. In short, political commentary and satire and critical journalism had begun to merit a binder's label.[19]

Pedro Pastor

In 1828, Pedro Pastor took over the workshop of the royal bookbinder Santiago Martín. He had been an apprentice to Martín, who had entrusted him with running the workshop during a bronchial illness that proved fatal.

Martín recognised Pastor's zeal and attention to detail by leaving him his house and all his tools—presses, gilding tools and materials—so that he could continue with the master's work. In March that year, he asked to be allowed to officially occupy the post which had fallen vacant.[20]

By 1829, he was already submitting bills as royal bookbinder for serial bindings on texts directly linked to the Royal Household and published that year. He bound the *Descripcion de las alegorías pintadas en las bóvedas del Real Palacio de Madrid* in two different sets, one of twenty-four copies, and the other of one thousand. The difference in price clearly indicates that the first group received more luxurious bindings [figs. 147 and 148].

Two bills even specify different grades within both the luxury bindings and the ordinary ones. Of the former, fourteen were bound in morocco leather in English style, with blind roll decoration and coats of arms, at a cost of one hundred and thirty *reales* each, and ten in morocco with blind-stamped coats of arms at one hundred and twenty *reales*. Then there were four hundred in ordinary dyed sheepskin at five *reales* each, and six hundred in paper covers at one hundred and twenty-five *reales* per hundred.[21]

In 1833, he bound various copies of printed sixteenth-century works in "fine" dyed sheepskin at fifty *reales* each, distinguishing between two different sizes, "marca mayor" and "folio regular". There were twenty-nine titles bound in thirty-three volumes. They were serial bindings described as "pasta fina" —brown speckled *pasta valenciana* with roll and other tooled decoration—for which he charged fifty or thirty-eight *reales*, depending on the size. Some of the tools employed for this job had already been used by Santiago Martín and were part of his legacy. The list also mentions a special assignment: the binding of the *Libro de la Montería* in morocco with a large coat of arms and silk endpapers, for which he charged one hundred and thirty *reales*. The stamp with the royal coat of arms that he impressed on the rear cover was made in London and signed "Book Sc. London". It is the same one that appears on a desk made for the king and may possibly have been commissioned by the binder during his stay in London.

The same bill has a separate heading that lists "Encuadernaciones para la Reyna N. Sª. y sus Augustas hijas" [bindings for Our Lady the Queen and her August daughters]. It mentions books in landscape format for "the girls" to play with. And for the queen, he bought specific issues to complete collections of works in instalments.[22]

A bill submitted that November gives an idea of Pastor's incessant work: two hundred and sixty-five titles, many of them comprising several volumes. He bound nearly all of them in "pasta fina"—brown or green mottled *pasta valenciana*—and he occasionally did half-bindings. He worked mainly on the holdings of older printed works that had entered the collection before 1808, although he also charged for binding periodicals and serial works published that year. Among the books for which he billed are some that retain the accession number of the Gondomar residence known as the Casa del Sol—which identifies them as having been in the count's collection—and others, like the personal papers, that are immediately recognisable as part of his holdings. There are also books from the

Fig. 147
Francisco José Fabre, *Descripcion de las alegorías pintadas en las bóvedas del Real Palacio de Madrid*. Madrid: por D. Eusebio Aguado, Impresor de Cámara de S.M. y de su Real Casa, 1829. Label of the binder Pedro Pastor. RB, Inf/1976

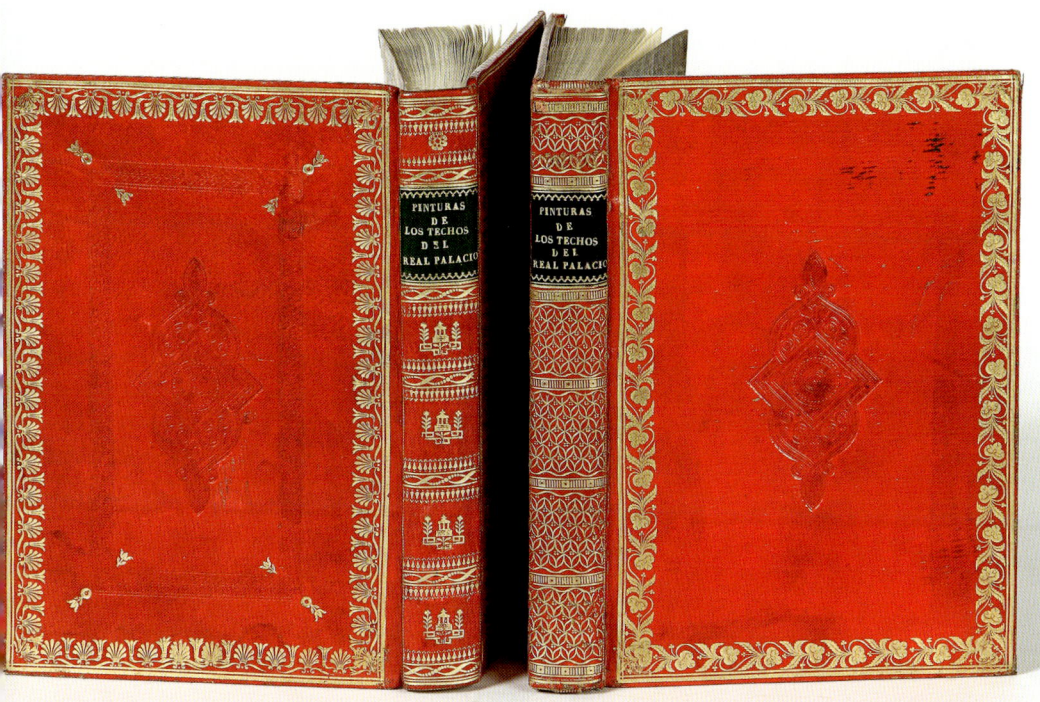

Fig. 148
Francisco José Fabre, *Descripcion de las alegorías pintadas en las bóvedas del Real Palacio de Madrid*. Madrid: por D. Eusebio Aguado, Impresor de Cámara de S.M. y de su Real Casa, 1829. Bound in long-grained red morocco with gold tooling by Pedro Pastor. RB, Inf/1976

library of the Infante Don Antonio Pascual or that were "Proprieté des trois". Another prominent feature of that bill is the binding of a collection of "Libros grandes de mapas y planos" [large books of maps and plans], consisting of thirty-five titles for which he put together and wrote the indexes. Some of the tools he used, such as the rolls, came from Santiago Martín's workshop. The only work bound in morocco is a fifteen-volume set of Walter Scott's writings printed by Fournier in Paris around that time.[23]

In 1838, he charged for several jobs that involved binding older printed works in blue and brown *pasta valenciana*, for which he continued to use earlier tools, as well as some new pallets. He defines these bindings as "pasta fina" and makes no mention of the gilding. This group of books includes some that originally came from the Gondomar collection, including Théodore de Bry's *Admiranda narratio fida tamen, de commodis et incolarum ritibus Virginiae*. He also made half-bindings for the *Diarios de Madrid* of 1833.[24]

By the following year, 1843, the situation had changed, and Pastor complained to the administrative department of the Royal Household that his services had not been required for some years and asked to be given work again. The librarian was informed that the tutor to HM had decided that Pedro Pastor should be considered for appointment whenever there was work to be done that called for his art.[25]

Royal Printing House, Royal Printers and Bookbinding

Imprenta Real

The Imprenta Real or royal printing house also had a bookbinding workshop whose manner of working makes it very difficult to know who did what, because the royal bookbinders were also involved in the institutional publications bound by its workshop, for which they used their own tools.

The bindings executed by this workshop, which were billed separately, were logically applied to the output of the Imprenta Real itself. The works bound at the Imprenta Real are particularly significant because the play on "serial but distinct" is established from the publication stage. Its products—within the basic division between deluxe and ordinary, and there are some variations—correspond to particular types of binding and form groups in which degree of luxury is inversely proportional to the number of copies.

The bill for the *Ordenanza de la Junta de Gobierno y de la Suprema de Apelaciones de la Real Casa y Patrimonio* distinguishes between two issues of the same edition: two thousand nine hundred superfine copies at seventeen *maravedíes* per sheet, and one hundred printed on Holland paper at one *real* per sheet.

Of the edition on Holland paper, seventy copies were bound in "pasta fina" at thirty *reales* each. Those bound in the more ordinary "pasta regular" were billed at ten *reales* each. Of the issue printed on the superfine English paper, two thousand six hundred were frame stitched and billed at two *reales* each.

The Royal Household made a further distinction and two copies from the luxury edition were bound by Pascual Carsi y Vidal and bear his label. The copy for Ferdinand VII was even more special, as it had a morocco finish. The copy for his wife, Isabel Francisca of Braganza, was bound in red-dyed "pasta fina" and received no other treatment. To these Empire-style deluxe serial bindings of the Imprenta Real, Pascual Carsi y Vidal added roll decoration on the inner covers, tooling on the spine and the cyphers of the king and queen in distinctive copies, producing unbeatable examples of singularity in the context of uniformity. Needless to say, he signed them as an artist.

The private royal collection also received a third copy with glued paper covers dyed the characteristic English hazel colour. This copy had paper endleaves and was frame stitched with long stiches.[26]

Six copies of the *Reglamento de las Reales caballerizas* of 1817 were given deluxe bindings of "pasta fina" with silk endpapers, for which the binder charged one hundred and sixty *reales* each. There were forty-four copies in medium-fine dyed sheepskin—"pasta entrefina"—worked with rolls and with decorated board edges, at sixteen *reales* each, and two hundred copies printed on English paper at three *reales* each. No copies of this work remain in the Real Biblioteca. Nor are there any copies of the *Ceremonial para el bautismo del Príncipe de Asturias* or the equivalent book published the same year, 1817, for the baptism of the infanta.[27]

The *Reglamento para el Monte Pío de Viudas y Huérfanos de los Empleados de la Real Casa y Patrimonio de S. M. bajo su inmediata protección* was printed the following year, in 1818. Four categories were established for this edition: twenty deluxe copies in English morocco leather with silk endpapers, at one hundred *reales*, including copies for their Majesties and Royal Highnesses; forty semi-deluxe copies in English morocco, at sixty *reales* each; forty copies in "pasta fina", at twenty-four *reales*; and five hundred copies with paper covers at half a *real*.

The copy for Isabel Francisca of Braganza, which remains in the Real Biblioteca, displays these characteristics. Over the luxurious material and roll decoration, the covers feature a curtain decoration with a mosaic pattern of *pasta española* and *pasta valenciana* and the queen's cypher. The "Y" surmounted by a royal crown on the lower outer corners denotes her ownership of this copy. The different types of dyed sheepskin distinguish the "curtains" on each cover in a spectacular play, forming an arrangement whose exquisite elements allow us to attribute this masterful example of curtain binding to Antonio Suárez.[28]

León Amarita

The problems of attribution associated with the Imprenta Real also apply to private printers who worked for the Royal Household producing official publications. Different issues were bound serially but distinctively, and this distribution called for foremost bookbinders who might play a major role in particular copies.

León Amarita printed the *Reglamento de la Real Casa* of 1822 in a leaflet in *cuarto marquilla* format, binding twelve copies in English morocco, at eighty *reales* each, and twenty-four in "pasta fina" at twelve *reales* each. Another two hundred and fourteen were fitted with half-bindings at six *reales* each. The two copies in the Real Biblioteca display Empire-style bindings in long-grained red morocco. They bear the label "Encuadernado por Antonio Suárez Jiménez, Librero de S. M. y de la Imprenta Nacional" [Bound by Antonio Suárez Jiménez, Bookbinder to HM and to the National Printing House]. Another copy, in neoclassical style, bears the inscription "Pardo" in gold lettering on the front cover. It has neither a label nor a signature, but its rolls and fleurons identify it as Suárez's work. The inscription at the bottom that assigns this copy to El Pardo Palace provides clues as to the possible distribution of the twelve deluxe copies billed by Amarita, which were probably intended for the palaces of the Royal Sites.[29]

Eusebio Aguado

Texts linked to the life of the royal family, produced by the Imprenta Real and the royal printers, were ideally suited to these differentiated multiple bindings. Eusebio Aguado, the head of a family of printers active throughout the century, also provides an example of the connections between royal publications and royal bindings. The examples of this genre of official publications include the *Reglamentos de la Real Portería de Damas*,

Fig. 149
Tabla de las festividades á las que el Rey N. Señor ... asiste asi á la cortina como á la tribuna de su Real Capilla de Palacio y de las que se celebran anualmente en la misma y en otras varias de Madrid .... Madrid: [n. n.], 1832. Cathedral-style binding in brown morocco with red, green and yellow morocco mosaic, by Antonio Suárez Jiménez. RB, XIV/2911

which he published in 1830 under the auspices of Queen María Cristina of Bourbon. Alejandro Rodríguez, bookseller and bookbinder to the royal stables and pages' household since 1814, when he was appointed to the post left vacant by Pedro Martínez, was entrusted with binding the entire print run. It was distinguished in many ways that ranged from the treatment of the pages—gold, silver, with small gold stars, fine gold and fine silver, fine with various patterns and engravings, fine with various patterns in gold and silver, and with foreign paper with different types of marbling for the small-format *Reglamentos*—to the bindings themselves and copies of the regulations for the ladies-in-waiting, stewardesses, duennas, seamstress, bathroom maids and sweepers. The binding thus reflected and embodied the hierarchy of the queen's female servants.

The binder lost his order of payment for the one thousand six hundred *reales* and had to request a duplicate in order to receive the money. An investigation was later carried out to make sure the mislaid order had not also been presented for payment.[30]

Funeral honours were another ideal prototype of books that were ideally suited to differentiated serial bindings executed by the leading binders. As in the previous case, Alejandro Rodríguez presented the office of the *Mayordomo Mayor*, the officer in charge of the king's household, with a bill for binding the entire run of the printed funeral services for Maria Josepha Amalia of Saxony, entitled *Oración fúnebre que en las ... honras celebradas de orden de ... D. Fernando VII ... por el alma de ... Doña María Josefa Amalia de Sajonia dijo el P. Eduardo José Rodríguez de Carassa, de la Compañia de Jesus ... en la Iglesia de S. Francisco el Grande de Madrid el día 28 de Julio de 1829*. The bindings he made ranged from seven luxury copies in morocco leather with all the adornments, at one hundred *reales*, to two thousand in paper covers and printed on fine paper, at eight *reales* per hundred, including some bound in "pasta fina" and another batch in the lower-grade "pasta entrefina".[31]

The bill for the *Oración fúnebre del rey de dos Sicilias*, the funeral prayers of the King of Two Sicilies—Francis I, who was married to Ferdinand VII's sister, María Isabel of Bourbon—specifies that the binding was carried out under the direction of the chaplain of honour, Antonio García Bermejo. It is another example of exclusive serial binding and of various degrees of luxury within its multiplicity. It was printed by Aguado in 1831 and the entire run was bound by Antonio Suárez. The binder divided the edition into six types of binding, with prices ranging from three hundred and twenty to two *reales* each. Twelve copies were bound in the most modern and luxurious style of the time—"gold tooled and inlaid with morocco of several colours and gilt plaques, with watered silk endleaves and on paper pressed to achieve a glossy finish"[32]—and received Suárez's artist-bookbinder label: "Enquadernado por Antonio Suárez, Librero de la Cámara de S. M. y de la Imprenta Real" [Bound by Antonio Suárez, chamber bookbinder to HM and to the Royal Printing House]. The two thousand two hundred and twenty-five copies he bound in paper covers with foreign marbled paper, white endpapers and spines did not receive his label.[33]

Aguado also printed calendars for the festivities attended by the king in the Chapel Royal, and other annual events held there and in other Madrid venues. He printed the *Tabla de las festividades á las que el Rey N. Señor ... asiste ... así á la Cortina como á la tribuna de su Real Capilla ...* in 1832. This edition, too, was bound by Suárez, including deluxe copies—only twelve—for the king and queen and other members of royalty, at one hundred and twenty *reales* each [fig. 149]. He also bound two hundred and twenty-six functional copies with a fine finish featuring white endleaves and a blue paper cover, at six quarters. The technique of cathedral-style mosaic used by Antonio Suárez for the luxury copies now in the Real Biblioteca is always defined by him as "the most modern style".[34] Those copies bear his label "Enquadernado por Dn. Antonio Suarez, librero de Cámara de S. M. y de la Real Imprenta".

Dynasties and Models: the Ginestas, the Family of an Experienced Liberal

Miguel Ginesta Clarós 18??–50

Miguel Ginesta Clarós was bestowed with the title of chamber bookbinder to Queen Isabel II in November 1839. The merits he listed in his application for the post that year identify him as a binder with a scholarship from Charles IV who had won a gold medal and diploma from the Sociedad Matritense for his binding of Ibarra's 1772 edition of Sallust in Spanish.

In 1803, he had received a scholarship from the king to study bookbinding at the Imprenta Nacional, the national printing house, under Pascual Carsi Vidal. In 1810, he had been appointed an officer at the printing house of the former Consolidation of Royal Bonds. He continued to work there when it became a renewal office, remaining until 1823. In 1814, he was appointed bookbinder to the Imprenta Real, where some of the works he produced began to forge his reputation.

His travels around France and England had not only provided him with an outstanding training but also with the possibility of procuring advanced machinery. In 1833, he was paid nine thousand *reales* for a binding he made for the queen regent, Cristina of Bourbon. The money was meant to cover the expenses of that trip to study advanced techniques, which he justified by bringing back machines that were then unknown in Spain. He had been employing those techniques and that technology in his work for the palace and the time had come to recoup his investment with "the pleasures enjoyed by other artists".[35]

Miguel Ginesta lost his job in 1823 as a result of his liberal ideas, which he never denied. In fact, in 1841, in a request submitted to the administrative department of the Royal Household that he be allowed to bind books for the Real Biblioteca, he proudly stated that he had bound the original Constitution of 1812 in the archives of Cadiz, as well as three copies of the Constitution of 1832 executed in Congress, at the personal request of Agustí Argüelles, president of Parliament. He referred to himself as "addicted to the Constitution"[36] and claimed that, since 1810, his ideas had not kept him from enjoying the esteem of his fellow citizens.

He had sacrificed the greater part of his life to serving his country: as a soldier—fighting in the sieges of Badajoz and Cadiz, and as an interim officer of the War Audit of the left-wing national militia army between 1820 and 1823—and as a writer and craftsman. Like so many other Spanish artists, he was in dire poverty and his works had been scattered to the winds.

Ginesta was a determined man, proud of his profession and of his ideas. He had no qualms about appealing to the guilty conscience of official carelessness to request that he be entrusted with organising an "object" that he knew perfectly: "the Library of HM is one of the places that houses many treasures".[37] At the time the royal collection was in an appalling state and, if not properly seen to, moths, and even rats, would finish off what remained of it.

A sign of his advanced mentality and social awareness was his idea that a bookbinder is an artist in contact with the aesthetics and technology of his time, as well as his consideration that a professional has an educational responsibility that makes him duty bound to train a technical team. His newspaper advertisements reveal the sort of young people he trained in his workshop on the Calle de la Independencia: apprentices between twelve and fourteen years of age from honourable families who should, if possible, have a good grasp of grammar and counting and should be accompanied by their parents to the recruitment process. At the end of his life, in 1850, another newspaper advertisement warned that, without his signature or prior payment, his suppliers should not provide materials to anyone claiming to act in his name. An apprentice already fired for fraud had compromised Ginesta Clarós and led him to discover a few flaws in a system of admission based on uprightness.[38]

He taught his son Miguel [Ginesta de Haro] "to follow the progress and fashions which art and taste are continuously changing".[39] He fully trained two craftsmen and helped other disciples set up their businesses. In 1841, his workshop was at the forefront thanks to the investment he had made in acquiring valuable, advanced equipment. In 1843, he asked the Spanish consul in Bayonne to seal and secure a crate of calfskins and shagreen that he was importing from France, because in Spain he could not fine hides large enough for binding the books in the royal collection. He also requested authorisation to bring in special tools, taking great care that they arrive undamaged. Until the end of his life, Ginesta Clarós made modernising his workshop one of his priorities, importing machines for that purpose. His faith in progress and in the advantages of mechanisation led him to enter contests, not only as a bookbinder, but also as a manufacturer. His lined paper—with one or more lines, accurately repeated—was publicly acclaimed as a useful article for public and private establishments. The queen awarded him a bronze medal as a distinguished manufacturer at the public exhibition of 1845. The publicity this recognition earned him was something he also knew how to exploit by inviting journalists to visit the glass-covered arcade in San Felipe Neri, where they could see his famous lined books, along with some of his bindings. In 1847, the directorate general of customs and excises published a legal decision in response to Miguel Ginesta's request that he be allowed to import binding machines from abroad, paying only one percent customs duties on their value. His request was denied.[40]

His sensitivity and considerable foresight as a man of his time is especially clear in the argument on which his request to the Royal Household is based: the world of luxury bindings had disappeared and the new market that was opening up was the conservation and continuity of the Real Biblioteca.[41]

The *Guías de forasteros* were a prototype of uniformity and singularity in bookbinding and, as we have seen, they belonged to a long tradition in the private royal library, even before responsibility for binding them was given to Miguel Ginesta Clarós. That assignment marked the beginning of a close relationship between the library and his family that extended to four different reigns.

Ginesta Clarós's bills unmistakably reflect the situation he described in his request of 1841, when he declared that a particular concept of luxury bookbinding was obsolete. They show how bookbinding had created a uniform language with this serial, informative and useful publication aimed at two different types of clientele. Ensuring the fidelity of an exclusive market was a common strategy. The printing house devised its own strategy through its careful and special edition of the *Guía* which the binder incorporated into a tactical design for the same purpose: to create a base of elitist collectors who every year needed to complete and continue to add to this series of objects with which they could feel equal to, yet different from, their peers.

Press advertising was a means of building fidelity in this market and of opening it up to a new clientele. Using the newspapers in a systematic manner and anticipating the needs of a hurried, bureaucratic society are examples of Ginesta's business acumen. He advertised all possible modalities of deluxe serial binding, drawing no distinction between them and those he might then be executing as royal bookbinder. His state-of-the-art machinery ensured consistent quality and offered clients the illusion of owning something exclusive. Velvet, silk, calfskin, vellum, morocco and other known materials, along with books for commercial and office use—Ginesta offered all of these things as royal binder to HM in the so-called *Despacho de libros rayados* [Office of lined books].[42]

Ginesta's luxury bindings are clearly identifiable in the royal collection: velvet with gold decoration using either individual tools or panel stamps; gilt or worked edges. The signature "Ginesta" appears at the foot of the spine (1843, 1847, 1848; those of 1850, 1852, 1854 and 1855 are by Ginesta de Haro). Morocco bindings have blind-tooled fillet borders forming romantic frames.

Years later, Miguel Ginesta de Haro, a member of the second generation, continued with this dual criterion. His bill from 1860 lists two deluxe *Guías* at one hundred and ten *reales* each, and twelve in morocco, at twenty-five *reales* each.[43]

There were also specific commissions from the palace for luxury works acquired in instalments, with proof prints and special paper, such as the four volumes of *Galerie du Palais Pitti*, which he bound in simple half-bindings, including the corners, but signed at the foot of the spine. A notable printed work, the Academy's legendary edition of *Don Quixote*, which, inexplicably, was still not in the Real Biblioteca in 1850, was also acquired that year, although the copy is incomplete, lacking the map.

Luxury bindings were requested for both of those books because "they are works that HM might request for his own use".[44] On 9 July 1850, the queen approved the royal binder's estimate of eight hundred *reales*. The binding of *Don Quixote* in red morocco leather is a distinctive creation in cathedral style and bears the signature "Ginesta" at the foot of the spine.

In his final years, Ginesta Clarós modernised his workshop with imported technology. He was already a knight of the Order of Isabella the Catholic in recognition of his merits, and he was aware that his worth, his capacity for innovation and his liberal patriotism made him deserving of this honour that he requested of the queen in writing in November 1845. The bestowal of this distinction was published in a Royal Order signed by the minister and author Martínez de la Rosa. It claimed that, besides his artistic career, he had served in the Peninsular War, as an officer of the War Audit "in the Army of the left, in times of the Marquis of La Romana and under the orders of his auditor, D. Tadeo Delgado", and that he was later appointed an officer of public credit, where he served until the end. And, as always, "he was very fond of the Art he professes, to which he has devoted himself exclusively, seeking to distinguish himself by his earnest efforts as demonstrated by his works and their general acceptance everywhere".[45]

Fig. 150
Alphonse de Lamartine, *Historia de la revolución francesa de 1848 y de la fundación de la República*. Madrid (Imprenta de D. Higinio Reneses. Imprenta de Boix mayor y Compañía), 1850. 2 vols. Fine claret sheepskin bindings by Miguel Ginesta Haro.
RB, VII/1942 and VII/1943

Miguel Ginesta de Haro, 1850–78

On 28 September 1853, Ginesta de Haro requested the title that had been bestowed on his father sixteen years earlier. His application was based on his own merits, along with those of his father. The queen agreed and on 16 November she conceded him the title—of royal bookbinder "even of the chamber", according to the note the chief librarian sent to Ginesta the following day.[46] He was sworn in on 12 December and received his certificate as honorary chamber bookbinder.[47]

He shared his father's enthusiasm for technology, business acumen, concern for seeking new markets and capacity to capture new clients. In addition, he became a printer and in his obituary he is remembered as both royal binder to HM and as a printer. He also inherited his father's liberal mindedness and, like Ginesta Clarós, he defended advanced causes including the revocation of the printing law of 1867.[48]

During the 1850s, manuscripts and early printed works were bound systematically, although without any apparent priority.

Miguel Ginesta de Haro received his commissions in lists (1851: 9 April, 20 August, 4 November; 1853: 6 April, 18 June, October, 21 November, 31 December) which specified the type of binding. By then there was a set type of binding for serial works such as the *Colección de documentos inéditos*. The Real Biblioteca had established various types of bindings for these useful works: dyed sheepskin, *pasta valenciana*, half-binding, fine half-binding, cloth, and cloth with gilt edges.

These were mass-scale projects and the bindings were never signed; as such, they should be understood to be workshop products. Nevertheless, careful attention was paid to their aesthetic aspect, along with a constant pursuit of distinctive materials, including embossed or marbled papers for the half-bindings, and dyes for a personal type of *pasta valenciana* based on mottled greens. Special attention was paid to the decoration of the edges, which were finely marbled to match the endpapers, thus creating visual unity when the cover was opened [fig. 150].

Fig. 151
Giovanni Marchesini, *Mammotrectus*. Venetiis: p[er] Symone[n] papien alias Beuilaqua, 1492. Bound in red-dyed *pasta valenciana* by Miguel Ginesta Haro. RB, I/137
A. M. Pugin, *Les vrais principes de l'architecture ogivale ou chrétiene, avec des remarques sur leurs renaissance au temps actuel*. Bruges: [n. n.], 1850. Bound in *pasta valenciana* by Miguel Ginesta Haro. RB, IV/997

Fig. 152
Laffont de Montferrier, *Le coeur du poète, ou fleurs poétiques*. Paris (Perpignan: impie. de J.-B. Alzine), 1857. Bound in green-dyed *pasta valenciana* on a claret-brown background by Miguel Ginesta Haro. RB, VIII/18443

Fig. 153
Laffont de Montferrier, *Le coeur du poète, ou fleurs poétiques*. Paris: Garnier (Perpignan: Imp. J.-B. Alzine), 1857. Bound in beige-dyed *pasta valenciana* on a brown background by Miguel Ginesta Haro. RB, XIV/2694

Ginesta de Haro's work was valued in his own day as a sign of a patriotic attitude. The silver medal he was awarded at the Spanish Industrial Exhibition of 1850 was hailed by the press as a recognition of his effort to use only indigenous materials—leather, cardboard, dyes, "all are products of the Peninsula"—and to benefit society by achieving quality at affordable prices, producing bindings that were "inexpensive and made with indigenous materials."[49] Years later, in 1867, his participation in the Universal Exposition in Paris revealed his great potential for artistic binding. He presented a model of sixteenth-century French binding for a *Don Quixote* printed by the Imprenta Nacional (1862) and a personal, painstakingly executed binding in Mudejar style for *Arte y vocabulario arábigo,* a book printed in Granada in 1505. This was "possibly the first [binding] of its kind to be presented at a universal exposition".[50]

The speed of production attained by Ginesta's workshop by the middle of the century is clear in his delivery notes. During the two months from September to November 1852, it produced forty perfectly differentiated types of bindings of the following kinds:

- Fine half-binding: leather spine and cloth. Edges painted to match the finely marbled endpapers[51].
- Half-binding with marbled paper[52].
- *Pasta valenciana* in shades of green with plant motifs[53] [fig. 151].

The play of colours provided by the *pasta valenciana* leathers achieved different results, and this is particularly clear when Ginesta de Haro sought to differentiate two copies of the same work, as he did with *Le Coeur du poète*. The pattern resulting from the wrinkling

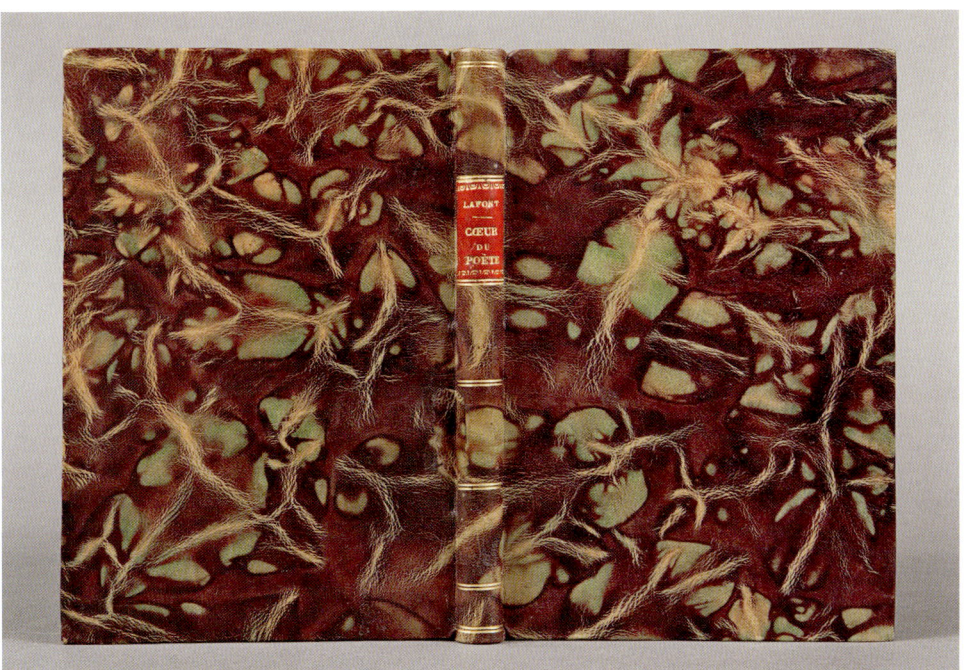

152

153

of the leather is evidenced by the use of bright green over a claret-hued brown. The binder's skill is also evident in the use of the same type of marbling for the edges, which matches the green leather in one case, and the endpapers in the other [figs. 152 and 153].[54]

A representative example of the Real Biblioteca's conception of serial royal bindings is one of the items listed among the books delivered to Ginesta de Haro in 1852 to be bound. *Cosas de Nueva España* is one of the most significant pieces in the private royal collection and is bound according to the model in use at that time, in *pasta valenciana*. However, since it is a valuable manuscript from the collection of Juan Bautista Muñoz that entered the royal collection during the reign of Charles IV, Ginesta had the professional sensitivity to respect its original margins and neither sheared nor painted its edges. Various incunabula were also bound in that batch. One of them was from another of the major collections that joined the library during the reign Charles IV: the collection of Diego Sarmiento de Acuña, Count of Gondomar.[55]

- Fine half-binding. Half-binding with embossed paper and edges painted to match the finely marbled endpapers. Although his commissions sometimes precisely specified the colour of the leather, the cloth and the edges, Ginesta de Haro had considerable leeway to vary the model within his serial bindings[56] [fig. 154].

- "Pasta fina" ["Fine" dyed sheepskin]. The colours can vary considerably, ranging from coral to the traditional brown. This type of binding is traditionally adorned with gold fillets and smooth spines alternate with raised bands. The edges are marbled to match the endpapers.

While Ginesta de Haro held the post, various items from the Gondomar collection must have had their parchment bindings replaced with "pasta fina" or *pasta valenciana* bindings, thus losing the accession numbers that identified their location in Gondomar's library in the Casa del Sol.

There was no doubt that Ginesta de Haro should be responsible for carrying on with the standardisation of the valuable holdings of manuscripts and incunabula carried out in the Juego de Pelota at the beginning of the century. Ginesta de Haro's reinterpretation of *pasta valenciana* expresses that same desire to identify the personal collection with a single aesthetic concept through a binding which, while simple in appearance, was enormously meticulous. The respect he showed by fitting simple bindings to notable printed works is evident in the incunabula and manuscripts. The dyed sheepskin he used is treated in an old-fashioned way, compared to Ginesta de Haro's customary work.[57]

His wish for continuity in the royal collection by seeking to follow the same bookbinding guidelines as the royal workshops is clear from the bindings he executed for some of the many early printed works in the Real Biblioteca, such as the 1585 Zaragoza edition of Zurita's *Anales de Aragón* printed by Portonariis, of which there were already some bound copies, including one that had been bound in the Juego de Pelota [XIX/4640].

In July 1859, Ginesta de Haro was supplied with the first volume from the collection of Joaquín Ibáñez García, "el chantre de Teruel" [XIV/1476], as a sample. When binding the second volume, which did not bear the stamp of the Ibáñez collection, he adapted his work to match the eighteenth-century binding, with

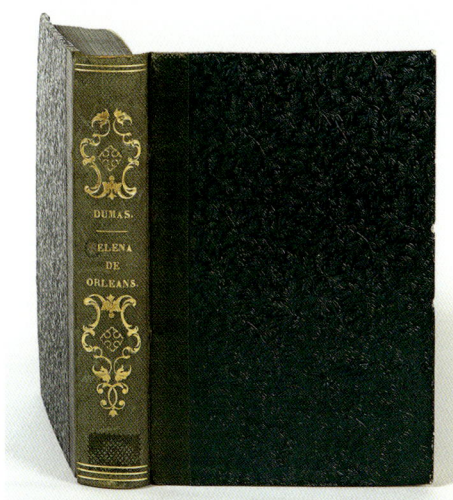

Fig. 154
Aléxandre Dumas, *Elena de Orleans: novela histórica*. Madrid, (impta. de la Biblioteca del Siglo), 1849. Half-binding by Miguel Ginesta Haro. RB, IX/6347

the same treatment of the mottled sheepskin and the suitable placement of the labels and tooling on the book's spine, for which he used the green-dyed sheepskin. He varied the endpapers, which are the usual ones from his workshop—fine-grained marbled paper—whereas those from the first volume, bound in the eighteenth century, are large grained. The second volume was supposed to have an extemporaneous binding and was larger than the first one, whose margins had been cut. As on other occasions, Ginesta de Haro showed his respect for the book's material qualities, preserving the original size of the title page by folding it at the top and outer edges to adjust it to the size of the textblock, which he sheared so that the two volumes would have the same height.[58]

This serial bookbinding did not differentiate between the historical collection inherited from earlier reigns and the ongoing collection because that was precisely its function. Authors presented their books to Isabel II with signed dedications, despite which the decision was made to bind them serially, "like the sample". The same is true of the multivolume set that Gómez de la Cortina sent the queen in 1857.[59]

- Morocco. The existence of several copies of the same work is inevitable in the royal private library because it brings together the private collections of different members of royalty, such as the infantes and the Princes of Asturias, as well those of noblemen or scholars, not to mention books that arrived by various means—directly, institutionally or as personal gifts. In the royally-printed editions Ginesta de Haro was commissioned to bind, he used colours to distinguish the copies he received. Such is the case of the *Catálogo de los objetos de la Real Armería* printed by Eusebio Aguado in 1863. Of the one hundred copies he received, he distinguished four by playing with colour of the covers—two and two—through the colours of the red and green morocco leather used. For the remaining copies, which belonged to a lower category but were "bonitos y esmerados" [pretty and carefully crafted], as he wrote in his note, he replaced the morocco with a Bradel binding in percaline. He maintained the same decorative system used for the luxury copies but continued to differentiate the colours —green and purple—and lowered the grade by changing the materials and using the blind-tooling technique.

Old printed works were also bound in more valuable materials such as morocco with gold and blind tooling and raised bands. These were very well executed bindings but they were not signed and were considered workshop products. The endpapers were made of red and cream fine comb-marbled paper whose colours matched the morocco.[60]

Miguel Ginesta Revuelta

This member of the third generation of the Ginesta family continued their serial binding work. In 1884, Miguel Ginesta Revuelta bound the royal album commemorating Alfonso XII's marriage to Christine of Augsburg.

La comitiva regia is an example of these mass-produced bindings of special copies carried out by two different firms simultaneously. This is another aspect of the industrialised serial binding performed by multiple-service companies such the paper warehouse, lithography and bookbinding firm Ojeda y Sanz, "Encuadernaciones de lujo y económicas" [deluxe and economic bindings]. It was located next to the palace, at number 3 of the Plaza de Isabel II. Another such business was Miguel Ginesta's "Obrador de encuadernaciones y libros rayados. Encuadernador de Cámara de S. M" [Workshop of bindings and lined books. Chamber bookbinder to HM]. This workshop was an excellent example of uniformity and singularity. Ojeda y Sanz charged three thousand two hundred and fifty pesetas for binding one hundred copies at thirty-two pesetas and fifty cents each. They were delivered to the office of the *Mayordomo Mayor* on 9 May 1885.

Miguel Ginesta was commissioned to make luxury bindings for one hundred copies and ordinary bindings for another nine hundred. The one hundred deluxe copies were to be bound in cloth bindings and eight hundred of the others were to be bound in boards. All of these were stamped with the supralibros of the royal crown and cypher. The remaining one hundred were simply cut, gathered and collated. From Ginesta's bill we can deduce that the thousand copies he received were raw, as he charged for cutting, gathering and collating all of them.

The cypher, featuring the initials A [Alfonso XII] and C [Christine of Augsburg], and the crown were engraved by Atanasio Carrasco, who billed the binder directly. The copies in the Real Bibioteca display several variants.[61]

On 5 December 1888, Miguel Ginesta Revuelta founded the company "M. Ginesta Hermanos" with his brother-in-law, Emilio Mollinedo, who became its manager. The duplicated accounts reveal a much smaller volume of commissions.

Book Semiotics. Private Tools: A National Cause for the Dream of Spain

The newspaper page bearing a description of the premiering of *Electra* in 1901 contextualises the social problems facing the government and what Spain was like for this play to become a symbol of the opposition. The Bishop of Cordoba's circular prohibiting its performance appeared in a local newspaper under "Pedradas" [Taunts], "Quejas" [Complaints] and "Gorrones" [Spongers], headlines of the social chronicle that also covered the premiere performance of Galdós's play.[62] Swamped by grave social, religious and nationalist problems, and reeling from the recent "disaster"—as the Spanish-American war and its outcome were known—Spain arrived at Alfonso XIII's coming of age. The year 1902 was marked by the need to launch a national ideological project aimed at creating a collective awareness of the figure of the king as a means of building cohesion among all political leanings.

Alfonso XIII's private library was an essential element in that huge-scale project, in which binding came to play a particularly important role, as it unquestionably entered one of the most interesting periods in its cultural history. Serial royal bindings became an ideal programmatic tool as vehicles for the project intended to legitimise the national monarchy. The project was launched by a scholarly conservative group linked to heritage assets. Conceived in a nationalist style, this type of binding, like architecture and art, stemmed from a "profound and deeply felt patriotic movement that seeks to revive the traditional and genuinely Spanish". It drew on historical sources—Mudejar or Renaissance, in the case of the Real Biblioteca's bindings—to create a "modern national style".[63]

Three key elements in this process were: the creation of new means of identification (tools, bookplates and binding models), scientific efforts to make the private royal library known to the public (its catalogues were published for the first time); and the establishment of a bibliographical treasure (the most valuable manuscripts and printed works were designated repositories of "the national essence").

Identifying Features:
Tools, Models and Bookplates

Specific tools were a key element of distinctive standardisation and they had been used as such since the times of the workshop in the Juego de Pelota; even so, they played an even more prominent role during the reign of Alfonso XIII. The Real Biblioteca still has the tools used until 1931 to identify books belonging to the king or other members of the royal family.

A box of tools, assembled first by Justo Luna Valbuena in 1908 and later, in 1923, by the bookbinding workshop of the widow and son of L. García, along with a compilation of their impressions and a set of sample bindings, including the cloths, are physical proof of the vitality of a binding tradition of the Real Biblioteca.

This blue morocco box-like case bearing a coat of arms and gold label, is lined in red chamois. Some of its tools date back to 1902, while others were made ten years later by Augusto Delbreil Laffite, engraver to the Royal Household, and José Rokiski. As we see below, these were made for a specific purpose[64] [fig. 155].

The case contains thirty-eight tools whose impressions are numbered in the *Muestrario de encuadernaciones y hierros*. Among them are:

INDIVIDUAL ARMORIAL
Castle, no. 1.
Fleur-de-lis (medium, no. 2; large, no. 10; small, no. 17; tiny, no. 14; small over pike, no. 15).
Lion, no. 3.

INDIVIDUAL RELIGIOUS
Labarum, no. 7.
Virgin Mary, no. 6.

ONOMASTIC
Alfonso, no. 4 [fig. 157].
Mercedes, [n. no.].
Cristina, no. 8 [fig. 158].
Teresa, no. 9.

COMBINATORY FOR NAMES:
Mª, no. 11
XIII, no. 13 [fig. 173].

CYPHER
Alfonso XIII, no. 18 [fig. 173].

Fig. 155
Box or case containing hand tools of the Real Biblioteca

ORNAMENTAL
Nos. 5 [fig. 161], 12 [fig. 159], 16.

MEDIEVAL-STYLE ALMOHAD
Roll, no. 19 [fig. 169].
Corner tool, no. 21 [fig. 165].
Military orders: Saint James, no. 20; Montesa, no. 23; Alcántara, no. 22; Calatrava, no. 25
Two-headed eagle with Hapsburg coat of arms, no. 24.
Corner tools: nos. 26 [fig. 166], 28 [fig. 167].
Cypher of Alfonso XIII, no. 27 [fig. 168].

COATS OF ARMS AND CROWNS
Coat of arms from royal medieval privilege, no. 33.
Royal crowns, nos. 29, 30, 31.
Royal coats of arms, nos. 32, 35, 36, 37.
Large coat of arms with mantling, no. 38.
Quartered shield of Leon and Aragon, no. 34

The set of samples contains eight samples of binding cloth, one of leather and six "models of binding" numbered on the spine labels: "pasta anticuada" [sheepskin dyed dark brown/black], granite-marbled sheepskin, standard Bourbon half-binding, raw drill and boards covered with Bourbon blue fabric. Each sample includes tools, spine bands, endpapers, royal coats of arms, cypher and lettering.

Beginning during the Restoration, the need to seek a national aesthetic became a state priority and the project for a decorative system to be used in the bindings of the Real Biblioteca was a response to the urgent appeal for a means of identifying with the supposed, imagined—and sometimes authentic—original Spanish roots.

The ideological supporters of this return to the national roots were part of a national scholarly and antiquarian movement and included the people in charge of the royal collections, servants of the Crown linked to the nobility and diplomacy and closely connected to the conservative party. They constituted an elite group during the reign of Alfonso XIII, having an international academic background and extraordinary connections abroad. They gave impetus to national recovery through the collections, fostering the scientific cataloguing of the artistic and bibliographical holdings of Spain's national heritage, the selective growth of those collections and the maintenance of historical and artistic assets. They did not hesitate to set in motion the creation of a new national heritage whose historical assets were used as models and reference points. Owing to their capacity to function as symbolic surfaces, the bindings in the king's private collection were a key facet of this programme of national identity.

The Count of Las Navas, director of the Biblioteca Real Particular, was a fundamental figure, along with the chief armourer, José María Florit y Arizcun, the group who attended the gatherings of the Instituto de Valencia de Don Juan and its creator Guillermo Joaquín de Osma y Escull, Count of Valencia de Don Juan. In *Recuerdo de la tertulia dominguera del Conde de Valencia de Don Juan. Arqueólogos anticuarios y biliófilos más o menos chiflados* (Madrid, Hanset y Menet fototipia, 1904), Florit immortalised its members in twenty cari-

Fig. 156
Bookplate of Alfonso XIII made by Alejandro Riquer

catures. This group was bound together by a conservative ideology, a sound culture and deeply Spanish understanding of life, all of which unified their tastes and facilitated their relations.[65]

Their programmatic construction effort within the movement to build a national historical image for the king through his artistic and cultural assets was based on the creation of a semiotic for Alfonso XIII's books. A sign language to express the ideological outlook of the king's private library through this traditional and supposedly Spanish aesthetic based on specific colours, materials and forms.

Key elements in the construction of that identity were the two most conspicuous marks of ownership: the bookplate and the supralibros.

One of the essential moments in the definition of the personal library was when they were devised. The decisions about their symbolic content included choices about their material expression.[66] In 1904, the Duke of Sotomayor, Carlos Martínez de Irujo y del Alcázar, who was chief officer of the palace at that time, commissioned Alejandro Riquer, Count of Casa Dávalos, to design a bookplate for the king's library. Riquer "conscientiously fulfilled" this request, which required three stamps to produce a *noucentista* colour image that became one of two forms of identifying Alfonso XIII's books on paper. The other was the return to the use of King Charles IV's bookplate, printed in bistre ink: modernity and tradition[67] [fig. 156].

Stage Costumes: The Catalogues

In the ten years which had elapsed since the Restoration, the French decorative taste in bookbinding had clearly fallen from favour. The identifiable and distinctive bindings for the new period called for designing "Spanish tools", even though the skill of French engravers was still required to actually make them. As in the case of the bookplates, it was considered indispensable to turn to a Spanish precedent for their design.

In the opinion of Hermenegildo Miralles, the bookbinder from Barcelona who worked for the Real Biblioteca, the French were the most reputable artists in the world, but they lacked a "feeling for line", so the results were no more than caricatures. Therefore, some of the tools he had made for his commissions from the Count of Las Navas had to be re-engraved.

The models designed for these bindings were taken from other books in the heritage collection. As these new royal bindings were devised in the context of a "neo" movement, both artist and client sought a return to historical sources in order to reproduce a glorious past in a paltry present. As Miralles put it, it was a matter of "studying and copying handsome Spanish books from which more tools will be engraved"[68] until patrons and mentors were satisfied. The bookbinder thus became an interpreter, while the scholarly bibliophiles, antiquarians and curators of the royal collections became the intellectual authors, proposing, guiding and judging the models. The regular gatherings headed by the Count of Valencia de Don Juan provided the guidelines and reference points at all times: Hermenegildo Miralles, in the correspondence he exchanged with the Count of Las Navas, offered to send books to Guillermo Joaquín de Osma so that he could present them to that highly esteemed group and they, in turn, could see how much effort he was making in an undertaking that brought neither money nor glory and produced things that were neither understood nor appreciated.

One of the group's central ideas was that Mudejar binding was the quintessence of Spanishness and that binders should return to it with utmost devotion, drawing on the assurances offered by new embossing and pyrogravure techniques imported from Germany that facilitated the reproduction of ancient decorative models. "A rare book bound by a Moor" also found its way to Valencia de Don Juan's gathering and the binder asked for the count's honest and personal opinion of it. Apparently, Miralles' twin aspirations were to receive the group's approval and to be knighted as a Spanish bookbinder. Friend and master are the terms with which he addressed

López Valdemoro in 1911, when he sent him a book decorated with "Spanish tools", although this was a bait to capture the Count of la Mortera as a client. The book in question, *Rincones de la Historia: Apuntes para la historia social de España*, had been written by the count himself and published a few years earlier. Miralles needed this nobleman and his friends to be the first to criticise his work. His tools were to the liking of the members of the gathering, but López Valdemoro felt that they failed to embody the essence of Spain, "not because they are lacking in character, but because it is too general in them".[69] Nor did he approve of the shot silk lining the inside covers, perhaps for the same reason, even though it had already been used in another binding made for Alfonso XIII: the poetry of Joan M. Guasche. The stamping and craftsmanship were as impeccable as those of the binding on the king's copy of the *Pirenenques*, which was only faulted by the count for being signed not among the tooling but more discreetly, in small type on the pastedown. The author had given that copy of *Pirenenques* to the civil governor of Barcelona, Buenaventura Muñoz, whose son sent it to the secretary of the office of the *Mayordomo Mayor* to Alfonso XIII so the king could admire it.[70]

But in that pursuit of local excellence, certain obstacles stood in the way of the achievement of purity and perfection through binding tools and models. The binder complained to the Count of Las Navas that Spanish leathers and paper were more difficult to come by. The only skins available were the dyed sort from Valencia, which were not to Miralles' liking. Among the types of paper, there were some commendable gold ones but there was a shortage of models to copy.

Moreover, the realities of the bookbinding trade in Spain clearly lay elsewhere. As always, binders had to seek out buyers beyond the elite group, and Hermenegildo Miralles mentioned to his mentor and favourite client that, along with the most luxurious bindings, he also worked on "cheap but pretty" bindings, for which he could not find enough clients either. He employed two hundred fifty workers at his bindery and sold one hundred thousand *duros* [five hundred thousand pesetas] worth per year. He had no time to seek out small jobs and his goal was to secure major commissions that would allow him to keep his factory fully occupied. Miralles analysed his situation in political terms and told the Count of Las Navas about the problems involved with both luxury and ordinary bindings, linking them to the situation of the movement for Catalan autonomy.

"The supporters of Catalan autonomy, like the freemasons, protect and help each other",[71] complained Miralles. He went on to claim that "because of who he is", the archivist and bookbinder Ángel Aguiló received a commission from the archives of the Crown of Aragon and from the University; and that Miquel y Rius, who published books in Catalan, was hired to bind books whenever possible. The convents and priests used the services of Subirana. Finally, there were those who bound books when the opportunity arose. According to Miralles, he himself was the only one who actually knew how to bind, but he foresaw that his declared opposition to Catalan autonomy would lead him to lose the business of the few book lovers who recognised the quality of his art. Isidre Bonsons, a habitual client, had stopped using his services because he found him too expensive and sent his books to Paris instead. According to Miralles, he was rich, fractious, disagreeable at times, had few books bound and understood nothing. And Madrid, where everything Catalan was viewed as separatist, was no paradise for Miralles either.[72] He did not get enough commissions from the capital to justify setting up a rapid delivery service in special boxes. Officialdom would not let books leave Madrid. And Miralles could not even consider the possibility of having a representative there. These comments are striking when we consider that, during the reign of Alfonso XII, Miralles had advertised himself in the press using his title of royal bookbinder to HM.[73]

Nevertheless, there is no doubt that the Count of Navas depended on Miralles to carry forward the emblematic project of "national bindings" for Alfonso XIII's library. When the chief librarian sent Miralles two volumes of the *Catálogo de la Real Biblioteca* published in 1910 on linen paper—vol. I: *Introducción. Noticia de algunas bibliotecas de Reyes de España*; vol. II: *Impresos. Autores Historia A-B*—he used it to propose a prototype for ordinary binding: a Bradel binding with parchment covers, a flat spine adorned with simple borders and corner pieces. In the centre, inside and out, the royal crown motif applied with the tool he had used for a luxury binding in pigskin and with Aldine tools, which had been to the count's liking. López Valdemoro, however, defined what he considered appropriate for a distinctive everyday binding: pigskin with no adornment whatsoever on the outside, blind-stamped title and bands; the inner cover in grained dark myrtle-green leather. Miralles had used that colour for a copy of *De libros*, a book from the "Yellow and Green" collection

Figs. 157 and 158
Name tools no. 4, "Alfonso", and no. 8, "Cristina"

published by the Count of Las Navas in 1908 and given to Osuna by its author. It featured tooled fleur-de-lis motifs and, in the central rhombus, a small circular royal shield and underneath, in a small Elzevirian line, the words "Biblioteca de Alfonso XIII" [Library of Alfonso XIII]; ribbed silk endpapers with neither watered effects nor a sheen, in the same colour as the leather; well-rounded corners. The result included a variant: the inner cover bore the king's cypher (tools no. 4 and no. 13 [figs. 157 and 160]) surmounted by the crown (tool no. 29).[74]

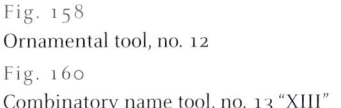

Fig. 158
Ornamental tool, no. 12

Fig. 160
Combinatory name tool, no. 13 "XIII"

Fig. 161
Ornamental tool, no. 5

The same concept underpins another copy, bound in navy blue shagreen with no external adornments, featuring five spine bands, gold lettering [fig. 162]; a claret-coloured, grained inside cover, mounted in relief, framed by the smoothed and polished blue shagreen, decorated with individual gold-tooled motifs (nos. 5 [fig. 161], 16 and 12 [fig. 159]) between fillets; endpapers of claret-colour ribbed silk, the same colour as the shagreen of the inside cover; board edges decorated with a gold fillet. The inside front cover displays the royal cypher: Alfonso (tool no. 4 [fig. 157]), XII (tool

NEXT PAGES

Fig. 162
Juan Gualberto López Valdemoro de Quesada, Count of Las Navas, *Catálogo de la Real Biblioteca: Impresos. Autores Historia.* Madrid, Ducazcal, 1910–31. Bound in blue shagreen with gold tooling. RB, I/J/616

no. 13 [fig. 160]) surmounted by the royal crown (tool no. 29). And on the inner back cover, the royal cypher: Cristina (tool no. 8 [fig. 158] surmounted by the royal crown (tool. no. 29). Endleaf and one flyleaf in shiny claret-coloured paper.

The catalogue of the Real Biblioteca was considered a crucial piece—the bibliographical expression of the figure of the king—and, as such, its binding was one of the elements that constituted its symbolic character. None of its luxury bindings is signed, a fact which emphasises its role as an institutional allegory. In the volume *Autores-Historia*, the Count of Las Navas described these bindings that were designed to embody an aesthetic of unmistakably monarchic symbolism at minimal expense: heraldic colours, marks with the coat of arms in various sizes and, at the foot of the spine cover, the circular stamp with the cypher of Alfonso XIII in gold (tool no. 18).

The same occurred with the catalogue of Latin codices in the library at El Escorial. Guillermo Antolín dressed the volumes he sent to the Royal Library "in the local fashion, in clothing approved by Philip II".[75] This was a simple but characteristic binding decorated with some blind tooling and gilt edges.[76]

The *Enciclopedia Espasa* is another example of these discreet and symbolic bindings. Miralles explained that it was "encuadernado tal como se hacen ahora para S. M. el rey" [bound the same way as is now done for HM the king] when he sent the first volume to replace the one bearing its original binding. Red shagreen, gold fillets, a royal crown on the front cover, inner edges adorned with a gilt plant-motif border, and burnished endpapers with a comb-marbled pattern.[77]

During those years, the Count of Las Navas also sought other binders fit to work for the Real Biblioteca. For him, this was a longstanding concern: in 1894, Jacinto Octavio Picón highly recommended Adriano Durand as "the finest bookbinder in Madrid, the one who most loves his art and the best I know".[78] At the time he was consulting bibliophiles specialised in binding: Félix Boix y Merino, director of the northern railway company and one of the most important collectors of his day; and José Lameyer González, a lawyer and conservative Member of Parliament whose collection, specialised in bindings, became a part of the Real Biblioteca in 1917. Boix, who was also a member of the gathering headed by Valencia de Don Juan, told him about "the inevitable Arias", the only professional in a mediocre business in which Antonio Corvera's successor based at the Calle del Espejo had been the most prominent practitioner.[79]

The "inevitable" Arias had been collaborating with HM's Real Biblioteca for quite some time. While Alfonso XIII was still a minor, he had already worked on pieces in his workshop on the Calle de Echegaray which were important in the serial project of nationwide scope that would take shape later on. Imitation calfskin and the blind-tooled neo-Renaissance decoration used for antique printed works, such as Fernández de Oviedo's histories of the Indies or the Real Biblioteca's first catalogue of codices, provided a foretaste of the characteristically Spanish style of bookbinding the Count of Las Navas so desired. The luxury binding on the first edition of Menéndez Pidal's catalogue—*Crónicas generales de España*—reflected the symbolic and founding value that has been attached to catalogues and their bindings in the cultural history of the king's private library since the Bourbon Restoration. It was accompanied by seven flexible half-bound copies with square spines and red headbands, which were also standardised with the royal coat of arms. The bills from the 1890s and the first years of the twentieth century bear witness to the serial bindings given to the collection of antique and contemporary printed works, featuring *pasta española*, white cloth, square spines and red headbands. These bindings were always identified by the coat of arms, either blind-stamped or in black. The same interpretation should be given to a set of office utensils that was of the standard sort yet distinguished with the king's coat of arms: the pen wipers that began to appear on the desks of HM's library during those years. The use of the armorial binder's tool became systematic and electrolytic etching was adopted as an engraving method for reproducing the dies bearing the coat of arms. In 1896, Antonio Gascón was paid seven pesetas for using this technique to reproduce it. The wear suffered by the tools of the royal crown can be traced through the periodic retouching work charged by the engravers through the binders' bills. This indicates that both systems were in use at the time to reproduce coats of arms on book covers.[80]

Binders sometimes teamed up to produce these "multiple yet distinctive" bindings. Some of the results were positive, others were merely curious. Hermenegildo Miralles was joined by Victorio Arias in binding the multivolume *México a través de los siglos*, a monumental work published by Espasa. The Count of Las Navas was especially interested in this work and exchanged long letters with the publisher. The last three volumes were bound by Arias, and although his bill assures that they were "equal to the notable bindings by Miralles",[81] the truth is that the white cloth and gilt headband, along with the attempt at a spine covering, are the only elements that even come close to them. Miralles' modernist design painted on parchment with brown moiré endleaves and brown squares, with Queen María Cristina's cypher on the label at the top of the spine, is in a different league to Victorio Arias' stark white cloth binding with the royal coat of arms stamped on the front cover (no. 37).

Among Arias' work at the end of the century are jobs typical of royal bookbinders: restoration work and repairs to printed works from the sixteenth century, such as *Carro de las donas* and the *Biblia complutense*, or special bindings for presentation copies in the library's purest tradition: the *Oficios Divinos de la Real Capilla*, which he bound in 1895 in Australian leather with a luxury finish for "the gift copy from the Library of HM to the Countess of Bernard".[82] Years later, he bound a special 1892 copy of the *Oficios* for Don Juan of Bourbon and Battenberg—the infante's name is printed on a flyleaf—with a luxury binding based on the "Bourbon uniform" model, featuring the royal coat of arms (no. 36) stamped on the inner cover. The two bindings dating from 1904 were in deep-red levant leather, edges and squares with fine gold fillets, deep-red moiré silk endpapers and the royal crown on the cover. The queen arranged for this book to be bound through one of her ladies in waiting, Rosa Arístegui y Doz, Countess of Mirasol. In 1906, he made two equal and outstanding bindings for Queen Victoria, in white double levant leather with white leather pastedowns and flyleaves, gold fillets forming a "V" and the royal crown, as well as a display of exceptional heraldic and

decorative elements. The *Oficios* continued to be a constant feature among his distinctive deluxe serial bindings. Justo Luna Valbuena was another of the men responsible for executing series of official bindings and that same year, 1906, he bound two copies in green morocco leather with yellow leather endleaves, gilt edges and a case, which he called a "Guardapolvos" [dust guard].

Arias made innumerable special bindings for the private library and there can be no doubt that Count of Las Navas relied on him to bind his most important works: the ones directly linked to the royal family. In 1904, soon after the poems of the Infanta Paz of Bourbon were printed in Freiberg, Arias bound four copies for the king and queen and infantes with silver ornamental tooled motifs (tools. nos. 16, 5 [fig. 161] and 12 [fig. 159]) and fine quality Australian leather and blue shagreen. The copy for Alfonso XIII was based on the medieval model in blue morocco leather and bears the king's name on the white leather inside cover (tool no. 4 [fig. 157]) [fig. 163]. Another family copy is bound in purple morocco and bears the coats of arms of Spain and Bavaria surmounted by a royal crown. This combination identifies it as a lady's copy that is related to the infanta [fig. 164]. The Duke of Rivas wrote a prologue for this new edition, which was published for charity. At the king's behest, he had previously written a prologue for Rivadeneyra's first Madrid edition in 1883.

Fig. 164
María de la Paz de Borbón y Borbón, *Poesías de Paz de Borbón*. Feiburg im Breisgau (Germany) [etc.]: B. Herder, 1904. Bound in purple morocco with gold tooling. RB, INF/1941

For that edition, the poet had covertly acted as a good literary editor, introducing variations in the text and trying to maintain the authoress' ideas, titles and order in this rather unremarkable group of poems. Alfonso was fully involved in this edition of works by his great-aunt. He reserved the first ten copies for his family, and he sent nineteen copies out of the run of one hundred and fifty to the royal poetess, together with a list of the people to whom he had also sent copies.[83]

On 20 February 1935, Arias' obituary appeared in *ABC*, where he was remembered as a master binder dedicated to a most noble craft and the recipient of international esteem and prizes.[84]

Fig. 163
María de la Paz de Borbón y Borbón, *Poesías de Paz de Borbón*. Freiburg im Breisgau (Germany) [etc.]: B. Herder, 1904. Bound in blue morocco with silver tooling on the inside covers. RB, I/J/639

The image of the figure of the king shaped by the Count of Las Navas through the royal collection of books was officially inaugurated in 1913. Alfonso XIII's visit in March of that year symbolises the type of personal link the king established with the Real Biblioteca. The last sheet of paper written by Marcelino Menéndez Pelayo had been placed in the palace library and the press assured its readers that, like God, the great master wrote in crooked lines, although his handwriting was uneven. For this last page, Félix Granda made a simple but elegant Renaissance-style mahogany frame; decorated in relief with chased silver and crowned with the royal coat of arms, it was described as "an honour to Spanish silversmithing of our time".[85] Luna Valbuena enhanced its value as a relic by lining the inside of the frame with chamois. The king had been interested in ensuring the immediate publication of the third volume of the general catalogue of *Autores-Historia*—it would come out in 1931—in whose prologue Menéndez Pelayo set out the concept of history upheld by the Catholic national historicism that he represented. Finally, the king had stopped in front of the large showcase that contained "the treasure": Villalón's grammar book, the *Libro de la Montería*, Isabella the Catholic's Book of Hours, the autograph work that Rossini dedicated to Isabel II and all the other precious objects that the Count of Las Navas particularly prized in the king's library.[86] A book was compiled to commemorate that memorable occasion, and the press clippings reporting the royal visit were bound by Justo Luna y Valbuena in the Bourbon colours and, as always, with the decoration in the inner part of the volume.[87]

Luna y Valbuena, like Hermenegildo Miralles and Victorio Arias, had become one of the participants in the Count of Las Navas' binding programme. It was he who bound the factitious volumes of poetry that Menéndez Pidal called the "Cartapacios salmantinos" [Salamanca portfolios] when he put them in order in 1906, rectifying the misarranged sheets. Luna y Valbuena based its binding on the medieval-style model using sheepskin imitating calf with blind-tooled fillets. He identified these volumes with the supralibros of Alfonso XIII, the royal coat of arms (tool no. 37) and the cypher of Alfonso XIII (tool no. 18 [fig. 173]).[88] Luna y Valbuena, who may have been recruited by the Count of Las Navas following the latter's round of consultations, had also bound by royal order twenty-eight volumes of the *Autores-Historia* catalogue in the brown/black dyed sheepskin termed "pasta anticuada" with gold decoration and varnished, to be given by the king and queen as presents. These were followed by a further twelve, also in "pasta anticuada" but without ornamentation. He bound two special volumes in "pasta rejilla" with square spines and red heads for the Count of Bernar, and he cut out a steel coat of arms with which to stamp them, retouched the royal crown and made a tool for "XIII" (no. 13 [fig. 160]). He also executed half-bindings for two volumes in red drill for the use of the Real Biblioteca, for which he charged eight pesetas. His serial "Bourbon uniform" half-bindings of periodical publications, with their scheme of two colours and the royal coat of arms, were in keeping the rich collection built up in previous reigns.[89]

The *Catálogo de medallas de la casa de Borbón* was another of these institutional assignments. These standardised but distinctive bindings which he executed in 1917 were for the royal family, and he made six sets in "pasta anticuada" with gold tooling, varnish and leather endleaves. But he also displayed his skill at devising clever combinations in several copies, showing how standard resources—tools, materials and models of bindings—could be handled in exclusive ways to strike a difference. These included a copy for Infanta Isabel of Bourbon; another for the King of Italy in morocco leather with endleaves of *écrasé* leather with gold-stamped decoration; three copies in white leather, with the steel coat of arms stamped in gold on the cover; and three in green shagreen with leather endleaves. There was also a copy with paper covers based on the "Bourbon uniform" model, another in white drill, and a special copy that marked the zenith of this allegorical binding system with its use of wild boar skin. Luna y Valbuena also made a case of *écrasé* leather for the tools he used in this binding, which had been crafted by José Rokiski.[90]

Figs. 165–68
Almohad medieval-style tools no. 21, corner tool; no. 26, corner tool; no. 28, corner tool; and no. 27, cypher of Alfonso XIII

Fig. 169
Almohad medieval-style tool no. 19, roll

The Soul of Spain in the Treasures of the Real Biblioteca

The prominent role played by the conservative group of antiquarians in the bindings of the Real Biblioteca is especially clear around this time. In 1912, Vicente Lampérez Romea and José María Florit made drawings for a set of tools that would broaden the existing choice, in an effort to create a standard method for identifying the king's most highly valued books. This proposal is especially interesting because it represented an invented aesthetic based on supposedly traditional styles whose application to antique pieces is underpinned by the same principles that guided the architectural restorations carried out by Lampérez, who had recently published his *Historia de la Arquitectura Cristiana Española en la Edad Media según el estudio de los elementos y los monumentos*. Tools 19, 21, 26 and 28 and the royal cypher no. 27 belong to this set, in which the reinterpretation of Almohad-style medieval decorative elements resulted in tools which were pastiches [figs. 165–9].

The tools were made by Augusto Delbreil Laffite, engraver to the Royal Household, who presented a bill for ninety pesetas in September for the "twelfth-century style tools for binding the *Liber canticorum*, the most ancient work in the Real Biblioteca".[91] The tools consisted of three elements: a centre tool with the cypher of HM King Alfonso XII [*sic*], for 20 pesetas (no. 27 [fig. 168]; a corner tool, for 15 pesetas (no. 21 [fig. 165]); and a roll for the edges costing 55 pesetas (no. 19 [fig. 169]).[92] This decorative system was so highly valued that it was, in fact, used for the binding of "a book as inestimable as the *Liber canticorum*", a codex that had belonged to Ferdinand I of Castile and had been bound "in the most vulgar modern marbled leather".[93]

The manuscript was intended for the royal hands of Sancha, queen consort of Ferdinand I, King of Leon: inside the initial, the words *Sancia regina* are merged with God. The text was modified when it entered the hands of the Infanta Urraca Fernández. The binding was executed in the library itself by Justo Luna y Valbuena in 1915 and his signature, "J. Luna. Madrid", is discretely added in gold letters at the foot of the inner front cover. He used large-grained levant leather and employed the Bourbon colours: blue for the covers and red for the interior. The maximum decoration was reserved for the inner covers: a border made with roll tool no. 19 on the red shagreen, corner tool no. 21 and, on the inner front cover, the cypher of Alfonso XIII, no. 27. The external decoration was in keeping with the sober style established by the Count of Las Navas and was adapted to a medieval-like aesthetic: blue shagreen with blind tooling beginning at the spine bands, three triangles ending in fleurs de lis (no. 2) and a spine with four bands and the title in gold lettering.

This codex left the Real Biblioteca for the University of Salamanca in 1954 as part of the items given in exchange for the granting of the title of *Doctor honoris causa* to Francisco Franco. In that exchange, the university's rector, Antonio Tovar, received holdings originally from the *colegios mayores*, which had entered the Real Biblioteca Particular of Charles IV when those university residences were closed in accordance with a Royal Order. This codex had been housed in the Monastery of Sant María de Aniago and arrived at the palace from the Colegio de

Cuenca. There is no record of the binding it may originally have had before it was bound in *pasta española*, as may be inferred from the Count of Las Navas' description, in the workshop in the Juego de Pelota as part of the mass-scale campaign begun by Santiago Martín around 1808 to standardise the bindings on works entering the collection from the "Biblioteca del Sol"—the library of the Count of Gondomar in Valladolid—and from the university residences that had been closed in Alcalá de Henares and Salamanca.

The codex's exceptional nature did not go unnoticed to any of the palace librarians. In Manuel Carnicero Weber's *Indice de los codices y manuscritos*, it is listed in his impeccable handwriting as a "precious codex of the 11th century. On vellum. 1 vol., 8vo, dyed sheepskin".[94] In the late nineteenth century, after examining it for his research on Mozarabic music, Marius Férotin had assured the Count of Las Navas that "very few monarchs possess such treasures in their palaces today".[95] And in the fifties, when Teofilo Ayuso requested permission to compare this Mozarabic psalter with his study on late codices from Burgos, López Serrano stressed in her reply that it had been written by Spanish monks and was "a book of outstanding interest because of the person to whom it belonged, its art and writing, and its liturgical text".[96]

The new binding on the *Liber canticorum* expressed the will to create a national core in the king's book collection and reflects the application of traditionalist policies to books. This was a comprehensive project that involved selecting substantive manuscripts and printed works as historical sources of the Crown and physically identifying them through bindings designed to reflect "the Spanish style".

Piece by piece, both contents and container were to form the national mosaic embodied by the monarchy. The design of the tools and the choice of the materials and decorative system constituted the expression of the Spanish character imagined by the Count of Las Navas: an ascetic austerity that holds in its interior the exuberance and unmistakably patriotic allegiance of its symbols.

Following this traditionalist line, the same contemporary interpretation of supposedly medieval binding was applied. The pieces chosen for rebinding form an eloquent and unambiguous group in which the chromatic symbolism employed on the outside of the *Liber canticorum*—drawing on the colours of Bourbon livery—gave way to natural leather, which was more reminiscent of the medieval period. For the most significant pieces, the skins of wild boars were used, as these animals were linked to royalty. The rest were bound in morocco leather. José Luna Valbuena and Victorio Arias were the binders but they only signed these more special works. The others can be identified as theirs because they are listed in their bills.

The manuscripts and printed works chosen by the Count of Las Navas to be covered in medieval-style bindings decorated with their own tools are an obvious public display of historicist conservatism applied to the national bibliographical heritage[97] [fig. 170]. His selection constituted yet another element in an ambitious and well-designed programme consisting of specific actions —distinctive bindings, systematic and thematic catalogues, critical editions—that were all carried out with the same objective: to define the national corpus in the private collection of the kings of Spain. Justo Luna

Fig. 170
Marcos Jiménez de la Espada, *Manuscritos de América propios de la Real Biblioteca* [*papeletas bibliográficas*]. Nineteenth century. Twentieth-century binding in hazel sheepskin imitating calf, by Justo Luna Valbuena. RB II/2909

Valbuena and Victorio Arias were the main executors of this project.

Liberals and neo-Catholics coincided in the effort to organise the documentary and literary sources in accordance with a civil web of history, and the Real Biblioteca brought together its leading philologists: Ramón Menéndez Pidal, who was in charge of the manuscripts; and Marcelino Menéndez y Pelayo, who was an essential reference point and guide. Literary nationalism took shape in the repositories of memory through well-designed operations like those undertaken at the Real Biblioteca.

Ramón Menéndez Pidal defined this operation in his preface to the first edition of *Crónicas generales de España* as "laying the foundations ... that have finally arrived to fill such a large gap in the historical and literary studies of our country".[98] The intention was for the catalogue to be presented as the cornerstone of a project under the patronage of the queen regent, underpinning the structure with the annals that had substantiated the shaping of Spain's history in the royal book collections since the Middle Ages. In 1898, Menéndez Pidal published his *Catálogo de Crónicas generales de España manuscritas*, which was distributed in the month of July to the monarchs, European heads of state and Spanish ambassadors. In previous months, the Count of Las Navas had offered it as an exchange with leading European libraries and scholars. The success of the operation was gauged in the articles about this catalogue and the correspondence compiled at the Real Biblioteca.[99] Those first notes were soon joined by the observations of critics such as Morel-Fatio, Schiff, Cirot and Fidel Fita, as well as the publication of the *Primera Crónica General*, all of which led to the reprinting of the catalogue of *Crónicas*. Improved, corrected and illustrated with facsimiles that enabled palaeographic studies to be carried out, the publication became a priority for López de Valdemoro. In June 1915, this third edition had begun to be printed, but two years later there were still no final proofs. The Count of Las Navas asked Menéndez Pidal to limit the proof readings, as the printer had raised the cost estimate by twenty-five pesetas per sheet as a result of the extra corrections.

Internal work on the Real Biblioteca's collection was also part of this plan: identifying the incunabula amounted to acknowledging the work of the early printing houses of Burgos, Granada, Murcia, Salamanca, Seville, Valencia and Zaragoza. The Count of Las Navas grouped them together on a single set of shelves, "so that they are more visible and well kept".[100] Because of their relevance to the construction of this national discourse, some of them were also included in the medieval-style binding project, although there was one exception: the neo-Renaissance binding on a work by Alonso de Cartagena. The material used was calfskin, as wild boar skin was used to distinguish works that substantiated the national discourse and the most significant manuscripts. The purpose of individualising works published by the earliest Spanish printing houses in the king's collection was evident, and these incunabula were labelled at the foot of the spine with the place and date of printing, thus mapping out

Fig. 171
Infante Juan, *Forma libellandi* .... Sevilla: por tres compañeros alemanes, 1498. Bookplate of Alfonso XIII. RB, I/198

the earliest printing centres of Spain on the bookshelves. The bookplate stamped under the coat of arms identifies these books as Alfonso XIII's—"Biblioteca de S.M." [Library of HM]—and was devised by Bernardo Rodríguez in accordance with a proposal by the Count of Las Navas in 1916. The letters were made in two sizes and the count himself supplied the engraver with a simpler typeface that would make the smaller size more legible[101] [fig. 171].

To the Count of Las Navas, the mention of these essential pieces in the king's presence during the national celebration of the Real Academia Española in 1922 had been a "great and pure spiritual satisfaction".[102] On several occasions, Julián Ribera had alluded to the

Fig. 172
Alonso de Cartagena, *Genealogía de los reyes d'España* …. Fifteenth century. Twentieth-century binding in hazel boar skin by Justo Luna Valbuena. RB, II/3009

Fig. 173
Tool no. 18, cypher of Alfonso XIII

Cancionero Musical, a treasure of the Real Biblioteca on which he had been able "to base extraordinarily important statements about the origins of popular music".[103] The Count regarded these scholarly recognitions as "enamels" reserved for publicly adorning the collection, and he therefore reproached Menéndez Pidal for using them for his own benefit instead of reserving them for a *Catálogo de la Poesía Castellana* that he had promised but never seemed to get around to making.[104] These manuscripts, to which López-Valdemoro listened and paid heed, cried out for solid and luxurious bindings to replace their unbecoming and vulgar coverings of *pasta española*. That same year, Justo Luna Valbuena, working in the Real Biblioteca, clothed in that "severe skin of wild boars" the *Cancionero Musical* and the *Genealogía de los reyes de Castilla* that had belonged to the Count of Gondomar [figs. 172 and 173], as well as the *Crónica dels reis d'Aragó* and the chronicle of Rodrigo Jiménez de Rada, both which came from the *colegios mayores* of Salamanca.[105]

When deciding which manuscript and printed sources embodied that "Spanish essence", the Count of Las Navas relied on a concept of Spain as a compound monarchy and included works documenting the history of its kingdoms and that of America. The attention paid to the "kingdom of Catalonia" clearly indicates that he also took a stand in the political debate surrounding the Catalan independence movement.[106]

Llinatges de Catalunya was one of the manuscripts chosen to be distinguished with this medieval-style binding. Massó Torrents had considered it an emblematic example of Catalan historiography in his *Manuscritos catalanes de la Biblioteca de S. M.* Pere Bohigas and Martí de Riquer studied it as a leading testimony of Catalan Renaissance miniatures and Catalan heraldry. The new binding was made by Justo Luna Valbuena, for which he took apart the manuscript, which was also originally from the Colegio de Cuenca and had been probably been re-bound in the Juego de Pelota workshop. He mounted the eighty-six folios on guards and modern paper and bound them in wild boar skin, following the same decorative scheme of plain tooled designs that extend from the bands to create a triangle ending in fleurs-de-lis (tool no. 2), and reserving the colours and luxury for the interior—the soul—of the book: inner covers of long-grained red morocco with gold tooling and fine fillets and red morocco endleaves. The inside decoration is a heraldic canting design embodying the national standardisation of this key work from the history of Catalonia: the two-headed imperial eagle of Toledo (tool no. 24) is set in a border of three fillets that form a frame whose corners are adorned with the four orders of knighthood (tools 20, 22, 23 and 25). At the base, the words "Biblioteca de S.M." surmount the central coat of arms. The recto of the endpaper is an extension of the inside cover in long-grained morocco with the gold cypher of Alfonso XIII (tool no. 18 [fig. 173]). The verso, made of glossy red paper, was intended to make it easier to leaf through.

The *Crónica del reis d'Aragò I comtes de Barcelona*, known as the *Crónica de San Juan de la Peña*, most likely came from the Monastery of Santa María de Ripoll and was another of the manuscripts that entered the collection from the Colegio de Cuenca. Massò Torrents' study in the *Révue Hispanique*—a leading vehicle for late nineteenth-century Hispanic studies—called it a key piece of Catalonian historiography in vernacular during the national period, and in those same years Menéndez Pidal considered it a constituent element of the chronicles of Spain. Justo Luna's binding also made it part of the set. In the same year, 1922, he billed for "Kings of Aragon, 14th Century", "Genealogy of the Kings of Castile, 15th Century" (one hundred pesetas each), "Musical Songbook" (eighty pesetas), bound at the Real Biblioteca, and a copy of *Crónicas generales de España*, all bound in wild boar skin but differing in the colour of the inside cover: red morocco and silk endpapers for the manuscripts (one hundred pesetas each), and green shagreen and silk endpapers for Menéndez Pidal's catalogue (sixty-five pesetas).[107]

This set of national emblems was an internal product created by another of the members of the ideological group that underpinned the development of the Real Biblioteca during the reign of Alfonso XIII: the individual tools of the military orders (nos. 20, 22, 23 and 25) and the armorial tool of the two-headed eagle with the coat of arms of the Hapsburgs (no. 24) were designed by José María Florit, chief armourer of the Palace as well as a member of Valencia de Don Juan's gathering. Florit personally took the drawings of these tools to the engraver in the second fortnight of May 1912, after showing them to the Count of Las Navas. The reasonable price—"they would cost about 75 pesetas"—and short time span—"they would take about ten days"[108]—as well as the craftsman's skill convinced him to order them without consulting the chief librarian. José Rokiski's workshop on Calle Barcelona in Madrid specialised in heraldic engraving, cyphers, crowns and chased and engraved gold and silver covers for albums and luxury bindings. In June, Rokiski charged seventy-five pesetas for five individual engraved tools called "tronquillos" for gilding the quarters of the Spanish coat of arms and the knights' crosses. In 1917, he made the centre tool, two corner tools and the Spanish coat of arms so that Justo Luna could bind copies of the *Catálogo de las medallas de la casa de Borbón*. Years later, in 1925, he submitted a bill for a bronze "tronquillo" bearing the coat of arms of Spain to gild the

Fig. 174
Henri Bouchot, *Les reliures d'Art a la Bibliothèque Nationale*. Paris: Édouard Rouveyre, éditeur, 1888. Mosaic leather binding by César Paumard. RB, XIV/CL/150

royal crown and the Golden Fleece (no. 36). This was used for five copies of the *Oficios divinos a que asiste la corte en la Real Capilla*, which were bound by Enrique García.[109]

Bookbinding established a distinctive language. The sources of historical nationalism were identified with this austere, natural clothing and a few significant though not necessarily Spanish printed works were bound in "pasta anticuada" if they had been printed between the sixteenth and eighteenth centuries, while contemporary works were distinguished by the colours of the Bourbon uniforms.

The latter bindings were decorated exclusively on the inside, following the scheme established by the *Liber canticorum*. Luna y Valbuena used calligraphic tools (nos. 5 [fig. 161], 16 and 12 [fig. 159]), the king's onomastic tool and his cypher (nos. 4 and no. 13 [figs. 157 and 160]) surmounted by the royal crown (no. 31).

As in the eighteenth century, institutional tools were also used to identify artistic bindings—signed individual creations executed with absolute freedom—with the king and his private book collection. Cesar Paumard

Fig. 175
Henri Bouchot, *Les reliures d'Art a la Bibliothèque Nationale*.
Paris: Édouard Rouveyre, éditeur, 1888. Inside cover in dark
green morocco with gold tooling. RB, XIV/CL/150

produced one of these singular yet standardised bindings for *Les reliures d'art à la Bibliothèque Nationale*, a book that had entered the library from the Lameyer collection. The Count of Las Navas described this binding as "highly notable" and hailed it as one of the Real Biblioteca's exceptional events of 1923.

In 1920, Paumard apologised to the Count of Las Navas for not having completed it on time. His letter was motivated not so much by the injured pride of someone who hates missing deadlines as by someone pained at not being up to the standard of a major project of the director of the Real Biblioteca, which called for all, or most, of Spain's binders to bind books from the Lameyer collection acquired in 1917. The desire to do a perfect job had led him to get carried away devising designs until hitting upon one that was fitting, and even then, he did not wish to begin working on it until he received the approval of the Count of Las Navas. The proofs are a pale reflection of what Paumard had in mind for this book: the crudeness of the sample would disappear with the gold and the yellow background decorated with a filigree pattern impressed by small tools. The combination of yellow and gold set off the mosaic, reducing its brilliance and the harsh appearance of the separate colours in the sketch, becoming instead a harmonious and agreeable background that enlivened the colours [fig. 174]. The edges, which were to be the work's *pièce de résistance*, met with an insurmountable obstacle: there was no quality gold available and even with the best that was to be had, the fore edges came out ugly in a coppery shade that was impossible to make use of in this binding in which gold was intended to be the most important element.[110]

Alfonso XIII, to whom this work was dedicated, thanked the artist and sent him a fine gold watch, a gentleman's Cyma purchased from Girod. In his reply, Paumard expressed the attitude of his professional colleagues towards the work being carried out by the Real Biblioteca, specifically the Count of Las Navas' support for contemporary Spanish artistic binding: gratitude for the fact that "the love of books and their protection were the stimulus for cultivating one of the most beautiful of the Applied Arts".[111] To be involved in the binding of the royal collection was an honour that was payment in itself. Following López-Valdemoro's guidelines, he reserved the king's name for the book's "soul" and the institutional tools identifying it with the monarch were therefore impressed on the inner cover, framed by Grolier-style tooling on morocco leather at a sober dark-green that continued in the ribbed silk endpapers[112] [fig. 175].

The Second Republic had no need to construct a new identity though the books belonging to what had been the king's private library until 1931. Responsibility for the collection was handed over to the state, and Jesús Domínguez Bordona, a renowned scholar trained in the Centro de Estudios Históricos, took charge of the collection of outstanding books on which he conducted advanced lines of research without feeling any need to make visible changes. He did so by recognising, respecting and continuing the work of his predecessor, with whom he shared both intellectual and professional interests. Domínguez Bordona considered that the main effort should be put into promoting knowledge of such an extraordinary collection. The exhibition in 1934 offered the public a chance to view bindings that he considered a singular heritage for all to see. That same conviction underpins the harmony between the candour and the luxury of the royal bindings brought together in this exhibition.

1. Jorge Soret (classification of tools in the database), Alejando Monreal and José Antonio Ahijado (digitalisation and documentation Archivo General de Palacio [hereinafter AGP]), José Cosials (digitisation), Juan José Alonso (Director AGP). José Luis Rodríguez, Valentín Moreno and Pablo Andrés Escapa (RB).
2. Razola, María (AGP, Personal, Cª669, Exp. 31); Villalpando, Fermín (AGP, Infante don Antonio Pascual, Cª 5, Exp. 4); Martínez Dávila, Francisco (AGP, Personal, Leg. 5243, Exp. 11); Gómez, Gabriel (AGP, Personal, Cª 438, Exp. 58); Gómez, Gabriel, AGP, Personal, Cª 438, Exp. 58); Tubella, Antonio (AGP, Personal, Cª 1303, Exp. 46); Rodriguez, Juan Romualdo (AGP, Personal, Cª 896, Exp. 66); Rodríguez, Alejandro (AGP, Personal, Cª 892, Exp. 8); Martín Pérez, Vicente (AGP, Personal, Cª 11936, Exp. 82); Arias Alonso, Pablo (AGP, Personal, Cª 1343, Exp. 8); García, Enrique (Archivo de la Real Biblioteca [hereinafter ARB], year 1920 and following).
3. ARB, ARB/1, carp.3, doc. 5. LÓPEZ-VIDRIERO 1996 and 2002.
4. [Por clasificar las obras que tenía S. M. y encajonarlas en cuarenta y tres cajones en cuya operación gastaron treinta y cinco días un oficial, dos mozos y el mismo Carsi.]
5. Carsi Vidal, Pascual, *Cuenta* (1814/07/08), AGP, Leg. 5233, Exp. 3. Payment was made on 14 October 1819, according to the acquittance. Among the books on that bill are the following examples of bindings: 1. In "jaspe menudo" [granite-marbled leather]: Bacallar y Sanna, Vicente, marques de San Felipe, *Vida de los dos Tobias: historia sagrada, escrita en 500 octavas ritmas castellanas*, Madrid, por el mismo Gabriel Ramirez ..., 1746 (RB, VI/497). 2. Salazar y Castro, Luis, *Jornada de los coches de Madrid a Alcala o Satisfacion al Palacio de Momo y a las apuntaciones a la Carta del Maestro de Niños*, Zaragoza, [n. n.], 1714 (RB, VIII/14785). 3. In "becerrillo fino" [fine calfskin]: Saussure, Théodore de, *Recherches chimiques sur la végétation*, Paris, Didot jeune, 1804 (RB, VIII/15614). For a more detailed bibliographic description of all the books in the Real Biblioteca (RB) mentioned in this text, consult the online catalogue at: www.realbiblioteca.es
6. For the amount of 1624 *reales*. Carsi Vidal, Pascual, *Cuenta*, 1816/11, AGP, RF7 Cª 402, Exp. 9 (for the amount of 1552 *reales*). *Cuenta*, 1818/04/27, AGP, Leg. 306¹, Exp. 4. Carsi Clark, Pascual, *Recibí*, 1819/04/03, AGP, Leg. 306¹, Exp. 4. Carsi Clark, Pascual, *Cuenta*, 1820, ARB/1, carp. 3, doc. 8.
7. *La biblia vulgata latina traducida en español, y anotada conforme al sentido de los santos padres y expositores cathólicos por el Padre Phelipe Scio de San Miguel ...*, Valencia, Joseph y Thomas de Orga, 1790–93. RB, III/2801–2810. ARB/5, carp. 2, doc. 68/5.
8. [A las más delicadas inglesas.]
9. AGP, Leg.18 (2).
10. AGP, Exp. Personal, Encuadernadores, Cª 628/44.
11. Nota de Sumillería de Corps al Mayordomo Mayor (1816/12/16). AGP, Exp. Personal, Encuadernadores, Cª 628/44.
12. The cost was thirty-three thousand and eight *reales*. The craftsmen received daily wages of twelve *reales* each. The mock books were billed at fifteen *reales* each. Martín, Santiago, *Cuenta*, 1816/12/12, AGP, Exp. Personal. Encuadernadores, Cª 628/44.
13. Suárez, Antonio, writing desk, Patrimonio Nacional [inv. no. 10032222].
14. He charged one *real* for each coat of arms. The work was done in July 1819. See Martín, Santiago, *Cuenta*, 1819/08/01, AGP, Leg. 5233, Exp. 3.
15. Also, a prayer book in silk with a case for the queen, which he billed at eighty *reales*.
16. Martín, Santiago, *Cuenta*, 1818/07/28, AGP, Leg. 523, Exp. 3. *Cuenta*, 1818/10/24, AGP, Leg 306¹, Exp. 3. *Calendario manual y Guía de forasteros de Madrid para el año 1819*, Madrid, Imprenta Real, 1819, RB, CS/4/1, nineteenth-century binding, by Santiago Martín (1819), asymmetrical "curtain" style. Other significant examples are found in the *Calendario manual de 1815*, RB, CS/4/1, nineteenth-century binding by Santiago Martín (1815), asymmetrical "curtain" style. However, the *Estado militar de España* for the years 1819 and 1820, featuring curtains on red morocco with gold tooling, smooth spine with tooling and gilt board edges, squares and edges, blue silk endpapers, are identified by their tooling as the work of Antonio Suárez and are very interesting because they include two figurative tools that are new in that artist's repertoire: a dolphin and a bird. See RB, I/L/81, I/L/82.
17. Colomarde, Francisco Tadeo, *Memoria dirigida a Fernando VII sobre diferentes asuntos del Ministerio de Gracia y Justicia*, RB, II/1796, nineteenth-century Empire-style binding. Red morocco. That same year, 1819, there is a document referring to the issuing of a bill for bindings made in May and June. The amount was one thousand six hundred and eighty-four *reales*: ARB/1, carp. 3, doc. 5. See also, Martín, Santiago, *Cuentas de abril y mayo*, 1819/05, AGP, Leg. 523, Exp. 3, for the amount of two thousand nine hundred and seventy-two *reales*, including the previous amount.
18. Martín, Santiago, *Cuenta*, 1820/04/1, AGP, Leg. 306¹bis, Exp. 2.
19. Martín, Santiago, *Primera [-segunda] Cuenta*, 1825/12/23, AGP, RF7, Cª 526. He continued to bind earlier printed works belonging to the infantes, including, for example: *Biblia. N.T. Evangelios*, Árabe-Latin, Romae, Typographia Medicea, 1591, RB, VIII/16128, nineteenth-century binding (1825), Santiago Martín (1825), *pasta española*; Marquille, Jaime, *Comentaria Iacobi de Marquilles super vsaticis barchin[onesis]*, Impressum barchinone: p[er] Ioh[an]em luschner ..., 1505, RB, I/D/5, nineteenth-century binding (1825), Santiago Martín, brown *pasta valenciana*.
20. Pastor, Pedro, *Instancia*, 1828/03/03, AGP, Exp. Personal, Encuadernadores, Cª 795/23.
21. For the amount of 3020 *reales*, 1829/12/23; for the amount of 2920 *reales*, 1830/03/30, AGP, Exp. Personal, Encuadernadores, Cª 795/23. Pastor, Pedro, *Cuenta*, 1829/12/14 and 1830/03, AGP, Leg. 5233, Exp. 3. His work included: RB, I/I/62, bound in long-grained red morocco, nineteenth-century (1829); RB, INF/1976, bound in long-grained red morocco, nineteenth century (1829), binder's label: "Pastor. Encuadernador de Cámara de SS. MM. y AA. Lo Encuadernó.

Calle del Espejo Nº 11. Madrid." Copies for everyday use, bound in *pasta española* (1829) stamped with plant motifs, smooth spine with gold tooling and a red morocco title label can be found in RB, VIII/10161, VIII/12285 and XIV/1933.

22 My thanks to Valentín Moreno Gallego for locating the plaque on the desk of the king consort Francisco de Asís at the Royal Palace of Aranjuez [inv. no. 10028779]. Alfonso XI, King of Castile, *Libro de la montería*, fourteenth century (*ex*). RB, II/2105, bound in red morocco by Pedro Pastor (1833). Pastor's bill is in AGP, Leg. 303[1], Exp. 1, Cuentas de 1833. The amount of this bill is 1320 *reales* (1833/08/01). Among the items on this list are: Ubaldi, Baldo degli, *Baldi Vbaldi Perusini ... In Primum [-undecimum] Cod[icis] Lib[ros] Com[mentaria]*, RB, III/8, nineteenth-century binding by Pedro Pastor (1833), in brown *pasta valenciana*. Other books located in the Real Biblioteca: III/15, IX/6621, IX/6620, MAP/349, III/2, IX/6041, V/2053-2054, V/2055-2056, IX/3471, V/2052, IX/3470, VIII/3217-3218, V/2059-60, III/14, V/1088, XIV/1144, VII/2406, VII/34.

23 For the amount of 8775 *reales*. Pastor, Pedro, *Cuenta*, 1833/11/16, AGP, Leg. 304[2], Exp. 4. Speed, John, *Theatrum Imperii Magnae Britanniae ...*, Amstelodami, ex officina Iudoci Hondij, 1616, RB, V/904, bound by Pedro Pastor (1834) in brown *pasta valenciana*. From the library of the Count of Gondomar. Other examples: RB, II/2358, a volume of various law papers bound by Pedro Pastor (1833) in *pasta valenciana*. Carranza Miranda, Bartolomé de, Archbishop of Toledo, *Comentarios del reuerendissimo señor Frai Bartholome Carrança de Miranda*, Antwerp, Martin Nucio, 1558, RB, IX/2356, bound by Pedro Pastor (1833) in brown *pasta valenciana*. Commelin, Johannes, *Horti medici Amstelodamensis ...*, Amsterdam, Blaeu, 1697–1701, RB, V/427–428, bound by Pedro Pastor (1833) in brown *pasta valenciana*. Scott, Walter, sir, *Ses oeuvres*, traduction de Mr. Defaucupret ..., Paris, H. Fournier, 1830–31, RB, IX/2553–2567, bound by Pedro Pastor (1833) in purple morocco.

24 For the amount of 5946 *reales*. RB, I/B/249. Pastor, Pedro, *Cuenta*, 1838/11/27, AGP Leg. 5233, Exp. 4.

25 Intendencia General de la Real Casa y Patrimonio, *Oficio al Bibliotecario Mayor*, 1843/08/21, ARB, Caja 1843–49.

26 Copy of Ferdinand VII: RB, I/F/322. Copy of Isabel Francisca of Braganza: RB, VIII/7691. Among the classified tools used for this binding, besides those belonging to Pascual Carsi Vidal, there are others that also coincide with those of other bookbinding workshops and artists: Gabriel Gómez Martín, Imprenta Real, Vidal, Santiago Martín and Antonio Suárez. Copy for everyday use: CAJ/FOLLFOL/253 (19). AGP, Leg. 5243, Exp. 11.

27 For these cases, the binding consisted of: English paper and fine endpapers, 2 *reales*, 500 copies. Vellum-paper with fine endpapers and gilt edges, 6 *reales*, 50 copies.

28 RB, I/G/95. Floral border with pods [SUA R FLO 03], beaded border—three pearls and a bead—[SUA R DEC 05]; for the curtain decoration: tassel [SUA F DEC 01].

29 RB, VIII/6309 and RB, I/F/533 (1).

30 Bill for 1672 *reales*. Rodriguez, Alejandro, *Cuenta*, 1830/08/20, AGP, Leg. 5233, Exp. 3. There are examples of some of these types of binding in the Real Biblioteca: CAJ/FOLLFOL/130 (2); CAJ/FOLLFOL/59 (17); C/892 (37). Rodriguez, Alejando, *Instancia*, 1831/03/29. AGP, Personal, Caja 892, Exp. 8.

31 Bill for 5356 *reales*. Rodríguez, Alejandro, *Cuenta*, 1829/10/03, AGP, Leg. 5233, Exp. 3. The Real Biblioteca holds one of the 41 that he billed at 16 *reales* "en pasta fina con ruedas y cantos": PAS/2952, nineteenth-century binding (1829), brown *pasta valenciana*, double fillet and roll-worked design in gold, gilt edges, large-pattern marbled endpapers.

32 [Fogueado embutido de tafilete de varios colores y placas doradas, con guardas de groc de aguas y en cuenta de batidos ensetinados a prensa.]

33 It came to 20353 *reales*, and was endorsed by Antonio García Bermejo. Suárez Jiménez, Antonio, *Cuenta*, 1831/04/25, AGP, Leg. 5233, Exp. 3. The different types of bindings on the copies in the Real Biblioteca fall into the following categories: "todo lujo" (I/I/388); "pasta fina" (I/179, VIII/3886, IX/9289, VIII/16417, PAS/2956, PAS/ARM3/664).

34 The bill was for 3169.22 *reales*. Suárez, Antonio, *Cuenta*, 1832/07/04, AGP, Leg. 5233, Exp. 3. The Real Biblioteca has copies with some of these types of bindings: "en tafilete morado con placas de oro y embutidas de tafilete por el estilo más moderno" (XIV/2911). Of the twelve copies he billed at 60 *reales* "de medio lujo en tafilete inglés encarnado con placas fogueadas de relieve por el propio estilo", the following are located: IX/5777, XIV/2376, I/F/257.

35 [Los goces que disfrutan los demás artistas.]

36 [Adicto a la Constitución.]

37 [La Biblioteca de S. M. es uno de los puntos en que se encierran muchas preciosidades.]

38 "Anuncios", *Diario de avisos de Madrid*, 1847/07/26. [Advertisement] "Don Miguel Ginesta Clarós ...", *El heraldo de Madrid*, 1850/27/02. "Comunicado", *Diario oficial de avisos de Madrid*, 1850/28/02.

39 [Para que siga los progresos y modas que el arte y el gusto están variando continuamente.]

40 "Exposición de los productos de la Industria española en 1845", *El heraldo de Madrid*, 1845/06/28. [Advertisement], *La Esperanza*, Madrid, 1845/11/05. "Comunicado", *Diario de Avisos de Madrid*, 1845/09/05. *El eco del comercio de Madrid*, 1847/04/21. *El genio de la libertad*, Palma de Mallorca., 1847/05/04.

41 Ginesta Clarós, Miguel, AGP, Personal, Cª 434, Exp. 15. España, Constitución, 1812. *Constitución política de la Monarquía española: promulgada en Cádiz á 19 de Marzo de 1812*, RB, PAS/2793, Empire-style binding in red morocco. It is not signed by the binder and the tools are as yet not identified as his.

42 [Advertisement], *Diario de Avisos*, 1844/12/13.

43 Ginesta de Haro, Miguel, *Factura a la Inspección de gastos de palacio*, 1860/28/04. AGP, Leg. 5233, Exp. 6.

44 [Son obras de las que puede pedir S. M. para su uso.]

45 Archivo Histórico Nacional, Estado, 6322, Exp. 85. [En el Ejército de la izquierda, en tiempo del E. S. marqués de

la Romana a las ordenes de su auditor D. Tadeo Delgado ... tuvo grande afición al Arte que profesa al cual se dedicó más y exclusivamente procurando distinguirse por su aplicación, como lo están demostrando sus obras y la aceptación general de ellas en todas partes.]

46 ARB/15, doc. 11. [Hasta de Cámara]

47 ARB/15, doc. 11. AGP, Personal, Cª 434, Exp. 15.

48 "Necrología española", *La ilustración española y americana*, 1878/03/19. "Exposición dirigida al señor Ministro de Hacienda por los impresores de Madrid", *La tipografía. Periódico mensual*, 1869/04.

49 [Todo es producto de la Península ... la baratura y la fabricación con materiales indígenas.]

50 CASTANEDA 1957, 572. "Miscelánea", *La guirnalda. Periódico quincenal dedicado al bello sexo*, 1867/02/01. [La primera acaso en su género que haya sido presentada en exposiciones universales.]

51 [Holandesa fina.] Some examples: Céan-Bermúdez, Juan Agustín, *Sumario de las antigüedades romanas que hay en España ...*, Madrid, Imprenta de D. Miguel de Burgos, 1832, RB, IV/1001; Bascle de Lagrèze, Gustave, *Le Trésor de Pau: archives du Chateau d'Henri IV avec des fac-simile*, Pau, [n. n.], 1851, Imprimerie et Lithographie de E. Vignancour, RB, VI/3019; Ott, A., *Manual de Historia universal, desde la edad media hasta nuestros días*, Madrid, Imprenta de D. A. Espinosa y Compañía, 1846–47, RB, V/1987–1988. Concerning payment of this bill, see ARB/5, carp. 2, doc. 16.

52 [Holandesa con papel jaspe.] Some examples: *Reconocimiento del Río Guadalquivir entre Córdoba y Sevilla*, Madrid, M. Rivadeneyra, 1847, RB, VIII/10723, IX/4981; Oñate, *Trois moyens de salut: arrosement par des puisards, bon fumier, assolements ou recoltes alternes*, RB, II/1549.

53 Some examples: *Cuatro discursos de Fernández de Navarrete*, forming a factitious volume: RB, I/F/194. Padecopeo, Gabriel, *Los Soliloquios amorosos de un alma a Dios ...*, Madrid, Imprenta de Musica por Juan de San Miguel, Calle del Barco, 1756, RB, III/3952; García Conde, Pedro, *Verdadera albeyteria ...*, Madrid, Antonio Gonzalez de Reyes ..., 1685, RB, VIII/6903; Pugin, A. M., *Les vrais principes de l'architecture ogivale ou chrétiene, avec des remarques sur leurs renaissance au temps actueil ...*, Bruges, [n. n.], 1850 (Impie. de Daveluy), RB, IV/997. Also, ARB/12, doc. 13.

54 Laffont de Montferrier, *Le coeur du poéte, ou fleurs poétiques*, 2 éd. Rev. et aug. Paris, Librairie Garnier Frères, 1857, RB, VIII/18443 and XIV/2694. Billed in 1858, cf. ARB/7, carp. 2, doc. 12.

55 Bernardino de Sahagún (O. F. M.), *Historia universal de las cosas de la Nueva España: repartida en doze libros en lengua mexicana y española* fecha por el muy reverendo padre fray Bernardino de Sahagún ..., Cámara de Seguridad, RB, II/3280; Caracciolo, Roberto, *Quadragesimale Roberti de peccatis*, Lugduni, per magi[stru]m Mathiam Huss, 1488. RB, I/138. *Epistolaí diaphórōn philosóphōn. rētórōn. sophistōn. ex pròs tois eikosi : òn tà onómata en tē exēs eurēseis selídi = Epistolae diuersorum philosophorum. oratorum. Rhetorum sex & viginti ...*, Venetiis, Aldus Manutius, 1499. RB, I/39; *Mammotrectus*. Venetiis, p[er] Symone[n] papien alias Beuilaqua, 1492. RB, I/137.

56 Dumas, Aléxandre, *Elena de Orleans: novela histórica*, Madrid, (impta. de la Biblioteca del Siglo), 1849. RB, IX/6347. Such is the case of *Eustache Le sueur, sa vie et ses œuvres. Dessins par MM. Gsell et Challamel*. Paris, publié par Challamel (impie. de Ducessois), 1849. An imperial quarto size volume specified as: spine in morocco and in cloth of the same colour, the upper edge gilt, the others uncut. The copy in the Real Biblioteca, however, belongs to the series in "holandesa con papel gofrado" and has the edges painted to match the endpapers, RB, IV/1008.

57 Adrián Cano de Abascal, María del Carmen, *Elogio de la Reina Nuestra Señora Doña Ysabel 2ª de Borbón ..., Año 1852*, RB, II/1754; Ruelle, Emile, *Histoire générale du moyen age redigée d'aprés le programme universitaire par M.M. Emile Ruelle ... et Alfonso Huillar-Bréholles*, Paris, Imprimerie de Beau, 1842–43, RB, VI/2992–2993; Prescott, William Hickling, *History of the conquest of Mexico ...*, London ..., MDCCCXLVII (Printed by S. & J. Bentley, Wilson and Fley), RB, VII/1196–1198; Lamartine, Alfonso de, *Historia de la revolución francesa de 1848 y de la fundación de la República ...*, Madrid (Imprenta de D. Higinio Reneses. Imprenta de Boix mayor y Compañia, 1850, RB, VII/1942–1943; Sophocles, *Sophokleous Tragōdiai epta metexegēseōn ...*, [Venetiis, Aldi Romani Academia, 1502], RB, VIII/1175; Patrizi, Francesco, Bishop of Gaeta, *De discorsi ... sopra alle cose appartenenti ad una cittá libera, e famiglia nobile ...*, Vinegia, [heirs of Aldo Manuzio], 1545 (in casa de' figliuoli di Aldo), RB, IX/9655; Manuzio, Aldo, the younger, *Eleganze, insieme con la copia della lingua toscana, e latina ...*, Venetia, [Aldo Manuzio], 1565, RB, VIII/3641; Terence, *Terenti[us] cu[m] Directorio Vocabulorum Sententiaru[m], Glosa i[n]terlineali artis Comice, Come[n]tariis Donato, Guidone, Ascensio*, Argentina, per ... Ioanne[m] Grüninger, 1496, RB, I/67; Arrivabene, Lodovico, *Il magno Vitei ...*, Verona, appresso Girolamo Discepolo 1597, RB, VIII/4745. See also: ARB/5, carp. 12, doc. 13; ARB/5, carp. 2, doc. 16; ARB/5, carp. 3, doc. 6.

58 Zurita, Jerónimo, *Los cinco libros primeros [-postreros] de la primera parte de los Anales de la Corona de Aragon ...*, caragoca [sic], en casa de Simon de Portonariis, 1585, RB, XIX/4630, XIV/1476, XIV/1477. See also: Ginesta de Haro, Miguel, *Cuenta*, 1859. ARB/7, carp. 3, doc. 12.

59 Gómez de la Cortina, Joaquín, *Catalogus librorum Doctoris D. Joachini Gomez de la Cortina, March de Morante, qui in aedibus suis existant* [Matriti, apud Eusebium Aguado], 1854–62, RB, VIII/10885–10892. Examples of bindings based on a model "like the sample" are those made in black grained morocco. Sometimes, as in the case of *Lettres sur l'empire de Russie publiées dans le Journal des Débats en 1838 et 1839 par N[i]t[ag]*, Paris, [Béthume et Plon], 1840, RB, IX/9400 (1–2), specifying that the coats of arms should not be stamped on the covers. Ginesta de Haro's solution for this factitious volume beginning with Demidov, Anatolii *Esquisses d'un voyage dans la Russie méridionale et la Crimée ...*, Paris, Everat et comp. 1838, was to attach a double spine label with gold lettering to differentiate the works. Lesseps,

Ferdinand de, *Percement de l'isthme de Suez exposé et documents officiels …*, Paris, (Typographie Henri Plou, 1855–56), RB, IV/783–785. See ARB/7, carp. 1, doc. 4.

60 Palacio Real (Madrid), Armería, *Catálogo de los objetos de la Real Armería*, Madrid, Eusebio Aguado, impresor de Cámara de S. M. y de su Real Casa, 1863, RB, INF/891, I/J/102, VIII/383, I/I/67, XIV/1388, PAS/ARM/571; 1864, ARB/9, carp. 1, doc.17. Gravelot, *Iconologie par figures ou Traité complet des allégories, emblêmes …, tome I [-IV]*, Paris, Lattré graveur ruë St. Jacques la Porte cochère vis-à-vis la ruë de la Parcheminerie à la Ville de Bordeaux …, [1722–88], (de l'Imprimerie de Clousier, rue de Sorbonne), RB, I/F/570–573. Bill of April 1858 in ARB/7, carp. 2, doc. 12.

61 Giménez, Manuel, *Comitiva regia en el casamiento de S. M. el rey de España Don Alfonso 12 con S.A.I. y R. la archiduquesa Dª María Cristina de Austria …*, [Madrid], Imp. en la Litª. de A. Foruny, [1883], 64 prints. Pasting on cloth and luxury binding, 60 pesetas each. Engraving a royal cypher and crown for the said album, 120 pesetas. Covers for each copy, cut, gathered and collated, 4 pesetas per set. Cutting, gathering and collation of each copy, 2 pesetas. Ginesta Revuelta, Miguel, *Curatela de Miguel Ginesta*, 1884/11/11, AGP, Leg.5233, Exp. 15. Two are clearly identified as the binding billed by Miguel Ginesta, but they differ in the quality of their finish: RB, I/I/243, bound in red morocco; crowned royal cypher on the upper cover: "AC" stamped in gold, made by Atanasio Carrasco; on the covers, double gold fillet with fleur-de-lis ornamentation at the corners, gilt board edges and squares; white moiré endpapers; pastedowns; *Olim*: Vitrina Sala IV. The border on the square GIN_R_FLO_01. RB, IX/M/98, bound in red sharkskin; stencil-drawn and coloured on the front cover, the crowned royal cipher; "AC", by Atanasio Carrasco; on the covers, a double gold fillet with fleurs-de-lis at the corners; moiré endpapers. Other copies of this album were not bound by Ginesta and are also different from each other, making it impossible to identify the 100 copies bound by Sanz y Ojeda: RB, IX/M/289 bis, in a folder lined with brown cloth with the following inscription in gold: "COMITIVA REGIA / en el casamiento de S. M. el Rey de España / DON ALFONSO XII / el dia 29 de Noviembre de 1879"; attached to another paper support; *Olim*: IX-Mesa-458 Bis. Contains the original drawings from which the lithographs were made. RB, GRAB/389 bis, bound in boards; on the front cover, crowned royal cypher: "AC", made by Atanasio Carrasco. *Olim*: Grab. 389 (bis). Unbound. RB, VIII/M/258–259, bound in boards with red and yellow cloth; on the front cover, crowned royal cypher: "AC", made by Atanasio Carrasco; pastedowns; *Olim*: VIII-Mesa-258.

62 *El defensor de Córdoba : diario católico*, year III, number 473, 1901/04/08.

63 *Gran Enciclopedia Espasa* 1923, vol. XXI, *s. v.* "España", 1256. Regarding the attempt, a few years earlier, to create a national calligraphy, see Bouza 2011. Regarding the involvement of this elite in the construction of a bibliophile movement with a national character, see López-Vidriero 2011.

64 He charged 35 pesetas for the case, "1 estuche para los hierros de encuadernación de la Real Biblioteca, en imitación tafilete azul y gamuza roja", Luna Valbuena, Justo, *Factura*, 1908/07/14. ARB, año 1909. Also, Taller de encuadernación de la viuda e hijo de L. García, *Factura*, 1923/10. ARB, año 1923. That year, the workshop bound numerous books in "pasta rejilla" or "pasta anticuada" with a red headband and coat of arms.

65 The people portrayed were: Don Juan and Don José María Florit; Don Guillermo J. de Osma.; Don Juan Catalina Garcia; Don Dimitri Schevitch; the Count of Las Navas; Don Alejandro Pidal y Mon; the Marquis of Laurencín; the Prince of Savoy; the Marquis of Valverde de la Sierra; Don Antonio Vives; Don Narciso Sentenach; Don Pablo Bosch; Don Eduardo Bosch; Don Félix Bosch; Count Crecente; Don Pelayo Quintero; the Baron of La Vega de Hoz; Don Francisco de Laiglesia; and Don José Antonio Balenchana. RB, GRAB/175.

66 I refer readers to the bibliography compiled by Concha Lois in the present volume (see the section "Real Biblioteca. Madrid" in her article), where she lists studies of marks of ownership in the royal collections.

67 Riquer, Emilia, *Carta al conde de las Navas*, Palma de Mallorca, 1926/12/10. ARB, año 1926. He proposes selling the stamps to the Real Biblioteca. When organising the services for his household, Alfonso XIII appointed Carlos Martínez de Irujo y del Alcázar, Duke of Sotomayor, as chief officer of the Palace and *Sumiller de Corps*. The latter was a title that had not been conferred on anyone for some time.

68 [Visitar y copiar hermosos libros españoles de los que se grabarán más hierros.]

69 [No por faltos de carácter sino por ser éste en ellos demasiado general.]

70 Guasch, Joan M., *Pirenenques: [Poesias]*, Barcelona, Bartomeu Baxarias, 1910, RB, I/J/336. Muñoz y García Lomas, Juan, *Carta a Ramón M. Bremón*, 1911/01/24. ARB, año 1911.

71 [Los catalanistas como los francmasones se protegen y se ayudan entre ellos.]

72 "A mí mismo me han dicho cosas … y eso todo un señor director de una Biblioteca o Museo y poeta, Catalina [Juan Catalina García López, director of the Museo Arqueológico]", in ARB, año 1911.

73 "A los señores suscritores a la Sagrada Biblia", *Lauburu. Diario de Pamplona*, 1885/05/19. "Noticias", *La Dinastia* (Barcelona), 1884/12/31.

74 Navas, Juan Gualberto López Valdemoro y de Quesada, Count of las, *De Libros: (menudencias)*, [Madrid, n. n., 1908], (Est. Tip. de Fortanet), Biblioteca Amarilla y Verde; tercer limón, Palacio real Madrid). *Catálogo de la Real Biblioteca: Impresos. Autores Historia*, Madrid, Ducazcal, 1910–31.

75 [Al modo de los de aquí, traje aprobado por Felipe II.]

76 Antolin García, Guillermo (O.S.A.), *Carta al conde de las Navas*, El Escorial, 1922/10/02, ARB, año 1922. *Catálogo de los códices latinos de la Real Biblioteca del Escorial*, Madrid, [Imprenta Helénica], 1910–23.

77 Miralles, Benjamín, *Carta al conde de las Navas*, Barcelona, 1915/04/21, ARB, año 1915.

78 Octavio Picón, Jacinto, *Carta al conde de las Navas*, Madrid, 1894/01/28, ARB/25, doc. 22 [1894]. Bascarán y Federico, José de, *Lecciones sobre el material de artillería*

que se usa en España, [Madrid?, n. n., 1873?], (Imprenta del Cuerpo de Artilleria?), RB, IX/9026–9027. According to CASTAÑEDA (1957, 542) the bookbinder was Adriano Durand. Accounted-for invoice 1894/03 reads: "Al encuadernador Durand, por la encuadernación de dos tomos del Dictionnaire français-allemand et allemand-français." This French-German dictionary was probably RB, VIII/5972, ARB/22, carp/1–22, doc. 188–3. [El mejor encuadernador de Madrid, el que más amor profesa a su arte y el que mejor lo conoce.]

79 Referring to Santiago Martín. Boix y Merino, Félix, director of the Compañia de los caminos de hierro del Norte, *Carta al conde de las Navas*, Madrid. 1915/03/29, ARB, año 1915.

80 Real Biblioteca, *Cuenta justificada*, 1896/06, ARB/23, doc. 21. For example, in his bill of 1904/11/10, Victorio Arias included: "Corona real, dos pesetas, importe del grabador en retocarla." ARB, year 1904. The pen wipers, in black leather, blind-stamped coat of arms, at 3 pesetas each. Arias, Victorio, *Factura*, 1897/09 and 1897/11/02, ARB/24, doc. 18.

81 [Iguales de la notable encuadernación de Miralles.]

82 [El ejemplar de regalo de la Biblioteca de S. M. a la señora condesa de Bernard.]

83 At present, one hundred and forty-seven books signed by Victorio Arias have been located. This should be considered an open number. There are abundant bills by "Victorio Arias, Encuadernaciones de lujo" beginning in 1892: these are half-bindings in *pasta española*, with light-colored cloth. The present essay only mentions those bindings that are relevant to the standardisation effort: neo Renaissance "uniform" bindings. Arias, Victorio, *Factura*, 1895/02/11, ARB/22, carp. 2, doc. 21. Fernández de Oviedo, Gonzalo, [*Sumario de la natural historia de las Indias*], Toledo, a costas del autor ..., 1526, RB, I/B/22. Fernández de Oviedo, Gonzalo, [*Historia general y natural de las Indias. Libro 1–20*], Sevilla, Juam [*sic*] Cromberger, 1535, RB, I/B/23. Also in calfskin with Renaissance ornamentation: Copy of the letter, 1503. Busto, Bernabé, *Arte para aprender a leer y escribir perfectamente en romance y latín* ..., [Spain, n. n., c. 1533], RB, I/B/119. Nebrija, Antonio, [*Reglas de orthographia enla lengua castellana* ..., Leon, [n. n.], 1527, RB, I/B/120. Arias, Victorio, *Factura*, 1898/01/03 and 1898/05/01, ARB/25, doc. 22. *Oficios Divinos a que asiste la Corte en la Real Capilla*, Madrid, ([Imp. de Manuel Tello], 1892, RB, VIII/14981–14982. Arias, Victorio, *Factura*, 1904/11/10, ARB, año 1904. Queen Victoria Eugenia's bindings are not in the Real Biblioteca: "... en el interior en la guarda tres hilos dorados cortados por leones, castillos y corona real, en el centro de la guarda. Portada, escudo de Battenberg, en la contraguarda tres hilos dorados, construcción nervios naturales y guardapolvo de piel blanca, cabeza dorada." He charged 180 pesetas. Arias, Victorio, *Factura*, 1906/11/13, ARB, año 1907. *México a través de los siglos* ..., Barcelona, Espasa y Compañia, (n. d., 1884), RB, VI/33–37. Menéndez Pidal, Ramón, *Crónicas Generales de España*, Madrid, Sucesores de Rivadeneyra, 1898, RB, IX/8882. Luna Valbuena, Justo, *Factura*, 1906/12/22, ARB, año 1907. Borbón y Borbón, María de la Paz de, Infanta of Spain, *Poesias de Paz de Borbón*, Freiburg in Breisgau, B. Herder, 1904. Alfonso XIII's copy: RB, I/J/639. The royal family's copy: RB, INF/1941. The Real Biblioteca also holds copies with other types of bindings: INF/CAJ/FOLL/6 (17–21), C/872 (7). Arias, Victorio, *Factura*, 1904/03/30, ARB, año 1904. Rivas, Enrique Ramírez de Saavedra, duque de, *Carta de Enrique Ramírez de Saavedra, duque de Rivas, a Paz.* (Madrid, 1883/06/12), RB, II/4557, doc. 679. Alfonso XII, King of Spain, [*Carta de Alfonso XII a Paz*], (Madrid, 1883/06/24), RB, II/4557, doc. 757.

84 "Noticias necrológicas", *ABC*, 1935/02/20, p. 32.

85 [Honor a la orfebrería española de nuestros tiempos.]

86 LÓPEZ-VIDRIERO 2012 [in press]. The binder charged 4 pesetas to line the board. Luna Valbuena, Justo, *Factura*, 1913/08/04, ARB, año 1913

87 [Don Alfonso XIII en su Biblioteca particular, 22 marzo 1913]. [Press clippings], RB, VI/F/417, binding by Justo Luna y Valbuena (1915), blue and red "Bourbon uniform" model in long-grained red morocco. Title lengthwise: "Don Alfonso xiii en su Biblioteca particular, 22 marzo 1913." Tools: Cypher of Alfonso XIII (tool no. 18), calligraphic tools (nos. 5, 16, 12); king's cypher (nos. 4 and 13) surmounted by the royal crown (tool no. 29). See ARB, año 1915. That same year, he made another binding with the same characteristics, for Clodd, Eward, *Storia dell'alfabeto* ..., Torino, [Vincenzo Bona], 1903, RB, VIII/7373 *cf.* ARB, año 1915. Twentieth-century binding (1915), Justo Luna Valbuena. Blue and red "Bourbon uniform" model. Tools: Cypher of Alfonso XIII (tool no. 18), calligraphic tools (nos. 5, 16, 12); king's cypher (nos. 4 and 13) surmounted by the royal crown (tool no. 29). On the back of the catalogue card: "Presente del E. S. Conde de las Navas Las anotaciones marginales, en lapiz así como el calco son de mano del célebre arqueológo, catedrático y académico Dn. M. Gómez Moreno, a quien perteneció el libro y quien lo regaló al Conde 1913."

88 His bills began appearing in the late nineteenth century and by the first years of the twentieth century they reflect continuous work on the collection of contemporary printed works and magazines. ARB, años 1901–4. [Factitious codices], RB, II/1577–1578. Twentieth-century binding (1907), Justo Luna Valbuena. Medieval-style model. Hazel-coloured calf-like sheepskin. Tools: supralibros of Alfonso XIII (tool no. 37) and cypher of Alfonso XIII (tool no. 18). He charged 15 pesetas per volume. Luna Valbuena, Justo, *Factura*, 1907/12/30, ARB, año 1907.

89 He charged 15 pesetas per volume on the bindings of gold-stamped "pasta anticuada", 9 pesetas for plain "pasta anticuada", 6 pesetas for those of "pasta rejilla" and 2 pesetas for those made of drill. He charged 9 pesetas for cutting the steel coat of arms, and 8 pesetas for retouching a royal crown and making a tool with "XIII". Luna Valbuena, Justo, *Factura*, 1911/01/31, 1911/03/03 and 1911/02/14, ARB, año 1911. Two items could fit this description: RB, IX/8883, varnished mottled leather, blind-tooled border, large coat of arms in blind on the front cover (tool no. 38); and INF/2091, cypher of the infanta, lettering of Isabel of Bourbon surmounted by the royal crown (tool no. 29). In 1912, he bound one hundred and forty volumes of sixty-

eight magazines. Luna Valbuena, Justo, *Factura*, 1912/11/30 and 1912/12/20, ARB, año 1912.

90 Identified in the Real Biblioteca are: the copy belonging to Infanta Isabel of Bourbon, with double endpapers of glossy paper, supralibros featuring the large royal coat of arms (tool no. 38), on the inside cover, bookplate of the Infanta "Isabel", gilt upper edge, RB, INF/2093. A copy in blue *écrasé*, endpaper of red shagreen with gold tooling (tools 16, 12, 5) and bookplate of Alfonso XIII (tools 1, 13 and 31) and ribbed silk endpapers, RB, ARM29/214. One in white drill, endpapers and flyleaves in red glossy paper; royal coat of arms on the inside cover (tool no. 32), RB, VIII/HVD/44. Special copy on linen paper, wild boar skin, bookplate of Alfonso XIII (tools 1, 13 and 31), endpaper in ribbed green silk and gilt edges, RB, VIII/3397. Luna y Valbuena, Justo, *Facturas a la Real Biblioteca de S. M.*, 1917/05/28, 1917/07 and 1917/09, ARB, año 1917. Rokiski, José, *Albarán a Justo Luna*, Madrid, 1917/09/15, ARB, año 1917.

91 [Hierros estilo siglo XII para encuadernar el *Libro canticorum*, obra la más antigua de la Real Biblioteca.]

92 *Memoria de los trabajos realizados en la Real Biblioteca, año 1912*, ARB, año 1912.

93 [Libro tan inapreciable como el *Liber canticorum* ... en moderna y groserísima pasta española.]

94 [Es códice precioso del siglo 11. En vitela. 1 vol., 8º, pta.]

95 [Muy pocos monarcas poseen hoy día tales alhajas en sus palacios.]

96 *Liber canticorum*, Biblioteca General Histórica de la Universidad de Salamanca [hereinafter BGUS], Ms. 2668 (olim: S. 2, Est. 1, P. 5). *Índice de los códices y mss. de la Bibl.ᵃ particular de S. M. la reina nra sra ... Dᵃ Isabel 2ᵃ*. 185?, vol. 4. See also: Uriarte y Badía, Manuel de, [Letter from Manuel de Uriarte to the Count of las Navas, Madrid, 1898/06/01]. López Serrano, Matilde, "Liber canticorum o Libro de los Cánticos", 1 sht., *c.* 1950. This is a sheet of folded paper joined to the catalogue card. Luna y Valbuena, Justo, *Factura*, Madrid, 1915/07/22, ARB, año 1915. On 1906/31/10 the *Cuenta justificada* of HM's library lists "al Sr. Delbreil, grabador, por s/c de objetos que menciona, 110 pesetas", but the bill itself is missing. ARB, año 1907. [Un libro de extraordinario interés por la persona a quien perteneció, su arte y su escritura y su texto litúrgico.]

97 Some examples:
MANUSCRIPTS:
Crónica de 1344, BGUS, MS. 2656. See *Catálogo de manuscritos* 1997–2002, vol. II, 1039. Twentieth-century binding (1909) by Justo Luna Valbuena. Medieval-style model. In the bill, Luna describes it as: "piel abecerrada, rótulo e hilos gofré (estaba en muy mal estado y ha habido que poner hojas blancas entre el texto para su conservación)." He charges 25 pesetas, *Factura*, 1909/07/03, ARB, año 1909.

Jiménez de la Espada, Marcos, *Manuscritos de América propios de la Real Biblioteca: Papeletas redactadas por ...*, RB, II/2909. Twentieth-century binding (1911) by Justo Luna Valbuena. Medieval-style model. Hazelnut-coloured calf-like sheepskin. Tools: fleur-de-lis (tool no. 15), supralibros of Alfonso XIII (tool no. 32). Luna Valbuena, Justo, *Factura*, 1911/08/01, ARB, año 1911.

Cantón, Antonio, *Règne de Philippe III Roi d'Espagne*, nineteenth century (1857), [Dedicated by the author to HM Isabel II], (Algiers, 15–XI–1857), RB, II/2979. Twentieth-century binding. Medieval-style model. Hazel calf-like sheepskin. Tools: royal coat of arms (tool no. 35), supralibros of Alfonso XIII and cypher of Alfonso XIII (tool no. 18).

Zurita, Alonso de, *[Historia de la Nueva España]*, sixteenth century (1585), RB, II/59. Twentieth-century binding (1907) by Justo Luna Valbuena. Medieval-style model. Hazelnut colored calf-like sheepskin. Tools: supralibros of Alfonso XIII (tool no. 37). Luna y Valbuena, Justo, *Factura*, 1907, ARB, año 1907.

Cortes de Aragón (1502). Sixteenth century (in.), RB, II/1614. Twentieth-century binding (1915) by Justo Luna Valbuena. Medieval-style model. Hazel calf-like sheepskin, stitched in the antique manner. Tools: supralibros of Alfonso XIII (tool no. 37) and cypher of Alfonso XIII (tool no. 18). Luna Valbuena, Justo. *Factura*, 1915, ARB, año 1915.

Valera, Diego de, *Espejo de la verdadera nobleza*, fifteenth century, RB, II/2078. Twentieth-century binding (1909) by Justo Luna Valbuena. Medieval-style model and blue and red "Bourbon uniform" model. Shagreen. Tools: fleur-de-lis (tool no. 15), cypher of Alfonso XIII (tool no. 18), supralibros of Alfonso XIII (tool no. 32). In his invoice, Luna describes it as: "sagren azul oscuro, guardas de badana roja, con hilos dorados, rotulo e hilos gofré, cabeza y pie dorados y 4 hojas vitela portada y final." He charges 50 pesetas. *Factura*, 1909/07/31, ARB, año 1909.

Cancioneros de poesías varias, sixteenth century, RB, II/1577–1581. Twentieth-century binding (1907) by Justo Luna Valbuena. Medieval-style model. Hazel calf-like sheepskin. Tools: supralibros of Alfonso XIII (tool no. 37), cypher of Alfonso XIII (tool no. 18), fleur-de-lis (tool no. 15). In his bill, the binder describes it as: "Poesías varias. Badana abecerrada, hilo gofré, poner escartivanas." Luna Valbuena, Justo, *Factura*. 1907/12/31, ARB, año 1907.

Crónica General de España. [Chronicle of 1344], fifteenth-sixteenth centuries, RB, II/875. Twentieth-century binding (1909) by Justo Luna Valbuena. Medieval-style model. Hazel calf-like sheepskin. Tools: supralibros of Alfonso XIII (tool no. 37) and cypher of Alfonso XIII (tool no. 18). Luna Valbuena, Justo, *Factura*, 1909/07/03, ARB, año 1908.
INCUNABULA:
Salustio Crispo, Cayo, *Obra selecta*, Taurini, per Nicolaum de Benedictis et Iacobinum Suigum, 1494, RB, I/62. Bound in brown leather. Tools: royal supralibros of Alfonso XIII (tool no. 37).

Boethius, Anicius Manlius Torquatus Severinus, *De consolatione philosophiae*, Venetiis, Per Bonetu[m] Locatellum ..., 1498, RB, I/75. Twentieth-century binding. Medieval-style model. Hazel calf-like sheepskin. Tools: supralibros of Alfonso XIII (tool no. 32) and cypher of Alfonso XIII (tool no. 18), fleur-de-lis (tool no. 14).

Eiximenis, Francesc (O .F. M), *[Lo Crestiá. llibre 1. Español]*, Granada, Meynardo Ungut [y] Joha[n]nes de nure[m]berga, por ma[n]dado y expensas del muy reuerendissimo señor don fray Hernando de Talauera, 1496, RB, I/7. 20th-century binding (1909) by Justo Luna Valbuena. Medieval-style model. Hazel calf-like sheepskin. Tools: royal supralibros of Alfonso XIII (tool no. 35); fleur-de-lis (tool no. 17) and royal cypher of Alfonso XIII (tool no. 18). Luna Valbuena, Justo, *Factura*, 1909/08/31, ARB, año 1909.

ANTIQUE PRINTED WORKS:

Dante Alighieri, *[La Divina comedia. Selección. Español]*, Burgos, por Fadrique alemán de Basilea, 1515, RB, I/B/21. Twentieth-century binding (1909) by Justo Luna Valbuena. Medieval-style model. Hazel calf-like sheepskin, red headband, royal supralibros of Alfonso XIII (tool no. 37) and royal cypher of Alfonso XIII (tool no. 18). Luna Valbuena, Justo, *Factura*, 1909/08/31, ARB, año 1909.

Iciar, Juan de, *Nueuo Estilo de escreuir Cartas mensageras sobre diuersas materias ...*, Çaragoça, a costa de Miguel de çapila mercader de libros, 1552 (por Agostin Millan impresor de libros), RB, I/B/121. Twentieth-century binding (1912) by Justo Luna Valbuena. Medieval-style model. Calf-like sheepskin. Tools: royal supralibros of Alfonso XIII (tool no. 37). Luna Valbuena, Justo, *Factura*, 1912/07/31, ARB, año 1912.

Beccadelli, Antonio, *Libro de los dichos y hechos del Rey doñalonso*, Impresso en Vale[n]cia, en casa de Juan Joffre, i[m]presor, 1527, RB, I/B/349. Twentieth-century binding (1912) by Justo Luna Valbuena. Medieval-style model. Calf-like sheepskin. Tools: fleur-de-lis (tool no. 17), cypher of Alfonso XIII (tool no. 18). Luna Valbuena, Justo, *Factura*, 1912/07/31, ARB, año 1912.

Another variant type of binding for these holdings was the "pasta anticuada" employed by Justo Luna y Valbuena for:

Nebrija, Antonio, *Artis rethoricae compendiosa coaptatio ex Aristotele, Cicerone [et] Quintiliano ...*, Granatae, [Elio Antonio de Nebrija], 1583, RB, I/B/200. Bound in mottled leather. Tools: royal supralibros of Alfonso XIII (tool no. 32) and royal cypher of Alfonso XIII at the foot (tool no. 18).

Cicero, Marcus Tullius, *Rhetoricorum M. Tullii Ciceronis ad Herennium libri IIII, eiusdem de Inuentione lib. II*, Impressum Lugduni, [Iacobus Giunta], 1535, RB, I/B/201. Bound in mottled sheepskin. Tools: royal supralibros of Alfonso XIII (tool no. 32).

García Matamoros, Alfonso, *De ratione dicendi libri duo ...*, Compluti, excudebat Ioa[n]nes Brocarius, 1548. RB, I/B/199. Bound in brown leather. Tools: royal supralibros of Alfonso XIII (tool no. 32).

98 MENÉNDEZ PIDAL 1898, VII. [Echar el cimiento ... que al fin venga a llenar un vacío tan grande en los estudios históricos y literarios de nuestra patria]

99 España. Casa Real. Intendencia General. *Oficio, 1899–01–02*, ARB/25, doc. 157. [Reviews of the "Catálogo de la Real Biblioteca. Manuscritos. Crónicas Generales de España" by Ramón Menéndez Pidal]. (n. p., 1898–99), ARB/25, doc. 156. MENÉNDEZ PIDAL 1906.

100 [Para tenerlos así más a la vista y custodia.]

101 CAMARA DE SEGURIDAD

1. Breydenbach, Bernhard von, *Le saint voiage et pelerinage de la cite saincte de hierusalem ...*, [Lyon, Gaspard Ortuin], 1489, RB, I/180. Twentieth-century binding (1909) by Justo Luna Valbuena. Dyed sheepskin. Tools: royal supralibros of Alfonso XIII (tool no. 36) and royal cypher of Alfonso XIII (tool no. 18). In his bill, Luna describes it as "pasta anticuada sencilla, cabeza dorada, los planos divididos y reforzados". He charged 11 pesetas. *Factura*, 1909/07/31, ARB, año 1909.

2. Breydenbach, Bernhard von, *[Sanctaru[m] peregrinationu[m] in montem Syon ad venerandu[m] xp[ist]i sepulcru[m] in Jesusalem atque in monte[m] Synai ad diua[m] virgine[m] et martire[m] Katherina[m] opusculum ...*, Civitate Moguntina, p[er] Erhardu[m] reiiwich de Tratecto, 1486, RB, I/179. Twentieth-century binding (1909) by Justo Luna Valbuena. Dyed sheepskin. Tools: royal supralibros of Alfonso XIII (tool no. 36) and royal cypher of Alfonso XIII (tool no. 18). In his bill, Luna describes it as "pasta anticuada sencilla, cabeza dorada, los planos divididos y reforzados". He charged 11 pesetas. *Factura*, 1909/07/31, ARB, año 1909.

3. Breydenbach, Bernhard von, *Viaje dela tierra sancta ...*, Çaragoça de Arago[n], Paulo Hurus, 1498, RB, I/181. Twentieth-century binding (1909) by Justo Luna Valbuena. Dyed sheepskin. Tools: royal supralibros of Alfonso XIII (tool no. 36) and royal cypher of Alfonso XIII (tool no. 18). In his bill, Luna describes it as "pasta anticuada sencilla, cabeza dorada, los planos divididos y reforzados". He charged 11 pesetas. *Factura*, 1909/07/31, ARB, año 1909.

4. *[Libro de Horas]*, fifteenth century, RB, II/2099. Twentieth-century binding (1909) by Justo Luna Valbuena. Blue and Red "Bourbon uniform" model. Shagreen. Tools: cypher of Alfonso XIII (tool no. 18), supralibros of Alfonso XIII surmounted by the royal coat of arms (tool no. 32). In his bill, Luna describes it as "sagren azul oscuro, guardas de badana roja, con hilos dorados, rotulo e hilos gofré, cabeza y pie dorados y 4 hojas vitela portada y final". He charged 50 pesetas. *Factura*, 1909/07/31, ARB, año 1909.

5. Deza, Diego de, Archbishop of Sevilla, *Fatris Didaci de Deça ordinis predicatorum vite regularis ... In defensio[n]es sancti Thome ab impugnationibus magistri Nicholai magistriq[ue] Mathie p[ro]pugnatoris sui ...*, Hispalis, per Meynardum ungut Alemanum et Stanislaum polonu[m] socios, 1491, RB, I/42. Twentieth-century binding. Medieval-style model. Hazel calf-like sheepskin. Tools: royal supralibros of Alfonso XIII (tool no. 32) and royal cypher of Alfonso XIII (tool no. 18).

6. Sallustius Crispus, Gaius, *[Obra selecta]*, Taurini, per Nicolaum de Benedictis et Iacobinum Suigum, 1494, RB, I/62. Twentieth-century binding. Medieval-style model. Hazel calf-like sheepskin. Tools: royal supralibros of Alfonso XIII (tool no. 37) and royal cypher of Alfonso XIII (tool no. 18)

7. *Vita [et] processus Sancti Thome cantuariensis martyris super ... libertate ecclesiastica*, Parisii, Joham philippi alemanu[m], 1495, RB, I/44. Twentieth-century binding in granite-marbled leather. Tools: gold royal supralibros of Alfonso XIII (tool no. 37).

8. Eiximenis, Francesc (O.F.M), *[Lo Crestiá. Llibre 1. Español]*, Granada, por Meynardo ungut [y] Joha[n]nes de nure[m]berga, por ma[n]dado y expensas del muy reuerendissimo señor don fray Hernando de Talauera, 1496, RB, I/7. Twentieth-century binding. Medieval-style model. Hazel calf-like sheepskin. Tools: supralibros of Alfonso XIII (tool no. 35), fleur-de-lis (tool no. 17) and cypher of Alfonso XIII (tool no. 18).

9. *Rhetorica ad Herennium. M.T.C. Rhetoricorum: libri cu[m] tribus co[m]mentis*, [Lugduni], per Iacobinu[m] Suigu[m] [et] Nicholaum de benedictis socios, 1497, RB, I/32. Twentieth-century binding. "Pasta anticuada". Tools: supralibros of Alfonso XIII in gold (tool no. 32), cypher of Alfonso XIII (tool no. 18).

10. Cartagena, Alonso de, *Doctrina [et] instrucio dela arte de cauallería*, Burgos, Juan de Burgos, 1497, RB, I/131. Twentieth-century binding. Neo-Renaissance model. Hazel calf-like sheepskin.

11. Boethius, Anicius Manlius Torquatus Severinus, *De consolatione philosophiae* ..., Venetiis, per Bonetu[m] Locatellum, impensis ..., Octauiani Scoti, 1498, RB, I/75. Twentieth-century binding. Medieval-style model. Hazel calf-like sheepskin. Tools: supralibros of Alfonso XIII (tool no. 37) and cypher of Alfonso XIII (tool no. 18), fleur-de-lis (tool no. 14).

12. Infante, Juan, *Forma libellandi* ..., Sevilla, por tres compañeros alemanes, 1498. RB, I/198. Twentieth-century binding. Medieval-style model. Hazel calf-like sheepskin. Tools: supralibros of Alfonso XIII (tool no. 37) and cypher of Alfonso XIII (tool no. 18).

13. *Leyes del estilo y declaraciones sobre las leyes del fuero*, Burgos, Faderiq[ue] alema[n], 1498, RB, I/108. Twentieth-century binding. Medieval-style model. Hazel calf-like sheepskin. Tools: supralibros of Alfonso XIII (tool no. 37) and cypher of Alfonso XIII (tool no. 18).

14. Pacheco, Francisco, *[Dibujos]|c.1599]*, RB, IX/M/83 (1–7). Twentieth-century binding (1911) by Justo Luna Valbuena. Medieval-style model. Hazel calf-like sheepskin. Tools: supralibros of Alfonso XIII (tool no. 37). In his bill, the binder specifies: "Retratos. Pacheco. Dibujos originales. Badana abecerrada, rótulo y escudo gofre." He charged 20 pesetas. Luna Valbuena, Justo, *Factura*, 1911/08/01, ARB, año 1911. See also: Navas, Juan Guadalberto López de Valdemoro, Count of las, *Carta a Bernardo Rodríguez*. Madrid, 1916/10/04. Rodríguez, Bernardo, *Carta al conde de las Navas*, Madrid, 1916/10/10. Rodríguez, Bernardo, *Carta al conde de las Navas*, Madrid, 1916/11/02. ARB, año 1916.

102 [Pura y grande satisfacción espiritual.]
103 [Sentar afirmaciones de extraordinaria importancia acerca de los orígenes de la música popular.]
104 Navas, Juan Guadalberto López de Valdemoro, Count of las, *Carta a Ramón Menéndez Pidal*, Madrid, 1917/01/16. ARB, año 1917.
105 *Cancionero Musical*, RB, II/1335. Twentieth-century binding (1922) by Justo Luna Valbuena. Medieval-style model. Hazel colored wild boar skin. Tools: fleur-de-lis (tool no. 17), royal cypher of Alfonso XIII (nos. 4, 13 and 29).
Cartagena, Alonso de, *Genealogía de los reyes d'España* ..., RB, II/3009. Twentieth-century binding (1922) by Justo Luna Valbuena. Medieval-style model. Hazel wild boar skin. Tools: fleur-de-lis (tool no. 2), cypher of Alfonso XIII (tool no. 18), royal cypher of Alfonso XIII (nos. 4, 13 and 29).
Jiménez de Rada, Rodrigo, *[Historiae]*, fourteenth century, *olim*: RB, II/1620 and now BGUS, Ms.2674. Twentieth-century binding (1922) by Justo Luna Valbuena. Medieval-style model. Hazel wild boar skin. Tools: cypher of Alfonso XIII (nos. 4, 13 and 29), fleur-de-lis (tool no. 2). The binder defined it as: "piel de jabalí, contratapa de piel tafilete rojo y guarda de seda. Dicho libro se encuadernó en la Real Biblioteca." See also: Luna y Valbuena, Justo, *Factura*, 1922/07/02, ARB, año 1922.

106 LÓPEZ-VIDRIERO 2009, 5–19.
107 [Reyes de Aragón, siglo XIV ... Genealogía de los Reyes de Castilla, siglo XV ... Cancionero Musical.]
Llinatges de Catalunya, BGUS Ms. 2490. See *Catálogo de manuscritos* 1997–2002, vol. II, 850. The bill specifies: "encuadernación, restauración y montaje ... consta de 86 folios; colocarlos en escartivanas, cartulinas y márgenes; encuadernación en piel de jabalí, guardas de legítimo tafilete rojo, contratapas con hierros e hilos y cortes dorados, trescientas pesetas." It was paid in six instalments of fifty pesetas. Luna y Valbuena, Justo, *Factura*, 1914/07/03, ARB, año 1914.
Crónica dels reis d'Aragó, BGUS, Ms.2664. See *Catálogo de manuscritos* 1997–2002, vol. II, 1061. Luna y Valbuena, Justo, *Factura*, 1922/07/02, ARB, año 1922.

108 [Sería cosa de alrededor de 75 pesetas ... tardaría unos diez días.]
109 Rokiski, José, *Factura a la Intendencia General de la Real Casa y Patrimonio*, Madrid, 1912/05/12 and 1925/03/31, ARB, años 1912 and 1925. Taller de encuadernación de la viuda e hijo de L. García, *Factura a la Real Biblioteca*, 1925/05/30, ARB, año 1925.
110 Paumard, Cesar, *Carta al conde de las Navas*, Madrid, 1920, ARB, año 1920.
111 [El amor al libro y su protección eran el estímulo para cultivar una de las más bellas de las Artes Aplicadas.]
112 J. A. Girod, S. A., *Factura*, 1923/02/27. Real Biblioteca, *Cuenta justificada del importe de los gastos que se han satisfecho en la Biblioteca de S. M.* 1923/02. Paumard, Cesar, *Carta al conde de las Navas*, Madrid, 1923/05/18. ARB, año 1923. Also: BOUCHOT 1888. RB, XIV/CL/150). Twentieth-century binding (1923) by César Paumard. Leather mosaic, ribbon border inside gold fillets with tooled finial and interior Grolier-style polychrome border in mosaic; spine with ribbon border set in fillets and vertical floral decoration in polychrome mosaic. Tools: onomastic, "Alfonso XIII" surmounted by the royal crown. Real Biblioteca (Madrid), *Memoria del año 1924*, 1925/01/25. ARB, año 1925.

From Industry to Art. Two Changes of Century in the Bindings of the Real Biblioteca

Dolores Baldó

The present study on modern and contemporary bindings in the Real Biblioteca revolves around these two apparently opposite terms, industry and art. Having been granted the privilege of exploring the shelves of the Real Biblioteca without restrictions of any kind, I gradually came across a significant number of industrial bindings dating from the turn of the nineteenth century into the twentieth; they were significant in number but also, and above all, in quality and representativeness. The artistic nature of this industrial production—once again the two terms are connected—became evident from the outset. It was also clear from the beginning that the main group of works that should be included in this study was the set of contemporary artistic bindings on the oeuvre of the winners of the Reina Sofía Prize for Ibero-American Poetry, executed between the twentieth and twenty-first centuries. Industrial bookbinding versus artistic bookbinding? Or are both types simply the result of a process of evolution and adaptation to the social, technical, artistic and cultural changes of the age?

> ... there are wines for different times of day and for different types of company. Industrial bookbinding was historically justified and is perfectly entitled to feature not only in the history of bookbinding but in the history of artistic bookbinding. And it naturally marks a step forward in the evolutionary history of the decoration of book covers.[1]

In general, the nineteenth century was a very dynamic period which witnessed an important and essential economic change that ended up consolidating the bourgeoisie as the main social and economic driving force. The decisive factor in this transformation was the major development in technology. Until not long before merchants and manufacturers had relied solely on the forces of nature and on their own work. Little by little, man learned to harness new sources of energy to achieve a higher output. The new work unit, the factory, took the place of craft production. Working conditions, means and methods of production and prices of products ceased to be established and regulated by guilds and were now at the mercy of the law of supply and demand. These new mechanical procedures were perfected quickly and progressively and began to supplant workers in the production process in what has been called the "mechanical transformation of the nineteenth century". What is more, the start of this century saw the beginning of a steady population increase which created a demand for products and consequently spurred commercial and industrial activity.

Focusing on the field of the graphic arts, a significant series of discoveries and inventions took place which, when applied jointly to the field of graphic arts, led to more technical breakthroughs than in the four centuries that had elapsed since the invention of the printing press. For example, the replacement of earlier presses with the new flat and rotary presses and the use of the system of continuous rolls of paper instead of loose sheets, among others, brought a fairly substantial increase in the speed of printing while also cutting costs. The Frenchman Louis Robert made the first attempt at a continuous paper making machine and patented the design. But the first machine was actually built in England in 1803 by the Fourdrinier brothers using Robert's patent. It was finally introduced to France in 1816. These machines did not catch on for some time owing to their high price. They were not used in Spain until the 1840s.[2]

These advances in industrial development led to the presentation of a new gold blocking press by the firm Cope & Sherwin in London in 1829. The old wooden press was replaced by an iron one with tubes which, when white hot, heated the engraved dies. These tubes were later replaced by gas burners.

In 1849, Massiquot presented a machine which cut stacks of paper with extreme precision at the Exposition Universelle of Paris: this was the paper cutter that began to replace the device used until then for cutting book edges. Earlier on, in 1845, shears had begun to be used to cut cardboard. The sewing machine for stitching gatherings appeared later, in 1889.

In addition to these advances, new printing methods began to be used such as lithography, chromolithography and, eventually, photography, leading to the progressive decline of traditional illustration methods for economic reasons. Photogravure eventually superseded lithography as it enabled texts, drawings and photographs to be reproduced directly. This fact had a very direct influence on books, as photomechanical methods gradually became widespread owing to their lower cost, and this gave rise to a substantial increase in the number of published works.

This boom in printing was also accompanied by a shift in the contents of published works. It may be said that up until this point the chief function of books had been to preserve ideas and thought, constituting a sort of repository of human memory. They not only continued to serve this purpose of preserving written and created works but now became an important vehicle for new ideas and for intellectual creation—and in addition, a source not only of knowledge but also a means of entertainment.

The greater equality that resulted from the French and American revolutions brought an improvement in public education and, accordingly, the possibility of reading and writing, as a result of which the reading public also increased. It may be said that, in general, a deep concern for children's education spread, along with the idea that it should be extended and made compulsory. In France, for example, primary education was established and made universal following the enactment of the Guizot Law in 1833. All communes with more than five hundred inhabitants were required to open a primary school. Fifteen years later the number of primary schools had increased from ten to twenty-three thousand. Universal schooling in England and Wales was introduced in 1870 for primary education and in 1900 for secondary education. The deplorable state of education in Spain, which had the highest illiteracy rates in Europe at the time, began to change with the Moyano Law of 1857 universalising primary education and regulating secondary and university education. It is evident that all this spurred a huge increase in demand for reading matter, particularly for children, including religious, educational and leisure books.

In short, the use of the new machinery that replaced much of the earlier labour resulted in greater production and lower costs and this allowed publishing companies to turn to mass production in order to meet the substantial demand for books that was beginning to arise. This means that, in order to achieve a selling price affordable to everyone, it was necessary to print and bind thousands of copies and do so in a manner that was simple but appealing. Once again, we find commercial concerns influencing our field of interest, in this case the decoration and design of bindings.

It should be stressed that some of the earliest printers and publishers, Aldo in Venice and Caxton in London, had already devised a few more or less uniform and characteristic bindings for certain works that were placed on sale no sooner had they been printed. A series of blocks were designed with different motifs in order to compose the decoration of some covers. This avoided the arduous and costly task of working with single tools. In France Geoffroy Tory also decorated a few lower-priced editions with blocks designed to be reproduced repeatedly. These first decorations imitated those used in artistic bindings.[3]

Beginning in the sixteenth and seventeenth centuries, publishers sometimes commissioned very simple bindings for copies released onto the market, as often the customer, having bought the book, preferred to decide on and commission a binding to his liking. These publisher's bindings were commonly made of calfskin with some gold tooling, or of laced-on parchment and/or vellum sometimes with the title hand painted. The Jansenists, spurred by their asceticism and rigour, eliminated all ornamentation from leather. After that leather came to be used only for the spine, and the boards were covered with paper. Taking this process one step further, books were then entirely covered in paper over the boards. The poor result of this binding only in paper led to the use of cloth, a stronger and more hardwearing material than paper. As can be seen, publisher's bindings gradually changed and adapted to the requirements that booksellers and publishers needed to meet.

The technique used for bookbinding was also adapted to this new output which required greater economy of means. The use of case binding became widespread. With this system the bookblock is not joined to the boards with cords, as in traditional binding, but only by the endpapers. First the gatherings are stitched together to form the bookblock, to which the endpapers are glued. This bookblock is cut so that the edges are perfect. After this rounding and backing takes place, although sometimes the spine is left straight. The gatherings that made up the book were stitched using the traditional method, on a loom. These operations, not yet mechanised, were usually performed by women.

At the same time, the case consisting of the two boards and the spine, all made of cardboard and joined by paper or fine card, was prepared. Mechanically manufactured and laminated card began to be used. The case was glued to the material chosen to cover the book (leather, cloth or paper, entirely or a combination). The binding was decorated before covering the book, with the material laid flat. After decorating it the book was attached to the cover. The case was joined to the book by gluing the endpapers.

But until almost halfway through the nineteenth century binders worked, at the same time and using practically the same tools, for both bibliophiles and publishers, and it is therefore difficult to distinguish between bindings made for a particular copy or those repeated for a large number of them. Romantic bindings date from this period. Publishers of deluxe editions began to devise bindings in keeping with the prevailing style of the Romantic period, the neo-Gothic. These bindings were decorated with blocks engraved with "cathedral style" architectural motifs which could be repeated in several copies. We find that they underwent the same adaptation. Single tools ceased to be used and leather was even replaced by other simpler and cheaper materials such as velvet, moiré and satin.

These early trade or industrial bindings fully espoused the decorative motifs and compositions employed by binders in their artistic counterparts. At the time, in most of these workshops' bindings were decorated either by copying some of the earlier styles in what was called retrospective style or by interpreting these antique styles. Very simple designs using the classical patterns of lines were also common. We find bindings decorated with arabesques, corner motifs, interlacing, "fanfare"

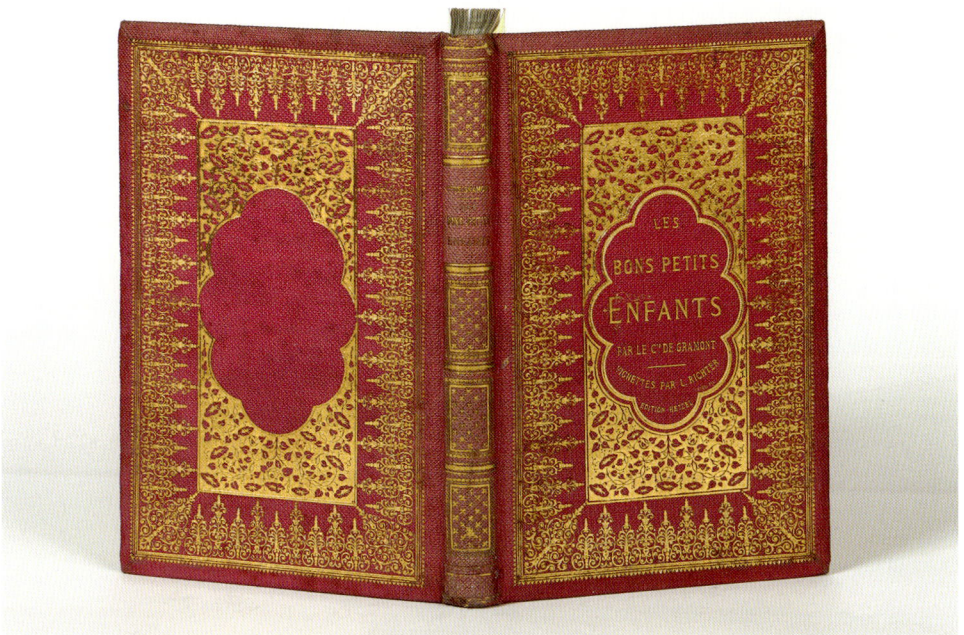

Fig. 176
Comte de Gramont, *Les bons petits enfants*. Paris:
J. Hetzel (J. Claye), (n. d.: 1863). RB, Inf. 262

rocaille, and Empire styles and the only one which, as Henri Béraldi states, could be called original—the cathedral style [fig. 176].

Publishers gradually found themselves forced to be more creative in order to attract readers and spur them to buy their works. The major change that took place then was the progressive shift away from leather as the covering material used. In the early nineteenth century, specifically the 1820s, a new material for covering books produced in large quantities began to catch on in England. This was percaline, a cotton fabric suitable for stamping and gilding. It became fashionable in France in the thirties. These textiles were initially in dark colours such as burgundy, black and navy. The decoration was applied by blocks with which the motif was blinded in and later completed with gold or silver and also with mosaics of coloured inlaid leather or paper. Around halfway through the century dark percaline began to be replaced by a brighter red percaline which showed off the gold much more. By the end of the century rich colours including blue, white, green and, above all, red were popular.

As we have seen, these new fabrics and the leathers and papers used for these bindings were decorated by means of metal blocks, usually made of bronze, copper, tin and/or

Fig. 177
Charles-Réné Forbes, Comte de Montalembert, *Sainte Elisabeth de Hongrie*. Tours: Alfred Name et Fils, 1878. RB, Inf. 905

zinc. They were engraved with decorative motifs that were transferred by means of pressure and heat before the book was covered. This process was performed by an engraver who reproduced an artist's design on the block using a steel point. The design was normally gold stamped in relief. Blind and gold stamped decoration proliferated between 1840 and 1860 and initially featured relief designs heavily gilded on dark background cloth and, gradually, on lighter fabrics. A sort of medallion in the centre of the covers was introduced around 1845 and reproduced scenes relating to the bound work. Once again, after executing the decorative design, engravers left empty spaces to which different motifs such as the title and author of the work could be incorporated. This possibility of interchanging motifs made it possible—by altering, say, small decorative elements or the background colours—for a single block to be used for different works. In these bindings the clustered gold motifs were progressively lightened, giving way to colour and simpler decorative compositions. The ornamentation ended up being simple geometric motifs around the central medallion [fig. 177].

The next step, taken around the 1870s, was to introduce colour through lithography and subsequently through chromolithography.

Traditional lithographic engraving was completed with colour. In 1837 Godefroy Engelmann registered a patent for using four stones for engravings: three with the primary colours and a fourth with black.[4] This rendered the process more difficult, as the polychrome decoration of the chromolithograph needed to coincide with the design impressed by the block. By the middle of the 1890s the golden age of chromolithography was nearing its end. The changes in readers' tastes and the development of photogravure were making chromolithography obsolete. The emergence of photography and, with it, photogravure, allowed for an even broader range of colours around the 1890s.

The sole aim of producing large quantities at a lower price led to a significant fall in the quality of the books published during those years. Even so—or rather as a result of it—at the same time interest grew in carefully decorated and edited books, in short in bibliophile books that were the complete opposite of the mediocrity of printing and the horrible uniformity introduced by mass production. A radical change also took place in the concept of the illustrator's role. Illustration ceased to be a mere visual rendering of the text it accompanied and began to be more fully considered an art. It came to be regarded as the personal and subjective interpretation of the artist who made the illustration. The same artists also designed the decorations of the bound covers. We should therefore examine and stress the magnificent quality of some of these bindings which the world of bibliophiles, then as it does today, considered to be genuine luxury items.

Most of these bindings which we have found and chosen from the Real Biblioteca are French and Spanish and nearly all of them belong to the holdings of the Infanta María Isabel of Bourbon.

It is easy to realise that craft workshops were truly incapable of executing manually the impressive number of books that began to be produced following the development of the new machines. The development of mechanisation in the nineteenth century led to the establishment of industrial binderies to provide a service to these thriving publishing companies. The main French publishers of the industrial era were located chiefly in Paris: Louis Hachette, Pierre Jules Hetzel, Pierre Larousse, Ernest Flammarion and a few others.

In 1838 Engel opened his bindery along with his brother-in-law Schaer. Lènegre set up his workshop in 1840 with the collaboration of Magnier, who established his own business a few years later in 1860. Lènegre's bindery was the first to apply coloured decoration to cloth. All these workshops were based in Paris, while the firm Mame, another important centre of industrial production, established itself in Tours around 1885 and specialised in the production of religious books. Devauchelle describes in great detail the characteristics of these early French industrial binderies of the second half of the nineteenth century, the number of workers they employed, their wages, working hours and even the days they worked.[5]

Most of the blocks used to apply the gold decoration to these bindings were produced by the workshop of Auguste Souze, who was apprentice and later head of the workshop

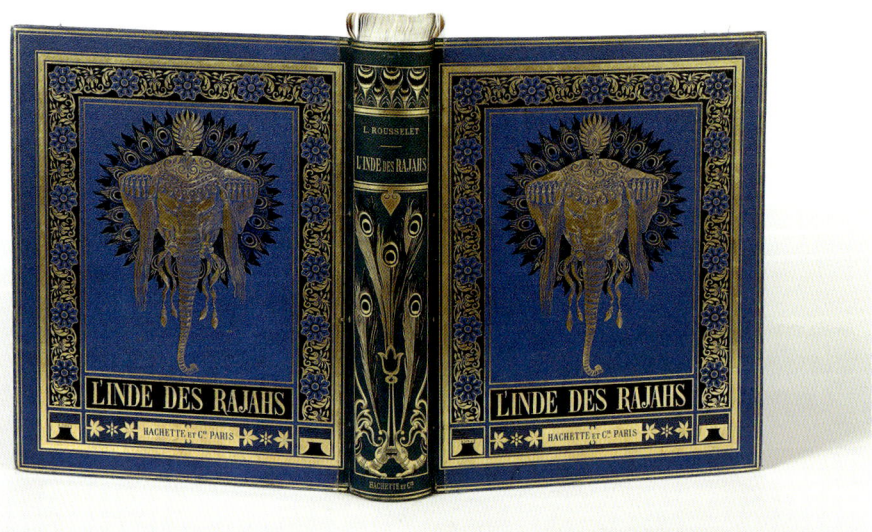

Fig. 178
Louis Rousselet, *L'Inde des Rajahs: Voyage dans l'Inde Centrale et dans les presidences de Bombay et du Bengale.* Paris: Hachette et Cie., 1875. RB, Inf. 1913

belonging to the firm Tambon and later founded his own workshop in 1857. Although he retired in 1892, the workshop continued to be held in great esteem thanks to the work of his nephew Paul Souze. They produced blocks for publishers such as Hachette and Hetzel, among others. The decorative motifs of the blocks are often designed by well-known artists and therefore this type of trade binding was and continues to be highly valued by bibliophiles. For example, H. Catenacci designed Hachette's *Bibliothèque Rose* and Gustave Doré also designed for this publishing house. Adolphe Giraldon created the decoration of the *Bibliothèque des écoles et des familles*, also for Hachette. Meanwhile, Louis-Maurice Boutet de Monvel produced designs for works bound by Engel.

We have already discussed the change in the contents of works. A certain amount of secularisation took place around then and, although religious publishing remained fairly important, its place was taken by school books as the major classics. The success of the firm owned by Louis Christophe François Hachette was built on the launch of specific collections for children and young people. It was he who began to use the term "library" in the sense of a collection. The first collection created by Hachette came out in 1856, after a train journey with Napoleon III and the Count of Ségur, during which the latter told them that his wife made up stories and tales for their children. And so the first work published was *Nouveaux contes de fées*, by the Countess of Ségur. Four years later the collection was given the name of *Bibliothèque Rose,* as it was bound in pink percaline decorated with fairly classical gold motifs. The *Bibliothèque des petits enfants,* bound in blue percaline with gold decorative motifs, was intended for younger children aged between four and eight [fig. 178].

Mame was also famed for its moralising stories for young Catholics.

The other great Parisian publisher of the day, Hetzel, earned sizeable profits from publishing the works of Jules Verne. When Verne wrote his first novel he offered the publication to Hetzel, who created the collection of *Voyages Extraordinaires* for Verne. He started out by publishing them in instalments in several Paris dailies. But he also brought out an exquisitely illustrated deluxe version in large format, a more economical and smaller version with considerably fewer illustrations, and a third —the cheapest—without illustrations. They were bound by Lènegre, although a few were done by Engel. The title pages bear the signature of A. Souze, the designer of the gold-stamped cover decoration [fig. 179].

Moving on to a different subject and focusing on Spain, although we have already stressed the impressive economic, political and cultural growth experienced by the industrialised countries as a result of the bourgeois revolution of the nineteenth century, the impact of this revolution was considerably weaker in Spain as, apart from a few hubs of industry, the rest of the country continued to live in a backward and impoverished agricultural world. It might be said that at the time Catalonia was the only Spanish region to have achieved a level of industrial and cultural

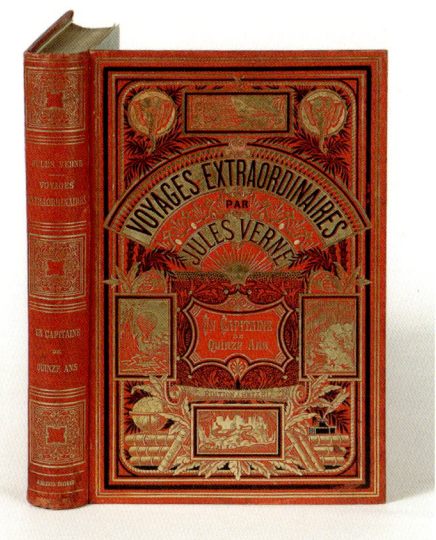

Fig. 179
Jules Verne, *Un capitaine de quince ans.* Paris: J. Hetzel et Cie., (n. d.: 18...). RB, Inf. 459

development comparable to that of the rest of Europe.[6]

In Catalonia in particular, these changes signified progress towards the European situation, spurred by the modernist movement. The modernist aesthetic trend had very little influence on the rest of the country. This was due simply to the fact that whereas Catalonia made a genuine effort to seek a new style of its own but close to European culture, in the rest of Spain these efforts resulted in a backward step and "a traditionalist bloody-mindedness with certain exaltations of localism".[7] It may be said that the Universal Exposition held in Barcelona in 1888 marked the start of modernism in Catalonia, driven by the rise of a powerful bourgeois class which grew progressively wealthier as industrialisation

Fig. 180
Julio Broutá, *La ciencia moderna: Sus Tendencias y cuestiones con ella relacionadas*. Barcelona: Montaner y Simón, 1897. RB, Inf. 1516

professionals travelled to Europe, especially France, to learn about the new machinery and the new techniques. They learned so much that, according to Emilio Brugalla,[8] the works presented by the Catalan firm Bastinos at the Paris exposition of 1889 were scarcely any different from those shown by the French workshops.

At the time, the importance of artistic bookbinding was slowly waning owing to the unstoppable rise in trade bookbinding as a result of the increased output from the use of state-of-the art machinery. Fortunately, faced with the need to keep pace with mass production using mechanical procedures, some Catalan firms not only succeeded in maintaining the quality of trade bindings but even caused it to stand out for its aesthetic features. As we will see, they achieved this through the interesting collaboration of prominent artists who produced the cover designs that were then engraved on blocks and reproduced in the bindings. Catalan printing and publishing developed substantially at the time owing, among other things, to the huge possibilities of the Latin American market. By about 1900 the modernist aesthetic had become widespread in trade binding, much earlier and with considerably more force and importance than in artistic binding.

The promoter of trade binding in Catalonia was Pedro Doménech i Saló, who was the first to use industrial machinery in 1860: large presses, shears, cutters and all kinds of modern material that facilitated the execution of bindings. He was aided by his sons Eduard and Lluís Doménech i Montaner, the latter an accomplished architect who illustrated

progressed, and also fostering a nationalist spirit in keeping with what was happening in Europe. The term "Catalan modernism" did not designate a single movement as in the case of the Modern Style or Art Nouveau, but rather the convergence of a series of trends such as the style derived from the powerful neo-Gothic tradition in Catalonia, that of Romantic or post-Impressionist realism, the particular Catalan versions of symbolism and those related more closely to Art Nouveau. Publishers' trade bindings were the first to adopt the modernist aesthetic and with astonishing results. Many publishing companies built or extended large premises in which to install their graphic arts workshops. Many and designed many of the covers of the bindings produced by this workshop, where the young Hermenegildo Miralles worked in the industrial bindings section, later going on to run a very important industrial and artistic bindery. Among many other collections, Miralles was responsible for binding the "Biblioteca Universal" published by Montaner y Simón. Among others, Josep Pascó and Josep Roca i Alemany worked with Miralles as designers and engravers of decorative blocks [fig. 180].

Another pupil of Doménech, Josep Ruiz, ended up setting up his own workshop. Other important binderies were those of Miquel y Ríus, J.R. Bastinos, Henrich & Cía., Maucci, Montserrat, Casa Subirana and Daniel Cortezo, among others. A prominent firm during the transition to the twentieth century was Casa Montaner y Simón, established in 1868 by Ramón Montaner and Francisco Simón. For example, they produced the first work whose covers displayed chromolithographic decoration, Juan Vilanova y Piera's *Historia Natural*, between 1872 and 1876. A series of large-format works illustrated by Gustave Doré enjoyed great success, including *The Holy Bible*, *Paradise Lost*, *The Divine Comedy* and *Don Quixote*, among others.

During this period many artists were involved in these works. They designed the illustrations but also the covers of the bindings: Apeles Mestres, Josep Pascó, Josep Llimona, Alexandre de Riquer, Josep Triadó, Adriá Gual and Arturo Mélida, among others. They produced delightful compositions, some neo-Gothic and others modernist and decorative very much in the Japanese style then in vogue in Europe [fig. 181].

Fig. 181
José Zorrilla, *Leyendas de D. José Zorrilla*. Madrid: Manuel Pedro Delgado, 1901. RB, Inf. 3450

Returning to the "libraries"/collections started by Hachette in Paris, four published in Catalonia are particularly worthy of mention owing to the excellence of their trade bindings and because major artists and engravers worked on them. The "Biblioteca Arte y Letras", brought out between 1881 and 1888, passed through the hands of several publishers such as Celestí Verdaguer and Eduard Doménech, Francisco Pérez, Daniel Cortezo and finally Manuel Maucci. Francesc Jorba, Josep Tersol and Josep Roca i Alemany were some of the artists who engraved the cover illustrations. The "Biblioteca Clásica española" (1884–90) was notable for displaying the same design for the whole collection, devised by the architect Joseph Vilaseca and engraved by Josep Roca y Alemany. The copies of the "Biblioteca Verdaguer" (1882–84) were decorated with a composition by the artist Apeles Mestres. Finally, the "Biblioteca Universal" published by Montaner y Simón beginning in 1887, was a more commercial collection than the previous ones but many of its covers, graced with noticeably modernist designs, were devised and engraved by Triadó, Pascó, Riquer, Gaspar Camps, Adrià Gual, Tamburini and others.[9]

We will now move away from industrial binding and on to artistic binding in which, during the turn of the century, after a brilliant period in which Spanish binders had created and developed two local decorative styles—bindings made from dyed leather, *pasta valenciana* and *pasta española*, and "curtain" bindings—the prevailing and almost only decorative style was the so-called "retrospective" style characterised by inspiration from and/or imitation of the leading classical styles.[10] The general trend was therefore to espouse the classical models, especially those of the seventeenth and eighteenth centuries, but adapting them in some cases to achieve new compositions. Spanish Mudejar, Renaissance and Gothic models were also widely imitated.

In the second half of the nineteenth century, Madrid binderies were considerably greater in number and importance than those of Barcelona, chiefly because bookbinding activities were closely connected with the Court, which was located in Madrid. The leading Madrid binderies of the day were those of Ginesta, Victorio Arias, Antonio Menard, Adrian Durand and Hipólito Paumard, all of whom employed the retrospective binding style mentioned above.

But it should be stressed that in Spain, or rather in Catalonia, the first decades of the new twentieth century witnessed a major flourishing of the art of bookbinding—which had been almost completely abandoned in previous years—spurred by the modernist style. A significant role in this comeback was played by prominent people mentioned early in connection with a more industrial type of binding, such as Hermenegildo Miralles, whose workshop employed well-known gilders who worked with small tools, such as Pierre Schultz and Pierre Guèrin. The work of Ramón Miquel i Planas and his main collaborators, the designer Joaquín Figuerola, the gilder Rafael Ventura and the binder Miquel Bonet, was of key importance in this period, as was that of Josep Roca i Alemany and his technique of carving and embossing leather.

The new languages already in vogue in nearby countries such as France had few repercussions in Spain. When they first appeared on the scene, the artistic movements of the so-called "historical avant-gardes" overturned the established order of art in general and of bookbinding in particular.

> It may be said that the Cubism of Picasso, Braque and Gris, the Futurism of Marinetti and Soffici, the Suprematism of Malevich, the Constructivism of Tatlin and El Lissitzky, the Dadaism of Tristan Tzara, Hans Arp, Man Ray and Schwitters, the De Stijl of Mondrian and Van Doesburg, and the Surrealism of Breton, Max Ernst, Dalí

and Magritte were the forerunners of a formal and conceptual break from which artistic bookbinding borrowed in order to create its own language. We are referring to the adaption of abstract forms, the psychological use of colour; the typographical revolution thanks to which letters acquired a function in their own right, enhancing the visual possibilities of their form and arrangement on covers; and finally, the use of collage and photomontage to achieve a certain sensation of three-dimensionality.[11]

Aside from the modernist or retrospective styles, only Emilio Brugalla (1901–1987), after serving an apprenticeship in industrial binderies and at the Escuela de Artes y Oficios, encouraged by his teacher Hermenegildo Alsina, was capable of moving to Paris to see and learn about the bookbinding scene. Owing either to ignorance of the changes and trends occurring outside the country or to most bibliophiles' distaste for these new forms, the Madrid binderies of the first half of the century continued to produce retrospective decorations, motifs representing names, and, very rarely, modernist-inspired ornamentation—all of them very fine examples of craftsmanship but lacking in creativity. A prominent figure on this scene, from which innovation was largely absent, was César Paumard with his particular technique of relief gilding and his decorative book edges.

Halfway through the century, Antolín Palomino (1909–1995), who is regarded as Paumard's successor, began to produce a large number of works with tooling and mosaic. Like his contemporaries, he continued to use retrospective decoration although he made a few forays into contemporary language.

Outside the two major cultural centres of the day, Madrid and Barcelona, and with the huge difficulty that this entailed, José Rodríguez Galván (1905–1989) was notable for his work in Cadiz. A well-rounded artist—something not particularly common among Spanish bookbinders—he was familiar with and respected, above all, the work of the French artists who had revolutionised and were then revolutionising the bookbinding world. In addition to ornamentation inspired in varying degrees by classical designs, Galván devised and executed others in a fairly modern language.

Up until then members of the royalty and nobility had been the main patrons of artistic bindings. Following the fall of the monarchy, this patronage disappeared and was replaced by that of official institutions and private entities and individuals. In general these private patrons shared the widespread taste for the retrospective style and very few were capable of moving forward and releasing binders from its fetters in order that they could express themselves with greater freedom and draw on their own creative abilities.

This takes us back to the Real Biblioteca and its bindings. Going back briefly in history, Matilde López Serrano informs us that a certain collection of books began to be formed through gifts and acquisitions during the reigns of Philip V, Louis I and Ferdinand VI. The private (and not the public) Biblioteca Real began to take shape in the final years of the reign of Charles III and the first years of that of Charles IV. "Charles IV was the first Bourbon to possess a private royal library, properly installed and organised and served by specialised staff."[12] Each of the successive monarchs progressively enriched this collection, also attaching importance to bindings with their booksellers, bookbinders-booksellers and court binders and financing with their patronage some editions of important works. With the advent of the Republic in 1931, the Cuerpo Facultativo de Bibliotecarios took over the Real Biblioteca until Patrimonio Nacional, established in 1940 as the public body responsible for state property subject to the use and service of the king and members of the royal family, returned all the holdings that had been evacuated during the Civil War, and this important institution resumed its functioning.

Out of all the collections—and there are many indeed—we wish to point out one that is fairly unusual, that of contemporary artistic bindings bearing a queen's cypher. In addition to kings, some infantas and queens also had, and devoted efforts to, their own private libraries. This collection includes an outstanding Bible owned by Philip II's sister Doña Juana and armorial bindings belonging, among others, to Barbara of Braganza, Isabella Farnese, María Amalia of Saxony, María Luisa of Parma, María Cristina of Habsburg, Isabel II, María de las Mercedes and Victoria Eugenia. This collection features magnificent examples of the work of court binders such as Antonio de Sancha, his son Gabriel de Sancha, Santiago Martín and Antonio Suárez, among others, decorated with the cyphers of their owners and fully representative of this retrospective trend of the time.[13]

But from 1931 onwards the collection of bindings bearing queens' cyphers and the future of the rest of the Biblioteca was interrupted by a series of only too well known events—namely the Republic and the Spanish Civil War. It was not until 1992, when María Luisa López-Vidriero, as director of the Real Biblioteca, reactivated the collection, now with the cypher of the current queen, Doña Sofía. She considered that four centuries of collecting deserved to have the added value of being continued, at a time when artistic bookbinding in Spain was making something of a comeback after remaining at a creative—but not technical—standstill for many years.

Having made this decision, it was then necessary to choose the works for which these bindings would begin to be commissioned and the binders who would execute them. According to María Luisa López-Vidriero, the intention was to carry on the tradition of adding artistic bindings to the Biblioteca and, furthermore, restore the meaning of presentation copy which royal libraries had traditionally accorded to books produced under the intellectual or financial patronage of the Crown. The publication of the oeuvre of the winners of the Reina Sofía Prize for Ibero-American Poetry, supported by Salamanca University and Patrimonio Nacional, was chosen for this reason. It was decided that it should be printed without luxuries and on organic, sustainable paper, and Salamanca University thus publishes a copy of these characteristics whose binding is intended for the collection of bindings bearing the cypher of Queen Sofía. The collection started out with the work of the poet Gonzalo Rojas, the first to be awarded the prize in 1992.

> The testimonial function of the collection makes it open to all trends with a single requisite: the excellence of the artist who executes the binding; and a sole requirement on the part of the Real Biblioteca: the inclusion of the cypher of Queen Sofía surmounted by the royal crown. As there is no official design for the cypher, the artist has full freedom of expression.[14]

The chosen binders, whose works are building up this collection, are commissioned for two consecutive years to execute the binding for the oeuvre of the winners of the Queen Sofía Prize for Ibero-American Poetry. The list to date features: Antolín Palomino (1992 and 1993), Antonio and José Galván (1994 and 1995), Ana Ruiz-Larrea (1996 and 1997), José Luis García Rubio (1998 and 1999), Manuel Bueno (2000 and 2001), Ramón Gómez Herrera (2002 and 2003), Andrés Pérez-Sierra (2004 and 2005), Juan Antonio Fernández Argenta (2006 and 2007), Dolores Baldó (2008 and 2009) and Rosa Fernández Iglesias and Mª del Carmen Villalba Caramés (2010 and 2011). These past twenty years have seen a change of century and have brought together several generations of binders whose works reflect the conceptual, aesthetic and technical changes that have taken place during this period: "it may be said that the major spiritual concerns that move the world are currently reflected in the domains of modern artistic bookbinding."[15] Studying these works and, accordingly, all these changes, will also enable us to trace the history of their time.

Books have traditionally been regarded as useful objects and, like any useful object, apparently lacking in artistic qualities. Fortunately, for some time bookbinding has been involved in the experimentations and pursuits of all the Fine Arts, it having been recognised that it entails artistic in addition to technical qualities. This gives rise to a dichotomy: on the one hand, bookbinding is an applied art at the service of books; and, on the other, bookbinding uses books as supports and creative objects. In the view of those who consider binding to be subordinate to books, binders are conditioned, without wishing, by the simple fact that they are working on an existing work, the book itself, with its text and illustrations, its pagination, its print type, etc. In the opinion of those who hold the second opinion, bindings possess an artistic value in their own right, independently of the work that is bound. There are also those who claim that the term "binder" is not appropriate for new generations with a theoretic and practical grounding in the arts, as it does not fully embrace all the aspects of the new discipline and it would therefore be more fitting to speak of artist/binder. As a result of the foregoing, nowadays we find binders who execute designs devised by others, binders who devise and execute their own designs and artists who design models for binders to execute. The involvement of designers in Spanish binding is quite rare. An example is the binding on the poetry of Sofía de Melo, designed by Miquel Ruíz and executed by Manuel Gómez Herrera, in this collection [fig. 200].

A major change resulting from the influence of the concepts of the artistic avant-garde of the early twentieth century is acknowledgement of the need to suggest and hint at the idea of the object rather than actually represent the object. Another concept upheld until now is to consider the cover and spine decoration to be independent elements although stylistically related. This is probably due to the fact that books were once bound in order to be protected and read and that now they are also bound to be seen; their decoration must be read with the covers open. The binding is conceived as a complete whole and not as two isolated covers joined by a spine. Therefore, the traditional raised bands are beginning to be eliminated as they impaired the free circulation of the decorative motifs [figs. 185–87].

As a result the book label, traditionally confined solely to the spaces between spine bands, can and should be extended across the covers and fully integrated into the decoration. The type is also part of the ornamentation, complementing it or consisting of the sole decorative element. It spreads across the boards, revealing the expressive possibilities of lettering in different sizes, colours and forms [figs 188–90].

The Russian constructivist Tatlin stated that the natural properties of materials condition the form and expressive power of the work. In most cases the leather itself provides the decoration of the binding by means of its pigmentation, dyes, flaws, arrangement on the boards, etc. We might speak of "natural decoration". But mention should also be made of the emergence and use of new treatments for leather whereby its appearance is altered by sanding to remove the grain, dye transfer, impressions, volumes, incisions with leather-covered backgrounds or acrylic painting, among others [figs. 191–94].

Other binders find leather somewhat limited as a sole means of expression and experiment with introducing other materials that are colder and have a radically different texture to leather: Plexiglas, polyester, fibre-glass, car paints applied with an airbrush, wood, acetate and polycarbonate [figs. 195–97].

But we also find the more traditional techniques known in the bookbinding world, such as the use of blind or gold tooling and mosaic, in some cases with modern aesthetic expressions and combined in perfect harmony with other modern materials and techniques [figs. 198–202].

It is very interesting to analyse the incorporation of the only compulsory motif established for the decoration of these bindings: the cypher of Queen Sofía. We might divide the collection very clearly into two groups: bindings whose decoration is based solely on this element and those in which the cypher is independent from the ornamentation. In the first group, the crowned letter S is the motif around which the whole design concept revolves. We find it extended over both covers and the spine, crossing from one side to the other, stylised, nearing abstraction, or standing out on both or only one of the covers. It may almost be said that they are bindings with supralibros, continuing this very old, traditional type which clearly and prominently displays these elements of identification on the covers of the binding, although those used in these contemporary works are not always evident at first sight.

In contrast, in the bindings decorated with other motifs, the initial is semi-concealed, gauffered on gilt edges [fig. 182], displayed on a sort of button added to the book edge [fig. 183], represented with tooling and mosaics [fig. 184], or stencilled with acrylic paint on the endpapers. The decoration of these bindings is not related to the cypher or supralibros.

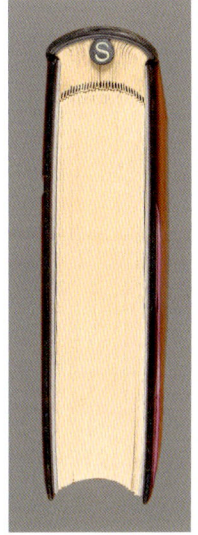

Fig. 182
Nicanor Parra, *Páginas en blanco*. Salamanca: Universidad de Salamanca; Madrid: Patrimonio Nacional, 2001. X Reina Sofía Prize for Ibero-American Poetry. Cypher of Queen Sofía on the edges. RB, XIV/2947

Fig. 183
Antonio Gamoneda, *Sílabas negras*. Salamanca: Universidad de Salamanca; Madrid: Patrimonio Nacional, 2006. XV Reina Sofía Prize for Ibero-American Poetry. Cypher of Queen Sofía on the edges. RB, XIV/2952

Fig. 184
Gonzalo Rojas, *Cinco visiones: selección de poemas de Gonzalo Rojas*. Salamanca: Universidad de Salamanca; Madrid: Patrimonio Nacional, 1992. I Reina Sofía Prize for Ibero-American Poetry. Cypher of Queen Sofía on the endpaper.
RB, XIV/2938

Figs. 185–87
The decorative motif is extended over the covers and spine

185
João Cabral de Melo Neto, *A la medida de la mano*. Salamanca: Universidad de Salamanca; Madrid: Patrimonio Nacional, 1994. III Reina Sofía Prize for Ibero-American Poetry. Bound by Antonio and José Galván. RB, XIV/2940

186
José Antonio Muñoz Rojas, *Yo sólo sé nombrarte*. Salamanca: Universidad de Salamanca; Madrid: Patrimonio Nacional, [2002]. XI Reina Sofía Prize for Ibero-American Poetry. Bound by Ramón Gómez Herrera. RB, XIV/2948

187
Pere Gimferrer, *Marea solar, marea lunar*. Salamanca: Universidad de Salamanca; Madrid: Patrimonio Nacional, 2000. IX Reina Sofía Prize for Ibero-American Poetry. Bound by Manuel Bueno. RB, XIV/2946

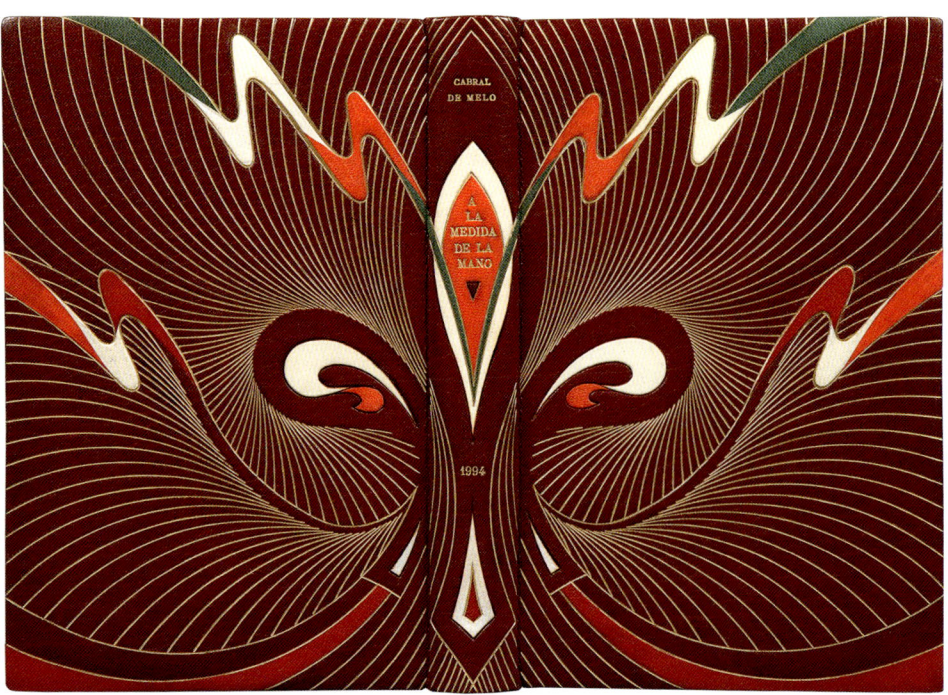

185

FROM INDUSTRY TO ART | 299

186

187

Figs. 188–90
Decoration with type as a prominent feature

188
José Caballero Bonald, *Años y libros*. Salamanca: Universidad de Salamanca; Madrid: Patrimonio Nacional, 2004. XIII Reina Sofía Prize for Ibero-American Poetry. Bound by Andrés Pérez-Sierra. RB, XIV/2950

189
Mario Benedetti, *Los espejos las sombras*. Salamanca: Universidad de Salamanca; Madrid: Patrimonio Nacional, 1999. VIII Reina Sofía Prize for Ibero-American Poetry. Bound by José Luis García. RB, XIV/2945

190
Blanca Varela, *Aunque cueste la noche*. Salamanca: Universidad de Salamanca; Madrid: Patrimonio Nacional, 2007. XVI Reina Sofía Prize for Ibero-American Poetry. Bound by Juan Antonio Fernández Argenta. RB, XIV/2953

188

189

190

Figs. 191–94
Alterations with sanding, transfers, impressions, volumes, dyes, etc.

191
Francisco Brines, *Para quemar la noche*. Salamanca: Universidad de Salamanca; Madrid: Patrimonio Nacional, 2010. XIX Reina Sofía Prize for Ibero-American Poetry. Bound by Obradoiro Penumbra. RB, XIV/2956

192
Pablo García Baena, *Rama fiel*. Salamanca: Universidad de Salamanca; Madrid: Patrimonio Nacional, 2008. XVII Reina Sofía Prize for Ibero-American Poetry. Bound by Dolores Baldó. RB, XIV/2954

193
Antonio Gamoneda, *Sílabas negras*. Salamanca: Universidad de Salamanca; Madrid: Patrimonio Nacional, 2006. XV Reina Sofía Prize for Ibero-American Poetry. Bound by Juan Antonio Fernández Argenta. RB, XIV/2952

194
Álvaro Mutis, *Summa de Maqroll El Gaviero: poesía, 1948–1997*. Salamanca: Universidad de Salamanca; Madrid: Patrimonio Nacional, 1997. VI Reina Sofía Prize for Ibero-American Poetry. Bound by Ana Ruiz-Larrea. RB, XIV/2943

191

192

193

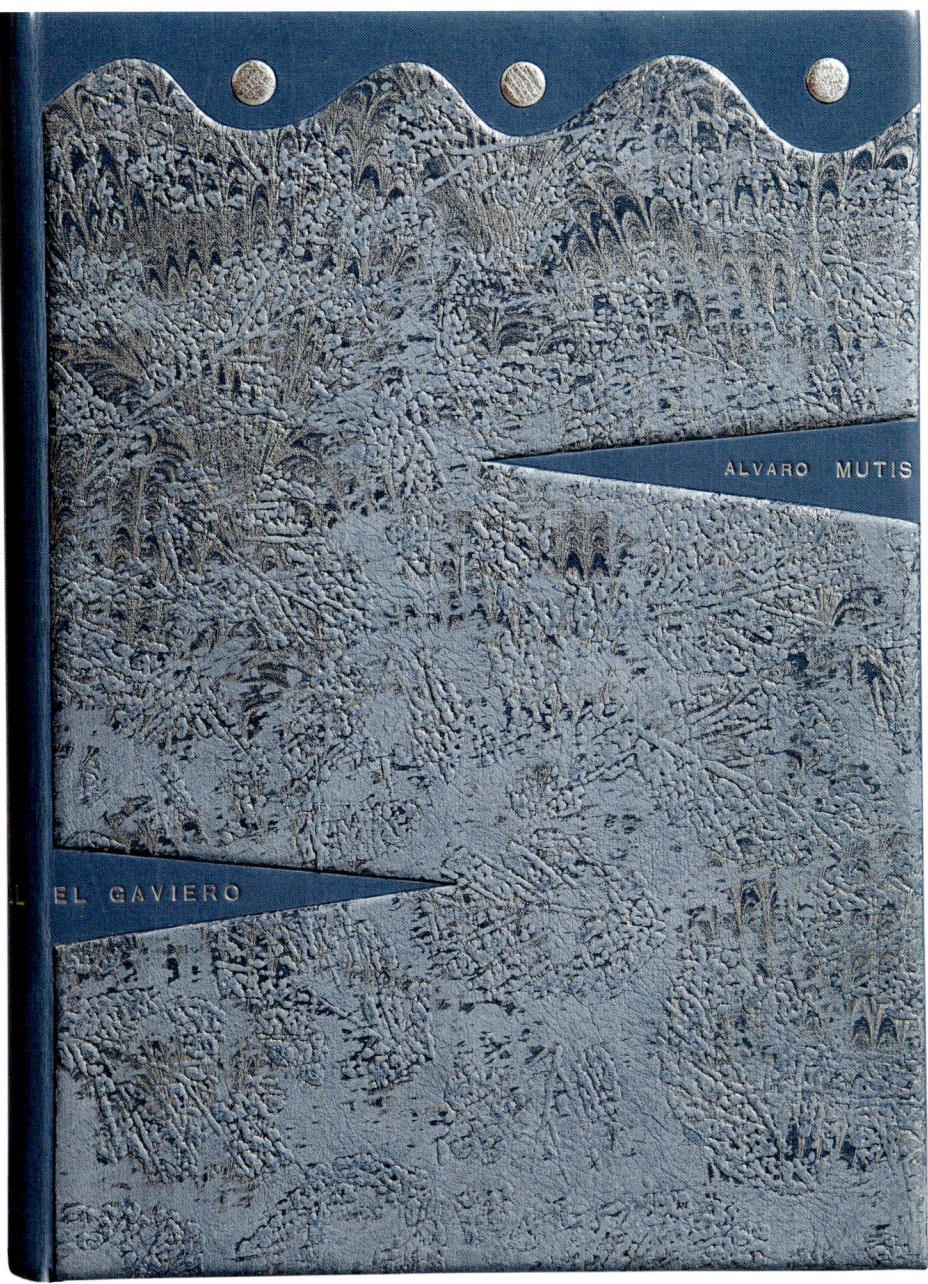

Figs. 195–97
Other materials such as wood, polycarbonates and acetate

195
José Ángel Valente, *El vuelo alto y ligero*. Salamanca: Universidad de Salamanca; Madrid: Patrimonio Nacional, 1998. VII Reina Sofía Prize for Ibero-American Poetry. Bound by José Luis García. RB, XIV/2944

196
José Emilio Pacheco, *Contraelegía*. Salamanca: Universidad de Salamanca; Madrid: Patrimonio Nacional, 2009. XVIII Reina Sofía Prize for Ibero-American Poetry. Bound by Dolores Baldó. RB, XIV/2955

197
Juan Gelman, *Oficio ardiente*. Salamanca: Universidad de Salamanca; Madrid: Patrimonio Nacional, 2005. XIV Reina Sofía Prize for Ibero-American Poetry. Bound by Andrés Pérez-Sierra. RB, XIV/2951

195

196

Figs. 198–202
The most traditional techniques in modern aesthetic expressions

198
Ángel González, *Luz, o fuego, o vida*. Salamanca: Universidad de Salamanca; Madrid: Patrimonio Nacional, 1996. V Reina Sofía Prize for Ibero-American Poetry. Bound by Ana Ruiz-Larrea. RB, XIV/2942

199
Gonzalo Rojas, *Cinco visiones: selección de poemas de Gonzalo Rojas*. Salamanca: Universidad de Salamanca; Madrid: Patrimonio Nacional, 1992. I Reina Sofía Prize for Ibero-American Poetry. Bound by Antolín Palomino. RB, XIV/2938

200
Sofía de Melo Breyner Andresen, *En la desnudez de la luz*. Salamanca: Universidad de Salamanca; Madrid: Patrimonio Nacional, 2003. XII Reina Sofía Prize for Ibero-American Poetry. Bound by Ramón Gómez Herrera. RB, XIV/2949

201
José Hierro, *Nombres propios*. Salamanca: Universidad de Salamanca; Madrid: Patrimonio Nacional, 1995. IV Reina Sofía Prize for Ibero-American Poetry. Bound by Antonio and José Galván. RB, XIV/2941

202
Nicanor Parra, *Páginas en blanco*. Salamanca: Universidad de Salamanca; Madrid: Patrimonio Nacional, 2001. X Reina Sofía Prize for Ibero-American Poetry. Bound by Manuel Bueno. RB, XIV/2947

198

199

200

201

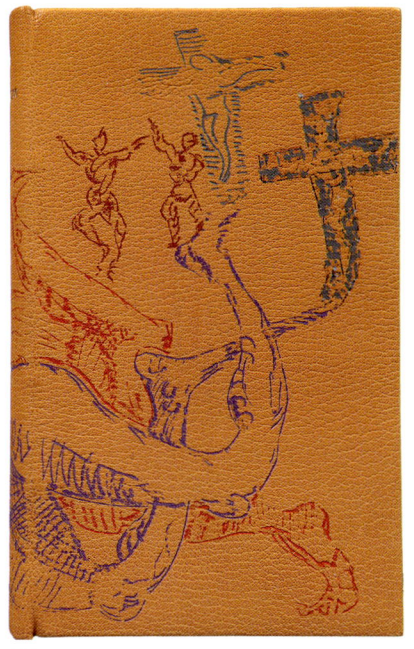

202

It is evident that, while the binders use the same elements and are subject to the same conditions, they focus their creative process on very different concepts and express themselves in very different aesthetic languages. In my opinion, this is one of the virtues of the collection of artistic bindings bearing the cypher of Queen Sofía.

It has been stated that "attention has not been paid to women's supralibros in Spain".[16] Actually, a study of the historical portion of the collection of bindings bearing the queen's cypher and its continuation with the contemporary part would provide an interesting insight into the development of women's presence in the world of books in general and in artistic bookbinding in particular.

1 Carrión 1996, 517.
2 Barbier 2005, 321.
3 Uzanne 1898, 120–21.
4 Trenc Ballester 1977, 12.
5 Devauchelle 1961, 113–14.
6 Baldó 1999, 135–38.
7 Satué 1993, 43.
8 Brugalla 2000, 99–100.
9 Quiney 2007, 41–46, and Trenc Ballester 1977, 73–76.
10 López Serrano 1947, 7–8.
11 Baldó 1999, 25.
12 López Serrano 1950, 23.
13 Moreno Gallego 2008, 63–67.
14 López-Vidriero 2002, 58.
15 Miquel y Planas 1933, 16.
16 Moreno Gallego 2008, 22.

A Thematic Bibliography of Bookbinding in Spain (from the Nineteenth to the Twenty-First Centuries): Historiography of Contemporary Studies

Concha Lois

Spanish literature on bookbinding emerged at the end of the nineteenth century in connection with various book-related activities: bibliophilism, the profession of librarian and the profession of bookbinder. Art historians study the styles and history of bookbinding in relation to other arts.

All these activities are interrelated: bibliophilism, taken to mean the love and care of books, is conducive to the development of the art of bookbinding. We find bibliophiles with their own workshops; the writings of bookbinders themselves on their work are essential sources for research; and librarians, as custodians of bibliographical heritage, are concerned with the proper description of the printed works and documents housed in libraries and organise or promote book exhibitions in order to make known the most valuable bindings.

The printed works on the art of book bindings are described in this article, grouped in accordance with the aforementioned activities. It also includes studies on techniques and workshops, manuals and studies on artistic styles, and works of historical interest.

The entries that feature under each heading or subheading are listed chronologically by date of publication, from oldest to most recent, and when there are several works by the same author they are listed chronologically. In such cases the name of the author is not repeated but listed only once together with the first of his or her works. When there are several editions of a work, only the first one is cited.

As for the bibliography, the works of Manuel Carrión (see the section on "Libraries, Librarians, Catalogues") and Checa Cremades (in the section on "Styles") include a select bibliography on bookbinding. A joint repertoire on the art of bookbinding can be consulted in the work by Carpallo Bautista (see the section on "Manuals, Techniques, Repertoires").

The database DIALNET, also quoted further on, provides a description of books, articles and parts of works published in Spain in recent decades, is sufficiently up to date, and allows access to the complete text of a large number of publications.

Early Studies

Escudero de la Peña, José María, "Encuadernaciones de la Edad Media y Moderna", *Museo Español de Antigüedades*, vol. VII (1876), 490.

Villanueva, Jaime, "Códices e incunables de la Catedral de Vich", *Boletín de la Real Academia de la Historia* (October 1894), 320–31.

Leguina, Enrique de, "El evangeliario de la Catedral de Vich", *Boletín de la Sociedad Española de Excursionistas*, year II, no. 12 (1894), 177–78.

"El Archivo de Simancas. Encuadernaciones de los siglos XV y XVII", *Blanco y Negro*, 31 October 1903.

Gudiol y Cumill, J., "L'orfebreria en l'exposició hispano-francesa de Saragoça", *Anuari* (1908), 103–49.

— "Encuadernaciones de Vich", *Museum*, year 3, no. 7 (1913), 240–50.

Debenga, Álvaro, "Estuche de cuero del Monasterio de las Huelgas", *Arte Español*, year IV, vol. II, no. 8 (1915), 4.

Pérez Llamazares, Julio, *El tesoro de la Real Colegiata de San Isidoro de León*, León, La Crónica de León, 1925, 275 pp., ill.

Ferrandis Torres, José, *Marfiles y azabaches españoles*, Barcelona-Buenos Aires, Labor, 1928, 270 pp., XXXVIII pp. of pls.

Font de Rubinat, Pedro, "La biblioteca y los libros de Poblet", in Luis Doménech y Montaner, *Historia y arquitectura del Monasterio de Poblet*, Barcelona, Montaner y Simón, 1929, 386–91.

Booksellers and Their Catalogues

The description of books from private collections and bibliophiles' interest in the most valuable examples makes booksellers' catalogues and lists compiled for sales essential sources of information for identifying and valuing, among other details of the books on sale, the bindings of interest, especially when they include facsimile reproductions of the copies on sale. Some of these catalogues are:

Vindel, Pedro, *Catálogo de la librería de Pedro Vindel*, Madrid, Librería de Pedro Vindel, 1901–3. 3 vols., facs.

— *Catálogo de una colección de cien obras raras procedentes de la Biblioteca del Marqués de Laurencín*, introduction by Félix Boix, Madrid, Imprenta de la Ciudad Lineal, 1927.

— *Catálogo ilustrado de la librería de Pedro Vindel: libros raros, curiosos y antiguos que se hallan en venta en esta Casa*, Madrid, Librería de Pedro Vindel, 1929, 384 pp.

— *Catálogo de libros escogidos y selectas encuadernaciones procedentes, en su mayor parte, de la colección que fué del Excmo. Sr. D. Félix Boix*, prologue by D. Vicente Castañeda, Madrid, Pedro Vindel, 1933 (Imp. de M. Minuesa de los Ríos), 5 shts., 50 pp.

Vindel, Francisco, *Cien obras de la colección Massó*, with 128 facsimiles, prologue by Francisco Vindel, Vigo, M. Roel, 1940, 148 pp., 1 sht.

Bibliophilism. Collectors, Bibliophiles

Bibliophilism evolved in Spain during the modernist period, as in other European countries, progressing from the discovery and collecting of rare books to the cultivation of book-related arts in order to make them more beautiful and perfect objects.

Bibliophiles foster the art of bookbinding and are therefore conducive to the perfecting of binding techniques. In addition, they promote the publication of studies on styles and techniques and the holding of conferences and exhibitions on books, which sometimes feature remarkable pieces from private collections.

AGUILÓ, Ángel, "La colección de encuadernaciones de Manuel Rico y Sinobas", *Revista de Archivos, Bibliotecas y Museos*, year 5, no. 11 (November 1901), 798–808.

The bibliophile, bibliographer and scholarly writer Ramón Miquel i Planas had his own bookbinding workshop in Barcelona:

MIQUEL I PLANAS, Ramón, *Bibliofilia: Recull d'estudis, observacions, comentaris y noticies sobre llibres en general y sobre qüestions de llengua y literatura catalanes en particular,* Barcelona, Miquel i Planas, 1911–21, 2 vols.

— *Restauración del arte hispano-árabe en la decoración exterior de los libros*, Barcelona, Miquel Rius, 1913, 23 pp., XXI shts. of pls.

— *La formación del libro*, Seville, Ortiz-Megías y Susillo, 1926, 89 pp.

— *Ensayos de bibiofilia: reunidos y publicados con motivo de los XXV años de vida editorial del autor*, Barcelona, Miquel Rius, 1929, 59 pp., 46 shts. of pls.

— *El arte en la encuadernación*, ed. Cámara Oficial del Libro, Barcelona, Cámara Oficial del Libro, 1933 (Imprenta Elzeviriana), 16 pp.

LAURENCÍN, Francisco Rafael de Uhagón, marqués de, "Series de los más importantes documentos del archivo y biblioteca del excelentísimo señor Duque de Medinaceli elegidos por su encargo y publicados a sus expensas por Antonio Paz y Meliá, informe del Marqués de Laurencín", *Boletín de la Real Academia de la Historia*, March 1916.

CASTAÑEDA Y ALCOVER, Vicente, *La exposición de encuadernaciones de la colección Lázaro Galdiano*, Madrid, Tipografía de Archivos, 1934, 15 pp., XVIII pls.

— "El arte del libro en Hispanoamérica", in *Voces de Hispanidad*, Madrid, Gráf. Afrodisio, 1940, 220 pp.

— *Taller español de encuadernación en 1050. Observaciones y comentarios*, Madrid, Vda. de Estanislao Mestre, 1946.

RICO Y SINOBAS, Manuel, *El arte del libro en España*, prologue by Francisco Hueso Rolland, Madrid, Escelicer, 1941, XIII pp., 1 sht., 500 pp., 1 sht.

GALBETE, Vicente, *Esbozo biobibliográfico de José María Azcona, erudito tafallés*, Pamplona, Institución Príncipe de Viana, 1965, LI pp.

PENNEY, Clara Louisa, *The Hispanic Society of America: An Album of Selected Bookbindings*, New York, The Hispanic Society, 1967, XV, 18 pp., 3 pls., pls. I–XL.

SÁNCHEZ MARIANA, Manuel, *Bibliófilos españoles*, Madrid, Biblioteca Nacional, 1993, 285 pp.

Bibliophiles' Associations and Conferences

The holding of conferences and meetings is conducive to studies and research on the art of bookbinding.

The Sociedad Española de Amigos del Arte promoted the 1934 exhibition of Spanish bindings, whose catalogue compiled by Francisco Hueso Rolland has been a source for much subsequent research.

The International Association of Bibliophiles has held international conferences whose papers contain information of great interest to studying bookbinding. The eighteenth took place in Madrid in 1993 and the twenty-second in Palma de Mallorca in 2001.

Since 1993, the Asociación para el Fomento de la Encuadernación de Arte has been publishing a specialised journal, *Encuadernación de Arte*, which is an ideal vehicle for disseminating articles on bookbinding as an artistic activity. As of 2011, thirty-eight issues have been published featuring articles by leading specialists on various aspects of bookbinding and interviews with binders, news on workshops and a wealth of information of interest to specialists:

Encuadernación de Arte: Revista de la Asociación para el Fomento de la Encuadernación, Madrid, AFEDA, 1993. [Half-yearly, nos. 1 (1993)–18 (2002), entitled *Encuadernación de Arte: Boletín de la Asociación para el Fomento de la Encuadernación* and published quarterly].

The complete index of this publication can be consulted in DIALNET, the database kept by various institutions and universities and coordinated by the University of La Rioja, and which allows access to the complete text of the articles.

The association has published a catalogue of its own library: Asociación para el Fomento de la Encuadernación de Arte. *Catálogo de la Biblioteca AFEDA, Asociación para el Fomento de la Encuadernación de Arte,* Madrid, AFEDA, 2003, 70 pp.

The first Congreso Nacional sobre Bibliofilia, Encuadernación Artística, Restauración y Patrimonio Bibliográfico took place in Cadiz in 1999, sponsored and organised by the Asociación para el Fomento de la Encuadernación de Arte. The second conference was held in Cadiz in 2004 and the third in 2009. The proceedings of all of them have been published, and exhibitions were held in connection with them. Another aspect encouraged by these conferences is the awarding of prizes to the best contemporary bindings:

El libro como objeto de arte: actas del I Congreso Nacional sobre Bibliofilia, Encuadernación Artística, Restauración y Patrimonio Bibliográfico, Cadiz, 21–24 April 1999, [Cadiz], Fundación Municipal de Cultura, Diputación Provincial de Cádiz, [1999], 452 pp.

El libro como objeto de arte: actas del II Congreso Nacional sobre Bibliofilia, Encuadernación Artística, Restauración y Patrimonio Bibliográfico, Cadiz, April 2004, [Cadiz], Ayuntamiento de Cádiz, [2008], 370 pp.

El libro como objeto de arte: actas del III Congreso Nacional de Bibliofilia, Encuadernación Artística, Restauración y Patrimonio Bibliográfico, Cadiz, 2009, Cadiz, Ayuntamiento de Cádiz, 2009, 524 pp.

Libraries, Librarians, Catalogues

In accordance with their duty to preserve and protect bibliographical heritage, libraries set out to inventory, show and study the bindings of the printed works and manuscripts they house. As custodians of major public and private collections, librarians have also been historians of bookbinding in Spain. They have likewise staged exhibitions to make known the most valuable bindings of the collections in their care and, above all, they have compiled catalogues, which are generally limited to the holdings of the particular library.

The study and description of bindings in Spain is currently governed by international standards and increasing attention is being given to the enforcement, dissemination and perfecting of these standards and to the establishment of the criteria and terminology used. All these unification efforts are leading to a more scientific methodology that is useful both to institutions and to private researchers. The Real Biblioteca is a pioneer in the establishment of a specialised database adapted to internationally accepted procedures which describes and reproduces the bindings it houses, thereby encouraging research on styles and periods.

Library of the Royal Monastery
of San Lorenzo de El Escorial

FERNÁNDEZ, Benigno, *Impresos de Alcalá en la Biblioteca de El Escorial, con adiciones y correcciones a la obra "Ensayo de una Tipografía Complutense"*, Madrid, Imprenta Helénica, 1913, 354 pp.

REVILLA, Alejo, *Catálogo de los códices griegos de la Biblioteca de El Escorial*, Madrid, Imprenta Helénica, 1936, 3 vols.

Library of Segovia Cathedral

VALVERDE DEL BARRIO, Cristino, *Catálogo de incunables y libros raros de la catedral de Segovia*, Segovia, Imprenta de El Adelantado, 1930, XXII pp., 2 shts., 510 pp., 2 shts., XXVIII shts. of pls.

Biblioteca Nacional, Madrid

Manuel Carrión who, as deputy director of the Biblioteca Nacional de España since 1975 has a good knowledge of its holdings, has compiled a history of Spanish bookbinding through the collections the institution houses. He has published several articles in the aforementioned journal *Encuadernación de Arte*.

CARRIÓN GÚTIEZ, Manuel, "La encuadernación española", in *Historia ilustrada del libro español: de los incunables al siglo XVIII*, ed. Hipólito Escolar Sobrino, Madrid, Fundación Germán Sánchez Ruipérez, 1994, 395–445 (Biblioteca del libro, 60).

— "Alta costura: la encuadernación de arte", in *La Biblioteca Nacional*, Madrid, Biblioteca Nacional, 1996, 177–83.

— "Decálogo de la encuadernación de arte", in *El libro como objeto de arte*: actas del I Congreso Nacional sobre Bibliofilia, Encuadernación Artística, Restauración y Patrimonio Bibliográfico, Cadiz, Fundación Municipal de Cultura, Diputación Provincial de Cádiz, 1999, 47–60.

— "El libro encuadernado como consumación", in *El libro como objeto de arte*: actas del II Congreso Nacional sobre Bibliofilia, Encuadernación Artística, Restauración y Patrimonio Bibliográfico, Cadiz, April 2004, [Cadiz], Ayuntamiento de Cádiz, [2008], 139–47.

RUBIO DE URQUÍA, Guadalupe, "La colección de encuadernaciones "Rico y Sinobas" de la Biblioteca Nacional", *Encuadernación de Arte*, 21 (2003), 35–37.

Real Biblioteca, Madrid

Matilde López Serrano, in charge of the palace library since 1939 and honorary director, has summed up the history of Spanish bookbinding and has published many works on binders, based on the rich collections in the royal libraries.

María Luisa López-Vidriero, director of the Real Biblioteca since 1991, has published studies on various aspects of bookbinding in the journal *Encuadernación de Arte*, and has encouraged research through two concurrent means: by establishing and keeping a database which analyses and describes in detail the bindings housed in the library, with digitised images, a glossary and added research; and by organising seminars and courses aimed at training professionals and experts in the study of bookbinding.

NAVAS, Juan Gualberto López Valdemoro y de Quesada, conde de las, "Hierros caligráficos", *Gutenberg, Revista de las artes gráficas*, no. 1 (February 1904).

— "Artes que embellecen el libro", *Gutenberg, Revista de las artes gráficas*, no. 2 (April 1904).

— "De la encuadernación. Generalidades. Bibliografía", *Revista de Archivos, Bibliotecas y Museos*, year IX (March-April 1905), 221–39.

— *De libros: menudencias*, Madrid, Est. Tip. de Fortanet, 1908, 274 pp.
— "De la Real Biblioteca: anaquelería-exposición", *Museum*, III, no. 10 (1913), 359.
— *De "Re Ligatoria": Noticia de la Colección Lameyer*, Madrid, Bernardo Rodríguez, 1917, 20 pp., 1 sht., eng. inserted.
— "De encuadernación: divagaciones", *Museum*, V, no. 8 (1917), 269.

López Serrano, Matilde, *Biblioteca de Palacio. Catálogo de cien encuadernaciones que envía la Biblioteca de Palacio a la Exposición del libro español en Buenos Aires, precedido de una noticia histórica sobre las encuadernaciones españolas*, Madrid, [n. n.], 1933, 16 pp.

— "La encuadernación en Madrid en la primera mitad del siglo XVIII", *Archivo Español de Arte y Arqueología*, vol. XIII (January-April 1937), 1–13.
— "La encuadernación madrileña en la época de Fernando VI", *Archivo Español de Arte*, vol. XIV (1940–41), 27–38.
— *La encuadernación en España*, Madrid, Escuela de Artes y Oficios Artísticos de Madrid, 1942, 34 pp., 5 pls.
— "Libreros encuadernadores de Cámara. I, Antonio Suárez", *Arte Español, Revista de la Sociedad Española de Amigos del Arte*, 14, vol. 27, no. 2–3 (1942), 7–14.
— "Encuadernaciones románicas de España", *Bibliografía hispánica*, vol. II, no. 2 (February 1943), 8–18.
— "Libreros encuadernadores de Cámara. II. Santiago Martín", *Arte Español, Revista de la Sociedad Española de Amigos del Arte*, XIV, vol. 27, no. 4 (1943), 14–22.
— "Exposición del centenario de Don Martín Fernández de Navarrete", *Revista de Bibliografía Nacional*, vol. V (1944), 547–48.
— *Exposición histórica del libro español, INLE, 28 de mayo al 6 de junio de 1944. Catálogo-guía*, Madrid, Estades, 1944, [2] shts. of pls., ill.
— "La Asociación de Bibliófilos de Barcelona", *Revista de Bibliografía Nacional*, vol. V (1944), 549–50.
— "Curiosidades de la encuadernación española: el encuadernador Gabriel Gómez, 1751–1818", *Coleccionismo. Revista mensual de Coleccionistas*, 3.ª época, XXI, no. 198 (31 January 1945), 68–71.

— "La encuadernación española en el s. XVIII", *Gráficas*, year II, no. 17 (November 1945), 4–5 and 28.
— "La encuadernación madrileña durante el reinado de Carlos III", *Archivo Español de Arte*, no. 67 (1945), 1–16.
— "El encuadernador Gabriel Gómez Martín. Nuevos documentos", *Revista de Bibliografía Nacional*, vol. VI (1945), 51–72.
— "Exposición de encuadernaciones de Emilio Brugalla", *Revista de Bibliografía Nacional*, vol. VI (1945), 388–89.
— "Exposición de libros portugueses", *Revista de Bibliografía Nacional*, vol. VI (1945), 383–85.
— "Notas características de la encuadernación moderna", in *Piel, Boletín del sindicato de la piel*, Madrid, May 1945.
— "Antonio de Sancha: encuadernador madrileño", *Revista de la Biblioteca, Archivo y Museo Municipales*, year XV, no. 54 (1946), 269–307.
— "Noticias de impresores madrileños I. Una tormenta doméstica en la familia Sancha", *Revista de Bibliografía Nacional*, vol. VII (1946), 391–409.
— "Evangeliarios de Navarra", *Príncipe de Viana*, no. XXVI (1947), 21–32.
— "Notas características de la encuadernación moderna", *Revista Bibliográfica y Documental*, vol. I (1947), 7–15.
— "Don Agustín Durán, encuadernador", *Revista bibliográfica y Documental*, vol. I (1947), 91–93.
— "Exposición de Casa Horta en el Ateneo barcelonés", *Revista Bibliográfica y Documental*, vol. I (1947), 295–97.
— "La encuadernación en la exposición de Artes Decorativas", *Revista Bibliográfica y Documental*, vol. I (1947), 303–6.
— "Exposición del libro español en la Biblioteca del Vaticano", *Revista Bibliográfica y Documental*, vol. I (1947), 307–8.
— "Encuadernaciones toledanas", *Arte y Hogar*, nos. 38 and 39 (1947–48), 34–35. Special issue.
— "Exposición histórica de la Orden Benedictina en la Biblioteca Nacional de Madrid, 1948, XIV Centenario de San Benito", *Revista Bibliográfica y Documental*, vol. II, no. 4 (October-December 1948), 469–71. There is an offprint, special edition of 25 numbered copies.
— "Don Pablo Font de Rubinat", *Revista Bibliográfica y Documental*, vol. III (1949), 349–51. There is

an offprint, a special edition of 25 numbered copies.
— *Galván, Encuadernaciones de Arte*, presentation by Matilde López Serrano, Cadiz, Talleres Tipográficos Salvador Repeto, 1949, 32 pp.
— *Biblioteca de Palacio: encuadernaciones*, introduction and notes by Matilde López Serrano, photographs by Juan Pando, Madrid, Afrodisio Aguado, 1950, 181 pp., 2 shts., 79 pls., eng. (Colección Artes decorativas en España, vol. II).
— "La encuadernación de arte en España desde 1939 a 1949", *Revista Bibliográfica y Documental*, vol. IV (1950), 242–63.
— "La encuadernación madrileña en la época de Carlos IV", *Archivo Español de Arte*, no. 90 (1950), 115–31.
— "El encuadernador catalán del siglo XIX Pedro Doménech", *Revista Bibliográfica y Documental*, vol. V, no. 1–4 (1951), 167–78.
— "Hand Binding in Spain", in *The Art of the Book. Some Record of Work Carried Out in Europe and the U.S.A., 1939–1950*, ed. Charles Ede, London, The Studio Publications, 1951, 201 and 204–5.
— "Encuadernaciones "de cortina": originalidades del libro español", *Reales Sitios*, year IV, no. 11 (1967), 22–31.
— *La encuadernación española: breve historia*, Madrid, Asociación Nacional de Bibliotecarios, Archiveros y Arqueólogos, 1972, 146 pp., 64 pls.
— "Une des originalités de la reliure espagnole: les types populaires", *Bulletin du bibliophile*, I, no. 15 (1974), 50–60, 1 pl. There is an offprint, Paris, Librairie Giraud-Badin, 1974.
— *Presencia femenina en las artes del libro español*, lecture delivered on 10 November 1975, Madrid, Fundación Universitaria Española, 1976, 38 pp., 1 sht., 16 shts. of pls.
— "Le décor 'de Cortina' dans la reliure espagnole de style Empire", *Bulletin du bibliophile*, no. 1 (1978), 22–34.
— "Biblioteca de Palacio. Encuadernaciones artísticas del mundo hispánico", *Reales Sitios*, year 17, no. 63 (1980), 49–56.
— "La encuadernación artística: las colecciones de Don José Lázaro Galdiano", *Goya*, 193–95 (1986), 14–21.
— *Piel de seda: encuadernación textil en España. Catálogo de la exposición celebrada en el Museo de Artes Decorativas, marzo-abril 1998*, Madrid,
Iberpapel; AFEDA, 1998, 107 pp. Tribute to Matilde López Serrano.

López-Vidriero, María Luisa, "Encuadernación en Palacio: lectura periférica y vestigio del tiempo", *Encuadernación de Arte*, 22 (2003), 4–22.

— "Las sílabas en la noche: Fernández Argenta en la colección de la Real Biblioteca", *Encuadernación de Arte*, 31 (2008), 39–42.

Moreno Gallego, Valentín, *Super libros reales: guía para la identificación heráldica en la Real Biblioteca*, Madrid, Patrimonio Nacional, 2008 [i.e. 2009], 187 pp., col. ills.

Biblioteca Histórica, Universidad Complutense

Sánchez Mariana, Manuel, and Antonio Carpallo Bautista, "Encuadernaciones históricas en la Biblioteca de la Universidad Complutense", *Encuadernación de Arte*, 21 (2003), 8–17.

Carpallo Bautista, Antonio, "Las encuadernaciones de la Biblioteca Complutense en el período de 1471 hasta 1503", in *Isabel I y la imprenta: consecuencias materiales, en el mundo cultural, de esta revolución tecnológica*, Madrid, Ministerio de Cultura, 2005, var. pag. Conference held at the Ministerio de Cultura in November 2004.

— "Encuadernaciones artísticas del siglo XVII en la Biblioteca Complutense", in *V Jornadas Científicas sobre Documentación de Castilla e Indias en el siglo XVII*, Juan Carlos Galende Díaz, dir., Madrid, Departamento de Ciencias y Técnicas Historiográficas, Universidad Complutense de Madrid, 2006, 9–64.

Universidad Complutense de Madrid. *Encuadernaciones en la Biblioteca Complutense, catálogo*, texts: Antonio Carpallo Bautista, selection of bindings: Manuel Sánchez Mariana, description of heraldic emblems: Alfonso de Ceballos-Escalera y Gila, marqués de la Floresta, Madrid, Servicio de Publicaciones de la Universidad Complutense, 2005, 206 pp., ill.

Library of the Fundación Lázaro Galdiano

The director of the library of the Fundación Lázaro Galdiano, Juan Antonio Yeves, helps promote knowledge of the art of bookbinding in Spain by studying and disseminating the bindings in the collection assembled by the bibliophile and collector after whom the museum is named.

Yeves Andrés, Juan Antonio, "Encuadernaciones españolas en la Biblioteca de la Fundación Lázaro Galdiano", *Encuadernación de Arte*, 2 (1993), 4–11.

— "Encuadernaciones heráldicas", in *El libro como objeto de arte: actas del I Congreso Nacional sobre Bibliofilia, Encuadernación Artística, Restauración y Patrimonio Bibliográfico*, Cadiz, Fundación Municipal de Cultura; Diputación Provincial de Cádiz, 1999, p. 329–40.

— "Colección de encuadernaciones artísticas de Romero de Lecea en la Biblioteca de Lázaro Galdiano", *Goya*, 315 (2006), 371–82.

— *Encuadernaciones heráldicas de la Biblioteca Lázaro Galdiano*, Madrid, Ollero y Ramos, Fundación Lázaro Galdiano, 2008, 462 pp., num. and col. ills.

Book Exhibitions of Private Institutions and Collections

The catalogues of book exhibitions, some intended expressly to show valuable bindings, have been and still are an essential source of knowledge and studies on bookbinding styles. One of the catalogues most widely used by Spanish specialists is the one compiled by Francisco Hueso Rolland for the exhibition organised in 1934 by the Sociedad Española de Amigos del Arte, which it hosted in May and June at Paseo de Recoletos no. 20, which also houses the the Biblioteca Nacional. This exhibition was staged to mark the seventh meeting of the International Library Committee, held on 28 and 29 May of that year. It consisted of four rooms devoted to Mudejar, Renaissance, eighteenth-century and Romantic bookbinding; contemporary bindings were on display in the entrance hall, in addition to endpapers from the seventeenth, eighteenth and nineteenth centuries. The national and local press gave the event considerable coverage during those two months and it was surprising to read that "one misses the skilled direction of masters … who might come to save … the excellent journeymen of whom there is no shortage and a workshop with fabrics, talent, tools and materials."

Almost contemporaneous with this exhibition was that of Spanish bindings organised in November 1934 in the library of the Royal Palace, of which a four-page leaflet entitled *Catálogo-guía* was published.

This section describes the catalogues for the main exhibitions, listed chronologically by date of publication, although some are also featured in the "Libraries" section under the name of the institution which organised the exhibition or the author of the catalogue.

Exhibitions

Breve noticia de la exposición agrícola industrial y de Bellas Artes celebrada en la ciudad de Palma a mediados del mes de septiembre del año 1860, Palma de Mallorca, Pedro José Gelabert, 1861.

Martín Mínguez, Bernardino, "Esmaltes en la exposición histórica europea", *Boletín de la Sociedad Española de Excursionistas*, year I (January 1894), 160 and 174.

Falcó y Osorio, Rosario, Duquesa de Berwick y de Alba, *Catálogo de las colecciones expuestas en las vitrinas del palacio de Liria*, le publica (sic) la Duquesa de Berwick y de Alba, Condesa de Siruela, Madrid, Sucesores de Rivadeneyra, 1898, 259 pp., 24 shts. of pls.

Cavestany y de Anduaga, Julio, "Industrias artísticas madrileñas (encuadernación)", in *Exposición del Antiguo Madrid. Catálogo general ilustrado*, Madrid, Sociedad Española de Amigos del Arte, 1926, 360 pp., I–LXX pls.

El libro de arte en España: catálogo de una selección de libros españoles, antiguos y modernos precedido de noticias históricas sobre la evolución del libro artístico en España, Madrid, Comisión organizadora para la Exposición del Libro Español en Buenos Aires, 1933, LIX shts. of pls., 95 pp., num. and col. ills.

Doce monografías sobre el libro español, Buenos Aires, [n. n.], 1933, 124 pp. Published in connection with the Exposición del Libro Español held in Buenos Aires in 1933

Hueso Rolland, Francisco, "Encuadernaciones españolas", *Revista Española de Arte*, year II, no. 8 (1933), 437–44.

— "Arte de la encuadernación en España", in *Biblioteca de Palacio. Catálogo de cien encuadernaciones que envía la Biblioteca de Palacio a la Exposición del libro español en Buenos Aires precedido de una noticia histórica sobre las encuadernaciones españolas*, Madrid, [n. n.], 1933, 1–8.

— *La exposición de encuadernaciones antiguas españolas*, Madrid, Sociedad Española de Amigos del Arte, 1934, 13 pp.

— *Exposición de encuadernaciones españolas, siglos XII al XIX. Catálogo general ilustrado*, Madrid, Imp. Blass, 1934, 258 pp., 63 shts., pls. I–LXI, eng. Title preceded by: Sociedad Española de Amigos del Arte.

— "El arte de la encuadernación", *Bibliografía Hispánica*, III, 2 (1944), 84–88.

Biblioteca de Palacio. *Exposición de encuadernaciones españolas. Catálogo-guía*, Madrid, Blass, 1934. [2] shts.

— *Exposición del libro español del siglo XIX*, Madrid, Blass, 1945, 4 shts.

— *Catálogo de la exposición conmemorativa del centenario de Goya, Patrimonio Nacional, Palacio de Oriente, junio 1946*, Madrid, Blass, 1946, 90 pp., 4 shts., pls.

El libro de arte en España: Catalogue of the exhibition held in connection with the XXIII Congreso Internacional de Historia del Arte, Granada, 3–8 September 1973, Granada, Universidad, 1975, 291 pp., ill. Title preceded by: Dirección General de Archivos y Bibliotecas. Departamento de Historia del Arte de la Universidad de Granada.

Biblioteca Nacional (España), *Cinco siglos de encuadernación artística, s. XV–XIX*, exhibition held in the Sala de Exposiciones of the Biblioteca Nacional de España, from December 1977 to January 1978, text of the leaflet: Amalia Sarriá, Madrid, Biblioteca Nacional, 1977, 1 sht. (6 pp.). Programme of the exhibition on the BNE's bindings from the Manuel Rico y Sinobas collection.

— *Encuadernaciones españolas en la Biblioteca Nacional*, texts by Isabel Ruiz de Elvira Serra; contributors: Carmen Crespo Tobarra, Cristina Guillén Bermejo, Madrid, Biblioteca Nacional, Julio Ollero, 1992, 157 pp., col. ills. Exhibition held at the Biblioteca Nacional, Madrid, June-August 1992

Sarria Rueda, Amalia, "Cinco siglos de encuadernación artística, s. XV–XIX", *Revista de Archivos, Bibliotecas y Museos*, LXXXI (1978), 191–93.

— *Encuadernación contemporánea en los fondos de la Biblioteca Nacional*: Madrid, from 10 June to 28 July 2000, Sala de Exposiciones, Biblioteca Nacional, curated by AFEDA, Madrid, El Viso, 2000, 62 pp., col. ills.

Ocho siglos de encuadernación española = Huit siècles de reliure en Espagne = Spaanse boekbanden uit acht eeuwen: Bibliotheca Wittockiana, 1985, n. p., n. n., 1985. (Barcelona, Escudo de Oro), 171 pp. Title preceded by: Europalia 85. España.

La encuadernación artística española actual [exhibition, Biblioteca Nacional, Madrid, February-April 1986], Madrid, Dirección General del Libro y Bibliotecas, 1986, 218 pp., num. and col. ills.

Gómez Herrera, Ramón, *Reliure d'art*, exhibition 10 October–16 November 1986, Ballens-Morgues, Gallerie de Ballens, 1986, 35 pp.

Imprenta Artesanal (Madrid), *Joyas de la encuadernación en la Imprenta Artesanal del Ayuntamiento de Madrid*, Centro Cultural La Elipa, from 10 December 1987 to 15 January 1988, Madrid, Imprenta Artesanal del Ayuntamiento, 1987, 102 pp.

— *Encuadernación artística en la Imprenta Artesanal del Ayuntamiento de Madrid*, Centro Cultural Galileo, Madrid, Ayuntamiento, Junta Municipal de Chamberí, 1992, 90 pp., ill.

Las encuadernaciones mudéjares de la Catedral de Segovia: XVIII Congreso Internacional de Bibliofilia: Thursday, 23 September 1993, (18th, 1993, Madrid), Segovia, Caja Segovia, 1993, 67 pp., [2] shts., [4] pp. of pls., ill.

La encuadernación artística española: su expresión en La Rioja [Logroño, Biblioteca Pública, April-June 1994], José Luis Magro Rastrero ... [et al.], Logroño, Biblioteca Pública Central de La Rioja, 1994, 103 pp., ill.

Encuadernaciones artísticas en las colecciones municipales [Madrid, Museo Municipal, November

1994–January 1995], Madrid, Ayuntamiento, Imprenta Artesanal, Ollero y Ramos, 1994, 209 pp., col. ills.

PALACIO REAL (MADRID). BIBLIOTECA, *Encuadernación e identificación:* Palacio Real de Madrid, 9 July 1996, directed by María Luisa López-Vidriero, catalogue: Carmen Crespo and María Luisa López-Vidriero, coordination and layout: J. L. Rodríguez Montederramo, n. p, n. n., 1996, III, 29 pp., [12] shts. of pls., [23] entries.

Raros y preciosos: encuadernación de arte actual en las bibliotecas europeas, febrero-abril 1997, Madrid, Fundación Central Hispano y Afeda, 1997, 159 pp., ill.

La artesanía se hizo arte: el taller de Galván, 1949–1999, Palacio de Exposiciones y Congresos, Cadiz, April 1999, ed. Rosario Martínez López, Madrid, Fundación Central Hispano, 1999, 228 pp.

Premio Nacional de Encuadernación Artística "José Galván" (1st, 1999, Cadiz), Palacio de Exposiciones y Congresos, Cadiz, April 1999, ed. Rosario Martínez López, prologue by José Bonifacio Bermejo Martín, with an introduction by Antonio Galván Cuéllar, photographs by Fernando Fernández, Cadiz, Fundación Municipal de Cultura, 1999, 159 pp. Held in connection with the I Congreso Nacional sobre Bibliofilia, Encuadernación Artística, Restauración y Patrimonio Bibliográfico.

BALDÓ SUÁREZ, Dolores, "Una exposición de encuadernaciones en la Embajada de Bélgica", *Encuadernación de Arte*, no. 15 (2000), 7–19.

Pequeños y exquisitos: tesoros en miniatura, Madrid, Museo Nacional de Artes Decorativas, from 12 April to 31 May 2000, Madrid, AFEDA, 2000, 124 pp.

El arte de la encuadernación: Casa de las Carnicerías, Ávila, 20 April to 4 May 2001, Instituto Municipal de la Música y la Cultura (Ávila), Ávila, Instituto Municipal de la Música y la Cultura de Ávila, 2001, 53 pp., col. ills.

Bibliofília a Catalunya: des del s. XIX, Fundació Jaume I, Barcelona, Fundació Jaume I, 2001, 119 pp., ill.

Presente y futuro de la encuadernación española: Biblioteca Nacional, Madrid, 16 October–1 December 2002, Bibliotheca Wittockiana, Brussels, 16 January–15 March 2003, Madrid, AFEDA, 2002, 150 pp., col. ills. Exhibition of the bindings awarded with the national binding prize, the Reina Sofía poetry prize and the José Galván national prize, showing works by Antolín Palomino Olalla, Hermanos Galván, Ana Ruiz-Larrea Cangas, José Luis García Rubio and Manuel Bueno.

Els vestits del saber: enquadernacions mudèjars a la Universitat de València, La Nau, Universitat de València, March-June de 2003, Sala Duc de Calàbria, texts: María Isabel Álvaro Zamora, María Luz Mandingorra Llavata, Donatella Giansante, València, Universitat de València, 2003, 202 pp., chiefly col. ills. (Projecte thesaurus, 11).

Encuadernaciones artísticas: homenaje a Antonio de Sancha: X Aniversario de la Asociación para el Fomento de la Encuadernación de Arte, Madrid, AFEDA, 2003, 93 pp., col. ills. Travelling exhibition.

Manuel Rico y Sinobas, Valladolid 1819–Madrid 1898: una memoria recuperada [exhibition], Sala Museo de la Pasión, 7 May to 8 June 2003, entries: Irene González Negro *et al.*, Valladolid, Junta de Castilla y León, Consejería de Educación y Cultura, Ayuntamiento de Valladolid, 2003, 253 pp., num. and col. ills.

Arte del libro: la encuadernación española en Nueva York: Instituto Cervantes, New York, 4 to 27 November 2004, Madrid, AFEDA, 2004, 52 pp., num. and col. ills.

Els vestits dels llibres: from 1 July to 10 September 2004, Centre Català d'Artesania, Serra, Ramon, Barcelona, Centre Català d'Artesania de la Generalitat de Catalunya, 2004, 56 pp., col. ills.

Diseño y encuadernación para el libro de un peregrino: from 12 February to 20 March 2005, Museo das Peregrinacións, Santiago de Compostela, Madrid, Asociación para el Fomento de la Encuadernación de Arte, 2005, 64 pp., chiefly col. ills.

La encuadernación de arte desde el mundo cervantino: el Quijote en el Museo Cerralbo, 1905–2005, Asociación para el Fomento de la Encuadernación de Arte, Museo Cerralbo, Madrid, Asociación para el Fomento de la Encuadernación Arte, 2005, 225 pp., num. and chiefly col. ills.

QUINEY, Aitor, *Hermenegildo Miralles: arts gràfiques i enquadernació*, exhibition held at the Biblioteca de Catalunya, April 2005, Joana Escobedo, Francesc Fontbona, Barcelona, Biblioteca de Catalunya, 2005, 300 pp., num. and col. ills.

Encuadernación de arte: escuelas y talleres: from 16 May to 15 June 2006, Centro Cultural Quinta de la Fuente del Berro, Madrid, texts: Íñigo Henríquez de Luna, Guadalupe Rubio de Urquía and Raquel Escudero Arribas, Madrid, AFEDA, 2006, 53 pp., chiefly col. ills.

Bookbinders

The writings of bookbinders themselves and studies of their work by other authors are documents which provide considerable knowledge of bookbinding as a technique and as an art.

Rovira y Adán, Jaime, "Don Pedro Doménech y Saló, encuadernador", *Revista Gráfica*, Barcelona, 1901–2, 56.

Canals, Carlos, "Brugalla, la pasión bibliófila", *El día de El Mundo*, Tuesday 17 August 1933, 49.

Brugalla Turmo, Emilio, *Tres ensayos sobre el arte de la encuadernación*, Barcelona, José Porter, 1945, XVI, 97 pp., L pls.

— "La encuadernación en sus diversos momentos", lecture published in *Gráficas*, year X, no. 107 (19 May 1953), 221.

— "Los encuadernadores buscan nuevos conceptos", *Gráficas*, no. 137–38 (November-December 1955), 558–59.

— "El arte de encuadernar y su evolución", lecture delivered at the Diputación Provincial de Barcelona in connection with the book fair of 1965, in *Catálogo de la producción editorial barcelonesa, 1964–1965*, Barcelona, Biblioteca Central, 1966, 55–72, X plates.

— "La encuadernación tradicional en España y la encuadernación original en el palenque europeo" (lecture delivered at Ascona (Switzerland) on 18 August 1967), in *Atti. Quinto Congresso Internazionale di Bibliofili* (Venice, 1–7 October 1967), Venice, 1967, p. 143–62.

— "'Los bibliófilos' de Mariano Fortuny (Cincinati Art Museum)", *La Vanguardia*, 21 April 1976.

— *Brugalla: 254 reproducciones de sus destacadas encuadernaciones elegidas entre más de dos mil, realizadas en el período de cincuenta años (1926–1976): precedidas de veintiocho ensayos ilustrados sobre temas del libro, de la bibliofilia y del arte de la encuadernación, seguidos de varios juicios críticos sobre la obra y actividades de Brugalla*, Bilbao, La Gran Enciclopedia Vasca, 1977, 559 pp., 1 sht., pl., num. and col. eng. Limited edition.

— "Contrastes de la Bibliografía: Divagaciones en torno al amor al libro y a su indumento", *Memorias de la Real Academia de Ciencias y Artes de Barcelona*, tercera época, vol. XLV, no. 2 (1980), 119–71.

— "Definición simbólica de la encuadernación suntuaria", *Academia*, no. 54 (1982), 167–84.

— "El simbolismo universal de la encuadernación", *La Vanguardia*, Barcelona, Sunday 28 March 1982.

— "El arte en el libro y en la encuadernación", *Revista de llibreria antiquària*, nos. 7–11 (1984–86).

— *En torno a la encuadernación y las artes del libro: diez temas académicos*, Madrid, Clan, 1996, 481 pp., ill. (Técnicas artísticas; 7)

— "El llibre i l'art d'enquadernació", in *Bibliofília a Catalunya: des del s. XI*, Barcelona, Fundació Jaume I, 2001, 94–97.

— *La encuadernación en París en las avanzadas del arte moderno*, Madrid, Ollero y Ramos, 2003, 219 pp., ill.

García Ubeda, Antonio, "Brugalla, un encuadernador español", *Gráficas*, year X, no. 106 (1953), 166–67.

— "Loable actividad de Emilio Brugalla", *Gráficas*, year XII, no. 131 (May 1955), 228.

Brugalla, Santiago, *Emili Brugalla, enquadernador: conmemoració del centenari del seu naixement*, Barcelona, Biblioteca de Catalunya, 2001, 361 pp., col. ills.

Palomino Olalla, Antolín, *Autobiografía, conocimientos y recuerdos sobre el arte de la encuadernación*, Madrid, Ayuntamiento, 1986, 68 pp., pls.

Waridel, Brigitte, "L'art de Ramón Gómez Herrera, relieur espagnol", *Librarium*, 30 (1987), 20–26.

Lloréns Cifre, José, *Antología de la encuadernación artística de José Lloréns Cifre, presentando algunas obras de José Ricardo Lloréns Martí*, Valencia, J. Lloréns, 1988, 120 pp.

Gómez Herrera, Ramón, *Color a flor de piel: Ramón Gómez, encuadernador, [exhibition]*, ed. Manuel Carrión Gútiez with the collaboration of Rosario Martínez López, Cadiz, Ayuntamiento de Cádiz, 2004, 189 pp., chiefly num. and col. ills.

Zapata, Esteban, "Camacho. Restauración de Libros, Encuadernaciones y Documentos gráficos",

photographs by Diego Martín, *Noticias bibliográficas*, 97 (2004), 32–33.
— "Encuadernadores de hoy: Carlos García Bermejo", photographs by Diego Martín, *Noticias bibliográficas*, 109 (2006), 23–24.

Masid Valiñas, Germán. "Manuel Martín Barranco, la huella de un jaspeador de papeles", *Encuadernación de Arte*, 28 (2006), 51–67.

Manuals, Techniques, Repertoires

Sabrel, M., *Manual completo del encuadernador de todas clases, teórico y práctico: contiene: el modo de alzar, satinar... aumentado con el Arte del rayador de papel para libros de oficinas y de comercio*, Barcelona, Librería de Manuel Saurí, 1868, 248 pp., 8 fld. shts. of plates.

Monje Ayala, Mariano, *El arte de la encuadernación*, Barcelona, Labor, 1944, 408 pp.

Sierra Rustarazo, Pablo, "Encuadernaciones españolas", *Información Comercial Española*, 94 (1944), 2–26.

Gijón, Esmeralda, "Cursillo sobre las artes del libro español", *Revista de Bibliografía Nacional*, VI (1945), 389–92.

Angulo, Julio, "El arte de las bellas encuadernaciones", *Revista Nacional de Educación*, year IX, 2.ª época, no. 85 (1949), 23–31.

Zumalabe Mendiburu, José Miguel, *El arte de la encuadernación*, San Sebastián, V. Echeverría impresor, 1949, 163 shts., ill.

Domenech y Montaner, Lluis, "Consideraciones sobre encuadernación", *Gráficas*, XI, no. 125–26 (1954), 546–47.

Amades, Joan, *El paper de guardes*, Barcelona, Gráfica Catalana, 1971, 11 shts., eng. Issue of 400 copies, the first 250 numbered.

Alfonso Jiménez, José Luis, *Conocimientos teóricos básicos de encuadernación*, Madrid, Gráficas Schelsinger, 1991, 183 pp.

Enciclopedia de la encuadernación, ed. and coord. José Bonifacio Bermejo Martí, Madrid, Ollero & Ramos, 1998. 353 pp., ill.

Torrente Secorún, José Vicente, *Manual del dorado de libros*, Madrid, Clan, imp. 2000, 214 pp., num. and col. ills.

Carpallo Bautista, Antonio, *Análisis documental de la encuadernación española: repertorio bibliográfico, tesauro, ficha descriptiva*, Madrid, Asociación para el Fomento de la Encuadernación de Arte, 2002, 319 pp.

Calderón Cabeza, María Victoria, "Encuadernación de Arte: Conservación y Restauración", in *El libro como objeto de arte:* actas del II Congreso Nacional sobre Bibliofilia, Encuadernación Artística, Restauración y Patrimonio Bibliográfico, Cadiz, April 2004, [Cadiz], Ayuntamiento de Cádiz, [2008], p. 125–38.

Camacho Navarrete, Iván, "El estudio de la encuadernación de los incunables a través de su restauración", in *Isabel I y la imprenta: consecuencias materiales, en el mundo cultural, de esta revolución tecnológica*, Madrid, Ministerio de Cultura, 2005, var. pag. Conference held by the Ministerio de Cultura in November 2004.

— "El estudio de la encuadernación a través de su restauración", *Noticias bibliográficas*, 103 (2005), 17.

Cambras, Josep, *Encuadernación*, Barcelona, Parramón, 2006, 143 pp., num. and col. ills. (Decorative techniques).

Artistic Styles

Prieto Vives, Antonio, "La simetría y la composición de los tracistas musulmanes", *Investigación y Progreso*, year 6, no. 6 (March 1932), 33–45, 70 figures.

— "Temas de composición de los tracistas musulmanes. La estrella", *Investigación y Progreso*, year 6, no. 7–8 (July and August 1932), 115–19.

— "Temas de composición de los tracistas musulmanes. La flor", *Investigación y Progreso*, year 6, no. 9 (September 1932), 138–43.

Almela i Vives, Francesc, *El libro valenciano*, Valencia, Miguel Juan, 1933, 50 pp.

Lasso de la Vega, Miguel, marqués del Saltillo, "Encuadernaciones heráldicas españolas", *Revista Española de Arte*, vol. III, no. 1 (January-March 1934), 1–35.

Entrambasaguas, Joaquín, "Las encuadernaciones alemanas", *Bibliografía general española e hispanoamericana*, no. 3 (1941), 5–7.

Ferrán Salvador, Vicente, *La encuadernación en Valencia durante los siglos XVI, XVII y XVIII*, Valencia, n. n., 1963, 39 pp. Offprint of *Anales del Centro de Cultura Valenciana*.

Foot, Mirjam M., "A Spanish Mudejar Binding of the End of the Fifteenth Century", *The Book Collector*, 36 (1987), 100–2.

Cockx-Indestege, Elly, Jan Storm van Leeuwen and Claudine Lemaire, "Reliures espagnoles à Bruxelles: considérations et réflexions en marge d'une exposition", *Le livre & l'estampe*, 34, 129, (1988), 9–60; *Le livre & l'estampe*, 35, 130 (1988), 131–56.

Rozsondai, Maria, "Ein spanischer Einband im Mudéjar-Stil, ca. 1480", *Philobiblon*, 35 (1991), 237–39.

Ruiz de Elvira Serra, Isabel, *Las encuadernaciones mudéjares de la Catedral de Segovia*, Madrid, XVIII Congreso Internacional de Bibliofilia, 1993, 67 pp., ill.

Checa Cremades, José Luis, *La encuadernación renacentista en la Biblioteca del Monasterio del El Escorial: introducción al estudio de la decoración exterior del libro en la España de Felipe II*, Madrid, Ollero y Ramos, 1998, 146 pp.

— "Pintura y encuadernación (siglos xiv–xvii)", *Encuadernación de Arte*, 17 (2001), 34–53.

— "Sobre la noción de estilo aplicada al estudio de la historia de la encuadernación", *Gutenberg-Jahrbuch* (2002), 223–33.

— *Los estilos de encuadernación: (siglo iii d.J.C. – siglo xix)*, Madrid, Ollero y Ramos, 2003, 517 pp., 24 pp. of pls.

— *La encuadernación clásica*, Madrid, Ollero y Ramos, 2006, 241 pp., col. ills.

— "La Encuadernación plateresca del Renacimiento Español, fuentes literarias y artísticas de un estilo", *Encuadernación de Arte*, 29 (2007), 51–66.

Linage Conde, José Antonio, "En torno a las encuadernaciones en los monasteries", in *El libro como objeto de arte: actas del I Congreso Nacional sobre Bibliofilia, Encuadernación Artística, Restauración y Patrimonio Bibliográfico*, Cadiz, Fundación Municipal de Cultura; Diputación Provincial de Cádiz, 1999, 285–302.

Mateo Ripoll, Verónica, "La encuadernación del libro renacentista en la biblioteca del seminario de Orihuela", in *El libro como objeto de arte: actas del I Congreso Nacional sobre Bibliofilia, Encuadernación Artística, Restauración y Patrimonio Bibliográfico*, Cadiz, Fundación Municipal de Cultura, Diputación Provincial, 1999, 303–24.

Calero Palacios, María del Carmen, "Consideraciones sobre algunos fragmentos de códices utilizados en encuadernaciones de obras del Sacromonte de Granada", in *Literatura y cristiandad: homenaje al profesor Jesús Montoya Martínez (con motivo de su jubilación): estudios sobre hagiografía, mariología, épica y retórica*, eds. Jesús Montoya Martínez, José Alonso García, María Luisa Dañobeitia Fernández, Antonio Rubio Flores, Granada, Universidad de Granada, 2001, 763–76.

Gómez Raggio, Francisco, *El libro de la encuadernación*, Madrid, Alianza Editorial, 2001, 484 pp., 16 pp. of col. pls, ill. (El libro de bolsillo. Aficiones, 7504).

Quiney, Aitor, "El estilo 'Le Gascon'", *Encuadernación de Arte*, 18 (2001), 56–69.

— "Louis Jou. Sus encuadernaciones", *Encuadernación de Arte*, 20 (2002), 5–18.

Garrigue, Marie, "Diseño y encuadernación, une école de reliure à Madrid", *Arts et métiers du livre*, 229 (2002), 70.

Canals Aromí, Maria Teresa, "Hermenegildo Miralles y Anglés, o el arte de transformar el papel", in *Actas del V Congreso Nacional de Historia del Papel en España, Sarrià de Ter, Girona, 2, 3 y 4 de octubre de 2003*, Girona, CCG, Sarrià de Ter, Ajuntament de Sarrià de Ter, 2003, 61–66.

Clavería, Carlos. "La encuadernación: análisis, identificación y valoración", in *Comercio y tasación del libro antiguo: análisis, identificación y descripción: (textos y materiales)*, Jaca, 1–5 September 2003: summer courses held by the Universidad de Zaragoza, Vicerrectorado de Proyección Social y Cultural, ed. Manuel José Pedraza Gracia, Zaragoza, Prensas Universitarias de Zaragoza, 2003, 117–32.

— *Reconocimiento y descripción de encuadernaciones antiguas*, Madrid, Arco Libros, 2006, 249 pp.

Espejo Arias, Teresa, "Tres catálogos de fotografías de José García Ayola: Un modelo de encuadernación del s. xix", *Cuadernos de la Alhambra*, 39 (2003), 153–68.

Herreras Morillas, José Luis, "La ornamentación de las encuadernaciones artísticas de los impresos de los siglos xvi y xvii de la Biblioteca de la Real Sociedad Económica de Amigos del País de Badajoz", *Boletín de la ANABAD*, vol. 54, no. 4 (2004), 103–18.

Díaz de Miranda, María Dolores, and Ana María Herrero Montero, "Encuadernaciones de los incunables españoles de la Catedral de Oviedo", in *Isabel I y la imprenta: consecuencias materiales, en el mundo cultural, de esta revolución tecnológica*, Madrid, Ministerio de Cultura, 2005, var.

pag., 24 pp., 4 shts. Conference held by the Ministerio de Cultura in November 2004.

Boudalis, Yorgos, "Influencias islámicas en las encuadernaciones griegas de época post-bizantina", *Erytheia*, 26 (2005), 127–76.

Gómez Ivanov, María Luisa, "La encuadernación del incunable de Lucena 'Repetición de amores e arte de axedrez: con CL juegos de partido': apuntes sobre el ajedrez en la Edad Media", *Medievalia*, Mexico, 37 (2005), 39–51.

Jurado, Augusto, *La encuadernación manual y la encuadernación artística en España, hoy*, Madrid, Comunicación Gráfica, 2005, 116 pp., ill.

Carpallo Bautista, Antonio, "Los estilos decorativos en la encuadernación del siglo xvii", in *Imprenta, libros y lectura en la España del "Quijote"*, ed. José Manuel Lucía Megías, Madrid, Artes Gráficas Municipales, 2006, 343–58

History of Bookbinding, Partial Studies

Amat Calderón, Elena, *Los libreros de Madrid en el siglo xvii*, Madrid, Sáez Hermanos, 1931, 53 pp.

Domínguez Bordona, Jesús, *El libro de arte anterior al siglo xviii en España*, Madrid, Blass, 1933, 14 pp.

Carreras Valls, R., *El llibre a Catalunya: els primers temps de l'impremta a Barcelona*, conferència donada a l'Institut Català de les Arts del Llibre el 23 d'abril de 1936, diada de la Festa del Llibre, adicionada amb notes inèdites de l'Arxiu Històric Notarial recollides pêl conferenciant R. Carreres Valls, Barcelona, G.B.S.A, 1936, 30 pp.

Thomas, Henry, *Early Spanish Bookbindings xi–xv Centuries*, London, Printed for the bibliographical Society, at the University Press, Oxford, 1939 (for 1936), XLVI, 65 pp., 1 p., 6 pls. (Illustrated monographs, no. XXIII).

Sánchez de Palacios, Mariano, *El bello arte de la encuadernación y dos ensayos sobre Goya*, Madrid, Escuela Nacional de Artes Gráficas, 1959, 55 pp., 3 pls.

Thompson, Lawrence, "Introductory Notes in the History of Bookbinding in Spanish America", *Libri*, vol. 10, no. 1 (1960), 10–22.

Ainaud de Lasarte, Juan, "Encuadernación", *Ars Hispaniae, Historia Universal del Arte Hispánico*, Madrid, Plus-Ultra, 1962, vol. 18 (*Miniatura. Grabado. Encuadernación*), 323–44.

López Castán, Ángel, "La encuadernación madrileña y la comunidad de mercaderes y encuadernadores de libros de la Corte en el siglo xviii»", *Villa de Madrid*, 24 (1986), 89–90.

Nieto Alcaide, Víctor, "La aparición del libro como objeto artístico: las encuadernaciones ricas", *Encuadernación de Arte*, 1 (1993), 7–13.

— "La encuadernación de oficio a arte", *Encuadernación de Arte*, 29 (2007), 25–33.

Historia ilustrada del libro español. La edición moderna, siglos xix y xx, ed. Hipólito Escolar; contributors: Jean-François Botrel [et al.], Madrid, Fundación Germán Sánchez Ruipérez, Pirámide, 1996, 608 pp., num. and col. ills. (Biblioteca del libro; 66).

Baldó Suárez, Dolores, *Arte y diseño en el libro: maestros encuadernadores, 1920–1970*, Capilla de San Martín, Palacio de la Aljafería, Cortes de Aragón, Zaragoza, 17 April–18 May, Madrid, Asociación para el Fomento de la Encuadernación de Arte, 1997, 72 pp., ill.

— *Arte y encuadernación: una panorámica del siglo xx*, Madrid, Ollero & Ramos, 1999, 246 pp., 72 pp. of num. and col. plates.

Moreno Gallego, Valentín, "Observaciones documentales para la historia de la encuadernación hispana", *Boletín de la Real Academia Española*, LXXIX (1999), 267–88.

La encuadernación, historia y arte: I Curso "El documento hispánico: Enrique IV-Fernando VII", organised by AFEDA and held with the collaboration and support of the Ilustre Colegio Notarial de Madrid and the Fundación Matritense del Notariado; coord. Guadalupe Rubio de Urquía, Madrid, AFEDA, 2001, 350 pp., ill. Course held at the Salón de Actos of the Ilustre Colegio Notarial, Madrid, in January and February 2000.

Soler i Fabregat, Ramón, *El libro de arte en España durante la Edad Moderna*, Gijón, Trea, 2000, 213 pp.

Rueda Laffond, José Carlos, "La fabricación del libro. La industrialización de las técnicas. Máquinas, papel y encuadernación", in *Historia de la edición en España, 1836–1936*, coord. Jesús A. Martínez Martín, Madrid, Marcial Pons, 2001, 73–110. (Historia).

Rivalan Guégo, Christine, "La imagen de cubierta en las ediciones de *Humo, dolor, placer* de Alberto Insúa", *Litterae*, Madrid, 3–4 (2003–4), 271–79.

— "Texto e imagen: la cubierta al encuentro del public", in *La memoria de los libros: estudios sobre la historia del escrito y de lectura en Europa y América*, coord. Pedro M Cátedra and María Luisa López-Vidriero, ed. María Isabel de Páiz Hernández, Salamanca, Instituto de Historia del Libro y de la Lectura, 2004, vol. II, 719–29. (Serie maior, 4–5).

Beny, Ana, and Pedro Barbáchano, "La encuadernación en el "scriptorium" de San Millán de la Cogolla (siglos x–xiv)", in *La memoria de los libros: estudios sobre la historia del escrito y de lectura en Europa y América*, coord. Pedro M Cátedra, María Luisa López-Vidriero, ed. María Isabel de Páiz Hernández, Salamanca, Instituto de Historia del Libro y de la Lectura, 2004, vol. I, p. 67–84. (Serie maior, 4–5).

Bécares Botas, Vicente, *Guía documental del mundo del libro salmantino del siglo xvi*, Burgos, Fundación Instituto Castellano y Leonés de la Lengua, 2006, 293 pp., ill., graphs. (Libros singulares, 7).

Prado Almansa, Lourdes de, José Bonifacio Bermejo Martín and Miguel Uceda Iniesta, *Imprenta artesanal C.C. Conde Duque*, Madrid, Dirección General de Educación y Juventud, 2006, 51 pp., col. ills. (Cuadernos madrileños. Museos).

References

Bookbinding, an Artistic Language
Víctor Nieto Alcaide

Álvarez Turienzo 1986. Teodoro Álvarez Turienzo, "Encuadernaciones escurialenses", in *IV Centenario del Monasterio de El Escorial. Fe y Sabiduría. La Biblioteca* [exh. cat.], Madrid, Patrimonio Nacional, 1986, p. 126.

Álvaro Zamora 2008. María Isabel Álvaro Zamora, "Encuadernaciones mudéjares", *Artigrama*, 23 (2008), 445–81.

Andrés 1985. Gregorio de Andrés, "Perfil histórico de la Biblioteca de El Escorial", in *El Escorial en la Biblioteca Nacional* [exh. cat. Madrid, Biblioteca Nacional], Madrid, Ministerio de Cultura, 1985, pp. 559–65.

Andrés González 2010. Patricia Andrés González, *Arte, fiesta e iconografía en torno a la Eucaristía. Juan de Arfe y su obra: la custodia Monumental de Valladolid*, Valladolid, Ayuntamiento de Valladolid, 2010.

Barbier 2005. Frédéric Barbier, *Historia del Libro*, Madrid, Alianza Editorial, 2005.

Benito García 2009a. Pilar Benito García, "Fiebre de seda en los palacios de Carlos IV", in *Carlos IV, mecenas y coleccionista*, Madrid, Patrimonio Nacional, Sociedad Estatal de Conmemoraciones Culturales, 2009, pp. 93–116.

Benito García 2009b. Pilar Benito García, "49. Alfombra del antiguo sitial de la Capilla Real de Aranjuez", in *Carlos IV, mecenas y coleccionista*, Madrid, Patrimonio Nacional, Sociedad Estatal de Conmemoraciones Culturales, 2009, pp. 194–95.

Bimbenet-Privat 1993. Michèle Bimbenet-Privat, "Rinceaux", in *L'Art décoratif en Europe. Renaissance et Manierisme*, Paris, Citadelles & Mazenod, 1993, pp. 113–89.

Blok 1982. Cor Blok, *Historia del arte abstracto (1900–1960)*, Madrid, Cátedra, 1982.

Borrás Gualis 1990. Gonzalo Borrás Gualis, *El arte mudéjar*, Teruel, Diputación Provincial, 1990.

Bouza Álvarez 2005. Bouza Álvarez, Fernando, *El libro y el cetro: la biblioteca de Felipe IV en la Torre Alta del Alcázar de Madrid*, Madrid, Instituto de Historia del Libro y de la Lectura, 2005.

Brugalla 2000. Emilio Brugalla, *Tres ensayos sobre el arte de la encuadernación*, Madrid, Ollero & Ramos, 2000.

Bury 2007. Richard de Bury, *The Love of Books: The Philobiblon of Richard of Bury*, trans. by E. C. Thomas, The University of Adelaide Library, eBooks@Adelaide, 2007.

Carducho 1979. Vicente Carducho, *Diálogos de la Pintura. Su defensa, origen, esencia, definición, modos y diferencias*, edited, prologue and notes by Francisco Calvo Serraller, Madrid, Turner, 1979.

Carrión 1994. Manuel Carrión Gútiez, "La encuadernación española", in *Historia ilustrada del libro español: de los incunables al siglo xviii*, edited by Hipólito Escolar Sobrino, Madrid, Fundación Germán Sánchez Ruipérez, 1994, pp. 395–445.

Carrión 1996. Manuel Carrión Gútiez, "La encuadernación española en la Edad Media", in *Historia ilustrada del libro español. Los manuscritos*, directed by Hipólito Escolar, Madrid, Fundación Sánchez Ruipérez, 1996 (2nd ed.), pp. 365–400.

Ceán Bermúdez 1800. Juan Agustín Ceán Bermúdez, *Diccionario histórico de los más ilustres profesores de las bellas artes en España*, Madrid, Imprenta Viuda de Ibarra, 1800, 6 vols.

Chambers 1988. Anne Chambers, *Guía práctica del papel jaspeado*, Madrid, Tellus, 1988.

Checa Cremades 1998. José Luis Checa Cremades, *La encuadernación renacentista en la Biblioteca del Monasterio de El Escorial: introducción al estudio de la decoración exterior del libro en la España de Felipe II*, Madrid, Ollero y Ramos, 1998.

Comisión Regia de España 1867. Comisión Regia de España. *Exposición Universal de París 1867: Catálogo general de la sección española*, Paris, Ch. Lahure, 1867.

Crespi de Valldaura 1994. Luis Crespi de Valldaura, "La encuadernación textil en España", *Encuadernación de Arte*, 5 (1994), 35–47.

Dacos 1969. Nicole Dacos, *La Découverte de la Domus Aurea et la formation de grotesques à la Renaissance*, London, The Warburg Institute; Leiden, E. J. Brill, 1969.

Delvaux 1981. Yves Delvaux, *Dix siècles de reliure*, Paris, Pigmalion, 1981.

Dudin 1772 René Martin Dudin, *L'Art du relieur doreur de livres. Descriptions des Arts et Métiers faites ou approuveés par messiurs de la Académie Royal des Sciences*, Paris, Saillant & Nyon et Dessaint, 1772.

Easton 1983. Phoebe Jane Easton, *Marbling: A History and a Bibliography*, Los Angeles, Dawsons Book Shop, 1983.

Francastel 1961. Pierre Francastel, *Arte y técnica en los siglos xix y xx*, Valencia, Fomento de Cultura Ediciones, 1961.

FUMAROLI 2010. Marc Fumaroli, "Retour à l'Antique: la guerre des goûts dans l'Europe des Lumières", in *L'Antiquité rêvée. Innovations et résistances au XVIIIe siècle* [exh. cat. Paris, Musée du Louvre; Houston, Museum of Fine Arts], Paris, Gallimard, 2010, pp. 23–55.

GALAY SARAÑANA n. d. José Galay Sarañana, *El lazo en el estilo mudéjar. Su trazado simplicista*, Zaragoza, Institución Fernando el Católico, n. d.

GARCÍA ÁLVAREZ 2001. César García Álvarez, *El simbolismo del grutesco renacentista*, León, Universidad de León, 2001.

GOMBRICH 1968. Ernest H. Gombrich, *Meditaciones sobre un caballo de juguete*, translated by José María Valverde, Barcelona, Seix Barral, 1968.

GRUBER 1993a. Alain Gruber, "Entrelacs", in *L'Art décoratif en Europe. Renaissance et Maniérisme*, Paris, Citadelles & Mazenod, 1993, pp. 21–111.

GRUBER 1993b. Alain Gruber, "Grottesques", in *L'Art décoratif en Europe. Renaissance et Maniérisme*, Paris, Citadelles & Mazenod, 1993, pp. 191–273.

HALDANE 1983. Duncan Haldane, *Islamic Bookbindings in the Victoria and Albert Museum*, London, 1983.

HOBSON 1999. Anthony Hobson, *Renaissance Book Collecting. Jean Grolier and Diego Hurtado de Mendoza, their Books and Bindings*, Cambridge, University Press, 1999.

HOBSON 2000. Anthony Hobson, "Diego Hurtado de Mendoza", *Encuadernación de Arte*, 16 (2000), 3–17.

HONOUR 1968. Hugh Honour, *Neo-classicism*, Harmondsworth, NY, Penguin, 1968.

HUESO ROLLAND 1935. Francisco Hueso Rolland, *Exposición de encuadernaciones españolas, siglos XII al XIX. Catálogo general ilustrado* [exh. cat. Madrid, Sociedad Española de Amigos del Arte], Madrid, Imp. Blass, 1935.

***Italian Renaissance Prints* 2007.** *Italian Renaissance Prints from the Swiss Federal Institute of Technology Zurich* [exh. cat.], Tokyo, The National Museum of Western Art, 2007.

JORDAN AND CONSTANTINI-LACHAT 1993. Marc-Henri Jordan and Francisca Constantini-Lachat, "Mauresques", in *L'Art décoratif en Europe. Renaissance et Maniérisme*, Paris, Citadelles & Mazenod, 1993, pp. 275–345.

JUNQUERA 1979. Juan José Junquera, *La decoración y el mobiliario de los Palacios de Carlos IV*, Madrid, Sala, 1979.

KUCHLY 1974. Louis Kuchly, *Joseph Beunat, le génial stucateur sarrebourgeois*, Sarrebourg, Société d'Histoire et d'Archéologie de Lorraine, Section de Sarrebourg, 1996.

LÓPEZ SERRANO 1946. Matilde López Serrano, "Antonio de Sancha, encuadernador madrileño", *Revista de la Biblioteca, Archivo y Museo Municipales*, XV, 54 (1946), 269–307.

LÓPEZ SERRANO 1967. Matilde López Serrano, "Encuadernaciones "de cortina": originalidades del libro español", *Reales Sitios*, IV, 11 (1967), 22–31.

LÓPEZ SERRANO 1972. Matilde López Serrano, *La encuadernación española: breve historia*, Madrid, ANABA, 1972.

LÓPEZ-VIDRIERO 2003. María Luisa López-Vidriero, "Encuadernación en Palacio: lectura periférica y vestigio del tiempo", *Encuadernación de Arte*, 22 (2003), 4–22.

MÉNDEZ PASCUAL 1999. Víctor Méndez Pascual, "El manuscrito de The Metropolitan Museum de Nueva York. Nuevas aportaciones al estudio de la lacería en la encuadernación mudéjar", *Encuadernación de Arte*, 13 (1999), 26–55.

MÜLLER PROFUMO 1985. Luciana Müller Profumo, *El ornamento icónico y la arquitectura 1400–1600*, Madrid, Cátedra, 1985.

NÈGRE 2004. Valerie Nègre, "Catalogues de fabricants et innovation dans le domain du bâtiment au XIX siècle", in Natacha Coquery, Liliane Hilaire-Pérez, Line Sallmann and Catherine Verna (eds.), *Artisans, industrie. Nouvelles révolutions du Moyen Age à nos jours*, Paris, ENS Editions (*Cahiers d'histoire et de philosophie des sciences*, 52), 2004, pp. 421–31.

NIETO ALCAIDE 1989. Victor Nieto Alcaide, "Renovación e indefinición estilistica, 1488–1526", in *Arquitectura del Renacimiento en España 1488–1599*, Madrid, Cátedra, 1989, pp. 11–96.

NIETO ALCAIDE 1998. Victor Nieto Alcaide, "Felipe II y la imagen del libro. Las encuadernaciones y la Biblioteca de El Escorial", *Reales Sitios*, 135 (1998), 46–55.

NIETO ALCAIDE 2000. Victor Nieto Alcaide, "La encuadernación bajo Felipe II (La decoración, el libro y el lugar)", in *Felipe II y las Artes. Actas del Congreso Internacional 9–12 de diciembre de 1998*, Madrid, Universidad Complutense de Madrid, 2000, pp. 673–78.

NIETO ALCAIDE 2007. Victor Nieto Alcaide, "La encuadernación, de oficio a arte", *Encuadernación de Arte*, 29 (2007), 25–33.

PASQUAL DIEZ 1988. Ramón Pasqual Diez, *Arte de hacer el estuco jaspeado o de imitar los jaspes a poca costa y con la mayor propiedad*, facsimile edition with introductory studies by José Ramón Nieto González and Salvador Mata Pérez, Valladolid, Colegio Oficial de Arquitectos de Valladolid, 1988.

RAQUEJO 1989. Tonia Raquejo, *El palacio encantado. La Alhambra en el arte británico*, Madrid, Taurus, 1989.

RUIZ GARCÍA 2004. Elisa Ruiz García, *Los libros de Isabel la Católica: arqueologia de un Patrimonio escrito*, Madrid, Instituto de Historia del Libro y de la Lectura, 2004.

RUSKIN 1853. John Ruskin, *The Stones of Venice*, Volume III: *The Fall*, London, Smith, Elder and Co., 1853.

SAGREDO 1526. Diego de Sagredo, *Medidas del Romano*, Toledo, Ramón de Petras, 1526.

SÁNCHEZ CANTÓN 1950. Francisco Javier Sánchez Cantón, *Libros, tapices y cuadros que coleccionó Isabel la Católica*, Madrid, C.S.I.C., 1950.

Sánchez Mariana 1994. Manuel Sánchez Mariana, "Las encuadernaciones del Marqués de Moya", *Encuadernación de Arte*, 4 (1994), 12–18.

Sebastián and Cortés 1973. Santiago Sebastián and Luis Cortés, *Simbolismo de los programas humanísticos de la Universidad de Salamanca*, Salamanca, Universidad de Salamanca, 1973.

Sigüenza 1927. José de Sigüenza (Jer.), *Fundación del Monasterio de El Escorial por Felipe II*, Madrid, Apostolado de la Prensa, 1927.

Stelzer 1964. Otto Stelzer, *Die Vorgeschichte der abstrakten Kunst*, München, R. Piper, 1964.

Thornton 1986. Peter Thornton, *L'epoque et son style. La décoration intérieure 1620–1920*, Paris, Flammarion, 1986.

Tschudi-Madsen 1967. Stephan Tschudi Madsen, *Art Nouveau*, Madrid, Guadarrama, 1967.

Vélez 1981. Pilar Vélez Vicente, "La encuadernación neomudéjar dentro del modernismo catalán", *Boletín del Museo e Instituto Camón Aznar*, VI–VII (1981), 161–99.

The Humble among the Distinguished
Carlos Clavería Laguarda

Aguerri 2002. Asunción Aguerri Martinez, "La colección Lope de Vega en Madrid", *Encuadernación de Arte*, 18 (2002), 45–49.

Aimone 2004. Pier V. Aimone, "Una biblioteca fatta per lo studio: le regole di conduzione di una biblioteca del XV secolo", in Luisa Secchi Tarugi (ed.), *L'Europa del libro nell'età dell'umanesimo*, Firenze, Franco Cesati, 2004, pp. 61–77.

Aries and Duby 1989. Philippe Aries and Georges Duby (eds.), *Historia de la vida privada*, III, Madrid, Taurus, 1989.

Canfora 2003. Luciano Canfora, *Vita di Chardon de la Rochette comisario alle biblioteche*, Messina, Università degli Studi-Libreria Antiquaria Gonnelli, 2003.

Carbonero 2003. Javier Carbonero Domingo, "La piel del tiempo. Aproximaciones a una exposición y un arte insólitos", in *Manuel Rico y Sinobas. Una memoria recuperada* [exh. cat. Valladolid, Sala Museo de la Pasión], Valladolid, Junta de Castilla y León, 2003, pp. 45–61.

Carena 2008. Carlo Carena, "Notizie inedite su Erasmo da Rotterdam in un incunabolo di lirici latini, e un suo nuovo ritratto", *La Bibliofilia*, 110, 3 (2008), 241–54.

Cátedra 2002. Pedro M. Cátedra, *Nobleza y lectura en tiempos de Felipe II. La biblioteca de don Alonso Osorio, Marqués de Astorga*, Valladolid, Junta de Castilla y León, 2002.

Culot 1979. Paul Culot, *Jean-Claude Bozerian. Un moment de l'ornement dans la reliure en France*, Bruxelles, Eric Speeckaert, 1979.

De Frede 2002. Carlo De Frede, "Maltrattatori di libri", *La Bibliofilia*, 104 (2002), 83–95.

De Marinis 1960. Tammaro De Marinis, *La legatura artistica in Italia nei secoli XV e XVI*, Firenze, Fratelli Alinari, 1960, 3 vols.

Dexeus 2003. Mercedes Dexeus Mallol, "La encuadernación en la cultura del libro", in *Manuel Rico y Sinobas. Una memoria recuperada* [exh. cat. Valladolid, Sala Museo de la Pasión], Valladolid, Junta de Castilla y León, 2003, pp. 65–79.

Escolar 1993. Hipólito Escolar, *Historia universal del libro*, Madrid, Fundación Germán Sánchez Ruipérez, 1993.

Etherington 2010. Don Etherington, *Bookbinding & Conservation: A Sixty-Year Odyssey of Art and Craft*, New Castle, Oak Knoll, 2010.

Incunabula 1994. *Incunabula from the Court Library at Donaueschingen, sold by order of his Serene Highness Joachim Prince zu Fürstenberg*, London, Sotheby's, 1994.

Goldschmidt 1928. E. Ph. Goldschmidt, *Gothic & Renaissance Bookbindings*, London, Benn, 1928.

Hobson 1953. Anthony Hobson, *French and Italian Collectors and their Bindings... in the Library of J. R. Abbey*, Oxford, The Roxburghe Club, 1953.

Hobson 1991. Anthony Hobson, "Introduzione", in *Legatura romana barocca: 1565–1700* [exh. cat. Rome, Museo di Roma], Roma, Edizioni Carte Segrete, 1991, pp. 13–14.

Legature 1977. [Michelini Tozzi], *Legature papali da Eugenio IV a Paolo VI* [exh. cat.], Città del Vaticano, Biblioteca Apostolica Vaticana, 1977.

López Serrano 1943. Matilde López Serrano, "Libreros encuadernadores de Cámara. II Santiago Martin", *Arte Español*, XIV, 27, 4 (1943), 14–22.

Mestre 1993. Gregorio Mayáns y Siscar, *Epistolario XII, Mayáns y los libreros*, edited by Antonio Mestre, Oliva, Ayuntamiento, 1993.

Mestre 2002. Antonio Mestre, "La formación de la biblioteca de un erudito de la ilustración", in Pedro M. Cátedra and María Luisa López-Vidriero (eds.), *De libros, librerías, imprentas y lectores*, Salamanca, Universidad de Salamanca, SEMYR (El Libro Antiguo Español, VI), 2002, pp. 219–40.

Montecchi 2002. Giorgio Montecchi, "Introduzione", in *Arte della legatura a Brera. Storie di libri e biblioteche. Secoli XV e XVI*, Milano, Edizioni Lonograf, 2002.

Morazzoni 1929. [Giuseppe Morazzoni], *La rilegatura piemontese nel '700. Note storiche di Giuseppe Morazzoni*, Milano, Walter Toscanini, 1929.

Naudé 2008. Gabriel Naudé, *Recomendaciones para formar una biblioteca*, Oviedo, KRK ediciones, 2008.

PETRUCCI NARDELLI 2007. Franca Petrucci Nardelli, *Legatura e scrittura. Testi celati, messagi velati annunci palesi*, Firenze, Leo S. Olschki editore, 2007.

PINTAUDI 1990. Rosario Pintaudi (ed.), *Angelo Maria Bandini. Dei principi e progressi della Real Biblioteca Mediceo Laurenziana*, Firenze, Edizioni Gonnelli, 1990.

RODRÍGUEZ-MOÑINO 1965. Antonio Rodríguez-Moñino, *Construcción crítica y realidad histórica en la poesía española de los siglos XVI y XVII*, Madrid, Castalia, 1965.

RUIZ 2004. Elisa Ruiz García, *Los libros de Isabel la Católica. Arqueología de un patrimonio escrito*, Salamanca, Instituto de Historia del Libro y de la Lectura, 2004.

SANTIAGO PÁEZ 2004. Elena Santiago Páez (dir. and coord.), *La Real Biblioteca Pública 1711–1760. De Felipe a Fernando VI* [exh. cat.], Madrid, Biblioteca Nacional, 2004.

SOTELO AND PACHECO 2001. M. E. Sotelo and R. Pacheco, "La Biblioteca de la Universidad Complutense de Alcalá (Siglos XVI–XIX)" in *Pasajes de cultura escrita*, Anexos de Signo 4, Alcalá de Henares, Universidad, 2001, 127–53.

TUZZI 2000. Hans Tuzzi, *Collezionare libri*, Milano, Edizioni Sylvestre Bonnard, 2000.

Keys to the Evolution of the Armorial Bindings of Patrimonio Nacional
Valentín Moreno Gallego

ANDRÉS 1969. Gregorio de Andrés, *El cretense Nicolás de la Torre, copista griego de Felipe II. Biografía, documentos, copias, facsímiles*, Madrid, Monasterio de San Lorenzo del Escorial, 1969.

CASTAÑEDA 1934. Vicente Castañeda, "La biblioteca del Marqués de Moya (Notas sobre el arte de la encuadernación en España)", *Anuario del Cuerpo Facultativo de Archiveros, Bibliotecarios y Arqueólogos*, I, (1934), 309–18.

CASTAÑEDA 1958. Vicente Castañeda, "La biblioteca del marqués de Moya: notas sobre el arte de la encuadernación en España", *Boletín de la Real Academia de la Historia*, 142 (1958), 79–142.

CÁTEDRA 2002. Pedro M. Cátedra, *Nobleza y lectura en tiempos de Felipe II. La biblioteca de don Alonso Osorio, Marqués de Astorga*, Valladolid, Junta de Castilla y León, 2002.

CLAVERÍA 2006. Carlos Clavería, *Reconocimiento y descripción de encuadernaciones antiguas*, Madrid, Arco Libros, 2006.

CSABA 1992. Csapodi Csaba, *Biblioteca Corviniana*, Budapest, 1992.

DI PIETRO LOMBARDA 2002. Paola Di Pietro Lombarda, "Mattia Corvino e i suoi emblema", in *Nel segno del Corvo*, Modena, 2002, pp. 117–28.

Documento pintado 2000. *El documento pintado: cinco siglos de arte en manuscritos* [exh. cat.], Madrid, Museo Nacional del Prado-AFEDA, 2000

DOMÍNGUEZ BORDONA AND AINAUD 1958. Jesús Domínguez Bordona and Juan Ainaud, *Ars Hispaniae*, vol. XVIII: *Miniatura. Grabado. Encuadernación*, Madrid, Plus Ultra, 1958.

GONZALO SÁNCHEZ-MOLERO 1998. José Luis Gonzalo Sánchez-Molero, *La "Librería Rica" de Felipe II: estudio histórico y catalogación*, [San Lorenzo del Escorial], R.C.U. "Escorial-María Cristina", Servicio de Publicaciones, [1998].

GONZALO SÁNCHEZ-MOLERO 2005. José Luis Gonzalo Sánchez-Molero, *Regia Bibliotheca. El libro en la corte española de Carlos V*, Mérida, Editora Regional de Extremadura, 2005, 2 vols.

GONZALO SÁNCHEZ-MOLERO 2010a. José Luis Gonzalo Sánchez-Molero, "La Heráldica de Felipe II, Príncipe, a través de las encuadernaciones de su librería rica", *Hidalguía*, 338 (2010), 76–117.

GONZALO SÁNCHEZ-MOLERO 2010b. José Luis Gonzalo Sánchez-Molero, "La Heráldica de Felipe II, Príncipe, a través de las encuadernaciones de su librería rica", *Hidalguía*, 343 (2010), 841–76.

GONZALO SÁNCHEZ-MOLERO 2011. José Luis Gonzalo Sánchez-Molero, "La Heráldica de Felipe II, Príncipe, a través de las encuadernaciones de su librería rica", *Hidalguía*, 344 (2010), 47–81.

GUIGARD 1870–73. Joannis Guigard, *Armorial du Bibliophile avec illustrations dans le texte*, Paris, Libraire Bachelin-Deflorenne, 1870–73, 2 vols.

HEVESY 1923. A. de Hevesy, *La bibliothèque du roy Mathias Corvin*, Paris, 1923.

HOBSON 1993 [2001]. Anthony Hobson, "The Library of Diego Hurtado de Mendoza", in *Actes et comunications. Association Internationale de Bibliphilie, XVIII Congrès, Madrid, 1993; Transactions. International Association of Bibliophiles, XVIIIth Congress, Madrid, 1993*, Madrid, El Viso for the Association Internationale de Bibliophilie, 2001, pp. 39–52.

HOBSON 1999. Anthony Hobson, *Renaissance Book Collecting: Jean Grolier and Diego Hurtado de Mendoza, Their Books and Bindings*, Cambridge, University Press, 1999.

HUESO ROLLAND 1935. Francisco Hueso Rolland, *Exposición de encuadernaciones españolas, siglos XII al XIX. Catálogo general ilustrado* [exh. cat. Madrid, Sociedad Española de Amigos del Arte], Madrid, Imp. Blass, 1935.

LÓPEZ-VIDRIERO 2003. María Luisa López-Vidriero, "Encuadernación en Palacio: lectura periférica y vestigio del tiempo", *Encuadernación de Arte*, 22 (2003), 4–22.

Menéndez Pidal 1982. Faustino Menéndez Pidal, *Heráldica medieval española, I. La Casa Real de León y Castilla*, Madrid, Hidalguía, 1982.

Menéndez Pidal 1988. Faustino Menéndez Pidal, "Panorama heráldico español. Épocas y regiones en el periodo medieval", in *I Seminario sobre Heráldica y Genealogía*, Zaragoza, Institución Fernando El Católico, 1988, pp. 5–21.

Moreno Gallego 1999. Valentín Moreno Gallego, "Observaciones documentales para la historia de la encuadernación hispana", *Boletín de la Real Academia Española*, LXXIX (1999), 267–88.

Moreno Gallego 2009. Valentín Moreno Gallego, *Super libros reales. Guía para la identificación heráldica en la Real Biblioteca*, Madrid, Patrimonio Nacional, 2009.

Moreno Gallego 2010. Valentín Moreno Gallego, "Heráldica y libro antiguo: breves reflexiones", *Boletín de la Real Academia de la Historia*, CCVII, I (2010), 39–74.

Pélisson-Karro 1998. Françoise Pélisson-Karro, "La Bibliothèque de Pierre-Daniel Huet, évêque d'Avranches, entre la maison professe des jésuites et la Bibliothèque du Roi", in *Mélanges autour de l'histoire des livres imprimés et périodiques*, Paris, Bibliothèque Nationale de France, 1998, pp. 107–30.

Pérez Pastor 1895. Cristóbal Pérez Pastor, *La imprenta en Medina del Campo*, Madrid, n. n. [Sucesores de Ribadeneyra], 1895.

Rico y Sinobas 1941. Manuel Rico y Sinobas, *El arte del libro en España*, Madrid, Escelicer, 1941.

Rubio de Urquía (coord.) 2001. Guadalupe Rubio de Urquía (coord.), *La encuadernación, historia y arte: I Curso "El documento hispánico: Enrique IV-Fernando VII" organizado por Afeda y realizado con la colaboración y patrocinio del Ilustre Colegio Notarial de Madrid y la Fundación Matritense del Notariado*, Madrid, Afeda, 2001.

Saltillo 1934. Miguel Lasso de la Vega y López de Tejada, marqués del Saltillo, "Encuadernaciones heráldicas españolas", *Revista Española de Arte*, III, 1 (1934), 2–35.

Sánchez Mariana 1994. Manuel Sánchez Mariana, "Las encuadernaciones del marqués de Moya", *Encuadernación de Arte*, 4 (1994), 12–18.

Vindel Angulo 1923. Pedro Vindel Angulo, *Grandeza y Gloria Hispana. Bibliófilos célebres. El Marqués de Caracena, 1608–1668*, Madrid, [Sobrinos de los Suc. de M. Minuesa], 1923.

Books for Reading. Commercial Bindings in Parchment and Paper in the Era of the Handpress
Nicholas Pickwoad

Carpallo Bautista 2010. Antonio Carpallo Bautista, *Las encuadernaciones de obra y fábrica del archivo de la catedral de Toledo*, Toledo, Instituto Teológico San Ildefonso, Cabildo Primado de Toledo, 2010.

Clarkson 1982. Christopher Clarkson, *Limp Vellum Binding and Its Potential As a Conservation Type Structure for the Rebinding of Early Printed Books. A Break with Nineteenth and Twentieth Centruy Rebinding Attitudes and Practises*, ICOM, 4th Triennial meeting, Venice, 1982 [reprinted 2005].

Cowie 1828. G. Cowie, *The Bookbinder's Manual: Containing a Full Description of Leather and Vellum Binding*, London, Cowie & Strange, 1828.

***Encuadernaciones artísticas* 2009.** *Encuadernaciones artísticas en el Archivo de la Nobleza* [exh. cat. Toledo, Hospital Tavera], Madrid, Ministerio de Cultura, 2009.

Penney 1967. Clara Penney, *An Album of Selected Bookbindings*, New York, The Hispanic Society of America, 1967.

Pickwoad 1995. Nicholas Pickwoad, "The Interpretation of Bookbinding Structure: an Examination of the Sixteenth-Centruy Bindings in the Ramey Collection in the Pierpont Morgan Library", *The Library*, 6th series, XVII, 3 (September 1995), 209–49. [Reprinted in *Eloquent Witnesses*, ed. Mirjam M. Foot, London, British Library, 2004, pp. 127–70.]

Pugliese 2001. Silvia Pugliese, "Stiff-Board Vellum Binding with Slotted Spine: a Survey of a Historical Bookbinding Structure", *Papier Restaurierung*, 2 (2001), 93–101.

Thomas 1939. Henry Thomas, *Early Spanish Bookbindings, XI–XV Centuries*, London, Bibliographical Society, 1939.

Diego Hurtado de Mendoza
Anthony Hobson

Agustín 1543. Antonio Agustín, *Emendationum et opinionum libri quattuor*, Venice, heirs of Lucantonio Giunta, 1543.

Agustín 1980. Antonio Agustín, *Epistolario*, edited by Cándido Flores Sellés, Salamanca, Universidad de Salamanca, 1980.

ANDRÉS 1790–93. Juan Andrés, *Cartas familiares del abate don Juan Andrés a su hermano D. Carlos Andrés...*, Madrid, Imprenta de Sancha, 1790–93.

ANDRÉS 1804. Juan Andrés, *Antonii Augustini archiepiscopi Tarraconensis* Epistolae *latinae et italicae nunc primum editae*, Parma, Aloysius Mussi, 1804.

ANDRÉS 1961. Gregorio de Andrés (O. S. A.), "Dos listas inéditas de manuscritos griegos de Hurtado de Mendoza", *La Ciudad de Dios*, 174 (1961), 382–89.

ANDRÉS 1964. Gregorio de Andrés, *Documentos para la historia del Monasterio de San Lorenzo el Real de El Escorial*, VII, Madrid, Imprenta Sáez, 1964.

ANDRÉS 1965–67. Gregorio de Andrés, *Catálogo de los códices griegos de la biblioteca de El Escorial*, Madrid, Imprenta Helénica, 1965–67, 2 vols.

ANDRÉS 1968. Gregorio de Andrés, *Catálogo de los códices griegos desaparecidos de la Real Biblioteca de El Escorial*, El Escorial, Imprenta del Monasterio, 1968.

ANTOLÍN 1910–23. Guillermo Antolín (O. S. A.), *Catálogo de los códices latinos de la Real Biblioteca del Escorial*, Madrid, Imprenta Helénica, 1910–23, 5 vols.

BATAILLON 1991. Marcel Bataillon, *Erasme et l'Espagne*, Genève, Droz, 1991.

BATTS 1975. M. S. Batts, "The 18th-Century Concept of the Rare Book", *The Book Collector*, 24 (1975), 381–400.

BERTARELLI AND PRIOR 1902. Achille Bertarelli and David-Henry Prior, *Gli exlibris italiani*, Milano, Hoepli, 1902.

BIBL 1898. Victor Bibl, "Nidbruck und Tanner", *Archiv für österreichische Geschichte*, 85 (1898), 385–430.

BUJANDA, DAVIGNON AND STANEK 1990. J. M. Bujanda, R. Davignon and E. Stanek, *Index des livres interdits*, VIII. *Index de Rome*, Sherbrooke & Geneva, Centre d'études de la Renaissance, 1990.

CASTELLANI 1896–97. C. Castellani, "Il prestito dei codici manoscritti della Biblioteca di San Marco in Venezia", *Atti del R. Istituto Veneto di scienze, lettere ed arti*, 7/8 (1896–97), 311–77.

CAVALCANTI 1967. Bartolomeo Cavalcanti, *Lettere edite e inedite*, edited by Christina Roaf, Bologna, Commissione per i testi in lingua, 1967.

CICERO 1541. Marcus Tullius Cicero, *De philosophia*, edited by Paolo Manuzio, Venice, apud Aldi filios, 1541.

COGGIOLA 1908. Giulio Coggiola, "Il prestito di manoscritti della Marciana dal 1474 al 1527", *Zentralblatt für Bibliothekswesen*, 25 (1908), 47–70.

CRAWFORD 1993. M. H. Crawford (ed.), *Antonio Agustín. Between Renaissance and Counter-Reform*, Warburg Institute Surveys and Texts; 24. London, The Warburg Institute, University of London, 1993.

DE MARINIS 1960. Tammaro De Marinis, *La legatura artistica in Italia nei secoli XV e XVI*, Firenze, Fratelli Alinari, 1960, 3 vols.

DELISLE 1868–81. Léopold Delisle, *Le Cabinet des manuscrits de la Bibliothèque Imperiale*, Paris, 1868–81, 3 vols.

DORMER 1680. Diego Josef Dormer (ed.), *Progresos de la historia en el reyno de Aragón y elogios de Gerónimo Zurita*, Zaragoza, Herederos de Diego Dormer, 1680.

DRAKE AND DRABKIN 1969. Stillman Drake and I. E. Drabkin, *Mechanics in Sixteenth-Century Italy*, Madison, University of Wisconsin Press, 1969.

DURME 1953. Maurice van Durme, *Antoon Perrenot Bisschop van Atrecht, Kardinaal van Granvelle, Minister van Karel V en van Filips II (1517–1586)*, Verhandlingen van de Koninklijke Vlaamse Academie van Wetenschappen, Letteren en Schone Kunsten van België, Klasse der Letteren; 18. Brüssel, Paleis der Academiën, 1953. [Spanish translation: *El cardenal Granvela, 1517–1586*, Barcelona, Teide, 1957].

***Exposición Mendoza del Infantado* 1958.** *Exposición de la biblioteca de los Mendoza del Infantado en el siglo XV con motivo de la celebración del V centenario de la muerte de Don Íñigo López de Mendoza, Marqués de Santillana*, Madrid, [n. n.], 1958.

FABRI DE PEIRESC 1992. N.-C. Fabri de Peiresc, *Lettres à Claude Saumaise et à son entourage (1620–1637)*, edited by Agnes Bresson, Firenze, Olschki, 1992.

FERRARY 1992. Jean-Louis Ferrary (ed.), *Correspondance de Lelio Torelli avec Antonio Agustín et Jean Matal (1542–1553)*, Como, Edizioni New Press, 1992.

FOOT 1978–2010. Mirjam M. Foot, *The Henry Davis Gift: A Collection of Bookbindings. A Catalogue of South European Bindings*, London, The British Library & Oak Knoll Press, 1978–2010.

FOSCARINI 1752. Marco Foscarini, *Della letteratura veneziana*, Padova, Stamperia del seminario, appresso G. Manfrè, 1752.

FOUCAULT 1962, see **NICANDER OF CORCYRA 1962**.

FOUCAULT 1972. J.-A. Foucault, "Après l'annés Erasme. Souvenirs d'un contemporain", *Bulletin de l'Association Guillaume Budé*, IV, I (1972), 102–3.

FOULCHÉ-DELBOSC 1898. R. Foulché-Delbosc, "Mechanica de Aristotiles", *Revue hispanique*, 5 (1898), 365–405.

GONZÁLEZ PALENCIA AND MELE 1941–43. Ángel González Palencia and Eugenio Mele, *Vida y obras de don Diego Hurtado de Mendoza*, Madrid, Instituto Valencia de don Juan, 1941–43, 3 vols.

GRAUX 1880. Charles Graux, *Essai sur les origines du fond grec de l'Escurial*, Paris, Durand frères, 1880.

HARLFINGER 1971. D. Harlfinger, *Die Textgeschichte des pseudo-Aristotelischen Schrift Peri atómon grammōn*, Amsterdam, 1971.

Hobson 1975a. Anthony Hobson, "The *iter italicum* of Jean Matal", in *Studies in the Book Trade in honour of Graham Pollard*, Oxford, The Bibliographical Society, 1975, pp. 33–61.

Hobson 1975b. Anthony Hobson, "Two Venetian Bindings for Diego Hurtado de Mendoza", *The Book Collector* (1975), 33–36.

Hobson 1979. Anthony Hobson, "Jacobus Apocellus", *Transactions of the Cambridge Bibliographical Society*, 7/3 (1979), 279–83.

Hobson 1989. Anthony Hobson, *Humanists and Bookbinders: The Origins and Diffusion of the Humanistic Bookbinding 1459–1559, with a Census of Historiated Plaquette and Medallion Bindings of the Renaissance*, Cambridge & New York, Cambridge University Press, 1989.

Hobson 1999. Anthony Hobson, *Renaissance Book Collecting: Jean Grolier and Diego Hurtado de Mendoza, their Books and Bindings*, Cambridge, Cambridge University Press, 1999.

Hoffmann 1983. Philippe Hoffmann, "La Collection de manuscrits grecs de Francesco Maturanzio érudit pérugin (ca. 1443–1518)", *Mélanges de l'École française de Rome, Moyen Age-Temps Modernes*, 95 (1983), 89–147.

Irigoin 1977. Jean Irigoin, "Les Ambassadeurs à Venise et le commerce des manuscrits grecs dans les années 1540–50", in *Venezia centro di mediazione tra Oriente e Occidente (secoli XV–XVI)*, eds. H.G. Beck, M. Manoussacas and A. Pertusi, Firenze, L. S. Olschki, 1977, vol. II, pp. 399–415.

Jenny 1964. Beat Rudolf Jenny, "Arlenius in Basel", *Basler Zeitschrift für Geschichte und Altertumskunde*, 64 (1964), 5–45.

Josephus 1544. Flavius Josephus, *Opera* [Greek], Basel, Hieronymus Froben and Nicolaus I Episcopius, 1544. [Edited by Arnoldus Arlenius].

Labowsky 1979. Lotte Labowsky, *Bessarion's Library and the Biblioteca Marciana*, Rome, Edizioni di Storia e Letteratura, 1979.

Laguna 1543. Andrés de Laguna, *Castigationes in tralationem octo ultimorum librorum De re rustica, Constantini Caesaris, per Ianum Cornarium physicum editam*, Coloniae, prope D. Lupum Ioannes Aquensis excudebat, 1543.

Legrand 1885–1906. Émile Legrand, *Bibliographie hellénique ou description raisonnée des ouvrages publiés par des Grecs aux XVe et XVIe siècles*, Paris, E. Leroux, 1885–1906.

Llorente 1817–18. Juan Antonio Llorente, *Histoire critique de l'Inquisition d'Espagne*, Paris, chez Truttel et Wurtz, Delaunay [et] P. Mongie, 1817–18, 4 vols.

Madius and Lombardus 1550. Vincentius Madius and Bartholomaeus Lombardus, *In Aristotelis librum de poetica communes explicationes*, Venetiis, in officina Erasmiana Vincentii Valgrisi, 1550.

Maicas 1986. Pilar Maicas, *Juan de Arce, humanista español*, Madrid, Fundación Universitaria, 1986.

Malaguzzi 2008. Francesco Malaguzzi, *De libris compactis. Legature di pregio in Piemonte. L'Astigiano e il Torinese*, Torino, Centro Studi Piemontesi, 2008.

Marcel 1899. Gabriel Marcel, "Les Origines de la carte d'Espagne", *Revue Hispanique*, 6 (1899), 163–93.

Menéndez y Pelayo 1945. Marcelino Menéndez y Pelayo, *Historia de los heterodoxos españoles*, Buenos Aires, Emecé, 1945, 6 vols.

Morales 1575. Ambrosio de Morales, *Las antigüedades de las ciudades de España*, Alcalá de Henares, Juan Íñiguez de Lequerica, 1575.

Morisse 1995. Gerard Morisse, "Johann Wild et l'Inquisition espagnole", *Gutenberg-Jahrbuch 1995*, 159–74.

Müller 1884. K. K. Müller, "Neue Mittheilungen über Janos Lascaris und die Mediceische Bibliothek", *Zentralblatt für Bibliothekswesen*, I (1884), 333 fols.

Nader 1979. Helen Nader, *The Mendoza Family in the Spanish Renaissance 1350 to 1550*, New Brunswick, NJ, Rutgers University Press, 1979.

Nicander of Corcyra 1962. Nicander of Corcyra, *Voyages*, ed. J.-A. de Foucault, Paris, Les Belles Lettres, 1962.

Nicander of Corcyra 1841. Nicander of Corcyra, *The Second Book of the Travels of Nicander Nucius, of Corcyra*, translated by J. A. Cramer, London, Printed for the Camden Society by J. B. Nichols and son, 1841.

Nixon 1956. Howard M. Nixon, *Broxbourne Library: Styles and Designs of Bookbindings from the Twelfth to the Twentieth Century*, London, Maggs Brothers, 1956.

Omont 1887. Henri Omont, "Deux registres de prêts de manuscrits de la bibliothèque de Saint-Marc à Venise (1545–1559)", *Bibliothèque de l'École des Chartes*, 48 (1887), 651–86.

Paschini 1958. Pio Paschini, "Cinquecento romano e riforma cattolica", *Lateranum*, 24/1–4 (1958), I–XII, 1–283.

Pettas 1974. William A. Pettas, "Nikolaos Sophianós and Greek Printing in Rome", *The Library*, 5/29 (1974), 206–13.

Piccolomini 1547. Alessandro Piccolomini, *In mechanicas questiones Aristotelis, paraphrases paulo quidem plenior [...] Eiusdem commentarium de certitudine mathematicarum disciplinarum*, Roma, Antonio Blado, 1547.

Pickwoad 1991. Nicholas Pickwoad, "Italian and French Sixteenth-Century Bookbindings", *Gazette of the Grolier Club*, 43 (1991), 55–80.

Pollard 1910–11. A. W. Pollard, "Book-Collecting", in *Encyclopedia Britannica*, 11th edition, 1910–1911, vol. 4, pp. 221–25.

Porro 1983. Antonietta Porro, "Pier Vettori editore di testi greci", *Italia medioevale e umanistica*, 26 (1983), 307–58.

REICHENBERGER 1969. A. G. Reichenberger, "The Marqués de Santillana and the Classical Tradition", *Iberomania*, 1 (1969), 5–34.

REUSCH 1886. F. H. Reusch, *Die Indices librorum prohibitorum*, Bibliothek des Litterarischen Vereins in Stuttgart; 176, Tübingen, 1886.

ROSE AND DRAKE 1971. Paul Lawrence Rose and Stilman Drake, "The *Mechanica* in the Renaissance", *Studies in the Renaissance*, 18 (1971), 65–104.

RUNCIMAN 1968. Steven Runciman, *The Great Church in Captivity: A Study of the Patriarchate of Constantinople from the Eve of the Turkish Conquest to the Greek War of Independence*, Cambridge, Cambridge University Press, 1968.

SCHIFF 1970. Mario Schiff, *La Bibliothèque du marquis de Santillane*, Paris, Libraire Emile Bouillon [Charlon-Sur-Saone: E. Bertrand], 1905. [Republished: Amsterdam, Van Heusden, 1970.]

SPEAKE 1993. Graham Speake, "Janus Lascaris's Visit to Mount Athos in 1491", *Greek Roman and Byzantine Studies*, 34 (1993), 325–30.

SPIVAKOVSKY 1970. Erika Spivakovsky, *Son of the Alhambra: Don Diego Hurtado de Mendoza (1504–1575)*, Austin & London, Texas Press, 1970.

ST CLAIR 1983. William St Clair, *Lord Elgin and the Marbles*, London, Oxford University Press, 1983. [Second edition; first edition: London, OUP, 1967].

THOMAS 1954. Henry Thomas, "Diego Hurtado de Mendoza and His Plaquette Bindings", in *Studies in Art and Literature for Belle da Costa Greene*, Princeton, Princeton University Press, 1954, pp. 474–80.

TINTO 1965. Alberto Tinto, "Nuovo contributo alla storia della tipografia greca a Roma nel secolo XVI: Nicolò Sofiano", *Gutenberg-Jahrbuch 1965*, 171–75.

TINTO 1970. Alberto Tinto, "The History of a Sixteenth-Century Greek Type", *The Library*, 5/25 (1970), 285–93.

TOOLEY 1939. R. V. Tooley, "Maps in Italian Atlases of the Sixteenth Century", *Imago Mundi*, 3 (1939), 12–47.

TREWEEK 1957. A. P. Treweek, "The Manuscript Tradition of the "Collectio Mathematica", *Scriptorium*, II (1957), 195–233.

VALENTINELLI 1868–73. Giuseppe Valentinelli, *Bibliotheca manuscripta ad S. Marci Venetiarum. Codices Mss. Latini*, 6 vols., Venetiis, ex typographia Commercii, 1868–73.

VÁZQUEZ AND ROSE 1935. Alberto Vázquez and R. Selden Rose, *Algunas cartas de don Diego Hurtado de Mendoza escritas 1538–1552*, New Haven, Yale University Press, 1935.

VOGEL AND GARDTHAUSEN 1909. Marie Vogel and Victor Gardthausen, *Die griechischen Schreiber des Mittelalters und der Renaissance*, Leipzig, O. Harrasowitz, 1909. [Republished: Hildesheim, G. Olms, 1966].

ZARCO CUEVAS 1924. Julián Zarco Cuevas (O.S.A.), *Catálogo de los manuscritos castellanos de la Real Biblioteca de El Escorial*, Madrid, Imprenta Helénica, 1924, 3 vols.

ZORZI 1987. Marino Zorzi, *La libreria di San Marco. Libri, lettori, società nella Venezia dei Dogi*, Venezia, Mondadori, 1987.

ZULUETA 1939. Francisco de Zulueta, *Don Antonio Agustin*, Glasgow, Jackson, 1939.

Three Aspects of French Bindings in the Spanish National Heritage Collections

Isabelle de Conihout and Pascal Ract-Madoux

BÉLY 2001. Lucien Bély, "La rivalité avec la France: les historiens et l'impossible duel entre François I et Charles Quint", in Francisco Sánchez-Montes González and Juan Luis Castellano Castellano (coords.), *Carlos V, europeísmo y universalidad* [international conference, Granada, May 2000], Madrid, Sociedad Estatal para la Conmemoración de los Centenarios de Felipe II y Carlos V, 2001, vol. 3, pp. 75–84.

BENNASSAR 1995. Bartolomé Bennassar, "Les relations entre Charles Quint et François Ier", in *François Ier, du château de Cognac au trône de France*, symposium in Cognac, September and November 1994, *Annales du GREH*, 16 (1995), pp. 229–36.

BROOKER 1997. T. Kimball Brooker, "Bindings Commissioned for Francis I's 'Italian Library' with Horizontal Spine Titles Dating from the Late 1530s to 1540", *Bulletin du bibliophile*, 1 (1997), 33–91.

CHECA 1997. Fernando Checa, *Las maravillas de Felipe II*, Madrid, Banco Bilbao Vizcaya, 1997.

CHECA 2010. Fernando Checa (dir.), *Los inventarios de Carlos V y la familia imperial /The Inventories of Charles V and the Imperial Family*, Madrid, Fernando Villaverde Ediciones, 2010, 3 vols.

COLIN 1975. Georges Colin, "Sur quelques reliures de Christophe Plantin découvertes récemment", *The Book collector*, 24, 1 (Spring 1975), 58–64.

COLIN 1990. Georges Colin, "La Fourniture de reliures par l'Officine plantinienne", *Gutenberg Jahrbuch* (1990), 346–59.

COLIN AND NIXON 1968. Georges Colin and Howard Nixon, "La Question des reliures de Plantin", in *Studia Bibliographica in honorem Herman de la Fontaine Verwey*, Amsterdam, Hertzberger, 1968, pp. 56–89.

Cockx-Indestege and Storm van Leeuwen 2005. Elly Cockx-Indestege and Jan Storm van Leeuwen (eds.), with the collaboration of Dirk Imhof, *Estampages et dorures: six siècles de reliure au Musée Plantin-Moretus* [exh. cat. Antwerp, Museum Plantin-Moretus], Anvers, Musée Plantin-Moretus, 2005.

Deprouw 2011. Stéphanie Deprouw (dir.), *Geoffroy Tory: Imprimeur de François 1er, graphiste avant la lettre* [exh. cat. Ecouen, Musée de la Renaissance], Paris, RMN, 2011.

Gonzalo Sánchez-Molero 1998. José Luis Gonzalo Sánchez-Molero, *La "Libreria rica" de Felipe II. Estudio histórico y catalogación*, San Lorenzo de El Escorial, EDES, 1998.

Gonzalo Sánchez-Molero 2006. José Luis Gonzalo Sánchez-Molero, "'Au roy catolique': Un poema desconocido de Jean-Antoine de Baïf a Felipe II (1573)", *Bibliothèque d'Humanisme et Renaissance*, LXVIII, 3 (2006), 553–61.

Haan 2010. Bertrand Haan, *Une paix pour l'éternité, la négociation du traité du Cateau-Cambrésis*, Madrid, Casa de Velázquez, 2010.

Hobson 1970. Geoffrey D. Hobson, *Les Reliures à la fanfare. Le problème de l'S fermé*, Amsterdam, 1970 [second edition augmented by A. R. A. Hobson].

Hobson 1989. Anthony Hobson, *Humanists and Bookbinders: The Origins and Diffusion of the Humanistic Bookbinding 1459–1559, with a Census of Historiated Plaquette and Medallion Bindings of the Renaissance*, Cambridge & New York, Cambridge University Press, 1989.

Hobson 1999. Anthony Hobson, *Renaissance Book Collecting: Jean Grolier and Diego Hurtado de Mendoza, their Books and Bindings*, Cambridge, Cambridge University Press, 1999.

Jacquart 1981. Jean Jacquart, *François Ier*, Paris, Fayard, 1981.

Jordan Gschwend 2010. Annemarie Jordan Gschwend, "Ma meilleur sœur: Leonor of Austria, Queen of Portugal and France", in Fernando Checa (dir.), *Los inventarios de Carlos V y la familia imperial /The Inventories of Charles V and the Imperial Family*, Madrid, Fernando Villaverde Ediciones, 2010, pp. 2569–92.

Jordan Gschwend and Wilson-Chevalier 2007. Annemarie Jordan Gschwend and Kathleen Wilson-Chevalier, "L'épreuve du mécénat: Aliénor d'Autriche, une reine de France effacée?", in *Patronnes et mécènes en France à la Renaissance*, Saint-Etienne, Publications de l'Université de Saint-Étienne, 2007, pp. 341–80.

Knecht 2002. R. J. Knecht, "Charles V's Journeys through France, 1535–40", in J. R. Mulryne and E. Goldring (eds.), *Court Festivals of the European Renaissance, Art, Politics and Performances*, Aldershot, Ashgate, 2002, pp. 153–70.

Laffitte and Le Bars 1999. Marie-Pierre Laffitte and Fabienne Le Bars, *Reliures royales de la Renaissance. La librairie de Fontainebleau 1544–1570*, Paris, BNF, 1999.

Le Bris 2002. Sabrine Le Bris, "Dubuisson", in P. Fouché et al. (dirs.), *Dictionnaire encyclopédique du livre*, Paris, 2002, vol. I, p. 828.

Le Person 2005. Xavier Le Person, "A Moment of 'Resverie': Charles and Francis I's Encounter at Aigues-Mortes (July 1538)", *French History*, 19, 1 (2005), 1–27.

Michon 1951. Louis-Marie Michon, *La Reliure française*, Paris, Larousse, 1951.

Michon 1956. Louis-Marie Michon, *Les Reliures mosaïquées du XVIIIe siècle*, Paris, Société de la reliure originale, 1956.

Mousset and De Jonge 2007. Jean-Luc Mousset and Krista De Jonge (eds.), *Un prince de la Renaissance. Pierre-Ernest de Mansfeld 1517–1604* [exh. cat. Luxembourg, Musée National d'Histoire et d'Art], Luxembourg, 2007, 2 vols.

Nixon 1971. Howard Nixon, *Sixteenth Century Gold-Tooled Bookbindings in the Pierpont Morgan Library*, New York, The Morgan Library, 1971.

Paillard 1879. C. Paillard, *Le Voyage de Charles-Quint en France en 1539–1540 d'après les documents originaux*, Paris, V. Palmé, 1879.

Sallmann 2004. Jean-Michel Sallmann, *Charles V, L'Empire éphémère*, Paris, Payot, 2004.

Saulnier 1960. Verdun-Louis Saulnier, "Charles Quint traversant la France: ce qu'en dirent les poètes français", in J. Jacquot (ed.), Les Fêtes de la Renaissance, vol. II: *Fêtes et cérémonies au temps de Charles Quint (IIe Congrès de l'Association Internationale des Historiens de la Renaissance, Brussels, Antwerp, Ghent and Liege, 2–7 September 1957)*, Paris, Éditions du Centre National de la Recherche Scientifique, 1960, pp. 207–33.

Vekene 1978. Émile van der Vekene (ed.), with the collaboration of Pavlina Hamanová and Howard M. Nixon, *Les Reliures aux armoiries de Pierre Ernest de Mansfeld* [exh. cat. Luxembourg, Bibliothèque nationale de Luxembourg], Luxembourg, Éd. de l'imprimerie Saint-Paul, 1978.

Voet 1969–72. Leon Voet, *The Golden Compasses. The History of the House of Plantin-Moretus*. Amsterdam, London, New York, 1969–72, 2 vols.

Bodonian Bindings
Pedro M. Cátedra

Barocelli 1988. Francesco Barocelli (ed.), *Il Correggio e la Camera di San Paolo*, Milano, Electa, 1988.

Beraldi 1895–97. Henri Beraldi, *La reliure du xixe siècle*, Paris, L. Conquet, 1895–97, 4 vols.

Bertini 1982 and 1983. Giuseppe Bertini, "P. M. Paciaudi e la formazione della Biblioteca Palatina di Parma (Ricerca sugli aspetti materiali della fondazione di una biblioteca nella seconda metà del xviii secolo)", *Aurea Parma*, 66 (1982), 243–64; 67 (1983), 14–41, 161–79. There is an "estratto" of all the instalments with consecutive pagination, which is used here.

Caroselli 2010. Francesco Caroselli, *Legature del Settecento nella Biblioteca Provinciale dei Cappuccini di Bologna. I fondi dei conventi emiliani*, Bologna, Biblioteca Frati Minori Cappuccini, 2010.

Cátedra 2010. Pedro M. Cátedra, *G. B. Bodoni y los españoles, I. Epistolario de Leandro Fernández de Moratín y Giambattista Bodoni, con otras cartas sobre la edición de "La comedia nueva" (Parma, 1796)*, Parma and San Millán de la Cogolla, Instituto de Historia del Libro y de la Lectura, Instituto Biblioteca Hispánica del CiLengua, Parma, Museo Bodoniano and Biblioteca Palatina, 2010.

Cátedra in press [a]. Pedro M. Cátedra, *La encuadernación en Parma en el último tercio del siglo xviii: el fondo bodoniano de la Real Biblioteca*. In press.

Cátedra in press [b]. Pedro M. Cátedra, "Las bibliotecas bodonianas del Conde de Floridablanca y del infante don Antonio Pascual de Borbón, con el epistolario entre Giambattista Bodoni y Manuel Losada y Quiroga". In press.

Cátedra in press [c]. Pedro M. Cátedra, *Bodoni y los españoles, III. Los clásicos griegos de Bodoni. Epistolario de Manuel María Rodríguez Aponte & Giambattista Bodoni*. In press.

Ciavarella 1965. Angelo Ciavarella (ed.), *Manuale tipografico del cavaliere Giambattista Bodoni*, Parma, Franco Maria Ricci, 1965, 3 vols.

Ciavarella 1979. Angelo Ciavarella (ed.), *De Azara - Bodoni*, Parma, Museo Bodoniano, 1979, 2 vols.

Ciavarella et al. 1990. Angelo Ciavarella, Corrado Mingardi, James Moseley and Bernard Chevalier, *Il "Cimelio" di Bodoni. L'opera e il suo stampatore*, introductory volume to the facsimile edition of the Cimelio, copy illuminated by Pasini and intended for Napoleon and his wife, Verona, Valdonega, 1990.

Ciravegna 1942. Marino Ciravegna, "G. B. Bodoni e l'abate di Caluso", *Annali Alfieriani*, 1 (1942), 229–43.

De Lama 1816. G. De Lama, *Vita del cavaliere Giambattista Bodoni, tipografo italiano, e catalogo cronologico delle sue edizione*, Parma, Stamperia Ducale, 1816, 2 vols.

Gorreri 1990. Silvana Gorreri, "Bodoni e le legature", in *Bodoni. L'invenzione della semplicità*, Parma, Ugo Guanda, 1990, pp. 231–51.

Gorreri 1994. Silvana Gorreri, "Louis Antoine Laferté: legatore francese in Parma (Un contributo alla storia della legatoria del Settecento in Italia)", *Rara Volumina*, 2 (1994), 45–64.

Gorreri 1995. Silvana Gorreri, "Legature bodoniane e alla bodoniana", in Giancarla Bertero (ed.), *La collezione bodoniana della Biblioteca Civica di Saluzzo*, Collegno, Gianfranco Altieri Editore, 1995, pp. 60–63.

Gotor 1992. José Luis Gotor, "José Nicolás de Azara, editor de clásicos con Bodoni", in *Italia e Spagna nella cultura del '700*, Roma, Accademia dei Lincei, 1992, pp. 87–118.

Jimeno Puyol 2010. Dolores Jimeno Puyol (ed.), *José Nicolás de Azara. Epistolario (1784–1804)*, Madrid, Castalia, 2010.

López-Vidriero 2002. María Luisa López-Vidriero, *Speculum Principum. Nuevas lecturas curriculares, nuevos usos de la Librería del Príncipe en el Setecientos*, Salamanca, Instituto de Historia del Libro y de la Lectura, 2002.

Mingardi 1990. Corrado Mingardi (ed.), *Essai de caractères russes di Giambattista Bodoni*, Milano, Edizioni il Polifilo, 1990.

Mingardi 1994. Corrado Mingardi, "L'impresa bodoniana della Camera di San Paolo nei disegni di Francisco Vieira", *Bolletino del Museo Bodoniano*, 8 (1994), 201–18.

Moreno 2008. Valentín Moreno, *Super libros reales: guía para la identificación heráldica en la Real Biblioteca*, Madrid, Patrimonio Nacional, 2008.

Raggi 2005. Giuseppina Raggi, "Vieira, Rosaspina, Bodoni: Uma relação ininterrupta entre a Emilia italiana e Portogallo", in *Francisco Vieira o portuense 1765–1805*, Porto, Museu Nacional Soares dos Reis, 2005.

Servolini 1958. Luigi Servolini, *Autobiografia di G. B. Bodoni in duecento lettere inedite all'incisore Francesco Rosaspina*, Parma, Comune di Parma, 1958.

Brugalla 1977. Emilio Brugalla, *El arte en el libro y en la encuadernación*, Bilbao, La Gran Enciclopedia Vasca, 1977.

Brugalla 1986. Emilio Brugalla, "El arte de la encuadernación en España", in *La encuadernación artística española actual* [exh. cat. Madrid, Biblioteca Nacional], Madrid, Ministerio de Cultura, Dirección General del Libro y Bibliotecas, 1986, pp. 27–33.

Brugalla 1996. Emilio Brugalla, *En torno a la encuadernación y las artes del libro: diez temas académicos*, Madrid, Clan (*Técnicas artísticas*, 7), 1996.

Brugalla 2000. Emilio Brugalla, *Tres ensayos sobre el arte de la encuadernación*, Madrid, Ollero & Ramos, 2000.

Carrión 1992. Manuel Carrión, "La encuadernación artística española", in *Encuadernaciones españolas en la Biblioteca Nacional* [exh. cat.], Madrid, Biblioteca Nacional; Julio Ollero, 1992, pp. 9–16.

Carrión 1996. Manuel Carrión, "La encuadernación española en los siglos xix y xx", in *Historia ilustrada del libro español. La edición moderna, siglos XIX y XX*, directed by Hipólito Escolar Sobrino, Madrid, Fundación Sánchez Ruipérez, 1996, pp. 491–539.

Cotoner 2002. Luisa Cotoner Cerdó, "La biblioteca 'Arte y Letras', primera aproximación", *Quaderns. Revista de traducció*, 8 (2002), 17–27.

Devauchelle 1961. Roger Devauchelle, *La Reliure en France des ses origines à nos jours*, Paris, Jean Rousseau-Girard, 1961, 3 vols.

Devauchelle 1995. Roger Devauchelle, *La reliure*, Paris, Éditions Filigranes, 1995.

Devaux 1977. Yves Devaux, *Dix siècles de reliure*, Paris, Pygmalion, 1977.

Escolar 1966. Hipólito Escolar, *La edición moderna siglos xix y xx*, Madrid, Fundación Sánchez Ruipérez, 1966.

López Serrano 1947. Matilde López Serrano, "Notas características de la encuadernación moderna", *Revista Bibliográfica y Documental*, I, 1 (1947), 7–15.

López Serrano 1950. Matilde López Serrano, *Biblioteca de Palacio: encuadernaciones*, Madrid, Afrodisio Aguado, 1950.

López Serrano 1951. Matilde López Serrano, "El encuadernador catalán del siglo xix Pedro Doménech", *Revista Bibliográfica y Documental*, V, 1–4 (1951), 167–78.

López Serrano 1972. Matilde López Serrano, *La encuadernación española: breve historia*, Madrid, ANABA, 1972.

López-Vidriero 2002. María Luisa López-Vidriero, "*Deka te basilea*. Juego de números", in *Presente y futuro de la encuadernación española*, Madrid, Afeda, 2002, pp. 57–58.

Miquel y Planas 1915–20. Ramón Miquel y Planas, "El renaixement de l'encuadernació d'art a Barcelona", *Bibliofilia*, 2 (1915–20), 383–87.

Miquel y Planas 1933. Ramón Miquel y Planas, *El arte en la encuadernación*, Barcelona, Cámara Oficial del Libro, 1933.

Moreno Gallego 2008. Valentín Moreno Gallego, *Super libros reales: guía para la identificación heráldica en la Real Biblioteca*, Madrid, Patrimonio Nacional, 2008.

Quiney 2007. Aitor Quiney, "Josep Pascó. Un esteta vinculado a las artes del libro catalán", *Encuadernación de Arte*, 29 (2007), 35–49.

Rovira y Adán 1901–02. Jaime Rovira y Adán, "Don Pedro Doménech y Saló: encuadernador", *Revista Gráfica* (1901–02), 56–60.

Satué 1993. Enric Satué, *El diseño gráfico*, Madrid, Alianza Forma, 1993.

Trenc Ballester 1977. Eliseo Trenc Ballester, *Las artes gráficas de la época modernista en Barcelona*, Barcelona, Gremio de Industrias Gráficas, 1977.

Uzanne 1898. Octave Uzanne, *L'art dans la décoration extérieure des livres en France et à l'étranger*, Paris, L. Henry May, 1898.

Vélez 1999. Pilar Vélez, "La encuadernación industrial del modernismo en Catalunya", *Encuadernación de Arte*, 13 (1999), 71–74.

Wood 1899–1900. Esther Wood, "La reliure commerciale anglaise", *Le Studio* (1899–1900), 1–9.

Patrimonio Nacional Bindings Reproduced in This Book

Figs. 2 and 3
Firdwasi, [*Shah-Nama / Abul Qasim Mansur Firdusi*]. Fifteenth century (1485). RB II/3218.
Fifteenth-century Persian binding in brown sheepskin with an envelope flap. Outer and inner covers, flap and reverses decorated and polychromed; the side of the flap that is folded over the bookblock edges is divided into cartouches; marbled endleaves; silk guards.

Fig. 6
Liber Missarum reginae Elisabeth Catholicae. Fifteenth-century manuscript. RBME Vitrinas 8.
Gothic-Mudejar binding covered in a crimson taffeta case whose covers bear two circular badges in translucent enamel surrounded by a border of small pearls in gilt silver, with the arms of Castile and Aragon before the conquest of Granada. The binding itself, covered by the case, is decorated with four stamps of animals in volutes and surrounded by Mudejar bandwork.

Fig. 11
Francisco Jover, *Sanctiones ecclesiasticae tam synodicae quam pontificiae in tres classes distinctae ... / per Franciscum Iouerium* .... Parisiis: apud Audoënum Paruum ..., 1555 (ex chalcographia Ioannis Sauetier). RBME 83.IX.12.
Artistic gold-tooled and illuminated binding, possibly by Christopher Plantin; illuminated shield with the coats of arms of England and Spain on both covers.

Fig. 13
Saint Thomas Aquinas, *Regimiento de príncipes.* Fifteenth-century manuscript. RB II/3569.
Gothic-Mudejar fifteenth-century (last quarter) binding in goatskin over wood; in cartouches: "Ave María"; brooch marks. Edges gilt; vellum endleaves. Inverted binding.

Fig. 15
Breviarium Caroli imperatoris. Toledo, 1515–45. 4 vols. Sixteenth-century manuscript (1515–35). RBME Vitrinas 4–7.
Bound in wooden boards covered in claret cordovan with Mudejar decoration consisting of a central bandwork star that extends across the whole cover. The work is comprised of four volumes which are differently decorated, though in the same Mudejar style. They bear the stamp of the Monastery.

Fig. 16
Torello Saraina, *Torelli Saraynae Veronensis leg. doct. De origine et amplitudine ciuitatis Veronae; eiusdem* .... Veronae ...: ex officina Antonii Putelleti, 1540. RBME 39.I.37.

Natural-colour calfskin binding over wooden boards with a triple frame stamped with rolls of heads and floral motifs. The central rectangle contains two vases with plants and the royal seal of Spain, all in blind. Gilt edges displaying the grid motif of the Monastery.

Figs. 18 and 23
Carissimo in Christo filio nostro Ferdinando hispaniarum Regi Catholico, Benedictus PP. XIV .... Italy (?): n. n., c. 1753. RB I/E/84.
Eighteenth-century (second half) Rococo binding in red morocco; on the covers, double gold fillet and gold floral border with decorated corners by Antonio Sancha, framing a large oval with green mosaic work, floral adornments and in the centre the supralibros of Philip V; fully ornamented spine *alla greca*; gilt board and bookblock edges; marbled endleaves with gold-stamped decoration. Royal bookplate of the period of Ferdinand VII.

Fig. 19
Universidad de Salamanca, *A los Reyes nuestros señores D. Fernando VII y Doña María Josefa Amalia de Saxonia, en testimonio de amor, júbilo y homenage por su venturoso enlace / la Universidad de Salamanca.* [Spain: n. n.], [1819]. RB I/G/354.
Nineteenth-century Empire-style binding in dyed sheepskin. On the front cover: gold tooling and mosaic in *pasta valenciana*, in the centre the crowned cypher (FMA) of King Ferdinand VII and Queen Maria Josefa Amalia. On the back cover: gold tooling and frame with a curtain figure. Gilt board edges, squares and bookblock edges. Bound by Antonio Suárez.

Fig. 20
Planes o Estados que manifiestan el número de pleytos, causas y expedientes ... despachados en el año 1816 por las salas civiles y del crimen de la Real Audiencia de Valencia .... Valencia: Benito Monfort, 1817. RB I/G/355.
Eighteenth-century Empire-style Valencian "curtain" binding in morocco. In the corners, squares of ochre *pasta valenciana*; curtain in blue and yellow *pasta valenciana*. Gilt board edges, squares and bookblock edges; orange moiré endleaves. Label: "Vicente Beneyto lo enquadernó en Valencia". Royal bookplate of the period of Ferdinand VII.

Fig. 21
Noticia de la función fúnebre en que el Regimiento provincial de Oviedo solemnizó el once de Marzo de ... mil ochocientos diez y nueve la muerte de ... Doña María Isabel Francisca de Braganza, Reyna de España. Oviedo: Petregel y C., 1819. RB XIV/2905.

Empire-style Spanish "curtain" binding. Red long-grained morocco; gold decoration and *pasta valenciana* mosaic work in several shades of ochre and blue. Roll-worked frame, the most prominent roll featuring elements of the collar of the order of Charles III, characteristic of the binder Miguel Ginesta. Ochre and pale blue curtains. Decorated spine without raised bands; gilt board edges, squares and bookblock edges; blue paper endleaves with dots and gold stars.

Fig. 24

Decretos del Rey Don Fernando VII: año primero de su restitucion al trono de las Españas: se refieren todas las reales resoluciones generales que se han expedido por los diferentes ministerios y consejos desde 4 de mayo de 1814 hasta fin de diciembre de igual año / por Don Fermin Martin de Balmaseda. Vol. 17. Madrid: en la Imprenta Real, 1832. RB I/G/241.

Cathedral-style panel-stamped red morocco binding by Antonio Suárez Jiménez; covers with triple gold fillet framing a Gothic window decorated in blue, green and purple; smooth, fully decorated spine with black morocco labels: "Decretos del Rey y Reina Q.D.G., 1932", "17"; gold roll decoration on board edges and squares; edges gilt. Binder's label: "Encuadernado por Antonio Suarez, Librero de Cámara de S.M. y de la Real Imprenta".

Fig. 25

[Uniformes del Ejército de Rusia]. Nineteenth century (1857). RB FOT/26.

Nineteenth-century Romantic-style armorial binding. Malachite and gold-plated silver. Case made out of a whole sheet of malachite. In the centre, the cypher "YII" surmounted by the royal crown. On the back cover, decorative corner pieces. The covers are articulated by means of three green velvet spine straps with applied gold mounts. Fore-edge gilt. Interior lined in moiré. On the inside of the upper border, goldsmith's stamps: "J.V.", "84" and stamp with the arms of St Petersburg on the front; "A.M. [Alexandr Nikolaevich Mitin] 1857", "84", "J.V." and stamp of the arms of St Petersburg on the back. Gift of Mariano Téllez-Girón, general and ambassador of Spain in Russia, together with a table and armchair (inv. nos. 10052205, 10052206).

Fig. 26

Fina García Marruz, *¿De qué, silencio, eres tú silencio? /Fina García Marruz; edición e introducción de Carmen Ruiz Barrionuevo; selección de Fina García Marruz*. Salamanca-Madrid: Ediciones Universidad de Salamanca; Patrimonio Nacional, 2011. RB XIV/2957.

Artistic binding displaying the royal cypher. Executed in 2011 by Obradoiro Penumbra in beige *veau*, painted. Three-dimensional composition of bands made of inlaid pieces of Asturian jet. Black leather endbands to match the jet. Pastedowns made of the same painted leather. Suede flyleaf. Guards made of the same paper as the book. On the front cover, at the lower end, the title in small letters; on the back cover, in the middle and diagonally, the name of the author in small letters. At the bottom of the front turn-in, the date; at the bottom of the back turn-in, "o.penumbra". Rigid case in printed buckram reflecting the initial design for the decoration of the book.

Fig. 27

Clemens Reynerus, *Apostolatus benedictorum in Anglia siue Disceptatio historica de antiquitate Ordinis Congregationisque monachorum nigrorum S. Benedicti in regno Angliae ...*. Duaci: ex Officina Laurentii Kellami ..., 1626. RB IX/6424.

Bound in dyed sheepskin. Stamp of Joaquín Ibáñez, chantre of Teruel. Royal bookplate of the period of Ferdinand VII. Manuscript bookplate: "Collegij Soctis Iesu Louany".

Fig. 28

Constitución política de la Monarquia española: promulgada en Cádiz á 19 de Marzo de 1812. Cadiz: dicho año en la Imprenta Real, [1812]. RB III/7062.

Original nineteenth-century binding (1812) in gold paper with semé pattern in relief; edges gilt.

Fig. 29

Constitución política de la Monarquia española: promulgada en Cádiz á 19 de Marzo de 1812. Cadiz: dicho año en la Imprenta Real, [1812]. RB PAS/2793.

Empire-style red morocco binding; on the covers, composition formed by small squares at the corners in green mosaic joined by gold fillets, surrounded on the inside by roll-impressed gold plant motifs; spine with tooling in the manner of bands and small adornments representing a boat in the spine panels; board edges gilt; inner covers in green tissue paper decorated with a gold border; edges gilt. Royal bookplate of the reign of Ferdinand VII.

Figs. 30 and 31

Epistolai diaphórōn philosóphōn. rētórōn. sophistōn. ex pròs tois eikosi: ōn tà onómata en tē hexēs heurēseis selidi = Epistolae diuersorum philosophorum. oratorum. Rhetorum sex & viginti: quorum nominainse quenti in venies Pagina. Venetiis: apud Aldum, 1499.

RB I/39:

Bound in *pasta valenciana* by Miguel Ginesta Haro (September 1852); marbled edges; marbled endleaves. Stamp: "inventariado por las Cortes. 1874".

RB I/45:

Bound in leather; blind-tooled fillet frame on the covers with plant motifs at the corners surrounding the supralibros of the Monastery of El Escorial; spine with raised bands, blind tooling and paper label: "Epistolae diversiorum Graec"; edges gilt and crown gauffered on the fore-edge. Royal bookplate of the period of Ferdinand VII. Manuscript annotation on side edge: "50, Ep., Epistolai".

RB I/51:
Nineteenth-century binding in *pasta valenciana*, probably by Santiago Martín; gilt board edges and yellow bookblock edges; marbled endleaves.

Fig. 32
Marco Polo, *Historia de las grandezas y cosas marauillosas de las Prouincias Orientales* .... En Caragoça: por Angelo Tauanno, 1601. RB VI/586.
Parchment binding. Manuscript bookplate: "de Don Francisco Blanco y de Domingo Guynez Gossez del Pi". Stamp of Joaquín Ibáñez, chantre of Teruel.

Fig. 33
Etymologikon mega kata alphabēton, pany ōphelimon/ [Márkou mousoúrou ...]. En Enetíais: analōmasi ... Nikoláou bla[st]ou [to]u krē[tò]s [: ... Annēs thyga[tr]òs t[ou] ... Louka notara: ... pónō dé k[aí] dexiótēti, Zacharí[ou] kalliérgou t[ou] krētós, 1499.
RB I/2:
Bound in dyed sheepskin with a gold border of plant motifs on the covers; spine with gold tooling and red morocco label: "Etimologia graecae"; gilt board edges and marbled edges; marbled endleaves. Stamp: "Inventariado por las Cortes. 1874".
RB I/3:
Bound in brown leather and, on the covers, "tree" marbled leather. Gold border of plant motifs on the covers, probably by Pascual Carsí; spine with gold tooling and red morocco label: "Etymol otikon"; gold board edges and marbled edges; marbled endleaves. Manuscript annotation on back of endleaf: "H. 6691".
RB I/4:
Nineteenth-century binding in *pasta valenciana*. Floral border in gold on the covers, probably by Santiago Martín; yellow edges; marbled endleaves.

Fig. 34
Rodrigo Sánchez de Arévalo, Bishop of Palencia, *Compendiosa historia hispánica: in qua agitur de eius situ & descriptione* .... [Romae]: Vdalricus Gallus ... eundem librim impressi, [1470]. RB I/119.
Bound in green dyed sheepskin; gold fillet, cat's tooth roll and wavy ribbon border decoration on covers; spine with raised bands and gold tooling and red morocco label: "Roderici santii hist. hispanic."; gilt board and bookblock edges; marbled endleaves. Stamp of Joaquín Ibáñez, chantre of Teruel. Label of Charles IV's library: "Rey N. S. I-J-3". Royal bookplate of the period of Ferdinand VII glued over the previous label. Stamp: "Inventariado por las Cortes. 1874".

Fig. 35
Abraham Ortelius, *Theatro de la tierra universal / de Abraham Ortelio, Cosmographo d'el Rey Nuestro Señor: con sus declaraciones traduzidas d'el Latin.* Anveres: por Christoval Plantino, 1588. RB V/1553.

Eighteenth-century binding in mottled sheepskin. Provenance: Count of Gondomar according to II/2619, f. 19v. Royal bookplate of the period of Ferdinand VII.

Fig. 36
Scipione Ammirato, *Discorsi del Signor Scipione Ammirato Sopra Cornelio Tacito* .... In Vinezia: per Filippo Giunti, 1599. RB V/2396:
Binding in *pasta española*; spine with gold tooling and red morocco label: "Ammira Sopra C. Tacit."; gilt board edges and red bookblock edges. Stamp of Joaquín Ibáñez, chantre of Teruel. Royal bookplate of the period of Ferdinand VII.
RB PAS/ARM1/24:
Bound in parchment; manuscript in ink on spine: "Ammirato, Discursos del Ammirato". Manuscript annotation on front cover: "nº 40". From the Count of Gondomar's library.
RB III/340:
Nineteenth-century binding in *pasta valenciana* with gold border on covers by Santiago Martín; gilt board edges and marbled bookblock edges; marbled endleaves.

Fig. 37
María Jesús de Ágreda, *Sacra Rituum Congregatione ... a Sanctissimo Domino Nostro Benedicto XIV deputata in causa tirasonen. beatificationis et canonizationis ... Sor. Mariae à Jesu de Agreda* .... Romae: ex Typographia Rev. Camerae Apostolicae, 1747. RB III/1691.
Eighteenth-century Italian Rococo-style binding in morocco. In the centre, supralibros of Charles III; gilt board edges and squares; gilt edges with guards; brocade paper endleaves painted yellow with pomegranate and flower decoration, oxidised, signed: "Augsburg bey G.C. Stoy". Label: "Caxon I. G.". Label of Charles IV's library: "Rey N. S. III. L. 2", glued over the previous one. Royal bookplate of the period of Ferdinand VII.

Fig. 38
Ottavio Antonio Baiardi, *Prodromo delle antichita d'Ercolano alla maesta del re delle Due Sicilie Carlo infante di Spagna.* In Napoli: nella Regale Stamperia Palatina, 1752. RB VIII/9704.
Eighteenth-century Neapolitan Rococo-style binding in morocco. On the cover, royal supralibros of Charles III. Gilt squares and bookblock edges; brocade paper endleaves painted green. Label: Caxon I. D. Label of Charles IV's library: "Rey N. S." Royal bookplate of the period of Ferdinand VII. Stamp: "Inventariado por las Cortes. 1874".

Fig. 39
Biblia sacra vulgatae editionis: tomus III. Parisiis: apud Fredericum Leonard, typographum regium, 1705. RB IV/2966.
Eighteenth-century Rococo-style binding in morocco; on the covers, medallion in coloured paint, protected by a sheet of transparent talc, with the royal supralibros of Philip V; gilt board edges, squares and bookblock edges; blue silk endpapers. Royal bookplate of the period of Ferdinand VII.

Fig. 40
Philipp Clüver, *Philippi Cluveri Sicilia antiqua ... item Sardinia et Corsica* .... Lugduni Batavorum: ex Officina Elseviriana, 1619. RB V/32.
Seventeenth-century binding in mottled leather. On the cover, supralibros of Pierre-Daniel Huet, bishop of Avranches.

Fig. 41
Miguel de Medina, *Disputationum de indulgentiis, aduersus nostræ tempestatis haereticos, ad patres s. Concilij Tridentini* .... Venetiis: ex officina Stellæ, Iordani Zileti, 1564. RBME 6.V.43.
Toledan binding in purple calfskin with a roll-impressed animal border between a double Franciscan cord motif and another border of the same cord. In the centre, an oval medallion displaying the coat of arms of Spain above the crowned imperial eagle. Quadruped animals at the corners. Gilt and gauffered edges. Traces of ties for fastening.

Figs. 43 and 44
Livre d'Heures d'après les Manuscrits de la Bibliothèque Royale. Paris: Auguste Fontaine, 1878. RB XIV/2922.
Nineteenth-century armorial binding (1878). Grolier-style neo-Renaissance. Natural morocco colour. On the covers, ribbon border in blue leather, interwoven with a gold fillet forming an oval central medallion surrounded by four rectangular caissons; in the corners, coats of arms of Spain in gold. In the upper caissons, gold-tooled fleurs-de-lis. In the central medallion, the royal shield of Spain (quartered shield of Saint Ferdinand) in leather mosaic work with the heraldic colours, gold olive branches all over the surface. Spine with raised bands, decorated with caissons of alternate gold-tooled lion, castle and fleur-de-lis motifs. Gold label with the title inscribed in the second panel: "Livre /d'heures". Inside covers of blue morocco with gold semé pattern of castles, lions and fleurs-de-lis. On the head and tail edges, the Bourbon shield; on the fore edge, the Spanish coat of arms. Signed at the foot of the front inside cover: "Chambulle-Duru". Register embroidered in silver, four white moiré ribbons adorned with silver fleurs-de-lis.

Fig. 45
Mateo de las Nogueras y Fuente, *Oracion panegyrica, en aplauso de Maria Santissima, con el titulo de el Rosario*. En Madrid: en la Imprenta de Lorenzo Mojados, 1743. RB PAS/2861.
Eighteenth-century Rococo-style binding in morocco. In the centre of the covers, royal arms of Philip V; edges gilt; marbled endleaves. Label of the library of Charles IV: "Rey N. S. II E 5". Royal bookplate of the period of Ferdinand VII glued over the previous label.

Fig. 46
Francisco Satorre y Carbonell, *Suaristica, aristotelea, contentiosa, et experimentalis Philosophia*. Valentiae: Chalcographiâ Josephi Thomae Lucas ..., 1755. RB I/E/135.
Eighteenth-century Rococo-style binding in morocco; on the covers, supralibros of Ferdinand VI, probably by Antonio de Sancha, after the English model in royal heraldry. Royal bookplate of the period of Ferdinand VII.

Fig. 47
Giovanni Antonio Cavazzi, *Relation historique de l'Ethiopie occidentale* .... A Paris: chez Charles-Jean-Baptiste Delespine le Fils ..., 1732. RB V/2452.
Eighteenth-century neoclassical-style binding in natural morocco. Supralibros of Paulin Prondre de Guermantes, President of the Cour des Comptes (1713); red edges, blue silk register; marbled endleaves. Bookplate: "De LL. AA. RR. les Princes d'Espagne". Royal bookplate of the period of Ferdinand VII. Stamp: "Inventariado por las Cortes. 1874". Stamp: "P.F.C." Stamp: "Propriété des trios".

Fig. 48
Recueil de différentes recettes. Eighteenth-nineteenth centuries. RB II/4572.
Seventeenth-century Baroque-style binding "à la Duseuil" in French *veau*. On the cover, royal coat of arms of Anne of Austria. Gilt edges and squares. Reused binding.

Fig. 49
See figs. 126–29

Fig. 50
Regula et constitutiones fratrum sacri ordinis beatae Mariae de Mercede redemptoris captivorum. [Salmanticae]: Cornelius Bonardus excudebat Salmanticae, 1588. RBME 10.V.22.
Calfskin binding with gold tooling, double polygonal frame with scroll and animal roll. Royal coat of arms in the centre of the cover, in a rectangle. Edges gilt and gauffered.

Fig. 51
Hermann Silberberg, *[Marche de couronnement]*, [c. 1902]. RB MUS/MSS/1410.
Leather binding; in the centre of the front cover, royal coat of arms of Alfonso XIII in relief and painted in colour; edges gilt; green and gold flowered paper endleaves. Stored in a brown card case lined with quilted green moiré.

Fig. 52
Antoine-Siméon-Gabriel Coffinieres, *Le Code Napoléon expliqué par les décisions suprêmes de la Cour de cassation et du Conseil d'État*. A Paris: chez Garnery, Libraire, rue de Seine, Hôtel Mirabeau ..., 1809. RB VIII/16346.
Nineteenth-century neoclassical binding in morocco; on the front cover, royal supralibros with the imperial coat of arms and eagle, probably of Joseph Bonaparte; gilt board edges, squares and bookblock edges. Royal bookplate of the period of Ferdinand VII. Stamp in red ink: "J. B. Grand Electeur". Stamp: "Inventariado por las Cortes. 1874".

Fig. 53
Juan de Herrera, *Sumario y Breve declaracio[n] de los diseños y estampas de la fabrica de San Lorencio el Real del Escurial.* Madrid: por la viuda de Alonso Gomez, 1589. RB I/B/107.
Sixteenth-century Baroque-style binding in parchment with tie fastenings by Juan de Sarriá; on the cover, coat of arms of Francisco Pérez de Cabrera y Bobadilla, Marquis of Moya. Bookplate with the coat of arms of Richard Ford. Ford's manuscript signature on bookplate.

Fig. 54
Pontificale Romanum / Clementis VIII Pont. max. iussu restitutum atque editum, nunc primùm typis Plantinianis emendatiùs recusum. Antuerpiae: ex officina Plantiniana: apud Balthasarem Moretum, & viduam Ioannis Moreti, & Io. Meursium, 1627. RBME 61.V.13.
Bound in parchment. Manuscript bookplate of the RBME on title page.

Fig. 55
Achille Gagliardi, S. I., *Catechismo della fede cattolica, con vn compendio per fanciulli.* In Milano: nella Stamperia di Michel Tini, 1584. RB IX/8282.
Parchment binding with cloth fastenings; manuscript in ink on spine; edges gilt. From the library of the Count of Gondomar. Stamp: "Inventariado por las Cortes. 1874". Note pasted over colophon on final page [4] "ad instanza di Pietro Tini libraro al segno del Giglio". *Olim* ms. Gondomar: "Sal. 3ª, Est. 14, Cax. 3ª".

Fig. 56
Domingo de Soto (O. P.). *Annotationes in commentarios Ioannis Feri Moguntinensis super Euangelium Ioannis ....* [Salamanca]: excudebat Andreas à Portonariis, 1554. RB I/D/163.
Sixteenth-century archival binding in parchment; manuscript in ink on spine: "Soto in Feru[m] in Ioan". Provenance: Count of Gondomar.

Figs. 57 and 58
Libro de memoria de los libros que se imbian a las Indias este año de 1595, [1595–1613]. RBME 186.VI.4.
Parchment binding.

Fig. 59
Jean Hotman, *The Ambassador / [by Hotman].* Printed at London: by V[alentine] S[immes] for Iames Shawe, 1603. RB PAS/ARM4/59.
Seventeenth-century parchment binding. Cut down. Provenance: Count of Gondomar.

Fig. 60
Christoph Gewold, *Genealogia Serenissimor. Boiariae Ducum et quorundam genuinae effigies à Wolffg. Kiliano Aug± aeri inscisae /[Christophoro Gewoldo].* Augustae Vindelicorum: apud Saram Mangiam viduam, 1620. RB IX/5080.

Seventeenth-century stitched parchment binding. Spine with manuscript annotation: "Genealogia Ducum Bavaria". Provenance: Count of Gondomar.

Fig. 61
Iustificacion del medio, que la señora duquesa de Medina de Rioseco propone, para el desempeño de la casa del almirante de Castilla su hijo, y paga de sus acreedores. En Madrid: por Luis Sanchez ..., 1607. RBME 67.IX.2.
Stitched parchment binding. Manuscript bookplate of the RBME. Bookplate of Fray Pedro de los Ángeles on the endleaf.

Figs. 62 and 68
Johannes de Sacro Bosco, *La sphere / de Iehan de Sacrobosco; traduicte de Latin en langue Francoyse ... [par Martin de Perer].* A Paris: par Iehan Loys, 1546. RB I/D/225 (1).
Sixteenth-century parchment binding; manuscript in ink on spine: "Sphere de Jo. de Sacrobosco in franc." Provenance: Count of Gondomar.

Fig. 63
Wolfgang Musculus, /*Commentariorum in Euangelistam Ioannem heptas prima [-tertia & postrema].* Basileae: apud Bartholomaeum Westhemerum, 1545. Vol. 2. RBME 66 IX.20–21.
Parchment binding. Parchment endleaf from reused French medieval document.

Figs. 64 and 65
Manuel Abad Illana, *Historia del gran padre y patriarca San Norberto, fundador del Orden candido Premonstratense ....* En Salamanca: por Eugenio Garcia de Honorato y S. Miguel ..., 1755. RBME 64.IX.3.
Parchment binding.

Figs. 66 and 67
Albertus de Saxonia, *Questiones subtilissime Alberti de Saxonia in libros de celo et mundo.* Venetijs: Boneti d[e] locatellis Bergome[n]sis: impensa v[er]o nobilis viri Octauiani scoti, 1492. RBME 81.IX.21.
Parchment binding.

Fig. 69
Andreas Schottus (S. I.), *Itinerarii Italiae Germaniaeque libri IIII ....* Coloniae Agrippinae: sumptibus Bernardi Gualtheri, 1620. RB PAS/ARM1/223.
Seventeenth-century binding in parchment of the period with thongs. On the spine cover: "Schotti/Itinerar." Provenance: Count of Gondomar.

Fig. 70
Pierre François Sweerts, *Selectae christiani orbis deliciae ex vrbibus, templis, bibliothecis et aliunde.* Coloniae Agrippinae: sumptibus Bernardi Gualteri, 1625. RB PAS/ARM1/304.
Bound in parchment over cartonnage. From the library of the Count of Gondomar. *Olim* ms. Gondomar: "Sal. 2ª, Est. 10, Cax. 1º".

Fig. 71
Michele Timoteo, *In Diuinum Officium trecentum quaestiones in decem tractatus partitae* .... Venetiis: apud Franciscum Zilettum, 1581. RB PAS/ARM1/198.
Bound in parchment with leather fastenings; manuscript spine with leather comb linings: "Timotei in Diuinum officium". From the library of the Count of Gondomar. Manuscript bookplate on endleaf: "Ex libris M. J. osiis". *Olim* ms. Gondomar: "Sal. 3ª, Est. 12, Cax. 1º".

Fig. 72
Francisco Cartagena, *Doctoris Francisci Carthagenae sacrae theologiae professoris, De Praedestinatione et reprobatione Angelorum & hominum. Tractatvs in discvrsvs dvodecim divisvs* .... Romae: Apud Vincentium Accoltum, 1581. RB PAS/ARM1/135.
Sixteenth-century parchment binding with leather fastenings; spine with manuscript parchment inner reinforcement and leather outer reinforcement. Label in ink: "Carta[gena] De predestinatione et ...". Provenance: Count of Gondomar.

Fig. 73
Marcin Kromer, Bishop of Ermland, *De falsa lutheranorum siue Euangelicorum nostri temporis, et vera Christi religione libri duo primi de quatuor Polonica lingua ante octo et novem annos conscriptis atque editis, nunc recens Latina lingua donati & aucti*. Parisiis: apud Gulielmum Guillard & Almaricum Warancore, 1560. RB PAS/ARM6/197.
Parchment binding with remains of leather fastenings; manuscript in ink on spine: "Martin Cromerus de falsa lutheranos, et vera Cristi religione". From the library of the Count of Gondomar. *Olim* ms. Gondomar deleted: "Sal. 3ª, Est. 10, Cax. 1º".

Fig. 74
Xenophon, *[Select Work]*. [Lyon]: expensis honesti viri Bartholomei trot, 1511. RB PAS/ARM1/38.
Parchment binding with remains of leather fastenings. From the library of the Count of Gondomar. Manuscript annotation on endleaf: "arco. 5, libro. 56". *Olim* ms. Gondomar: "Sal. 1ª, Est. 1, Cax. 1º".

Fig. 76
Ubaldino Malavolti, *I servi nobili*. In Siena: appresso Salvestro Marchetti, 1605. RB PAS/ARM4/70.
Parchment binding with ties. On the spine: "I Serui Nobili". From the library of the Count of Gondomar. *Olim* Gondomar: "Sal. 1ª, Est. 12, Cax. 1º".

Fig. 77
Antonio Pérez, *Pentateuchum fidei, siue Volumina quinque* .... Matriti: apud Viduam Ildephonsi Martin, 1620. RBME 70.IX.2.
Parchment binding with loop and toggle fastenings.

Fig. 78
José de Sarabia y Lezana, *Annales de la sagrada Religion de Santo Domingo* .... En Madrid: por Juan Garcia Infanzon ..., 1709. Vol. 2. RBME 65.IX.18–19.
Parchment binding with leather loop and white glass bead fastening. Censor's note on endleaf: "Prohibido según el suplemento del índice expurgatorio de 1738".

Fig. 79
Bulario de la Sagrada Religion de la Hospitalidad de San Juan de Dios aprobada por San Pio Quinto .... En Madrid: en la imprenta de Geronimo de Estrada y Junco, 1702. RBME 67.IX.4.
Parchment binding with leather loop and coloured glass bead fastening.

Fig. 80
Manuel Mariano Ribera, *Real patronato de los serenissimos señores Reyes de Espana en el Real y Militar Orden de Nuestra Señora dela Merced* .... Barcelona: por Pablo Campins ..., 1725. RBME 65.IX.13.
Parchment binding with leather loop and ivory bead fastening.

Fig. 81
Luis de Salazar y Castro, *Historia genealógica de la casa de Silva* .... En Madrid: por Melchor Alvarez y Mateo de Llanos, 1685. Vol. 2. RBME 64.IX.4–5.
Parchment binding with leather loop and "turk's head" knot fastening.

Figs. 82 and 83
José Ortiz Cantero, *Directorio cathechistico, glossa vniversal de la doctrina Christiana ... tomo primero* y *Directorio cathechistico, el Christiano ilvstrado en la fe ... tomo segundo*. En Madrid: por Diego Martinez Abad ..., 1705–8. RBME 73.IX.2–3.
Parchment binding. Two volumes with the label written in ink on the spine, dividing the contents between the two volumes. Bookplate of the RBME on title page.

Fig. 84
Hermenegildo de San Pablo (Jer.), *Origen y continuacion de el Instituto y Religion Geronimiana* .... En Madrid: en la Imprenta Real, 1669. RBME 66.IX.23.
Seventeenth-century parchment binding.

Fig. 85
Juan Gómez Bravo, *Catalogo de los Obispos de Cordoba, y breve noticia historica de su Iglesia Catedral, y Obispado / escrito por el Doct. D. Juan Gomez Bravo ... con un Apendice de los Obispos, que lo han sido de esta Ciudad, despues de la muerte del autor de esta obra ... Tomo I*. Cordoba: en la oficina de Juan Rodriguez ..., 1778. RBME 72.IX.10.
Parchment binding with fore-edge ties.

Fig. 86
Theophilactus Simocattus, *Historia de rebus gestis Mauricii imperatoris*. Manuscrito, 1453. RBME Φ.I.12.
Plaquette binding. Provenance: Diego Hurtado de Mendoza.

Figs. 87 and 88
Dante Alighieri, *Comedia del diuino poeta Danthe Alighieri: con la dotta e leggiadra spositione di Christophoro Landino ...; aggiuntaui di nuouo vna copiosissima tauola ....* In Vinegia: ad instantia di M. Gioanni Giolitto da Trino, 1536. RBME 24.XIII.13.
Bound in goatskin with vertical lines and plaquettes. Provenance: Diego Hurtado de Mendoza.

Figs. 89 and 90
Albert Krantz, *Wandalia*. Coloniae Agrippinae: Iohannes Soter alias Heil ex Bentzheim & socij impresserunt, 1519. RBME 42.VI.24.
Bound in red and black goatskin with gold tooling and plaquettes. Provenance: Diego Hurtado de Mendoza.

Fig. 91
Alessandro Caravia, *Il sogno dil Caravia*. In Vinegia: nelle case di Giouann'Antonio di Nicolini da Sabbio, 1541. RBME Mesa 11–II–7.
Sixteenth-century Renaissance-style binding in red morocco. On the covers, blind- and gold-tooled fillet frames, the interior with fleurons and gold corner pieces, a lozenge inscribed with tortoises in the corners, and in the centre a symmetrical composition of plant motifs and volutes in gold, all flanked by small blind-tooled leaves; spine with raised bands flanked by gold fillets, which extend over the covers forming wedges, and blind-tooled fillets; paper endleaves. Provenance: Diego Hurtado de Mendoza

Fig. 93
Aristotle, *Opera, graece*. Vol. I. Venetiis: Aldus Manutius, 1495, vol. I. RBME 54.IV.3.
Venetian plaquette binding. Copy dedicated to Alberto Pio, Prince of Carpi. Provenance: Diego Hurtado de Mendoza.

Fig. 94
Claudius Ptolomy, *Geographia*. Roma: Bernardino dei Vitali para Evangelista Tosini, 1508. RBME 69.V.5.
Bound in red goatskin with gold tooling. Copy dedicated to Cardinal Robert Britto. Provenance: Diego Hurtado de Mendoza.

Fig. 95
Giacomo Sannazzaro, *De partu Virginis*. Neapoli: per Antonium Fretiam Corinaldinum ..., 1526. RBME 64.VI.13.
Bound in red goatskin with plaquettes. Provenance: Diego Hurtado de Mendoza.

Fig. 97
Guillaume Budé, *Guillielmi Budaei Parisiensis Secretarij Regij libri V de Asse ....* Venetiis : in aedibus Aldi, et Andreae Asulani soceri, 1522 mense Septembris. RBME 177.IV.14.
French binding in dark blue morocco with gold-tooled decoration.

Fig. 98
Titus Lucretius Carus, *T. Cari Lucretii poetae ac philosophi vetustiss. De rerum natura libri VI*. Lugduni: apud Seb. Gryphium, 1534. RBME 16.V.31.
Medium-blue morocco binding, artistic gold tooling with supralibros of the RBME.

Fig. 99
Marcus Tullius Cicero, *M. T. Ciceronis orationum: volumen primum*. Parisiis: apus Simonem Colinaeum, 1538, mense Iulio. RBME 63.IV.2.
French artistic binding.

Fig. 100
Marcus Tullius Cicero, *M. T. Ciceronis orationum: volumen tertium*. Parisiis: apud Simone[m] Colinaeum, 1532, mense Octobri RBME 63.IV.3.
French artistic binding.

Fig. 101
Marcus Tullius Cicero, *M. Tullii Ciceronis ad Titum Pomponium Atticum, ad M. Brutum & ad Quintum fratrem, epistolaru[m] libri XX ....* Parisiis: apud Simonem Colinaeum, 1532, mense Iunio (1532, mense Maio). RBME 75.IV.3.
French binding in blue morocco with gold tooling and title on the spine.

Figs. 102 and 103
Angelo Poliziano, *Angeli Politiani Opera ....* Lugduni: apud Seb. Gryphium, 1536–37, 3 parts in 2 vols. RBME 37 VI.31–32.
Bound in white sheepskin with different gold ornamentation on both volumes. Bookplate of the RBME engraved on all four covers.

Fig. 104
Saint Thomas Aquinas, *Divi Thomae Aquinatis ... Commentarij in Soliloq[ui]a, sive hymnos davidicos ... / recognitione Campestri ... restituti*. Lugdu[ni]: In edibus Jacobi myt: impensis Jacobi q. Fra[n]scici de giu[n]ta et sociorum florentinoru[m], 1520, ad Idus Augusti. RBME 177.V.11.
French calfskin binding with gold-stamped decoration. Bookplate of the RBME.

Fig. 105
Marcus Fabius Quintilianus, *M. Fabii Quintiliani Institutionum oratoriarum libri XII; eiusdem Declamationum liber ....* Lugduni: apud Seb. Gryphium, 1536. RBME 80.IV.1.
French artistic binding in bronze green morocco with gold tooling.

Fig. 106
Aulus Gellius, *Auli Gellii luculentissimi scriptoris Noctes Atticae*. Lugduni: apud Seb. Gryphium, 1534. RBME 56.IV.22.
Bound in bronze green morocco with gold tooling; on the spine: "A. GELLIUS".

Fig. 107
Ambrosius Aurelius Theodosius Macrobius, *Macrobii Aurelii Theodosii viri consularis In Somnium Scipionis libri II; Saturnaliorum libri VII / nunc denuo recogniti & multis in locis aucti*. Excud. Lugd.: Seb. Gryphius Germ., 1532. RBME 56.IV.23.
Bound in bronze green morocco with blind tooling.

Fig. 108
Marcus Tullius Cicero, *M. Tullij Ciceronis Rhetoricorum libri quatuor ad Herennium; item M. Tullij Ciceronis de inuentione libri duo*. Parisiis: ex officina Simonis Colinaei, 1539. RBME 80.IV.5.
Artistic binding in bronze green morocco with gold tooling.

Fig. 109
Guillaume Budé, *Annotationes Gulielmi Budaei ... in quatuor & viginti Pandectarum libros ...: per autore[m] diligentissime recognitae & auctae*. Basileae: apud Thomam Volffium, 1534. RBME 74.IV.10.
French binding in citron morocco with gold tooling.

Fig. 110
Decius Junius Juvenal, *Iun. Iuuenalis et Auli Persii Flacci satyrae / iam recens recognitae, simul ac adnotatiunculis ...*. Lugduni: apud Seb. Gryphium, 1538; Iacopo Sannazaro, *Opera omnia ...*. Lugduni: apud Seb. Gryphium, 1536. RBME 17.V.1.
French artistic binding.

Fig. 111
Paulus Jovius, *Histoires de Paolo Iovio ... sur les choses faictes et auenues de son temps en toutes les parties du monde / traduictes de latin en françois par le seigneur du Parq Champenois*. À Lion: chez Guillaume Rouille ..., 1552–55. RBME 40.I.13.
French artistic binding in citron morocco and black paint, with coloured coat of arms on both covers and gold decoration on covers and spine.

Fig. 112
Jean-Antoine de Baïf, *Euvres en rime / de Ian Antoine de Baif ...*. A Paris: pour Lucas Breyer ..., 1572–73. 4 vols. RBME Mesa 5.II.11–14.
French artistic binding in red morocco with gold tooling. Copy dedicated to Philip II by the author.

Figs. 113 and 114
Francisco Tarafa, *Francisci Taraphae Barcinonen. De origine ac rebus gestis Regum Hispaniae liber, multarum rerum cognitione refertus*. Antuerpiae: in aedibus Ioannis Steelsij, 1553 (typis Ioannis Latij). RBME 40.VI.13.
Artistic binding, possibly by Christopher Plantin, illuminated with the royal coat of arms painted on the front cover.

Fig. 115
Rerum à Carolo V Caesare Augusto in Africa bello gestarum commentarij: elegantissimis iconibus ad historiam accommodis illustrati .... Antuerpiae: apud Ioan. Bellerum ..., 1554. RBME 40.VI.18.
Artistic binding possibly by Christopher Plantin, illuminated.

Fig. 116
Gian Michele Bruto, *De rebus a Carolo V Caesare Romanorum Imperatore gestis, Ioannis Michaëlis Bruti oratio*. Antuerpiae: apud Ioannem Bellerum ..., 1555. RBME 39.VI.12.
Flemish artistic binding in blue morocco, with gold-tooled border and ornamentation and inscribed on the front cover: "D. Philippo Princ. Opt. M."

Fig. 117
Ludovico Ariosto, *Orlando furioso: dirigido al Principe Don Philipe nuestro Señor / traduzido en romance castellano por Don Ieronymo de Vrrea*. Imprimiose en ... Anuers: en casa de Martin Nucio, 1549. RBME 30.V.24.
Artistic binding possibly by Christopher Plantin. Censored copy.

Fig. 118
Juan Cristóbal Calvete de Estrella, *El felicissimo viaie del muy alto y muy Poderoso Principe Don Phelippe, Hijo d'el Emperador Don Carlos Quinto Maximo ...*. En Anuers: en casa de Martin Nucio, 1552. RBME 34.I.15.
French artistic binding with gold tooling.

Fig. 119
Christopher Plantin, *Ode au trespuissant et serenissime Prince Philippe II ... Colit ardua virtus*. [Antuerpiae: Christopher Plantin, 1556]. RBME Mesa 9.II.6.
Artistic binding by Christopher Plantin with dedication on front cover: "Diuo Philippo Regi Optimo Max."

Fig. 120
Hubertus Goltzius, *Viuae omnium fere imperatorum imagines a C. Iulio Caes. vsque ad Carolum V et Ferdinandum ...*. Excus. Antuerpiae: cura & aere Huberti Goltz ...: in officina Aegidij Copenij ..., 1557. RBME . 40.IV.5.
French binding in dyed sheepskin with gold tooling and illuminated royal coat of arms.

Fig. 121
Juan de Orozco, *Ioannis Oroscii Regii in Pinciana Curia Consiliarij ... Ad responsa prudentum commentarij ...*. Salmanticae: in aedibus Andreae Portonariis ..., 1558. RBME 32.IV.1.
French artistic binding with royal coat of arms illuminated by hand; on the back cover: "D. Phlippo Hispaniarum Regi Catholic".

Fig. 122
Ivo, Bishop of Chartres, *Pannormia, seu Decretum, D. Iuonis Carnothensis episcopi restitutu[m], correctum, &*

emendatum .... Louanii: ex officina Antonij Maria Bergagne ..., 1557. RBME 25.VI.20.
Binding with boards covered in calfskin, gold tooling, polychromed covers. Edges gilt.

Fig. 123
Flavius Josephus, *Los siete libros de Flauio Iosefo los quales contienen las guerras de los Iudios, y la destrucion de Hierusalem y d'el templo / traduzidos ... por Iuan Martin Cordero* .... En Anuers: en casa de Martin Nucio ..., 1557. RBME 33.V.17.
French artistic binding in dyed sheepskin with painted royal coat of arms.

Fig. 124
Tommaso Fazello, *F. Thomae Fazelli Siculi ... De rebus Siculis decades duae* .... Panormi: ex officina Ioannis Matthaei Maydae, 1558, mense Maio. RBME 60.IX.13.
French artistic binding in green and red morocco, with gold decoration and coloured coat of arms on both covers.

Fig. 125
Pedro Alfonso de Burgos, *Dialogi de immortalitate animae ... / per F. Petrum Alfonsum Bergensem Montis Serrati Monachum* .... Barcinone: apud Claudium Bornat, 1561. RBME 6.V.54.
French binding with bandwork and mosaic.

Figs. 126–29
Almanach Royal: année ... / Laurent d'Houry, éditeur. À Paris: De l'Imprimerie de la Veuve d'Houry; de l'Imprimerie de Le Breton, 1738–58. Bindings by Pierre-Paul Dubuisson. RB PAS/ARM3/30–75.
Brocade: copies grouped together owing to their use of brocade paper in the endleaves. Covers in various shades of morocco with gold decoration, representing the transition from late Baroque to early or mid-Rococo. On the covers, gold fillets or borders, à la dentelle or stamped, featuring different motifs framing a royal coat of arms or cypher in the centre of the cover or simply fleurs-de-lis. Brocade paper endleaves with prominent gold decorative details on paper in shades of blue, pink, green, etc., sometimes with oxidised edges. Copies: PAS/ARM3/33 (1738), 36–37 (1741–42), 40 (1745), 50 (1755).
Mica: deluxe copies linked by their design and decorative techniques, particularly the use of transparent sheets of talc. Pronouncedly Rococo-style bindings in leather decorated with a combination of mosaic work in different coloured leather and metallised paper in bright colours, as well as with gold and transparent sheets of talc to protect the painted ornamental and armorial motifs. The covers display an oval space in the centre for a royal coat of arms or cypher, always of Ferdinand VI; blue or pink silk endleaves. Some signed: "Du Buisson, le Fils relieur Doreur rue St. Jaque a Paris ..." Copies: PAS/ARM3/44–49 (1749–54), 51–53 (1756–58).

Figs. 132–34
Quintus Horatius Flaccus, *Q. Horatii Flacci Opera*. Parma: in aedibus Palatinis, typis Bodonianis, 1791. RB IX/7185.
Eighteenth-century neoclassical style binding in morocco. On the cover, royal supralibros and gold stamp: "S.D.S.Y.D.A." Gilt board edges, squares and bookblock edges; signed on fore-edge square of back cover: "Domenico Guarnaschelli legatore di libri". Royal bookplate of the period of Ferdinand VII. Stamp: "S.D.S.Y.D.A."

Fig. 135
Attributed to Thomas a Kempis, *De imitatione Christi libri quatuor*. Parmae: in aedibus Palatinis, typis Bodonianis, 1793. RB IX/8413.
Late eighteenth-century or early nineteenth-century neoclassical binding in mottled sheepskin in shades of green and ochre; on the covers, *pasta española* frame delimited by gold borders, floral corner adornments; gold tooling on spine, board edges and squares, edges gilt. Copy dedicated to Maria Luisa of Parma.

Fig. 136
Attributed to Thomas a Kempis, *De imitatione Christi libri quatuor*. Parmae: in aedibus Palatinis, typis Bodonianis, 1793. RB IX/7196.
Late eighteenth-century or early nineteenth-century neoclassical binding in granite-marbled sheepskin; on the covers, mottled sheepskin frame in shades of green and ochre delimited by gold fillets, floral corner decoration; gold tooling on spine, board edges and squares, edges gilt. Label of Charles IV's library: "Rey N. S. III. Ll. 1. Royal bookplate of the period of Ferdinand VII". Stamp: "Inventariado por las Cortes. 1874". Copy dedicated to Charles IV.

Fig. 137
Giovanni Gherardo De Rossi, *Pitture di Antonio Allegri detto il Correggio esistenti in Parma nel Monistero di San Paolo*. Parma: nel Regal Palazzo co' tipi Bodoniani, 1800. RB VIII/219.
Late eighteenth-century or early nineteenth-century neoclassical binding in mottled leather with gold fillet and double frame, one marbled and the other green with floral ornaments at the corners separated by gold rolls and a triple gold fillet on covers; gilt board edges, squares and bookblock edges. Royal bookplate of the period of Ferdinand VII.

Fig. 138
Giambattista Bodoni, *Manuale tipografico del cavaliere Giambattista Bodoni*. Parma: presso la Vedova, 1818. Vol. I. RB IV/5477.
Nineteenth-century binding in board. Uncut. Endbands in blue and white linen. Endleaves in blue-painted paper. Royal bookplate of the period of Ferdinand VII.

Fig. 139
Torquato Tasso, *La Gerusalemme liberata / di Torquato Tasso; tomo I [-II]*. Parma: nel Regal Palazzo co' tipi Bodoniani, 1794. Vol. I. RB VIII/6120.

Late eighteenth-century or early nineteenth-century neoclassical binding in morocco, probably by Francisco Cifuentes. Gilt board edges, squares and bookblock edges; and brown moiré endleaves. Stamp: "Inventariado por las Cortes, 1874".

Fig. 140
Giovanni Gherardo De Rossi, *Scherzi poetici e pittorici / [Giovanni Gherardo De Rossi; Giuseppe Tekeira, pittore]*. Parma: co'tipi Bodoniani, 1795. RB VIII/2322.
Late eighteenth-century or early nineteenth-century binding in *pasta valenciana* with gold border by Santiago Martin. Gilt board edges and marbled bookblock edges; marbled endleaves. Stamp: "S.D.S.Y.D.A." Stamp: "Inventariado por las Cortes. 1874".

Fig. 141
Tryphiodorus, *Tryphiodorou Aigyptiou tou grammatikou Iliou alosis*. Parmae: in Aedibus Palatinis, Typis Bodonianis, 1796. RB XIX/8290.
Bound in leather by Santiago Martín, with gold border of plant motifs on the covers; gold fillets, vases and tooling on the spine; gilt board edges, squares and bookblock edges; marbled endleaves. Stamp: "S.D.S.Y.D.A."

Fig. 142
Tryphiodorus, *Tryphiodorou Aigyptiou tou grammatikou Iliou alosis*. Parmae: in Aedibus Palatinis, Typis Bodonianis, 1797. RB VIII/6130.
Late eighteenth-century or early nineteenth-century neoclassical binding in leather by Francisco Cifuentes. Gilt board edges, squares and bookblock edges; brown moiré endleaves. Stamp: "S.D.S.Y.D.A.". Stamp: "Inventariado por las Cortes. 1874".

Fig. 145
[Guía de forasteros de Madrid]. Madrid: [n. n.], 1815. RB CS/4/1.
Bound in mottled sheepskin; half of the front cover features a curtain in greenish blue with gold tooling; in the diagonal half not covered by the curtain, a gold border, and beading all around the cover. Back cover with the same beaded border and an inner border in green leather mosaic; inner rectangle in claret-colour marbled leather, fine border of gold fillet and single beads and central lozenge with two curtain compositions facing different directions, the upper one in greenish blue and the lower one in shades of brown. Gilt board edges and squares, crimson satin endleaves, edges gilt, sky-blue silk register. Bound by Antonio Suárez Jiménez.

Fig. 146
[Guía de forasteros de Madrid]. Madrid: [n. n.], 1819. RB CS/4/1.
"Curtain"-style binding in greyish-white waxed board with a spaced border, green *pasta valenciana* mosaic at the corners and a floral border with oval shield motifs in the spaces; curtain in central rectangle in shades of brown, with gold tassels, outside the space a three-bead-and-chain border. On the back cover the curtain is replaced by a rectangle in green *pasta valenciana* with chestnut *pasta valenciana* at the corners. Spine with a gold-tooled composition at the bottom and red title label. Gilt squares, sky-blue endleaves, edges gilt. Bound by Antonio Suárez Jiménez.

Fig. 148
Francisco José Fabre, *Descripcion de las alegorías pintadas en las bóvedas del Real Palacio de Madrid*. Madrid: por D. Eusebio Aguado, Impresor de Cámara de S.M. y de su Real Casa, 1829. RB Inf/1976.
Bound in long-grained red morocco with gold border framed by a double gold fillet on the covers; on the inside covers, a figure composed of plant and geometrical motifs in blind; smooth spine with gold tooling and aubergine-colour morocco label; gilt board edges, squares and bookblock edges. Bookplate of the Infanta Isabel of Bourbon in ink. Blind stamp: "Secretaría de S.A. la Princesa de Asturias". Bookbinder's label: "Pastor. Encuadernador de Cámara de SS.MM. y AA.; Lo Encuadernó. Calle del Espejo Nº 11. Madrid".

Fig. 149
Tabla de las festividades á las que el Rey N. Señor ... asiste asi á la cortina como á la tribuna de su Real Capilla de Palacio y de las que se celebran anualmente en la misma y en otras varias de Madrid .... Madrid: [n. n.], 1832 (por Eusebio Aguado). RB XIV/2911.
Nineteenth-century cathedral-style binding in morocco with mosaic work. Covers stamped with Gothic-style rosettes and lobed motifs. Gilt board edges, squares and bookblock edges. Green paper endleaves with plant motifs in brown and gold. On the inside cover, bookbinder's label: "Enquadernado por D.n Antonio Suarez, librero de Cámara de S.M. y de la Real Imprenta".

Fig. 150
Alphonse de Lamartine, *Historia de la revolución francesa de 1848 y de la fundación de la República*. Madrid (Imprenta de D. Higinio Reneses. Imprenta de Boix mayor y Compañía, 1850. 2 vols. RB VII/1942 and VII/1943.
Bound in fine claret-coloured sheepskin; payment made in 1851 to Miguel Ginesta Haro. Smooth spine with gold tooling, labelled in gold. Marbled edges in blue, claret and black to match the endpapers.

Fig. 151
Giovanni Marchesini, *Mammotrectus*. Venetiis: p[er] Symone[n] papien alias Beuilaqua, 1492. RB I/137.
Bound in red-dyed sheepskin by Miguel Ginesta Haro (September 1852); gold tooling and black morocco label on spine: "Mamotretus 1491"; marbled edges; marbled endleaves. From the library of the Count of Gondomar. Stamp: "Inventariado por las Cortes. 1874". Manuscript bookplate: "Pro [... *n. p.*] Petro Squiviate". *Olim* ms. Gondomar: "Sal. 3ª, Est. 6, Cax 1º".

A. M. Pugin, *Les vrais principes de l'architecture ogivale ou chrétiene, avec des remarques sur leurs renaissance au temps actuel*. Bruges: [n. n.], 1850. RB IV/997.
Bound in *pasta valenciana* by Miguel Ginesta Haro (1850s) in lime green, blue marbled edges, paper endleaves in bird's eye-patterned coppery paper sprinkled with cobalt blue, discoloured spine with false gold raised bands; title lable in beige morocco.

Fig. 152
Laffont de Montferrier, *Le coeur du poète, ou fleurs poétiques*. Paris (Perpignan: impie. de J.-B. Alzine), 1857. RB VIII/18443.
Bound in green-dyed *pasta valenciana* over a claret-coloured background. Marbled edges match the colours of the sheepskin. Finely marbled endleaves. Smooth spine. Label in red leather with the author and title between pallets. Bound by Miguel Ginesta Haro in 1858.

Fig. 153
Laffont de Montferrier, *Le coeur du poète, ou fleurs poétiques*. Paris: Garnier (Perpignan: Imp. J.-B. Alzine), 1857. RB XIV/2694.
Bound in beige-dyed *pasta valenciana* over a brown background. Marbled edges match the colours of the finely marbled endleaves. Smooth spine. Label in red leather with the author and title between pallets. Bound by Miguel Ginesta Haro in 1858.

Fig. 154
Aléxandre Dumas, *Elena de Orleans: novela histórica*. Madrid, (impta. de la Biblioteca del Siglo), 1849. RB IX/6347. "Fine half-binding" by Miguel Ginesta de Haro, c. 1853.

Fig. 162
Juan Gualberto López Valdemoro de Quesada, conde de las Navas, *Catálogo de la Real Biblioteca: Impresos. Autores Historia*. Madrid, Ducazcal, 1910–31. RB I/J/616.
Bound in navy blue shagreen, board edges with gold fillet, wide squares decorated with ornamental tools of Alfonso XIII, inside covers in red shagreen with the king's name in the centre beneath the royal crown in gold on the front one and that of Christina of Bourbon on the back one. Spine with Catalan-style raised bands and title in second and third panels; date at the bottom of the spine, in gold. First flyleaves in burgundy ribbed silk and second endleaves in claret-coloured glossy paper; head edge gilt. Case in purple cloth lined with claret-coloured glossy paper. Bound by Victorio Arias.

Fig. 163
María de la Paz de Borbón y Borbón, *Poesías de Paz de Borbón*. Freiburg im Breisgau (Germany) [etc.]: B. Herder, 1904. RB I/J/639.
Bound in blue morocco with silver tooling. White leather inside covers, the front one with the supralibros of Alfonso XIII (tool no. 4). On the spine, in blind: "Paz de Borbón.- Poesías". Kept in a grey cloth case blind-stamped with the royal crown.

Fig. 164
María de la Paz de Borbón y Borbón, *Poesías de Paz de Borbón*. Freiburg im Breisgau (Germany) [etc.]: B. Herder, 1904. RB INF/1941.
Bound in purple morocco with a fine floral border on the covers and squares, front cover displaying the gold impaled coat of arms of the Infanta Paz of Bourbon, beneath the royal crown and above "Poesías de Paz de Borbón"; beige moiré endleaves, edges gilt, spine without lettering.

Fig. 170
Marcos Jiménez de la Espada, *Manuscritos de América propios de la Real Biblioteca* [bibliographical index cards]. Nineteenth century. RB II/2909.
Twentieth-century binding in hazel calf-like sheepskin by Justo Luna Valbuena. On the covers, fillet and tooling in blind extending from the spine bands and ending in fleurs-de-lis and, on the front cover, royal coat of arms (tool no. 32) and supralibros of Alfonso XIII; spine with raised bands and blind tooling; red head edge; red glossy paper endleaves, burnished.

Fig. 171
Infante Juan, *Forma libellandi* .... Sevilla: por tres compañeros alemanes, 1498. RB I/198.
Twentieth-century binding in hazel calf-like sheepskin. On the covers, blind-tooled plant border and, in the centre of the front cover, supralibros of Alfonso XIII, royal coat of arms (tool no. 37) and monogram of Alfonso XIII (tool no. 18); smooth spine with the author, title and year in blind, in gothic letters, separated by vegetal motifs: "Infante Forma libellandi MCCCCXCVIII"; blind-tooled floral border on squares; Italian comb marbled endleaves, burnished. On the inner cover, royal bookplate of Alfonso XIII printed in red by Bernardo Rodríguez after a design by the Count of Las Navas. The only complete copy known in Spain.

Fig. 172
Alonso de Cartagena, *Esta es la Genealogia de los reyes d'España Alphonsi de Cartagena episcopi Burgensis regum Hispanorum Romanorum imperatorum summorum pontificum nec non regum Francor[um], Anacaephaleosis / [trad. por Juan de Villafuerte]*. Fifteenth century (1450–75). RB II/3009.
Twentieth-century binding by Justo Luna Valbuena in boar skin. At the foot of the spine, monogram of Alfonso XIII. Inside cover in long-grained red morocco, with fillet and royal cypher of Alfonso XIII in the centre, both in gold; red silk flyleaf. Provenance: Count of Gondomar. *Olim ms.* Gondomar: "Sal. 2 Est. 7 Cax. 7".

Figs. 174 and 175
Henri Bouchot, *Les reliures d'Art a la Bibliothèque Nationale*. Paris: Édouard Rouveyre, éditeur, 1888. RB XIV/CL/150.
Eclectic twentieth-century binding in mosaic leather; Grolier-style inner border in polychrome mosaic; edges

gauffered in pointillé and polychrome border; gold tooling on board edges and squares; green morocco inside covers with gold-tooled Grolier decoration framing a central cartouche "Alfonso XIII" surmounted by the royal crown, in brown morocco; green moiré endleaves. Binding signed at the bottom of the front inside cover: "César Paumard", and at the bottom of the back inside cover: "Madrid 1922". Provenance: Lameyer collection.

Fig. 176

Comte de Gramont, *Les bons petits enfants*. Paris: J. Hetzel ([J. Claye], (n. d.: 1863). RB Inf. 262.
Industrial binding in pink grained publisher's cloth, gold-stamped on covers with a large border and central title frame in a polylobed medallion and floral ornamentation; edges gilt, spine fully decorated in gold; yellow paper endleaves.

Fig. 177

Charles-Réné Forbes, Comte de Montalembert, *Sainte Elisabeth de Hongrie*. Tours: Alfred Name et Fils, 1878. RB Inf. 905.
Industrial trade half-binding in red, spine in morocco with gold and blind decoration and title in central panel; front cover with floral border and coats of arms in the corners and at the centre of each side border; inside, heraldic composition in a lozenge above which a polylobed medallion holds an image of Saint Elizabeth of Hungary, all in black and gold. On the back cover, an almond-shaped central medallion with a cathedral. Gilt edges; cobalt blue endpaper illustrated with rampant lions, floral border and image of Saint Elizabeth of Hungary.

Fig. 178

Louis Rousselet, *L'Inde des Rajahs: Voyage dans l'Inde Centrale et dans les presidences de Bombay et du Bengale*. Paris: Hachette et Cie., 1875. RB Inf. 1913.
Industrial trade half-binding in cobalt blue; spine in gold-stamped morocco with a space for the title. Cloth covers gold stamped with a broad floral border and frontal head of an elephant decked out in Indian style; title at the bottom. Gilt edges, comb-marbled endpapers.

Fig. 179

Jules Verne, *Un capitaine de quince ans*. Paris: J. Hetzel et Cie., (n. d.: 18 ...). RB Inf. 459.
Red cloth binding by Lènegre with gold-impressed design after stamps by A. Souze. Bookplate of Isabel II. Stamp: "Biblioteca de Palacio-Madrid".

Fig. 180

Julio Broutá, *La ciencia moderna: Sus Tendencias y cuestiones con ella relacionadas*. Barcelona: Montaner y Simón, 1897. RB Inf. 1516.
Industrial binding in beige publisher's cloth over thick bevelled board; front cover displays an allegory of modern science in reddish-brown ink and title in a black and floral rectangular cartouche; at the lower end, signatures of the designers of the composition: "A. de Riquer, 97" and "F. Jorba". On the inner cover, double tinted fillet and, in the centre, the publisher's stamp; spine with title panels in black and the rest with tinted thistles.

Fig. 181

José Zorrilla, *Leyendas de D. José Zorrilla*. Madrid: Manuel Pedro Delgado, 1901. RB Inf. 3450.
Bone-coloured suede binding, signed at the bottom of the front cover: "Mélida, 1901", in gold. Front cover with gold fillet and title and author in broad gold medieval-style lettering in two strips across the upper and lower ends; in the centre, chiselled wood medallion of a winged ephebus strumming a large lyre; back cover with blind fillet and abbreviated model of the royal coat of arms in the centre. Gilt squares, off-white moiré endleaves, edges gilt.

Figs. 182 and 202

Nicanor Parra, *Páginas en blanco / Nicanor Parra; selección y edición de Niall Binns; introducción de Mª Ángeles Pérez López*. Salamanca: Universidad de Salamanca; Madrid: Patrimonio Nacional, 2001. RB XIV/2947.
Artistic binding with the royal cypher. Executed by Manuel Bueno in 2001. In gold-yellow morocco with polychrome tooling. Symbolic cover decoration relating to the poems and the author. In the lower half, two figures lie intertwined; small figures with clasped hands frame the upper part, evoking mythological beings. On the front cover two stylised representations of a crucifix are a reference to the anti-poet author. The heat-impressed decoration, without gold, uses the colours violet and red for the lovers, brown for the small figures and blue for the crucifixes. Edges gilt. The head edge is gauffered with the cypher of Queen Sofía, surmounted by the royal crown. Board edges decorated with fillets. Gold and palladium tooling and red bead mosaic on squares. In the upper corners, tool with the royal crown; in the lower corners, the queen's initial. Inside covers have pastedowns painted in the Taller Artesanal del Ayuntamiento de Madrid, made for Queen Sofía during a visit paid in 1988. Faded cypher "S" stencilled on the paper. Endleaves made of the same paper. Rounded spine. Author and title labelled in gold and palladium. Sackcloth dust jacket with label in gold-yellow morocco and the author and title in gold, book tool in palladium. Case lined in black imitation ostrich leather edged with yellow morocco. Signed "Manuel Bueno" at the top of the inside front cover and "M. Bueno" at the bottom of the case.

Figs. 183 and 193

Antonio Gamoneda, *Sílabas negras / Antonio Gamoneda; edición de Amelia Gamoneda y Fernando R. de la Flor*. Salamanca: Universidad de Salamanca; Madrid: Patrimonio Nacional, 2006. RB XIV/2952.

Artistic binding displaying the royal cypher. Executed in 2006 by Juan Antonio Fernández Argenta. In bronze hand-dyed cowhide leather over boards and sewn onto guards made from the same paper as the bookblock. Impressed decoration with bas-reliefs and edges painted in the same colour as the flyleaf. Four poems written by hand, in different shades, extend over the whole binding and the inside front and back covers. Pastedowns continuing the outer leather. Flyleaf in mauve split. Royal cypher impressed on a circular piece of leather mounted on the embroidery of the headband, supported by the central guard at the top and bottom. Matching jacket and cover. Everything protected by a case. Signed "argenta 2006" centre left of the front flyleaf.

Figs. 184 and 199
Gonzalo Rojas, *Cinco visiones: selección de poemas de Gonzalo Rojas / prólogo de Carmen Ruiz Barrionuevo*. Salamanca: Universidad de Salamanca; Madrid: Patrimonio Nacional, 1992. RB XIV/2938.

Artistic binding displaying the royal cypher. Commissioned in 1993 from Antolín Palomino. Executed in goatskin with classical-style decoration stamped in gold. In the centre of the front cover, the Spanish coat of arms, and on the back cover, a vase. Spine *alla greca* with gold and blind tooling simulating raised bands; on the label: "Gonzalo Rojas / Cinco visiones". Inside covers in paper with the cypher "S" surmounted by a hand-painted royal crown surrounded by roses and four gold faces. Endleaves and case in hand-painted paper with a swirled pattern. Signature "Palomino Olalla" at the bottom of the inside front cover.

Fig. 185
João Cabral de Melo Neto, *A la medida de la mano / Joao Cabral de Melo Neto; introducción, selección y traducción de Angel Crespo*. Salamanca: Universidad de Salamanca; Madrid: Patrimonio Nacional, 1994. RB XIV/2940.

Artistic binding displaying the royal cypher. Executed by Galván in maroon morocco-grained goat. Original hand-crafted decoration using gold gouges and mosaics, forming a fleur-de-lis. Inside covers in orange leather. On the front inside cover, the cypher "S" surmounted by the royal crown. Pastedowns in hand-painted paper. Edges gilt "sur temoins". Jacket in half-leather and modern paper, case in oasis goat. Signed "Galván" at the bottom of the inside front cover, 22 December 1994.

Fig. 186
José Antonio Muñoz Rojas, *Yo sólo sé nombrarte / José Antonio Muñoz Rojas; estudio introductorio de Emilia Velasco; selección y edición de J.A. Muñoz Rojas y Asunción Escribano*. Salamanca: Universidad de Salamanca; Madrid: Patrimonio Nacional, [2002]. RB XIV/2948.

Artistic binding displaying the royal cypher. Executed by Ramón Gómez Herrera in 2002 in white caribou skin with mosaic work featuring a symbolic decoration: the Impressionistic play of colours over the white cover reproduces concentric beams of light delimited by lines of colour that emerge from the earth. The warm colours range from bright yellows, clayey reds and shades of earth. White cowhide leather endleaves scattered with a mosaic of branches bearing olive-green leaves that provide a counterpoint to the cover with their formal naturalism. Cypher of Queen Sofía integrated into the mosaic landscape of leaves in the upper margin of the front inside cover. Green leather squares with fillets, lower edge gilt. Protective cover for the internal support made of green fabric reproducing the cypher of Queen Sofía. Ochre cloth dust jacket with a window through which the title of the work is visible in brown leather mosaic. Brown cowhide leather case with the name of the author in mosaic on the front cover.

Fig. 187
Pere Gimferrer, *Marea solar, marea lunar / Pere Gimferrer; introducción y edición de Luis García Jambrina; selección de Pere Gimferrer*. Salamanca: Universidad de Salamanca; Madrid: Patrimonio Nacional, 2000. RB XIV/2946.

Artistic binding displaying the royal cypher. Executed by Manuel Bueno in 2000 in royal blue morocco, in a nine-colour mosaic with gold and platinum tooling. Symbolic decoration evoking the sea, sun and moon of the title of the poetry book on both covers. The ship's prow on the back cover extends to the front cover in ten coloured sails. Gold- and platinum-tooled figures of sylphs all over the covers. Edges gilt. Top edge gauffered with Queen Sofía's cypher surmounted by the royal crown surrounded by tooled sylphs. Inside covers with gold tooling and pumpkin-colour mosaic beading and French paper to which tubes of paint were directly applied. Gold fillet on board edges. First endleaf painted in the Taller Artesanal del Ayuntamiento de Madrid for Queen Sofía during a visit paid in 1988. Faded cypher "S" stencilled on the paper. Second endleaf in grey and red marbled paper. Rounded spine. Title labelled in gold. Dust jacket half-bound in the same paper as the inside cover with strips of leather on front and back. Case made of the same paper as the inside cover, edged in leather, gold fillets with pumpkin-colour mosaic beading around the opening. Signed "Manuel Bueno" at the top of the front inside cover and "M. Bueno" at the bottom of the case.

Fig. 188
José Caballero Bonald, *Años y libros / José Caballero Bonald; edición e introducción de Luis García Jambrina; selección de J. Ramis Cabot y J.M. Caballero Bonald*. Salamanca: Universidad de Salamanca; Madrid: Patrimonio Nacional, 2004. RB XIV/2950.

Artistic binding displaying the royal cypher. Executed by Andrés Pérez-Sierra in 2004 in blue grained goatskin over boards with architectural decoration. Architectural image built on three levels using pieces of box calf in shades of blue, starting from a polarisation at a circular point in a break at the edge of the cover. The first level, from edge to edge, is embedded in the cover; it is in the same shade but establishes a play of textures, glossy/matte, rough/smooth. The second and third levels are superimposed in slight relief, emphasised by red and green staining. The play of textures is enhanced by the gradation from blue to turquoise. The label displaying the author and title is integrated into the design, on the second level of the front cover. The lettering, stencilled and painted in acrylics, prolongs the chromatic play of green and red and introduces the play of size. The leathers, headbands, guards and blank leaves are integrated into the chromatic play and display the various shades of blue, within the same range. Endleaves made of the same goatskin as the cover. Flyleaves made of split from one of the skins used in the binding. The bookblock is mounted on guards made of the same paper as the blank leaves to facilitate its opening. Queen Sofía's cypher, inside the circular piece on the front cover, is displayed in mosaic on two levels, in two shades of blue. Protective case in silk fabric. The inside of the case is made out of the same leather used in the decoration. The box calf fastening repeats the queen's cypher, inverting the use of blues. Signed "A. Pérez-Sierra" on the inner edge of the inside back cover and at the bottom of the inside of the case.

Fig. 189
Mario Benedetti, *Los espejos las sombras / Mario Benedetti; estudio introductorio y edición de Francisca Noguerol*. Salamanca: Universidad de Salamanca; Madrid: Patrimonio Nacional, 1999. RB XIV/2945.
Artistic binding displaying the royal cypher. Executed by José Luis García in two shades of box calf: light brown and beige. Allegorical decoration in which the rectangular patterns and alternating colours—four vertical strips brown/beige/beige/brown—evoke the mirrors and shadows alluded to in the title of the work. The decoration is based on horizontal and vertical incisions, with the outlines painted in acrylics in the same colour as the background leathers. The lettering is integrated into the design; the name of the author is displayed on the spine, at the top and bottom; the title is distributed over the covers following the outlines of the incisions. Lettering in films of colour to match the leather of the book. Rounded spine. Suede endleaves in two colours to match the bands of the binding. Queen Sofía's cypher, surmounted by the royal crown, stencilled and painted in acrylic with the Bourbon colours. Hand embroidered silk headbands. Matching box-like case lined in suede. Label in box calf displaying the author and title. Signed "J. L. García 1999" at the bottom of the front inside cover.

Fig. 190
Blanca Varela, *Aunque cueste la noche / Blanca Varela; edición e introducción de Eva Guerrero; selección de Ángel González Quesada*. Salamanca: Universidad de Salamanca; Madrid: Patrimonio Nacional, 2007. RB XIV/2953.
Artistic binding bearing the royal cypher. Executed by Juan Antonio Fernández Argenta in 2007 in black calfskin over boards, sewn on guards of the same paper as the bookblock. Decorated with inlays of impressed leather and incisions in black and red extending across the front and back covers and spine and over to the inside covers. The various titles that make up the anthology are displayed in black and red lettering on the surface of the cover, with the royal cypher in steel in the centre of the front cover. Pastedowns are a continuation of the cover, in the same leather. Flyleaves in matte black buffalo skin. Headbands hand embroidered with black silk and steel thread. Matching jacket in the same black cowhide leather with full covers and smooth spine displaying the author's name in the form of a setting half-sun and the title. Card case lined in red-edged lead-grey paper.

Fig. 191
Francisco Brines, *Para quemar la noche / Francisco Brines; Introducción, edición y selección de Francisco Bautista*. Salamanca: Ediciones Universidad de Salamanca; Madrid: Patrimonio Nacional, 2010. RB XIV/2956.
Artistic binding displaying the royal cypher. Executed in 2010 by Obradoiro Penumbra in dark violet matte *veau*, in the colour of the title and in female symbolism. Relief decoration. Inside cover in plain matte *veau*. Endleaves in dark violet suede. The royal cypher forms the relief decoration. False witnesses. Guards made of the same paper as the book and violet Japan paper. Lettering in pearl grey indicating the title, beginning on the front cover and ending on the back cover. Articulated box in off-white-grey *veau* and protective case fully lined in purple cloth. On the front cover "Brines" and on the back cover "Francisco". Signed "2010" at the lower end of the inside front cover and on the back inside cover "O. penumbra", in blind. On the front inside cover: "Para quemar" and on the back inside cover: "la noche".

Fig. 192
Pablo García Baena, *Rama fiel / Pablo García Baena; edición e introducción de Juan Antonio González Iglesias; bibliografía preparada por Antonio Portela*. Salamanca: Universidad de Salamanca; Madrid: Patrimonio Nacional, 2008. RB XIV/2954.
Artistic binding displaying the royal cypher. Executed in 2008 by Dolores Baldó in natural sanded matte shagreen with black *veau* appliqué work. Linear decoration with Indian ink and black ink transfers in geometrical shapes forming the royal cypher on the smooth spine. Inside covers in natural sanded matte shagreen, continuing that of the covers and the same linear pattern. Author and title on the front cover, in black film. False witnesses at the top and bottom edges. Endleaves in natural suede shagreen. Articulated case in black silk with natural shagreen suede ties on the front cover of the case, which forms two tabs that are fastened with two black antler points held in place by black silk straps. On the first tab, on the strip of suede, the

title; the royal cypher, transferred in black ink, is formed when the two tabs are closed. Inside base of the case in natural matte shagreen suede, unsanded. Signed "DOLORES BALDÓ" at the bottom of the inside front cover.

Fig. 193
See fig. 183.

Fig. 194
Álvaro Mutis, *Summa de Maqroll El Gaviero: poesía, 1948–1997 / Álvaro Mutis; introducción y edición de Carmen Ruiz Barrionuevo*. Salamanca: Universidad; Madrid: Patrimonio Nacional, 1997. RB XIV/2943.
Artistic binding displaying the royal cypher. Executed by Ana María Ruiz-Larrea in 1997 in lavender-blue box calf mosaic work. Symbolic decoration with a play of colours and forms that evokes features of the book—the ocean, waves, sails, travel—and alludes to the Spanish Royal Household (the royal crown, the heraldic blue, the Royal Household's connection with the sea and sailing). Queen Sofía's cypher in a mosaic pattern of silver-stamped leather work executed by hand and mechanically, forming a relief, occupies both covers. Two triangles in box calf bearing the name of the author and part of the title on the front cover, and the date and part of the title of the back cover, create the shape of the "S" [Sofía], with silver lettering. The upper part of the cover has silvered waves that evoke the royal crown, surmounting the cypher. Smooth spine displaying the title. Inside covers in *veau*. Suede endpapers. Jacket and case in box calf and Japanese paper. Jacket displays silver lettering with the author, title and year. Signed "A. Ruiz Larrea" on the inside front cover and 1997 on the inside back cover.

Fig. 195
José Ángel Valente, *El vuelo alto y ligero / José Ángel Valente; introducción, edición y selección de César Real Ramos*. Salamanca: Universidad de Salamanca; Madrid: Patrimonio Nacional, 1998. RB XIV/2944.
Artistic binding displaying the royal cypher. Executed by José Luis García in brown morocco with incisions in morocco and wood. Allegorical decoration in which the pieces form a lyre, in allusion to Apollo and poetry, which extends over the covers and spine. The lettering is integrated into the design of the instrument; the name of the author is on the spine, and the title on the front cover forms the outer part of the lyre. Rounded spine *alla greca*. Suede endleaves. The cypher of Queen Sofía, surmounted by the royal crown, is displayed on the front endleaf, stencilled and painted in acrylic with the Bourbon colours. Book-type case in cloth with leather edges, lined inside in suede. Label with author and title. Signed "J. L. García 1998" at the bottom of the inside front cover.

Fig. 196
José Emilio Pacheco, *Contraelegía / José Emilio Pacheco; introducción y selección de Francisca Noguerol*. Salamanca: Ediciones Universidad de Salamanca; Madrid: Patrimonio Nacional, 2009. RB XIV/2955.
Artistic binding displaying the royal cypher. Executed in 2009 by Dolores Baldó in graphite-grey *veau* with polycarbonate covers. Decorated by means of incisions that reveal parts of the transparent covers through which the engraving of the flyleaves is visible. Some of these incisions form the royal cypher. Leather headbands. Inside covers in anthracite-grey *veau* with the same incisions as the outside covers. Author and title in light grey film on the smooth spine. False witnesses on head and tail edges. Endleaves in suede with transferred decoration. Articulated case in black buckram with strips of suede embossed with the same motif as the endleaves and with the title and author. Inside base of the case in *veau* suede. Signed "DOLORES BALDÓ" at the foot of the flyleaf.

Fig. 197
Juan Gelman, *Oficio ardiente / Juan Gelman; edición e introducción de Mª Ángeles Pérez López; selección de Mª Ángeles Pérez López y Juan Gelman*. Salamanca: Universidad de Salamanca; Madrid: Patrimonio Nacional, 2005. RB XIV/2951.
Artistic binding displaying the royal cypher. Executed by Andrés Pérez-Sierra en 2005. Type designed by Cristina Pérez-Sierra Feduchy. In smooth, semi-matte box calf in coral red. Architectural decoration in three levels, symmetrical to the spine, with an industrially designed appearance. Circular cut-outs in each of the covers. Background of the cut-outs of the front cover in transparent methacrylate affixed with nails and washers to the board, piercing it through. Background of the cut-outs of the back cover in apple-green card. Royal cypher on methacrylate on the front cover; title and author on card on the back cover; flyleaves in rose-coloured pig suede over the first blank leaf with the same cut-outs as the front cover; second blank leaf in apple-green card fully integrated into the decoration of the first one. Headbands embroidered over the book in red and green silk thread. The bookblock is mounted on guards made from the same paper as the blank leaves to facilitate opening. Rigid case in box-calf and red cloth, lined inside in rose pig suede and outside in coral-red fabric; title and author displayed on the spine of the case over apple-green card. Signature "A. Pérez-Sierra" on the inner edge of the back inside cover.

Fig. 198
Ángel González, *Luz, o fuego, o vida / Ángel González; selección de Ángel González; edición de Víctor García de la Concha*. Salamanca: Universidad de Salamanca; Madrid: Patrimonio Nacional, 1996. RB XIV/2942.
Artistic binding displaying the royal cypher. Executed by Ana María Ruiz-Larrea in box calf and black morocco in mosaic. Symbolic decoration with a play of colours that recalls the elements of the book and the national heraldic colours. Queen Sofía's cypher in mosaic forming a relief on the covers; it is topstitched in red on the upper cover

and in yellow on the back cover. The royal crown is displayed in mosaic on the upper and lower ends of the inside covers. Front inside cover in red morocco with the crown in black and yellow; back inside cover in yellow with the crown in black and red. Suede endleaves impressed with the royal crown. Smooth spine with the author's name and date stamped in red at the top and bottom. Title in yellow and red. Jacket. Case in red and yellow. Signed "A. Ruiz Larrea 1996" at the foot of the front inside cover.

Fig. 199
See fig. 184.

Fig. 200
Sofia de Melo Breyner Andresen, *En la desnudez de la luz / Sophia de Mello Breyner Andresen; introducción, selección y traducción de Jacobo Sanz Hermida*. Salamanca: Universidad de Salamanca; Madrid: Patrimonio Nacional, 2003. RB XIV/2949.
Artistic binding displaying the royal cypher. Executed by Ramón Gómez in 2003 in white caribou skin with mosaic work in white, grey, blue, orange and yellow cowhide leather. Title in the form of a block of letters that occupies three-quarters of the covers. Elongated capitals, outlined to create a relief effect. In the minimalist composition, which evokes a typographic landscape illuminated by a light of different intensity, the rationalist inspiration of Miquel Ruiz's design is enhanced by the small coloured rectangular pieces inlaid in the letters. The metaphor of the title developed on the covers extends to the inside covers, where it contrasts with the figuration of the sea, so present in the author's oeuvre, in blue cowhide leather with mid-blue and white mosaic. Queen Sofía's cypher, in blue mosaic, in the lower corner of the back inside cover. Endleaves in dark blue cowhide leather. Protective cover for the bookblock in light grey cloth in dark blue mosaic, once again forming the queen's initial. Light grey cowhide jacket; author and title displayed lengthwise in white mosaic, the former parallel to the edge of the upper cover and the latter on the spine. In the centre of the covers, the cypher of Queen Sofía in dark blue mosaic. Dark blue cowhide leather case and sides in cloth displaying the initial on the front cover in light grey.

Fig. 201
José Hierro, *Nombres propios / José Hierro; selección de José Hierro y A. Sánchez Zamarreño; edición de Antonio Sánchez Zamarreño*. Salamanca: Universidad; Madrid: Patrimonio Nacional, 1995. RB XIV/2941.
Artistic binding displaying the royal cypher. Executed by Galván in blue morocco-grained goat with mosaic work in various shades. Modern-style decoration with elements symbolising proper names over patterned sea waves, a theme inspired by the poem entitled "Adagio para Franz Schubert". Gold and blind gouge decoration. Inside covers and flyleaves in sky-blue velvet leather. Cypher of Her Majesty the Queen in mosaic on the front inside cover. Edges gilt "sur temoins", case and jacket in half-leather and bands of blue morocco, modern paper painted expressly for this copy by the binder. Designed and crafted by hand. Signed "Galván" at the foot of the inside front cover, "2 January 1996".

Fig. 202
See fig. 182.

COVER [Uniformes del Ejército de Rusia], nineteenth century, RB, FOT/26 [fig. 25]; Paulus Jovius, *Histoires de Paolo Iovio ...*, 1552–55, RBME, 40.I.13 [fig. 111]; Juan de Orozco, *Ad responsa prudentum commentarij ...*, 1558, RBME, 32.IV.1 [fig. 121]; Dante, *Comedia*, 1536, RBME 24 XIII.13 [figs. 87 and 88]; Tommaso Fazello, *De rebus Siculis decades duae ...*, 1558, RBME, 60.IX.13 [fig. 124]; Saint Thomas Aquinas, *Regimiento de príncipes*, fifteenth century, RB II/3569 [fig. 13]; *Almanach Royal: année 1749*, 1749, RB, PAS/ARM3/44 [fig. 127]; *Planes o Estados que manifiestan el número de pleytos, causas y expedientes ...*, 1817, RB I/G/355 [fig. 20]; *Decretos del Rey Don Fernando VII ...*, 1832, RB I/G/241 [fig. 24]; Ivo, Bishop of Chartres, *Pannormia ...*, 1557, RBME, 25.VI.20 [fig. 122]; [*Guía de forasteros de Madrid*], 1819, RB CS/4/1 [fig. 146]

BACK COVER María Jesús de Ágreda, *Sacra Rituum Congregatione ...*, 1747, RB III/1691 [fig. 37]; *Libro de memoria de los libros que se imbian a las Indias este año de 1595*, [1595–1613], RBME 186.VI.4 [fig. 57]; *Carissimo in Christo filio nostro Ferdinando hispaniarum Regi Catholico ...*, c. 1753, RB I/E/84 [fig. 18]; Albert Krantz, *Wandalia*, 1519, RBME 42.VI.24 [figs. 89 y 90]; Michele Timoteo, *In Diuinum Officium trecentum quaestiones ...*, 1581, RB PAS/ARM1/198 [fig. 71]; Miguel de Medina, *Disputationum de indulgentiis ...*, 1564, RBME 6.V.43 [fig. 41]; *Tabla de las festividades á las que el Rey N. Señor ... asiste ...*, 1832, RB XIV/2911 [fig. 149]; Angelo Poliziano, *Angeli Politiani Opera ...*, 1536, RBME, 37.VI.31 [fig. 102]; Álvaro Mutis, *Summa de Maqroll El Gaviero: poesia, 1948–1997*, 1997, RB XIV/2943 [fig. 194]

ISBN [Patrimonio Nacional]: 978-84-7120-474-5
ISBN [Ediciones El Viso]: 978-84-95241-93-1
NIPO: 006-12-022-9
DL: M-13847-2012

© edition: Patrimonio Nacional
© texts: their authors
© photographs provided by Patrimonio Nacional: laboratorio fotográfico de Patrimonio Nacional
© photographs: their authors